Truth
Bee
Told

Truth Bee Told

By

B. Brian Blair

with Ian Douglass

Copyright Brian Blair 2021. All Rights Reserved.

Published by:
Darkstream Press/WOHW Publishing

www.wohw.com

All rights reserved. This book may not be reproduced in whole or in part in any form without written permission from the author.

This book is set in Garamond.

10 9 8 7 6 5 4 3 2 1

ISBN 978-0-578-30359-8

This book is dedicated to the memory of
Brett Leslie Blair
May 9, 1991 – July 22, 2021

B. Brian Blair: Truth Bee Told

Table of Contents

Foreword	2
Foreword #2	5
One – *Down… but NOT out*	7
Two – *Adjusting to life in Tampa*	21
Three – *Learning the ropes*	29
Four – *Making adjustments*	46
Five – *Ribs to go*	60
Six – *Maui Owie*	74
Seven – *Double blackballed*	85
Eight – *Hard decisions*	100
Nine – *Life lessons learned*	117
Ten – *Leaving the North of Mid South*	136
Eleven – *Getting stronger and growing up*	145
Twelve – *Hangin' and bangin'*	157
Thirteen – *Honing my craft*	170
Fourteen – *Never grow up*	188
Fifteen – *Sayonara*	204
Sixteen – *The Most Underrated*	221
Seventeen – *Changing directions*	243
Eighteen – *The Bees are born*	255
Nineteen – *To be fined, or NOT to be fined*	271
Twenty – *Peaks and valleys*	287
Twenty One – *The master ribbers*	299
Twenty Two – *When one door closes, another opens*	312
Twenty Three – *Meeting Mr. Electricity*	326
Twenty Four – *High-heeled hookers and cocaine*	340
Twenty Five – *The hardest thing to open is a closed mind*	355
Twenty Six – *Quitters never win*	372
Twenty Seven – *Bumps, bruises and addictions*	390
Twenty Eight – *Aging gracefully*	405
Epilogue	414
Epilogue #2	419
Afterword	423
Bonus Stories and Outtakes	425
Championships & Accomplishments	456
Author's Acknowledgements	460
Biographer's Acknowledgements	465
Credits	466

B. Brian Blair: Truth Bee Told
FOREWORD

I first met Brian Blair on a trip to Japan in the fall of 1984. He was friendly and easygoing, and when I watched him wrestle the fit, aggressive, and sometimes uncooperative Japanese wrestlers, I saw how talented a wrestler he was. With a strong amateur wrestling background, Brian was more than capable of holding his own in the ring. We became friends then, and I learned he was working the Florida territory with Tampa as his hometown.

Much to our chagrin, we both had learned we'd been offered tentative positions in the WWF/WWE, which was only just beginning its takeover of the wrestling world. In Japan, we talked and concluded it was a long shot at best for wrestlers of our size and age to make it into the WWE, but it wasn't a surprise to find ourselves there a few months later.

I'd been thrown together with Jim "The Anvil" Neidhart and formed into a heel tag team called the Hart Foundation, more as an effort to simply do something with us. Brian was in a similar situation when he was suddenly teamed up with an equally talented Minneapolis wrestler well known in the business: "Jumping" Jim Brunzell.

All of us were young and anxious to prove ourselves in the exploding WWE. Tag team wrestling has a completely different style, pace, and psychology, and it doesn't work for everyone, but we were all top pros in our own right. I found a balance of speed, strength, and intensity with The Anvil, and it was much the same for Jim and Brian, who called themselves The Killer Bees. Both Brian and Jim had excellent timing, great technique, and a full grasp of credible workmanship. Not to mention that Jim was one of the best high flyers back then.

I had the misfortune of starting my WWE run after suffering a debilitating knee injury, and I was still nursing it along. The quick assessment on me was that I didn't have what it took, and although I had been working there for some time, I feared my head was on the chopping block. I decided to bring my parents down to New York to watch me wrestle at least once in the greatest hall of them all: Madison Square Garden. It was February 17, 1986 and other than the subpar TV matches I'd worked with unskilled jobbers, Vince McMahon had never once had a chance to see me work a real match ever with a top team. Hart Foundation vs. The Killer Bees would turn out to be the first chance to show Vince what we all had.

It remains today as one of my all-time favourite matches as all four of us went on early that night and gripped the well-educated New

B. Brian Blair: Truth Bee Told

York fans with a fast-paced, bone-jarring, layer-upon-layer of intense wrestling brilliance with the Hart Foundation pulling every dirty trick in the book and the Killer Bees gamely fighting an uphill battle. We popped the sellout crowd from the very start, and for the next 20 minutes we rocked The Garden, forcing all the wrestlers in the backstage area to come out and watch us, including Vince McMahon.

We built the match higher and higher with the fans on the edge of their seats. When Jim Brunzell moved out of the corner from Neidhart hurling me into him; I hit the empty corner nearly breaking my collarbone. Brunzell shot through Anvil's legs tagging Brian, who tore into us both with an explosive comeback. One pop after another with the Hart Foundation hanging on by threads, the bell rang. It was a draw.

The Killer Bees bounced us out of the ring to a thundering ovation. Jimmy Hart, Anvil, and I limped back to the dressing room looking exasperated, but we knew that we had blown the roof off. I was satisfied that I at least showed my dad sitting in the front row how good we were.

Vince, who had barely spoken a word to me in the two years I had been there, grinned at me and thrust his hand into mine. "Incredible match. Thank you so much." Moments later, all four of us sat across from each other soaked in sweat in the dressing room and

B. Brian Blair: Truth Bee Told

smiled back and forth because we all knew we had proved ourselves and ultimately set a standard for tag team wrestling that, in my mind, has never been topped.

Looking back, these were my most enjoyable memories in the ring and I can probably say that the Killer Bees were one of the greatest WWE tag teams of all time – unlike any other. I know if it hadn't been for them that night, it's more than plausible that my chances would have run out and "The Hitman" would've quit or gotten fired only to fade away into the oblivion of pro wrestling history.

I loved working with The Killer Bees, and I say with all due respect, I owe them for *everything*.

Bret "The Hitman" Hart

FOREWORD #2

It's a great honor for me to write a foreword for the book of my close friend, Brian Blair. I should probably *read* the book first to make sure he doesn't say anything bad about me. (Just kidding, Brian!)

Brian and I have been friends for more than 40 years, and I love him like a brother. I got to know him just prior to his breaking into the wrestling business. We both grew up in Tampa and had so much in common.

Florida had a reputation as a place where you had to pay your dues first if you wanted to break into the wrestling business. In other words, you had your butt stretched and worn out by the people who trained you; it was *not* an easy transition to make. Eddie Graham was the promoter in Florida, and he believed everyone should have to prove to him that they were tough enough to fight to get into the business, and also tough enough to fight *for* the business. Brian did an awesome job of proving he had the passion and guts to hang in there.

Now, let Brian take you on a journey through his career, and get ready to laugh your butt off at some of his great stories and locker room experiences. This book will provide you with insight into his life and career as a pro wrestler. If you want to lose weight, grow hair, look younger or live longer, this is the *wrong* book.

But seriously, Brian grew up against all odds and he overcame them through faith and endurance. In the process, he not only became a main eventer in our business, but also a successful businessman. Brian owned four Golds Gyms, and I had the honor and the privilege to be one of his partners in one of the gyms. Brian also became a county commissioner for the third largest county in Florida.

Brian is a great friend, husband, father and son. In addition, Brian had to pick up the ball when our Legends Luncheon in Tampa needed the support of someone who cares so much for everyone in the wrestling business. This is to say nothing of the fact that he is also the president of the Cauliflower Alley Club. Brian has a *big* heart and a ton of compassion for those in need.

To top it off, Brian is my *best friend*, and I would dare to say that I probably know him better than anyone. That means you can take my word for it when I tell you he is an honest, hardworking man that puts others first. We also attend a large Baptist church together in Tampa, and he is my brother *in Christ*.

I promise you it will be hard for you to put this book down once you start. Brian lived the true American Dream, from rags to

B. Brian Blair: Truth Bee Told

riches, and he didn't get there the easy way. He did it through lots of blood, sweat and tears. Thank you for opening and reading my best friend Beeber's book.

God bless.

Steve "Gator" Keirn

Keirn and Blair – NWA U.S. Tag Team Champions

B. Brian Blair: Truth Bee Told

ONE – *Down… but NOT out*

As I sat there in that orange jumpsuit, planted on a wooden bench in the back of the Hillsborough County Circuit Court, I felt as if my life might as well have come to an end. My entire world had just been taken away from me. In a single instant, everything I had worked for in my 50 years of life had more than likely evaporated into the misty haze of Tampa's summer sky.

I had parlayed a career as a world-famous professional wrestler into a lucrative business career, and then transitioned from all of that into a promising political career. Just like that, everything was gone. What made it far worse was the thought that I might even lose my family on top of everything else. For this to happen to me at any point was tragic, but for it to occur on Father's Day 2009 added an excruciating dose of salt to my emotional wounds.

Unfortunately, my wounds weren't merely emotional. As I favored my aching ribs and hunched over in discomfort, I also looked to my left and right – through a pair of eyes that had been swollen from a combination of tears and the battering of teenaged fists – at the rows of orange-clad detainees who were waiting to face the judge just as I was. From there, I turned my gaze to the ceiling. As more tears welled in my eyes, I asked God to provide me with strength and direction. Decades earlier, I had prayed to God and asked him to turn me into Superman; not even Superman could have endured the pain I was feeling in that moment.

I didn't understand how things could have gone so horribly awry, and that I could have acquired so much only to lose everything. Then again, considering how I grew up, sometimes it's hard to believe that I ever could have gained it all in the first place. While my 2009 home was in a very comfortable neighborhood in Tampa, Florida, my life story begins a *very* long way from Florida. When I was born to my parents in the winter of 1957, they were living nowhere near the Gulf of Mexico or the central coast of Florida. Instead, they were living in Gary, Indiana, adjacent to the frigid waters of Lake Michigan.

Growing up in that neighborhood in the mid 1960s, I was one of very few White kids living in the area. When I say that I had Black friends growing up, I don't mean it in the same way that a lot of people will use the phrase to point out they know a single Black person from the gym or office who they occasionally speak with. I mean the overwhelming majority of my friends were Black.

B. Brian Blair: Truth Bee Told

Even though I was a racial minority in Gary as a White kid, for the most part, all of the Black kids treated me like I was their brother. I honestly didn't perceive that I was treated any differently on the basis of my skin color. At the time, I was too young to know that the differences in skin shades had any significance behind them; I simply accepted that the majority of my friends had faces that were a little darker than mine, and it was no big deal.

Don't get me wrong; life in Gary was certainly no post-racial paradise. There were times when I was called ugly words or phrases, like "honky" or "poor White trash." If that ever happened, my friend Willie Young would find the perpetrators and kick their asses for me. Of course, there were some asses that simply couldn't be kicked. I went to Etna Elementary School in Gary, and Mr. Reed – the Black math teacher in his mid-twenties – just flat-out hated me.

As a baby with my mother

Mr. Reed carried around a long pointer stick while he conducted class, and it seemed like he would make a special point of banging that pointer stick on *my* desk in particular. Almost without fail, if I looked down or looked away from Mr. Reed while he was teaching his lessons, that stick would come violently crashing down in front of me.

Things would get even worse for me if I ever spoke to Mr. Reed directly, but then looked away from his face in the process.

B. Brian Blair: Truth Bee Told

When that happened, he would step toward me and stick his finger straight at my nose.

"Boy, when I'm talking to you, you look me in the *eye!*" he would order, sternly. "Do *you* understand me?!"

"Yes, sir!" I would respond.

Mr. Reed replicated this interchange with a couple other White kids in the class as well, but I never noticed him having these discussions with any of the Black children. That was the first time in my life I ever wondered if someone was treating me differently because of the color of my skin. I was only in fifth grade, and I didn't really understand the concept of prejudice. The only real prejudice I'd ever felt at that point in my life that had any power behind it came at the hands of Mr. Reed.

As a kid, I had no clue what I could possibly have done to irk Mr. Reed so severely. Once I matured and learned more about U.S. history, I realized that Black people had to cope with a lot of unfair treatment for centuries, so now I wonder if Mr. Reed was just capitalizing on an opportunity to take out some of his festering resentment on the few White kids in his classes.

When I wasn't in Gary, that usually meant I was spending time on my grandparents' farm in Arkansas. They lived on a massive, 1,800-acre stretch of property about 115 miles north of Little Rock in Saint Joe – a town with around 125 inhabitants. It was a far cry from the city living and condensed neighborhoods of Gary, and a great place to get in touch with nature. It was heaven on Earth for a kid, and also a perfect backdrop for learning some valuable life lessons.

One of the lessons I learned the hard way had to do with tobacco, and it was taught directly by my grandfather. I noticed that while he performed his daily chores around the farm, he liked to dip Copenhagen. Since my grandfather was one of my heroes, I longed for the chance to chew tobacco exactly like he did. Without fail, I asked him every single summer if I could partake of his chewing tobacco.

"No way," was the answer I received for the first few summers.

Grandpa worked from the instant he awoke in the morning. He would start the day by venturing out into his half-acre garden for an hour, and when he got back, my grandmother would have his breakfast ready for him, which consisted of two eggs, bacon and toast. Grandpa enjoyed this breakfast six days a week, and on Sunday my grandmother would make pancakes for him. After breakfast, Grandpa would have a couple cups of coffee, and then he would go back outside and continue tending to his massive property.

B. Brian Blair: Truth Bee Told

When Grandpa wasn't out working, he was heavily into crossword puzzles, which enabled him to hone his knowledge of a wide array of subjects.

My grandmother, Edna, immigrated to the U.S. from Sweden many years before she married my grandfather, but she nearly didn't make it off the inbound ship alive. While she was in transit, she was injured in a fall from the upper deck of the ship to the lower deck, and nearly died from the impact. Fortunately, she successfully completed her immigration after spending several months recovering in a New York hospital.

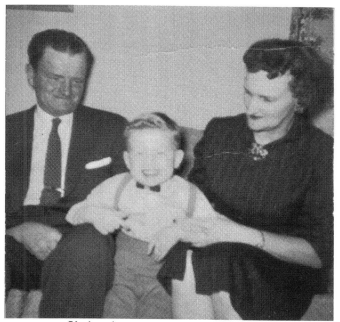

Sitting between my grandparents

My grandparents frequented a breakfast café in Saint Joe that was connected to the town's general store. In front of the store sat a set of rickety wooden steps that had been built out of Coke-bottle crates. My grandparents took me to eat there when I was nine years old, and while we were eating, the lady who owned the store came over to our table with a request.

"Would you be a dear and help me carry some empty bottles inside?" the lady asked with a smile.

I was eager to help, and quickly stood up to assist her with the collecting of beer bottles and Coke bottles that littered the ground

B. Brian Blair: Truth Bee Told

outside of her store. I made several trips with those bottles until only two remained to be brought inside. During my final trip, I held a soda bottle in my left hand, and my right hand held a Budweiser bottle.

As I climbed up that rotted set of soda-crate steps for the final time, the rotten wood finally gave way under my weight, and my foot plunged directly through the crate. I tumbled straight forward and instinctively stretched my hands out to brace myself for the impact, never considering the ramifications of slamming into the ground while holding a pair of glass bottles in my hands. When I struck the ground, the glass Budweiser bottle in my right hand shattered. A long, jagged fragment of glass was plunged straight through my tiny, nine-year-old right hand, between my pinky and ring finger.

Blood spurted everywhere. The owner of the café immediately grabbed some sugar and poured it all over my wound as crimson-colored blood continued to fight its way through the sugar granules. Once the woman had wrapped my hand in some bandages to the best of her capabilities, my grandparents rushed me to the closest doctor in town, who I only remember as "Dr. Williams."

There was no high-quality medical care to be found in Saint Joe, Arkansas. Dr. Williams held a cigarette between his lips as he treated me, and a long strand of ash dangled precariously from the tip of the cigarette and hovered over my gaping wound. The doctor then rinsed my hand beneath running water and cleaned my wound as I howled like a baby. My grandmother did her best to console me during this harrowing process.

"I've got to stitch him up," said Dr. Williams.

Unfortunately, Dr. Williams wasn't the most sure-handed doctor in the world. As he sewed up my wound, he made an erratic pattern in my skin. In addition to making a mess of my skin with the needle and thread, he also sewed one of my tendons to a nerve, resulting in my hand not being able to open or close without great difficulty. Almost all of the sensation in my right hand departed from me on that day.

My parents wanted to sue Dr. Williams, but my grandparents would have none of it.

"If you sue him, the people of Saint Joe will burn our ranch to the *ground*," insisted my grandfather.

My grandmother laid next to me in my bed every day for the remainder of that trip to console me while I suffered through a round of antibiotics and *excruciating* pain.

I never regained the feeling in my hand after that, to the extent that I could stick my right hand straight into a fire and not feel

B. Brian Blair: Truth Bee Told

any pain from it. Dr. Williams was a hack doctor, and probably an alcoholic. The Hippocratic Oath taken by all doctors requires them to promise to do no harm. Well, Dr. Williams did *plenty* of harm to me after being entrusted with the well-being of my hand.

My right hand remained curled up like a claw for many years. I suffered through several years of my early life as a veritable cripple and had to endure taunts from my young peers because of it.

"Brian has a corroded hand!" one of my female classmates announced after she caught a glimpse of my hand back in Gary.

I never forgot that statement. As a child, that comment *really* stung me.

Trying to write with a pen or pencil was a continual challenge. Before I could do any writing at all, I had to pick up the writing utensil with my left hand and place it gently in my right hand.

All of my other trips to the farm in Saint Joe were far more pleasant. During our stays out at the farm, there was plenty of work to be done, and Grandpa would recruit me to assist him with it. We would cut the hay, squeeze the hay, rake the hay, bale the hay, and then load the bales into the barn.

When I was 10-and-a-half years old, Grandpa entrusted me with the responsibility of driving his blue pickup truck a full 10 yards at a time as he filled it with bales of hay that weighed an average of 60 pounds each. From there, we would drive the pickup over to one of the barns, and Grandpa and I would unload the bales from the truck bed. One by one, I would hand him a bale from the back of the truck, and he would carry it into the barn.

On this particular occasion, I'm sure I felt like quite the grownup after experiencing the thrill of sitting behind the wheel of the pickup and driving it the shortest of distances. When we were finished unloading the truck, I climbed into the driver's seat. My grandfather then sat in the passenger seat and prepared to load some dip into his mouth.

Brimming with confidence, I decided to ask my grandfather a spirited question.

"Grandpa, I'm 10-and-a-half years old," I informed him. "That means I'm *half* a man."

In my young mind, I had reasoned that if a 21-year-old man was a full man, being 10-and-a-half years old made me *half* a man. My grandfather just eyed me curiously, wondering where my statement was headed.

"If I'm *half* a man, I think I should be able to have *half* a dip," I concluded.

B. Brian Blair: Truth Bee Told

Again, it all made sense in my young, pre-teen mind, and it appeared to have made sense to my grandpa as well. He hesitated for only a brief few seconds before extending the pack of Copenhagen to me.

I *couldn't* believe it. My hero was finally allowing me to join him in his ritual of dipping. I gleefully scooped up a pinch of chewing tobacco, being extra careful not to grab too much. My grandfather just looked at me with a face devoid of any expression that might have betrayed that he understood *exactly* what was about to unfold before him.

Fishing with my grandfather in Arkansas in 1964

I put the dip in my lip, and I was *so* proud of myself. I figured my grandfather must have been proud of me as well, because suddenly a blinding smile materialized on his face. I dutifully shifted the truck into second gear and started to drive it. The truck had barely made it to the second bale of hay before I began to feel nauseous, and sweat started to pour out of every pore in my body. In a panic, I quickly hit the brakes and parked the truck.

"Something's wrong, Grandpa!" I moaned. "I feel sick!"

B. Brian Blair: Truth Bee Told

My grandfather didn't say a word. Instead, he grabbed his fishing pole, departed on foot, and walked about 100 yards away to go fishing at Bear Creek – a four-mile-long tributary of the Buffalo National River. In the process, he left me lying in the truck for hours until I finally fell asleep. Thanks to that experience, I haven't touched a tobacco product since. My grandfather was a *genius*. I'm sure he knew he was curing me of my tobacco curiosity early in life, and he had the necessary patience to allow me to learn that lesson the hard way.

No matter how valuable the tobacco lesson would ultimately be to my development, my grandfather still felt guilty about letting me chew the tobacco when he knew I would get ill from doing so. Two days after the incident, we were heading off to work in the fields. As we were in the process of crossing the creek, Grandpa slowed the truck down. He'd seen a sizeable bass in the water below.

"Maybe around lunchtime we'll go fishing, Bee Bee," Grandpa told me.

"That'd be great!" I answered.

When lunchtime approached, Grandpa and I went over to the creek and began to fish. There in the waters at the bank of the creek was a spawning female bass who weighed about four pounds. Grandpa had forgotten to bring the minnow jug, so we didn't have any tantalizing bait to use. Undeterred, Grandpa placed every form of bait available to us in front of the bass, and it still refused to bite.

"Bee Bee, do you know what 'innovation' is?" Grandpa asked.

My young ears had never heard the word before.

"No, Grandpa," I replied. "What is 'innovation'?"

"I'm going to teach you what innovation is *right now*," smiled Grandpa.

As I watched closely, Grandpa collected four 1/0 fishing hooks and fastened them together with black tape. He weaved the tape in and out between the hooks before wrapping it tightly to form a barb. From there, he placed a leader on his fishing line and sank the makeshift barb into the water. Lo and behold, within a couple of minutes, Grandpa was able to position the barb underneath the bass, and then he jerked the line up and out of the water. When the barb emerged above the water's surface, it carried the bass along with it. It was the wildest thing I'd seen at that point in my young life.

The huge smile plastered on Grandpa's face indicated just how pleased he had been by his display of fishing prowess.

"*That's* innovation, Bee Bee," he said proudly.

Grandpa had just taught me the importance of thinking outside of the box… which in *this* case was a tackle box.

B. Brian Blair: Truth Bee Told

My grandfather had a saying: "Women, dogs, cats and kids; there oughtta be a law against 'em." Fortunately, even though he thought there ought to be a law against me, he was still willing to help me develop responsibly. Although my grandparents are now long gone and their property was absorbed into a national park, the lessons they taught me still linger in my memories to this day.

Another lingering memory stems from the time my parents told me I was old enough to be upgraded from Sunday school into the "big people's" church service at St. Mary's Methodist Church. I paid very close attention when the pastor preached to us about having faith. I took it to the bank when he said that God would eventually give us what we prayed for if we were good people. So many options raced through my mind about what I wanted God to give me.

My first thought was to have God give me a million dollars, but then I thought better of it since God might think better of giving so much money to a 10-year-old boy and then take it all back.

My next idea was to have God provide me with a Corvette, and I wasn't going to be too picky about the color. As far as I was concerned, God could provide me with either a blue Corvette or a red one. It was *His* choice. Then I realized I wasn't old enough to drive anyway, so I'd be forced to watch helplessly as my new sports car sat unused in our driveway.

Finally, I settled on having God turn me into Superman. I vowed to use my powers for good, so I couldn't imagine why God wouldn't grant my wish. For six straight months, I prayed diligently for God to transform me into a muscular, tights-wearing superhero. I figured I was merely assisting God with the transformation process when I tied a blanket around my neck and attempted to run through the walls. As you can imagine, my tiny body gave out *long* before the wall ever did.

I wasn't aware of the futility of that particular prayer until I was slapped with a cold dose of reality by my friend, Billy Kapinski. The two of us passed by several piles of snow as we made the stroll from my house at 1165 Arizona Street to Billy's house way on the other end of the street. As the foggy breath from our conversation filled the frigid air, Billy explained to me how he intended to become an attorney when he grew up. Billy reached this decision because he had overheard his parents complaining about how much money they owed the lawyer who was handling some legal dispute they were involved in.

"Being a lawyer sounds *boring!*" I told him. "*I'm* gonna be *Superman* when I grow up!"

B. Brian Blair: Truth Bee Told

"You can't *be* Superman, dummy!" replied Billy. "He's just a *fake* comic character! *Nobody* can be Superman!"

I was *devastated*. I'd already devoted six months of my young life to the dream of getting to wear tights and beat up bad guys for a living. It pained me to think that I would have to think of something else to do with my life.

The one thing I could find on television where the heroes even came close to being like Superman was professional wrestling. Indiana was part of the territory run by the American Wrestling Association before it transitioned into the home state of the World Wrestling Association. I sat riveted to the television screen as guys like Alex Karras, Moose Cholak, Dick the Bruiser and the Crusher wore tights and displayed their superhuman might on a weekly basis.

Dad worked incessantly to keep food on the table for us, which required him to work at two different jobs out of necessity. In fact, *both* of my parents worked extremely hard, but we simply didn't have a lot of money. For years, they drove us around in an old, blue station wagon. When they decided they finally had enough money and bought a brand new, citron gold 1966 Dodge Charger for $3,600, it was a *humongous* deal to us. Even at the age of eight years old, I could feel the excitement of my parents and understood what it meant for them to buy a new car. Not many families in my neighborhood could afford new cars, so I perceived that owning one meant that we weren't poor and everything was good in life.

We hadn't been poor in Gary per se, but my parents were still excited for us to leave Gary so that my father could find better job opportunities elsewhere. Mom and Dad collectively asked their four children – of which I was the eldest – where we wanted to move, and they gave us the choice of California or Florida.

We selected Florida, but by then the choice was well out of our hands. My father had already secured a job in Florida as one of the union carpenters helping to build the Tampa International Airport, which was a fact none of us knew at the time. Therefore, we were thrilled when my parents revealed that we would all be moving to Tampa, Florida, and they were probably relieved that we were all totally in favor of it.

As it turned out, the opportunity to move to Tampa couldn't have arrived at a better time. Just a few months before the move, my parents took me up to Chicago for a week. I'm not sure exactly what sort of business they were tending to, but we stayed at the home of my Uncle Harry, who always greeted me by handing me $2.

B. Brian Blair: Truth Bee Told

My mother and her five siblings – including Uncle Harry – had grown up in the 1930s on the South Side of Chicago, in what was an arduous, oppressive environment. Anti-Semitic sentiment ran rampant in Chicago during those days, and with a last name like Roth, it was extremely difficult for my mother and her siblings to hide the fact that they were of Jewish descent from people in the neighborhood who wished to do them harm. All the same, my grandparents admonished their children not to tell anyone they were Jewish out of the fear that they would find themselves on the receiving end of discriminatory violence.

As if living in an ethnically prejudicial environment wasn't challenging enough for my mother, there were parental and environmental problems to manage as well. Mom's father would frequently gamble away whatever money he made, which simply exacerbated the other problems the family faced. The conditions inside of the Roth family's home were so filthy at times that rats were able to thrive there, and my mother was actually bitten by one. She is petrified of rodents to this day.

Our impromptu trip to the Windy City allowed me to enjoy a one-week vacation in the company of my 18-year-old cousin Jimmy Roth and his similarly-aged neighbor Eddie Sullivan.

Jimmy was definitely on the mischievous side, and the fact that I looked up to him as an older cousin certainly increased the likelihood that I would be drawn into some form of malfeasance right alongside him. The preferred form of malfeasance Jimmy opted for during this specific trip was actually fairly complex. It all began when we absconded with my Uncle Harry's brand new 1969 Chevy Impala and cruised around Chicago in it. This car was absolutely gorgeous: It had a shiny blue finish, a white convertible ragtop, and an exquisite white-leather interior.

The three of us eventually arrived at the local mall and walked into Shoppers World.

"Hold onto this belt for me," said Jimmy, as he fastened a belt around my waist. "We're going to *take* this! Just play it cool and don't worry about it."

I knew stealing was wrong, but I was determined to fit in with the older boys. After we'd successfully made it out of Shoppers World with the ill-gotten belt in our possession, we ventured over to a nearby party store. As we walked through the aisles, Jimmy and Eddie took turns stuffing my pockets with water balloons and other party paraphernalia. Once again, we managed to escape from a store with

B. Brian Blair: Truth Bee Told

stolen goods in our possession. However, our crime spree had not yet reached its conclusion.

Directly in front of Shoppers World stood the mall's giant fountain, where patrons of the mall could make wishes before chucking their change into the shallow pool of water at the fountain's base.

"Take off your shoes, Brian!" demanded Jimmy. "We need you to wade in there and get all that change for us!"

I did exactly as I was told. I removed my shoes and socks, and then I swished around in the water and collected the change that was plainly visible at the base of the fountain. Once I'd plucked a coin from the pool, I placed it in my shirt, which I'd pulled out in front of me as a makeshift hammock for carrying the coins. By the time I'd completed my third pass through the water, my shirt was heavy from all of the coins that filled it, which amounted to around $50.

There was nothing particularly clever or secretive about what I was doing; we were in the middle of a busy mall, in front of a popular shopping destination. It was impossible that our theft of the fountain's change would escape notice, and our precarious pilfering quickly caught the attention of an old woman.

"Hey, you kids!" she yelled. "That money is for *poor* people! You can't just take that out of the fountain!"

"Let's get out of here!" urged Eddie.

I climbed out of the fountain, grabbed my socks and shoes and then darted away as fast as I could without allowing any of the change to escape from my shirt. As the three of us retreated, an old man came to our defense and responded to the accusations of the elderly woman.

"Leave that kid alone!" he said. "Does it look like he's got a million dollars? It's not like it's *your* money anyway, so why do *you* care?!"

As far as I could tell, we'd made a clean getaway. The funny thing is if anyone had been watching our activities that day, to the naked eye, it appeared as if I was the master criminal behind the heist. Every single item taken from the mall had been visibly stolen by *me*, including the belt, the balloons, some itching powder, and around $50 in assorted coins.

When we were in the clear, Jimmy unfastened the stolen belt and pulled it from my waist.

"How come we didn't pay for that?" I asked him.

"Because we didn't have the money," Jimmy answered, matter of factly.

B. Brian Blair: Truth Bee Told

That was the extent of Jimmy's reply. We were absolutely in the wrong, and I knew it, but at that moment I was happy that I'd made Jimmy happy. Any guilt that I was feeling quickly subsided as we engrossed ourselves in a water-balloon fight in the front yard of Uncle Harry's house. While we were distracted with hurling the stolen balloons at one another and watching excitedly as the water exploded all around us, the phone rang inside of the house.

We could faintly hear the voice of Uncle Harry as he answered the phone. His vocal tone gradually grew louder and more animated, and it ceased a few moments later with the sound of the phone's receiver being slammed down with great force.

"Jimmy!" Uncle Harry screamed. "You get your ass in here *right now!*"

Jimmy disappeared inside of the house, and we soon heard his distressed voice emanating from the home's upper level, punctuated by loud slapping noises.

"I *didn't* do it!" Jimmy pleaded with his father, who was obviously irate.

Uncle Harry was clearly disciplining my cousin with a belt. The security guard from Shoppers World had been on the other end of that phone call. The guard had intended to nail us for the theft while we were still on the mall's premises, but he had his attention diverted to the simultaneous theft of a more expensive item that was taking place elsewhere in the store. However, he was good enough at multitasking to have scribbled down our license plate number as the Impala pulled out of the mall's parking lot. From there, he tracked down Uncle Harry's phone number and ratted us out.

Uncle Harry had a serious conversation with Eddie and I afterwards about how we shouldn't follow Jimmy's awful example and continue to tread down a path of criminality.

As much trouble as Jimmy was in, it actually didn't seem to matter much to him at all. The very next night, Jimmy and Eddie visited a pool hall and returned to the house with a large, rectangular matchbox full of marijuana. The two of them rolled up a joint and puffed away at it for a while before they passed it over to me.

This was my first exposure to marijuana, and I had *no* idea what to do with it other than to replicate what they were doing. I puffed on the joint a few times and then quickly passed it back over to them. I wasn't sure what I should be feeling as a result of smoking pot, but I knew I was definitely too young to be doing that, and I would have been in *unimaginable* trouble if I'd been caught.

B. Brian Blair: Truth Bee Told

In the span of only two short days in Chicago, I had robbed three different stores *and* smoked weed... all before reaching my teenage years. Thank God my parents moved us from Gary to Tampa a few months later; there's no doubt in my mind that I would have wound up with a lengthy criminal record if we'd remained in Indiana. However, there was one positive outcome from our scandalous behavior: Owing to the fact that I was able to listen in on the whipping that my cousin Jimmy had received, and also owing to the follow-up conversation that Eddie and I had with Uncle Harry, I never stole another thing in my life.

Upon delivering the family to Tampa safe and sound, my father pulled the car into the driveway leading to a small, dilapidated trailer home with a tiny addition that had been tacked onto it, and then he parked the car.

"Here we are!" he said, turning to smile at his children in the back of the car. "What do you think?"

It was *horrible*. Luckily, my dad was just messing around with us; we wound up renting a decent house in an average neighborhood. I truly think my dad wanted to set our expectations very low by presenting us with the trailer home and revealing to us just how dire our situation could have been so that we would be relieved once he showed us the house on Tampania Avenue that we would actually be living in.

As quickly as they could, my parents ushered me into the care of the most reputable surgeon they could afford in Tampa, which was Dr. Greene. To the best of his ability, he cleaned up the mess Dr. Williams had made of my hand and helped it to achieve a vastly improved range of motion. I can't overstate how much this improved my life, especially when it came to my performance in sports. Without the surgical efforts of Dr. Greene, there is no way I ever would have had any athletic success in my life.

On the bright side, having to go so long without having a full range of motion in my right hand had forced me to become functionally ambidextrous, which also had its advantages. They were advantages that would serve me very well when my interests turned sharply toward pursuits of an athletic nature.

TWO – *Adjusting to life in Tampa*

There were some *enormous* social adjustments that I was forced to make after moving from Gary to Tampa. I spent the end of fifth grade and all of sixth grade at Tampa's Egypt Lake Elementary School. From there I went to Webb Junior High School, which was the first time I ever heard about busing programs, which were intended to integrate the school districts.

One of the boys I went to school with, Randy Payne, who was the epitome of a redneck, was loudly lamenting how the powers that be were about to start shipping "niggers" to our school, and added that their presence was somehow going to ruin everything that was good about our school.

Hearing Randy say *that* word in *that* way made me feel just like the character Navin in Steve Martin's 1979 comedy film *The Jerk*, when he beats up all the racist mobsters by the pool. Since the overwhelming majority of the friends I'd ever had in my life up to this point had been Black, this pissed me off immensely and resulted in an explosive argument between Randy and I.

"You don't even know any of those people yet!" I argued. "Everyone I know back in Indiana is Black, and those were all my best friends! You've *never* even been around any Black people!

"*That's* Gary, Indiana!" spat Randy. "*This* is Tampa, Florida!"

I'm sure Randy was just parroting the attitudes of the grownups around him in his home environment, but I perceived it to be a very personal issue between the two of us, and we almost came to blows over it. The thing that was so alarming about it all was that Randy had actually been a very good friend to me until conversations began to revolve around racial issues, and he revealed his racist thoughts about Black people.

One of the students brought to Webb Middle School through the efforts of the busing program was Gary Mathis, a huge Black kid who always seemed to have a chip on his shoulder, and who was on a constant quest for physical altercations. One day, the customary buzzer sounded to signal the end of class, except this time the sound of the buzzer was immediately followed by an unusual announcement over the loudspeaker.

"All teachers report to the cafeteria *immediately!*" blared the frantic message.

That particular interruption in the school day had been caused by a fight between Gary and Randy out by the big oak tree in the middle of the school courtyard. Their altercation prompted some of

B. Brian Blair: Truth Bee Told

the other boys to align themselves along racial lines and engage in fisticuffs of their own, and an all-out ethnic brawl had ensued on the level of the Jets and the Sharks in *West Side Story*.

To remediate the situation, the school's administrators rounded up all of the Black students, escorted them to the cafeteria, and monitored them until things settled down.

I couldn't understand why any of this was happening. The atmosphere in Gary had never been anywhere near this tense. The palpable tension in the middle school continued for about a month, and it was a rather unsettling feeling. Despite the anxiety of that period, I did manage to become friends with a few of the Black kids at school, including one girl who I would frequently study with and work on homework assignments with.

The tables turned when we continued on to Tampa Bay Tech High School, where there were more Black kids than White kids enrolled. I easily became friends with all of the guys on the football team, regardless of racial identity. However, during that first year at Tampa Bay Tech, I got into a fight with a Black kid at school who was a first-class instigator. Somehow, he held the belief that I simply wouldn't fight him no matter how much he antagonized me because he was surrounded by other Black kids, and that this somehow granted him immunity from harm. He *couldn't* have been more wrong.

This guy thought I wouldn't retaliate, and he was *very* surprised when I did. I locked my arms around him, quickly wrestled him to the ground, got on top of him, and punched him dead in the face. Within seconds, Mr. Kent, the principal, arrived on the scene and pulled me off of the guy. The other Black kids who were present for the fight knew this kid was a real asshole, and they weren't about to protect him from me when things didn't work out in his favor. Racial solidarity definitely has its limits if you're not worthy of the support.

Since I stood up for myself, I was heralded as someone in the school that you didn't want to pick a fight with, because I would take you up on it, and you might not be thrilled with the result.

By this time, I was already in love with professional wrestling. I was close friends with a boy named Tommy Demott, who lived at the end of Minnehaha Street and still does to this day. One of our favorite pastimes was to pretend we were pro wrestlers. We wrestled regularly in the front yard of our mutual friend Rick Costan's house, which was further up Minnehaha Street from where I lived.

Between the ages of 13 and 14 years old, imitating professional wrestlers was inarguably our favorite thing to do when school was out and our sports seasons had concluded. We would hang

B. Brian Blair: Truth Bee Told

out in the treehouse and then wrestle in Rick's backyard for hours on end. Aside from wrestling, I also enjoyed fishing, which is a love that my father and grandfather passed on to me. Tommy and I would go fishing on the Gandy Bridge and catch gigantic drumfish in the evenings.

Our fondness for fishing came in particularly handy when we dealt with Mr. Kleinbaum. He was an old, grouchy guy in the neighborhood who always came outside in his robe to hassle us. Every Sunday, Mr. Kleinbaum would emerge from his house like clockwork to fetch his newspaper between 11:00 a.m. and 11:30 a.m. Knowing this, Tommy and I caught a drumfish, cut the stomach out of the fish, and laid it across Mr. Kleinbaum's porch. The porch faced directly east, and there was nothing blocking it from the heat of the Florida sun. Before too long, the putrid remnants of the fish produced a fetid stench that seemed to saturate every inch of the Kleinbaum property.

Days later, Barry Kleinbaum, an old neighbor of ours who also happened to be Mr. Kleinbaum's son, tracked down Tommy and I on Minnehaha Street.

"Whoever put that fish in front of our house, you're in *big* trouble!" threatened Barry. "My dad stepped on that fish and slipped. He got hurt and couldn't read his paper. Now he's stuck in his chair and he'll probably have to go to the hospital! *And* our whole house smells like fish, and there are flies everywhere!"

These days, I feel sorry for whatever discomfort I caused that poor man. Honestly, at the time I thought it was one of the *funniest* acts I had ever committed. It was at this early age that practical joking became one of my foremost loves, and it would ultimately come in very handy just a few years later when I became immersed in the world of professional wrestling.

Long before high school began, I was already obsessed with playing sports and working out. I picked up my first Joe Weider magazine when I was 10 years old, started doing push-ups, and absorbed all the material about what I should be eating, along with how to gain strength and body mass while losing fat. I also began lifting weights. I started off with a 110-pound weight set consisting of cement weights with plastic coverings. Because I was reading the Joe Weider magazines, I learned how to lift properly so that I didn't get a hernia or stunt my growth; those were a couple of the things I was *extremely* concerned about.

Through diligent work, I became stronger, and in an era where relatively few athletes did regular strength training during their own free time, I became far stronger than most of my friends. It was

B. Brian Blair: Truth Bee Told

rewarding to be able to link my success and growth to the training I had been doing. It wasn't all about getting stronger; I also saw the secondary value of using fitness as a way to impress the girls.

However, it was even more important that I recognized how important fitness was for improving athletic performance. It seemed like the guys that were the highest achievers in sports all had very athletic bodies. The amateur wrestlers all appeared to possess chiseled physiques even if they didn't have huge, hulking bodies. It was obvious that they all worked out hard. Therefore, the value to me was in both aesthetics and in increasing my chances to succeed in sports.

Frankly, I couldn't have avoided playing sports even if I'd wanted to. My dad was a tremendous athlete, despite having been forced to play through a serious disability. At the tender age of three, he had lost the sight in his left eye due to a bout with glaucoma. He overcame this hindrance, and he may have been the only person ever to play NCAA basketball with one eye during his time at Valparaiso University. He played basketball there for one season, and he was also a very good pitcher for their baseball team. Despite his strong arm, my dad understandably had great difficulty holding runners on base because of his obvious lack of peripheral vision.

Dad took it upon himself to coach me in basketball for a couple of seasons, and I just couldn't become a good enough basketball player no matter how much time and effort I put into it. I wanted to impress my dad because he was so accomplished at both baseball and basketball. I was definitely a competent baseball player, but basketball was a sport I was simply wretched at. Every time I stepped onto a basketball court, I felt like I was letting my dad down by not excelling. Like most kids, I wanted to make my parents happy all the time, but there was no chance that I would ever make my father happy with the poor quality of my performances on the hardwood.

Ultimately, I decided the matter was worth speaking privately with my father about.

"Dad, I'm just not good at basketball," I lamented to him. "I want to try other sports."

Fortunately, Dad was okay with this. From there, I shifted my focus to football and wrestling, in addition to baseball, and I also threw the shotput and the discus for the track & field team. Progressively, I got better at each sport. This is when I formulated the goal to earn an athletic scholarship and to then become recognized as a professional athlete.

In that respect, things got off to a terrific start for me. While I was still attending Webb Junior High School, I won the first

B. Brian Blair: Truth Bee Told

Hillsborough County JHS Wrestling Championship by defeating Ronald Reddick, a ninth grader who stood 6'4" and weighed 250 lbs.

I also started both ways on our football team in 8th and 9th grade. Coach Phil Zimmerman was our awesome head football coach. He looked like Hercules, except he had a prosthetic leg and walked with a severe limp. He lost his leg during his days in the U.S. Navy when a mortar shell fell on his leg.

In addition to my athletic endeavors, Dad took an interest in my academic pursuits as well. One subject in particular was of foremost importance to him.

"Son, if you're going to be good in any subject, please be good at math because you don't want people to cheat you out of your money," he advised me.

Just that statement alone from my dad was enough to ensure that I would do everything I could to be good at math.

Sadly, my parents' union didn't last all the way to my arrival at Tampa Bay Tech. Their marriage suffered immensely during the carpenters' strike at Tampa International Airport. The strike lasted so long that Dad's unemployment benefits expired. After a while, I stopped seeing very much of him. He would come over to the house every so often and would tell all four of us kids that he was out looking for a job, but this was an obvious excuse. Some of our standard food items were conspicuously replaced by powdered eggs, powdered milk, prunes and Spam.

Eventually, our family had to accept government aid in the form of food stamps, which was one of the most humbling and sometimes humiliating experiences of my life, and also one of the most formative periods in my development.

One day my mom asked me if I wanted to go to the grocery store. It was a U-Save grocery store that happened to be on the other side of Sligh Avenue – a very busy street in Tampa both then and now.

"Nah, Mom," I replied. "But if *you* go, could you please get us some chicken or some hamburger?"

"No... I mean why don't *you* go to the grocery store," my mom reiterated.

I was dumbstruck.

"You mean by *myself*?" I asked in disbelief.

"Yes," she answered with a smile.

My mother had never let me walk to the grocery store by myself before; she had considered the walk across Sligh Avenue to be

B. Brian Blair: Truth Bee Told

too dangerous a trip for me to take solo. Clearly, I had reached a major milestone in my development into a responsible young man.

I assured my mother that I knew where everything was in the grocery store. I also made it clear that I would watch the cashier like a hawk to ensure that we didn't get cheated or double charged for any items while the groceries were being rung up at the cash register.

Mom handed me a list, and along with the list I expected to be provided with some cash. Instead of money, Mom handed me a strange-looking coupon.

"What is this?" I asked her.

"Hand it to the lady after she rings up the groceries," my mother instructed. "You should have some change coming back on a coupon that looks just like this."

My mother made the expected exchange sound simple enough, but something about the scenario she was describing didn't sit quite right with me. Nonetheless, I was excited to embark upon the trek to the grocery store on my own. I walked up Minnehaha Street and carefully hung a right straight towards Sligh Avenue.

As I promised my mom, I was extremely careful crossing Sligh Avenue and then making my way across Armenia Avenue to get to the U-Save grocery store. Once I'd successfully entered the store, I felt like a responsible adult for the first time in my life, even though I wasn't even 13 years old yet. I really enjoyed my excursion through the meat department, where I picked out some reasonably-priced chicken and some hamburger meat. From there, I scooped up all of the other items on the list and then made a beeline to the cash register.

There was only one person ahead of me in the line, and the cashier was in the process of checking them out.

"Hey, *Blair*!" I heard from behind me. "What are *you* doing here?"

I turned around to see Steve Epperson and a pair of his cronies. Collectively, they were the established bullies of Egypt Lake Elementary School. I couldn't afford to be distracted by them, however. The cashier soon began the process of ringing up my groceries, and I attentively watched her to ensure she did everything correctly. I didn't want to lose my newly-won privilege of being able to go grocery shopping on my own.

When the cashier concluded the process of tallying the price total, she announced how much money I needed to give her. I reached into my pocket, pulled out the coupon and then handed it to the cashier just as my mom had instructed. Recognizing the nature of the coupon, the cashier immediately pulled out another coupon and started to fill it out while another employee of the store commenced the process of bagging my groceries.

From behind me, I heard some faint whispers emanating from the area where Steve and his friends had been standing, and it sounded like it might have had something to do with the transaction that had just taken place at my register. As soon as the cashier handed me my coupon and my receipt, I hastily grabbed the groceries from the counter and walked home with them as quickly as I could. I never said anything to my mother about the awkwardness of that trip to the grocery store because I knew she was dealing with a lot of stress, and I did not want to add to her list of worries.

The following morning, Mom and I began our day in the usual manner: I did not want my friends to know that my mom drove me to school, so I had her drop me off at a place called the Journey's End about a quarter of a mile from Egypt Lake. As I always did, I gave her a kiss and told her that I would meet her right back in that same spot after school, and on time.

Everything seemed perfect to me at that moment. The prior evening, I had enjoyed my best meal in several months. As I approached Egypt Lake Elementary School, I could see that a sizable group of kids had gathered together close to the building's entrance. As I drew nearer, I saw that somebody had used green spray paint to irreverently decorate the front of the school with graffiti.

"There he is!" yelled one of the kids as I got closer.

This announcement was followed by laughter and plenty of whispering. Finally, I got close enough to read exactly what had been painted onto the front of the Egypt Lake school building, and the words made me want to dig a deep hole and jump into it. Someone thought it would be worthwhile to take a can of spray paint and expose my family's precarious financial state to the entire student body of Egypt Lake. In addition to calling me a series of nasty names, the vandal had gone to great lengths to make it clear to everyone that my family was "poor."

As I turned and walked dejectedly away from the wall, a few of my classmates began teasing me about my family's monetary struggles. I continued walking back in the direction I had come from, and when I got about 50 yards away from the school, warm tears descended from my eyes and I broke into a dead sprint. I ran all the way home, vowing to never return to Egypt Lake Elementary School ever again. I simply couldn't understand how or why people could be so cruel.

B. Brian Blair: Truth Bee Told

When I entered our house, my mother was very surprised to see me.

"What's wrong, Brian?" she asked. "Why aren't you at school?

"I'm sick and I had to come home!" I told her, and then I ran to my room.

Somehow, Mom found out what happened from my teacher and coach, Mr. Agliano. He had been my teacher for the last half of fifth grade and then again during sixth grade. Nobody in the school wanted to tangle with Mr. Agliano; he had big arms, was a lot taller than any of us, and he had a lot of thick hair all over his body.

When Mr. Agliano came to my house, he assured me that no one in the school would dare breathe a word to me about the inflammatory graffiti ever again, or about my family's financial predicament, under penalty of expulsion from the school. Thanks to his reassurance, I returned to school the next day. Looking back, this episode probably did more to shape the direction of my life than any other single childhood event. Not only did it teach me humility, but it also taught me that there were people in the world that were both extremely mean and extremely kind.

The memory of that incident lingered with me for well over a year, and it etched one thought in my mind that would remain present for my entire life: "I never want to be poor."

Ever since that time, I would always make it a point to do whatever I could to rid myself of any vulnerability to poverty. However, much of what I would soon do to earn money for my family was done out of absolute necessity.

B. Brian Blair: Truth Bee Told

THREE – *Learning the ropes*

My family desperately needed extra money, and I was *obsessed* with football. When I saw an advertisement in the newspaper requesting people to help sell concessions at Tampa Stadium during the University of Tampa's football games, I considered it the perfect answer to my prayers; a solution for family's needs coincided with my personal interests. What's more, we couldn't afford tickets to attend any of Tampa's football games. What could possibly have been better than getting paid to be in the building with a clear view of the entire field? At only 13 years of age, I secured what I considered to be a dream job selling soda during the home football games of the Tampa Spartans.

Part of what made selling soda such a golden opportunity for a teenage boy in Tampa was the fact that there were only two ways to enjoy serious sports action in Tampa during the 1970s. Either you attended the sporting events hosted by the University of Tampa, or you purchased tickets to watch Championship Wrestling from Florida's wrestling matches. There were no major league sports teams in Tampa, so college football and pro wrestling were the hottest tickets in town.

They called the stadium "The Big Sombrero" because it had two big sides. At the time, the University of Tampa was drawing about 30,000 fans to each of its Saturday night football games. My teenage mind couldn't comprehend that many people all occupying the same location simultaneously. I rightly assumed that there was a lot of money to be made off of them, and that I should be the one doing my very best to extract that money from them. My manager's name was Joe, and he could tell that I intended to be a workhorse. He put me straight to work selling drinks, and I hustled as hard as I could throughout the duration of that first game.

When the game concluded, Joe informed me that I'd just set a record for selling the most sodas of anybody that had ever worked for him. That bit of information got me *really* amped up. Whether Joe was telling me the truth or not, I had no idea, and it didn't really matter to me anyway. The end result was that I felt highly motivated to sell even *more* sodas. From there, I started earning about $100 during every game, which was a lot of money for a 13-year-old kid to bring home to his family back then... and we needed *every* penny.

Granted, this wasn't even my first job; early on I had a little mail route delivering sales flyers. For as long as I can remember, I always did what I could to make sure I worked. There was something

B. Brian Blair: Truth Bee Told

about growing up on the fringes of poverty that made me very self-conscious about whether or not I had income rolling in.

Before long, I developed a system for selling sodas at the optimal time. I recognized that when the Tampa Spartans were on offense, the fans were especially interested in watching them execute their plays, so I would stoop down and watch the plays unfold along with the rest of the fans in attendance. When the defense took the field, or during any other breaks in the action, I would spring to my feet and serve the fans who were now slightly less interested in the action and more interested in quenching their thirsts.

I soon identified the perfect vantage point from which to watch the action on the gridiron. The more action I took in, the more obsessed I became with the game of football *and* the University of Tampa Spartans. My obsession was justified, because the product that the University of Tampa put on the football field in those days was *incredible*. The top star on the team was John Matuszak, a defensive end who was a gargantuan man. He would eventually be selected first overall in the 1973 NFL Draft and win two Super Bowls with the Oakland Raiders.

The Spartans also had a few stars on offense during that era. One of them was a great quarterback named "Fabulous" Freddie Solomon. Even though he played quarterback in college, Freddie was transitioned into a wide receiver in the NFL, and won two Super Bowls with the San Francisco 49ers. The other star on offense was the fullback of the team, Paul Orndorff. Paul was drafted by the New Orleans Saints in the 12th round of the 1973 NFL Draft, but he would ultimately play a massive and enduring role in my life beginning just a few years later, and in a *vastly* different setting.

Those many Saturdays spent selling sodas at football games is how I originally became obsessed with the University of Tampa, and I started dreaming about playing football there just like all of my heroes.

As the money-motivated manager that he was, Joe would call me every week and make sure I was coming to the stadium to help him sell concessions. After my initial record-breaking sales performance, I can understand why he was so adamant about keeping me around. He was always very polite to me and treated me well, and I made it a point to return the favor, treat him with respect, and always reply by saying, "Yes, sir!" when I responded to him.

Even though my father was absent much of the time during my teenage years, he had already taught me the value of manners and treating people with respect. On top of that, politeness was already an integral part of my DNA.

B. Brian Blair: Truth Bee Told

A few weeks into my employment at Tampa Stadium, I even got to know some of the people that sat in my section on a personal basis. It didn't happen all that often, but I'd occasionally have people in my section who would wait for me to bring them sodas even if they had another soda guy standing right in their area. That was probably due to the fact that I would warn people if the ice had melted in the sodas I was holding, and that the sodas had become too watered down. It was nice to be recognized, and it felt rewarding when fans would specifically yell out, "Hey Brian! Come on up!"

Wrestling during my sophomore year against East Bay

Once I moved on to high school, I participated in several sports on the varsity level. This included football, baseball, track & field, and wrestling. At a weight of 212 pounds, I wrestled as our team's heavyweight in an era when there was no weight limit placed on the category. That means that I sometimes squared off against heavyweights from other schools who weighed in excess of 300 pounds, and who were *still* in formidable shape even at such colossal sizes.

However, the most memorable moment of my high school wrestling career wouldn't occur at a formal wrestling meet. Instead, it happened after I learned that I would be wrestling my old, racist nemesis Randy in a dual meet for practice. Our grudge hadn't subsided during the transition from middle school to high school, and I was excited for an opportunity to engage in legalized combat against him, to the extent that high school wrestling could be considered combat.

As we stared across the blue wrestling mat from one another, there was palpable tension in the air. Our dislike for one another was

B. Brian Blair: Truth Bee Told

public knowledge, and I couldn't wait to manhandle Randy in front of all of the other members of the wrestling team.

Unfortunately, things didn't work out exactly as I'd envisioned them. Randy knew more about technical wrestling than I did, and I wanted to beat him so badly that I made several foolish mistakes and played straight into his hands. He had learned a move called a Navy ride, which involved hooking my far leg and keeping my body pinned close to his. I simply didn't know how to escape from it. Randy stalled the contest until the very end, and I lost the match by a score of two to one.

To say I was crestfallen would be an understatement. Even though Randy outweighed me by at least 20 pounds, I was convinced that I could beat him. Inexperience and a lack of wrestling knowledge cost me a victory, and it taught me some humility as well. I was consoled by several of my teammates, all of whom knew that Randy had been a bully and a thorn in my side for years.

One of the teammates who consoled me was a great friend of mine named Steve Bush. He had a goal of dropping weight from 170 pounds to 158 pounds so that he could drop down to a weight class below that of our stud 170-pounder James Wyche and earn a spot as the 158-pounder on our wrestling team.

James and I, along with our coach Ken Lloyd, worked regularly with Steve as he trained incessantly to drop weight. Unfortunately, Steve just kept losing weight uncontrollably, well beyond the 12 pounds that he was required to lose in order to achieve his goal weight, and it seemed completely implausible that what he was doing in terms of dieting and exercising could have caused such dramatic weight loss.

It wasn't long afterward that we learned Steve had contracted Leukemia. He stopped coming to school, and I was able to visit him in the hospital only a few times before he quickly succumbed to his illness. This event dispelled any notions that my friends and I were immune to tragedy simply because we were young. In some ways, Steve's death has stuck with me for my entire life.

Despite my devotion to financially assisting my family, I didn't always make the most responsible decisions. One day during my first year of high school, my mother entrusted me with the family's prized 1966 Dodge Charger. Driving a sports car with a powerful engine attracts a lot of attention, which was one of the reasons I wanted to drive the Charger to school in the first place. Unfortunately, I fell prey to peer pressure and decided to race a guy named John Lemkuel.

B. Brian Blair: Truth Bee Told

One of my many jobs involved working alongside John's dad at a Sunoco gas station that was east of Dale Mabry on Kennedy Avenue. Tampa Bay Tech was a technical school, and I readily applied the lessons I learned in the auto shop class to the real world and fixed up cars. That included a 1969 Chevelle SS 396 that I worked on alongside one of my instructors.

John owned a tricked-out 1969 Camaro 350 with all of the gimmicks under its hood, and I really had no business racing against him in the family car. I *also* didn't want to back down from him. My teenage pride won out. The two of us lined our cars up at the appointed spot, and I put the Charger in neutral. One of our schoolmates stood in front of the vehicles to make sure we were arranged precisely where we were meant to be, and then he raised his arm into the ready position. When he dropped his arm to signal for us to go, I immediately dropped the car into drive and hit the gas pedal with everything I had. The transmission of the Charger *instantly* blew up.

I lied to my mom and made up a story about the transmission not working. I refused to tell her the truth of how I'd irresponsibly risked the functionality of the family car by racing it against a high school classmate. It was a huge family bill at precisely the wrong time, and it was *entirely* my fault. I still haven't come clean to my mother about what really occurred, and I feel guilty about it to this day.

When we could no longer afford the rent on the house, Mom found a place for all of us at Waterford Village Apartments on Waters Avenue. I slept at the apartment, but I was almost never there otherwise. I worked so many hours, studied so much and worked out so much that I had no time in the day for anything else.

In addition to my job at Tampa Stadium, which spanned three consecutive football seasons, I had a lot of other jobs. I welded mailbox posts for Bill Wahlenter, I sold cookware, pots, pans, and crystal for Richard Coppadonna of Exclusive Home Products, I worked at Kmart, and I also worked at a hooker bar called The Huddle Lounge. Things escalated to the point where I was working every night at the Huddle Lounge until 3:00 a.m. Then I would get up in the morning and drive my Yamaha 200 from Town 'N' Country to Tampa Bay Tech High School, rain or shine. It was a 10-mile journey each way.

With Mom out of the house working, and with me also scrambling to work every chance I could, the family needed a babysitter. Mom became friends with Terri Rubio, and Terri was charged with watching us, even though I felt that I could adequately

B. Brian Blair: Truth Bee Told

watch myself. Unbeknownst to us at first, Terri was one of the behind-the-scenes girlfriends of legendary baseball player Pete Rose.

On the baseball diamond with Pete Rose

To me, this was *unfathomably* cool. I was a *huge* baseball fan, and Pete was arguably the greatest player in all of baseball at the time. It was practically a point of pride for me that my babysitter was one of Pete Rose's mistresses. Terri would talk to him on the phone constantly, and I guess it just never really occurred to us that Pete was married with children, or the scandal that might ensue if it ever became public knowledge what Pete was doing behind his wife's back.

In that era when camera phones didn't exist, and when there wasn't an internet through which news and photos could be shared with millions of people in seconds, the affairs of celebrities could remain hidden from their loved ones even if they walked around with their mistresses in plain sight. As long as he was a few states away from home, even a guy as famous as Pete Rose could figuratively – and possibly even literally – get away with murder.

Not content to simply talk to his young mistress on the phone, Pete stopped over at the apartment on more than one occasion while I was there, and I was able to meet him and hang out with him personally. One time he brought me a signed photo of himself, and another time he came over and handed me a crisp $20 bill.

"Here, Kid... Go on and get a soda or something to eat," the baseball legend advised me. "Come home in an hour."

B. Brian Blair: Truth Bee Told

Twenty dollars was *huge* money to me at that age, and handing it over to me was Pete's indirect way of asking me to get lost. With that much *free* spending cash in my pocket, I felt like a millionaire.

"Yes, sir!" I said, as I accepted the money and headed for the door.

I did as I was told. They didn't think I knew what was happening, but I *absolutely* knew what was happening. Clearly, they wanted some time alone with one another, and I gave it to them.

Later on, Terri became pregnant and gave birth to a baby girl named Morgan Erin, who was named after baseball greats Joe Morgan and Henry "Hank" Aaron. Terri eventually sued Pete for paternity, but it took many years for Pete to finally admit that Morgan was his daughter.

On the rare nights that I had some free time, I liked to head over to a bar called The Other Place. There was a band that played there regularly called Ruckus, and the bass player was this massive, 6'6" blond guy with chiseled muscles and a moustache named Terry Bollea. Everyone in town knew who he was; he looked like a rock star and was larger than life. The bouncer was always kind enough to let me inside to hear Ruckus play, even though I was technically too young to be in there early on.

What was even cooler was that I would also see Terry at the wrestling matches sometimes. It was most affirming to see that I shared a fondness for professional wrestling with the coolest guy in all of Tampa. I tried to approach him and befriend him on more than one occasion, but the five-year age difference between us was huge when you're comparing a 16-year-old high school kid to a 21-year-old man. All the same, he was polite to me every time he saw me, whether it was at the matches at the Armory, or at The Other Place in between musical sets.

I had no way of knowing that both of our paths would lead us to full-time careers as professional wrestlers. There were two major factors that influenced the direction of my life and led me straight toward a career inside of the squared circle: One factor I had a tiny bit of control over, and the other factor happened by way of a pure quirk of fate.

The first factor had to do with the fact that I developed into a recognizable high school athlete around the Tampa area. I was one of the first four-sport lettermen in the history of Tampa Tech High School. Sports had been an outlet that helped me to get out all of the frustrations that came from growing up poor, having my mom and dad

B. Brian Blair: Truth Bee Told

being divorced, and the lingering resentment from some of the other disheartening things that had happened in my young life.

As a football star at Tampa Tech

I was also driven by the knowledge that I couldn't afford to attend college unless I received a full athletic scholarship. Fortunately, I was getting recruited by a lot of schools that had second-tier football programs, but which had solid academic programs, like Appalachian State in Boone, North Carolina, and Dartmouth College in Hanover, New Hampshire.

Of course, my teenage dream was to play football at the University of Tampa, so it didn't really matter to me whatsoever if any other universities had an interest in me.

Because of my athletic success, I was featured and interviewed a few times by Andy Hardy on Channel 13 during his coverage of local sports. The most consequential segment I was involved in brought to light how I had succeeded both athletically and academically despite being financially disadvantaged. This caught the attention of local wrestling promoter Eddie Graham, who had been watching the broadcast and thought that I conducted myself professionally while wearing a tie. The funny thing is, I had to borrow that tie from my dad just for the broadcast; I didn't even *own* a tie!

B. Brian Blair: Truth Bee Told

Eddie made it a priority to personally attend a lot of the local amateur wrestling dual meets and tournaments, and he was frequently flanked at these events by stars from Championship Wrestling from Florida. In addition to being a great public relations tactic, it was Eddie's way of letting local wrestlers know that there was a professional pathway connected to their sport of choice if they wanted to pursue professional wrestling after they'd finished with amateur wrestling. Eddie used these events to bridge the two sports, while also selling the Florida public on the idea that professional wrestling was legitimate competition.

On the Tampa Tech wrestling team

Mike Graham, Steve Keirn, Jack Brisco and Jerry Brisco all accompanied Eddie to one of my dual meets. I met all of them and shook each of their hands. Eddie and the four wrestlers were all extremely polite to me, but for some reason Steve Keirn really seemed to take a special liking to me.

The second factor that played a role in propelling me into the wrestling business was the fact that Buddy Colt lived in the same apartment complex that we did. I also worked regularly alongside his wife, Darlene, at the Huddle Lounge. In addition, Mom got to be very good friends with Darlene and hung out with her all the time at the apartment complex, which brought me into regular contact with Buddy.

B. Brian Blair: Truth Bee Told

Even though Buddy was a heel – or a bad guy – who often cheated by affixing an illegal device to his thumb when he faced my favorite wrestler of all time, Jack Brisco, it was impossible for me to hate him because he was so kind to me in person. Before too long, my list of money-making endeavors even included babysitting Buddy Colt's daughters, Vicki and Cindy.

Senior year of high school

After I'd made it clear that I would be interested in training to become a professional wrestler, Eddie asked Buddy to drive me down to 106 N. Albany Street – also known as either The Sportatorium or The Dungeon, depending on whether it was being used for entertainment or training at the time. The building held a wrestling ring and an upstairs office, and the heat inside of that building was *overpowering*. The sweltering temperature in The Dungeon could easily exceed 104 degrees where the wrestling ring was, which was partially due to the massive light that hovered above the ring. It must have been 2,000 watts, and it was *always* on. That's where all of the wrestling trainees and would-be wrestling stars went to get stretched by Hiro Matsuda.

Hiro was a highly accomplished professional wrestler who was broken into the wrestling business by the legendary Rikidozan, the father of professional wrestling in Japan. Hiro's fervent belief was that it was an honor to be a professional wrestler, and that anyone wishing

B. Brian Blair: Truth Bee Told

to make a career in the pro wrestling industry should pay a steep physical toll prior to entering it. All of this was reflected in Hiro's training techniques.

Hiro's idea of an initiation for his trainees was to make all of us do calisthenics until we begged for death. He started us all out with 500 Hindu squats and 500 pushups – in sets of 100 – with 20 seconds of rest in between each set. Then he made us crawl into the ring and get down on the mat for 10 straight minutes of amateur wrestling after we were already exhausted from the calisthenics.

Hiro's requests were absolutely preposterous, because in high school we would wrestle for three, two-minute periods with a one-minute break in between. In college, they wrestle for three, three-minute periods with a one-minute break in between. It would *never* make logical training sense to have someone get down on the mat and wrestle for 10 straight minutes unless you simply wished to punish them… which is precisely what Hiro intended to do.

Granted, none of us could adequately complete all of those squats and pushups anyway, so by the time my first 10-minute round of wrestling was over with, I'd had all the abuse I could physically handle. I rolled out to the floor outside of the ring and puked on my hands and knees. I vomited until there was absolutely nothing left inside of me that could come out. My first day of pro wrestling training was excruciatingly brutal. It was undeniably one of the *hardest* days of my entire life.

The next day, I did the exact same thing; I vacated the ring, and then vacated the contents of my stomach. On the third day I made a small improvement, inasmuch as I slid out of the ring and started dry heaving while I was down on all fours. I could feel the heat of Matsuda's glare on me and saw his bare feet out of the corner of my eye as he approached.

"Hey, boy…" Matsuda began, as he hooked my chin with his dusty foot and used it to lift my head until my eyes locked onto his. "Why you no puke?"

"Mr. Matsuda… sir… I haven't eaten since the last time I puked," I replied, struggling to get the words out.

Hiro quickly turned his face away from mine and removed his foot from beneath my chin. I didn't hear any laughter coming from him, but his ears perked up and his shoulders slid up and down. I soon got the feeling that my answer was satisfactory to him, because he dialed down the intensity of the training just enough so that I could survive… *barely*.

B. Brian Blair: Truth Bee Told

As savage as Hiro Matsuda's training methods could be, they weren't as painful as the methods of Karl Gotch, who would also come in and train with us from time to time. Gotch may have been the realest pro wrestler in the world, because his wrestling style was built around the idea that wrestling was a legitimate sport. In his eyes, the best pro wrestler in the world should be able to defeat any man alive in an honest-to-goodness fight.

Right when I was breaking in as a wrestler

If Hiro's preferred form of punishment was to push our bodies to the breaking point in terms of their capacity for physical endurance, Gotch preferred to push our bones to their literal breaking points without quite crossing the line. Somehow, he seemed to know the precise point at which an arm or a leg could be extended before it would snap into pieces.

B. Brian Blair: Truth Bee Told

The cavalcade of high-profile trainers also included Bob Backlund. Eventually Backlund would become the heavyweight champion of the World Wide Wrestling Federation, but at the time he came in to work with us, he was still relatively new to the wrestling business. Even so, Backlund had already been a two-sport NCAA Division II All-American, and also an All-American in two different weight classes of collegiate wrestling. His conditioning was absolutely otherworldly. Backlund could tire you out – or blow you up – simply by getting down on the mat with you and wrestling in a standard amateur style. He *never* got tired.

Even Gordon Nelson, who was in his late 40s at the time, would get in on the torture sessions. Gordon was generally regarded as a past-his-prime wrestler by that point, and his primary responsibility in the 1970s was setting up the ring truck. However, at his core Gordon was still the guy who had once been the best freestyle wrestler in Canada. He could casually hop into the training sessions at any point and perform a set of 500 squats just to make us look bad, and then he would carry on with the rest of his business for the day.

The ultimate irony behind all of this training was that my wrestling hero, Jack Brisco, hardly did any conditioning exercises at all. In fact, Jack was notorious for the brevity of his warmups prior to his matches. The famous 'Jack Brisco warmup' consisted of 25 jumping jacks, a quick bent-over hamstring stretch, and a few trunk twists, all with a cigarette dangling from his lip.

At no point in this training had anyone needed to reveal to me that pro wrestling was a work – or a performance-based sport with predetermined outcomes – because all of the training was rooted in legitimacy. All of the training had been conducted by real wrestlers – also known as "hookers" and "shooters" – who would exhaust you with calisthenics, and then teach you how to exchange real wrestling holds as if your life depended upon it.

I had initially thought my amateur wrestling background would serve me well during the training sessions, but I was wrong. I would instinctively set myself up to get hooked *all* the time. As soon as I would secure a tight waist hold on someone, they would slap a double wristlock on me. In short, if you tried to wrestle *properly* with these guys, you would always find yourself getting hooked in a painful submission hold.

It was an unbelievable treat for me when Paul Orndorff arrived to train with me during my second summer in The Dungeon, because he had been my hero from back when I was selling sodas to the fans at Tampa Stadium in my early teens. I never thought I'd ever

B. Brian Blair: Truth Bee Told

get to spend time with Paul, let alone train with him or wrestle him. Little did I know, I'd end up spending more time with Paul than with just about any other wrestler over the course of my career.

Paul was already much further along in his training when I started out. This meant that he had already learned how to take bumps, which is the art of learning how to fall to the mat without getting injured. I was at the point in my curiosity that I wanted to know what a bump felt like, and since Paul was ready to be shipped off to work for Bill Watts, I assumed he had already been told that wrestling was a "work" – meaning it was not real. After all, most of the pro wrestling we were watching on television was fundamentally different from the techniques we were learning in the ring at 106 N. Albany. Also, since I was spending most of my training sessions legitimately fighting for my life, it became much easier for me to spot cooperation between wrestlers during televised matches.

I told Paul that Hiro had already smartened me up to the fact that wrestling was a work, which is another way of saying it's choreographed with predetermined outcomes. Paul didn't believe me, and he was *right* not to believe me, because I was lying.

"Paul, slam me," I asked him.

"What do you mean, slam you?" Paul asked. "I'm not gonna *slam* you!"

"Come on!" I begged. "Hiro already told me how we have to cooperate with each other in our matches. We've already been through all that. Just slam me."

"Okay…" Paul shrugged.

Paul was so strong that he just casually hoisted me up and slammed me *hard* to the mat. I hadn't needed to provide him with any assistance whatsoever. As a result of that single slam, my hip was out of alignment for two weeks. In fact, I needed a chiropractor to slip everything back into place for me. Just in case I'd been lying about knowing that wrestling was a work, Paul went out of his way to ensure that my first bump was as memorable and painful as he could possibly make it.

Eventually, Hiro *did* teach me how to take bumps. When it's done properly, taking bumps is kind of like lifting weights, inasmuch as it's something your body gets used to if you do it regularly. If you lift weights for only one day, your muscles are going to be thoroughly sore the following day, and probably even more sore the day after that. But, if you lift weights every single day, the pain isn't going to be nearly as bad. Taking bumps works in the same fashion. If you're taking bumps every night, it hurts a whole lot less.

B. Brian Blair: Truth Bee Told

"*Must* learn to protect self," Hiro would say as he slammed us to the mat over and over again. "Chin to chest! Chin to chest!"

Hiro absolutely drilled into us that we always wanted to keep our chins to our chests. No matter what you do, you get your chin to your chest, because it's the best way to protect yourself from spending the rest of your life nursing a broken neck. That always has to be foremost in your mind. When you get slammed, suplexed or backdropped, you also want your forearms and your heels to hit the mat first. Even though the mat has a tiny bit of give to it, the surface of the ring is still composed of plywood placed over steel beams with half an inch of mat and canvas laid over the top of it. Landing on most wrestling mats is going to hurt no matter what you do. It's certainly *not* a trampoline.

One day I was sitting by the ring at the Sportatorium just after I'd finished up a round of training with Hiro. Eddie descended the steps from his upstairs office and beckoned for me to come over.

"Hey, Brian," Eddie greeted me with a wave of his arm. "Come on upstairs for a minute."

We both entered Eddie's office, and he walked me over to the chairs by the window.

"Have a seat," Eddie said, pointing outside. "*This* is pretty entertaining."

As instructed, I took a seat at the window and peered outside and out onto the street. The scene looked pretty normal, except for the presence of an attractive brunette standing out by the road, dressed in conspicuously skimpy shorts and a crop-top shirt.

"You see that girl over there on the corner?" Eddie pointed.

"Yes, sir," I answered.

"You see those guys behind that building across the way?" he asked.

"Yes, sir," I repeated.

"Those are cops, and that girl is wired up so that they can hear everything she's saying," Eddie informed me. "Watch what happens."

As we surveyed the scene, car after car would pull up and the drivers would proposition the girl. She would then instruct the drivers to meet her around the corner. As the drivers would pull around to the back, the girl would walk up to the driver's side window, and the drivers were totally oblivious to the presence of the police officers who would sneak up along the other side of the cars and then knock on the passenger's side window. Once a driver looked toward police officer number one, officer number two would switch places with the fake prostitute, then reach into the car and snatch the driver out onto the pavement.

When an arrest had been completed, the car would be towed, the driver would be carted off to jail, and everyone would reassume their original positions. Eddie and I must have watched this pattern repeat itself for more than an hour. A few of the times, Eddie personally knew the men who were falling into the trap.

Throughout the day, I would return to the ring to work with Hiro, but every time another John pulled up and was about to be apprehended by the police, Eddie would call for me to come back upstairs to the office. It was like he had access to his own private reality television series through the window of his office, and he wanted me to share in the experience.

Whenever free television tapings were advertised for the wrestling events, the full address of the building was always provided. That's why former CWF wrestlers are always so diligent about spelling out the 106 N. Albany address whenever they refer to the building. Sometimes the tapings were free, but if the Florida territory was really hot, they would charge five bucks for fans to get in.

If they *did* charge the five bucks, that meant I couldn't afford to go. In those cases, sometimes the wrestlers would help me get in, because even as a trainee, I had no special privileges when it came to show attendance. If they let me in for free, that meant there was theoretically still another $5.00 out on the street that could have made its way into a wrestler's pocket.

Steve Keirn was always great about getting me into the buildings when I couldn't afford a ticket. If the show was at the Fort Homer Hesterly Armory, Steve would pull up to the gate where the wrestlers drove in and then he'd order me to hop into this car. Once we got through to the building, Steve would have me carry his bag up to the dressing room, and then he'd shoo me off and tell me to go find a seat. He was extremely nice to me, and this got to be a regular occurrence. Then he started asking me if I wanted to hang out with him.

Steve was the first guy to really welcome me into the business as a true friend and not just as a trainee. He would invite me to go on his Hobi Cat over to the beach, or invite me out to eat with him at local restaurants. I always appreciated him for that. Steve is six years older than I am, which meant there was a good chance that I might end up competing against him for the same spot in a wrestling territory after he had established himself, and especially in Florida. Despite that, Steve still did everything in his power to make me feel welcome.

B. Brian Blair: Truth Bee Told

On one of the nights that Steve got me into the Armory, I found a seat by the railing of an elevated section that overlooked the ring to watch Jos Leduc fight against Dusty Rhodes in a Texas Bull Rope match. Jos and Dusty beat the absolute crap out of each other with the cowbells that were attached to the bull ropes. They brawled all over the building, and then gradually worked their way up the stairs into the section where I was sitting. The etchings carved into Leduc's forehead caused it to resemble a checkerboard even when he *wasn't* wrestling, and on that night, he bled like a stuck pig.

I was thoroughly frightened by seeing the blood gushing out of Jos' skull, and the gory nature of the contest caused me to have second thoughts about getting into the wrestling business altogether. They savagely clubbed one another while they were standing right next to me, and Jos' blood splattered all over my pants. Until then, I thought there might have been blood capsules involved in the matches, but it will alter your opinion in a hurry when you can personally see the blood oozing out of a man's flesh from less than two feet away, right before it decorates your clothing. I'd *never* been more frightened or intimidated in my life!

I had no clue that wrestlers would intentionally cut themselves with razor blades in order to produce authentic blood during the matches. I still wasn't yet allowed into the locker rooms, so I didn't get to watch anyone getting stitched up afterwards. Despite my presumption that wrestling results were predetermined, matches like this one could still occasionally convince me that everything about wrestling was real.

In the eyes of the wrestlers, I was just a step above the average fan, and I was sitting in an area of the building where fans wouldn't ordinarily be permitted to sit. At the same time, the wrestlers were a little more lenient with me because Keirn brought me into the building, and they all knew I was striving to become a wrestler just like them.

I was in the process of living out a dream, but I soon learned that wrestlers often paid physical tolls for being involved in their chosen profession, and sometimes the toll was absolutely devastating.

B. Brian Blair: Truth Bee Told
FOUR – *Making Adjustments*

Shortly after I had started training to become a pro wrestler during my senior year of high school, Buddy Colt and several other wrestlers were involved in a *catastrophic* plane crash on February 20th of 1975.

The wrestlers in the crash included Buddy, Bobby Shane, Austin Idol and Gary Hart, and they had been flying from Miami to Tampa. Buddy was personally flying the plane, but he didn't have an instrument rating; he was purely a visual-rated pilot. When a storm approached, Buddy got vertigo, missed Peter O. Knight Airport, and wound up crashing the plane into Tampa Bay, approximately 100 yards from shore where the water is around six-and-a-half-feet deep.

Bobby Shane died as a result of the crash. The rest of the wrestlers tried to grab him, but he freaked out because he couldn't swim and was never able to get his seat belt unhooked. He had been a very promising heel performer. Everyone who lived suffered some sort of serious injury, but Buddy's leg was so horribly mangled that he never wrestled again.

That was very traumatic for me, because Buddy and I had already become such close friends, and Buddy had vouched for me with Eddie Graham and personally driven me to my first day of training with Hiro Matsuda. Even though I hadn't been fully smartened up to the true nature of pro wrestling yet, and I still knew Buddy for being a dastardly heel on television, he had been a true mentor to me. When the plane crash occurred and Buddy's career was brought to an end as a result of it, I was absolutely *crushed*.

The plane crash was headline news in the area since it involved four prominent professional wrestlers. At the time, the only major-league sports team in the entire state of Florida was the Miami Dolphins. For all intents and purposes, wrestling was the *other* major-league sport in the state. Nearly everyone in Florida recognized the names of the guys involved in the plane crash.

During my senior year at Tampa Tech, I was named to the first team of the All Western Conference Football Team, and I signed a letter of intent to attend the University of Tampa alongside Priestly Davis, our stud of a running back who had broken his ankle halfway through our senior year. Despite his injury, he had a great reputation following his stellar junior year, so the injury hadn't hindered him during the recruiting process. However, the combination of transferring from the Sunshine Conference to the much larger Western Conference *and* losing Priestly for the season devastated our team. Our

B. Brian Blair: Truth Bee Told

record went from 6-4 my junior year to a winless 0-10 season during my senior campaign.

Despite our team's poor record, Coach Bob Anderson still went about his usual routine of sending game footage of his best athletes to several colleges in the hopes that he could help us acquire scholarship offers. Eleven different players from our team ultimately received scholarship offers to play at the collegiate level.

We're not talking about a run-of-the-mill set of collegiate athletes, either. One of our running backs was George Peoples, who transferred to C. Leon King High School after I graduated. He would ultimately go on to play for several seasons with the Dallas Cowboys. Our star defensive end, Phillip Darns, would go on to play with the New York Jets and Detroit Lions before ending his professional career with our hometown Tampa Bay Buccaneers.

Thanks to the combination of Coach Anderson's proactive promotional efforts and the quality of my play on the field, I'd managed to secure a scholarship to play football at my dream school. It was a childhood fantasy that had become a reality.

Unfortunately, the reality failed to last nearly as long as the fantasy. Within weeks of those two commitment letters being signed, it was announced that the National Football League would be expanding to the Tampa Bay region, and the Buccaneers football team would begin playing professional football games in the area. This didn't seem problematic at first, but it had *devastating* consequences.

Since the Buccaneers would be an NFL expansion team, it was obvious to everyone that they were going to have a losing season straight out of the gate, and probably several of them. If the Buccaneers were losing games on the field, it would have been even more difficult to garner the fan support they needed if they also had to compete for local fan support against the football dynasty at the University of Tampa. The Spartans were drawing between 30,000 and 40,000 people to their home games every Saturday night. They had also won 54 of the 75 total games they played in their prior seven seasons, and earned victories in each of the three bowl games the program had ever played in.

On the record, University of Tampa officials have stated that the football program was disbanded in order to help the academic reputation of the school, and also so that its team would not have to compete with an NFL franchise, but I'm convinced that money was exchanged behind the scenes to ensure the termination of the football program at the University of Tampa, and to help the NFL save face as it expanded into a fresh market.

B. Brian Blair: Truth Bee Told

When the University of Tampa dropped its football program just as I was sitting at the doorstep of my dream of playing there, it left me feeling completely *gutted*. Imagine spending all of those Saturdays selling sodas at Tampa Stadium as a teenager and fantasizing about the moment you would finally get to compete on that very same field. That dream was shattered the instant the NFL set their sights on Tampa, and it happened just as I was on the precipice of achieving that dream.

With my heart in pieces, I went back to Coach Anderson, who had already expended so much effort to help me get recruited, and I asked him what I should do. He made a couple of phone calls, including a call to Coach Vince Gibson at Louisville, which he knew had been my second choice.

A lot of schools had recruited me, but Coach Gibson stood out from the pack. Vince traveled all the way to Florida and drove right to my house. He brought a bouquet of flowers along with him and handed them to my mother. She *adored* that gesture.

"I appreciate you taking the time to come visit me, Coach," I told him once we were done. "I still think I'm going to play for the University of Tampa, though."

"I understand, Brian," Vince said. "You want to play in your hometown. Just remember me, and if things don't work out, you can always give me a call. I'd *love* to have you play at Louisville."

I really liked Coach Gibson. He was a really nice guy and a great talker. He and I hit it off immediately.

I was also a natural fit for the Louisville Cardinals given the way the team had been constructed. Gibson's 5'6" son, Stu, was the quarterback of the team, which meant his dad had to go to great lengths to accommodate his son's short stature. This resulted in Louisville's team keeping the middle of the field as short as possible, so none of the guards on the team were permitted to be taller than 6'2". Meanwhile, the tackles were allowed to be big and tall in order to keep the throwing lanes open. For example, Louisville's starting center during that era, Ron Olejack, was 6'3".

Vince Gibson called my mom and left a message for me to call him back. Unfortunately for me, by the time we reached Gibson, Louisville didn't have any scholarships remaining for the upcoming season. I was distraught at first, but Gibson gave me a couple of options.

"You can walk on, and I can do my best to help you out," said Gibson. "Of course, the NCAA places a lot of restrictions on us, so you'd have to *pay* for all your books."

B. Brian Blair: Truth Bee Told

It was nice of him to make that offer, but without any form of sustained financial support, that option was still out of the question. My family was broke, so providing me with a tiny bit of assistance here or there wasn't going to make a whole lot of difference.

Then Gibson said, "I have a good friend in Dade City at St. Leo College named Tilrow Morrison. He's a *tremendous* coach. He used to play at the University of Alabama under Bear Bryant. You could play for him for a year and then transfer up here. They have a great club football program. They travel all over the country and play a lot of the JV teams at big universities."

"That sounds great!" replied.

"There's just one catch," said Gibson. "They don't give scholarships."

"I can't afford to go to college without a scholarship," I reminded him.

"Let *me* work on that," Gibson said.

Vince spoke to Tilrow, and before much time elapsed, I received a call from Tilrow inviting me to visit the St. Leo campus, which is only about 40 miles from Tampa in an area that a lot of us call "the mountains of Florida." It's a very hilly place, and the school is situated along Lake Jovita.

The offer was *very* attractive to me; I would play football on St. Leo's club team for one year, and then I would be able to join the Louisville Cardinals. With that deal firmly ironed out, I enrolled at St. Leo College and joined their freshman club football team.

The next thing I knew, I was attending St. Leo College for free. I don't know how they pulled it off, and I don't particularly want to know since it might qualify as self-incriminating information. The one thing I do know is that they never once asked me to pay them a nickel. It was a small Catholic college with a shockingly large number of students from New York City taking classes there.

I never allowed myself to get too comfortable at St. Leo. In fact, I really didn't stay on campus any longer than I absolutely had to. St. Leo was only about 30 miles away from my house, so I drove to and from school every day.

I was immediately a starter on St. Leo's club team on offense, defense and special teams, while playing nose guard and offensive guard. I knew that Coach Gibson eventually wanted to bring me into the Louisville program as an offensive guard, but I was comfortable in any role. I just wanted to contribute as best I could and then get a free ride to a major university.

B. Brian Blair: Truth Bee Told

In my lone season with the St. Leo Monarchs, I was in constant motion during our games as I played nearly every down, seldom having a spare moment to catch my breath. My best trait as a player was that I was quick off the ball. That should *not* be interpreted as me saying that I was fast; I wasn't fast *at all*. I ran a 4.9 in the 40. Some people would call me slow, and I wouldn't argue with them if they did. I just wished they kept track of how quickly players got off the ball back then. That was the trait that allowed me to hold my own against the larger players I was constantly squaring off against.

We competed against the junior varsity teams of some major universities, including a game we played against the Duke Blue Devils. However, the most memorable experience from my time at St. Leo happened when we played Gallaudet College, which is now called Gallaudet University. While it's known to many people as the place where the movie *The Exorcist* was filmed, the most significant claim to fame of Gallaudet is the fact that it's the only institution of higher learning at which all of the programs are tailored exclusively to accommodate the deaf and hard of hearing. We rode the bus all the way from Florida to D.C. to play a football team that wouldn't be able to hear anything that was transpiring around them.

When we arrived at Gallaudet, we were led to the cafeteria where we were told we would be eating alongside the Gallaudet football players and the other students in the cafeteria. It was as quiet as can be, and it was an odd experience. Everyone around us was communicating exclusively in sign language, and we all felt out of place as the only people relying on spoken words to communicate. It's a unique environment that can be a little unnerving if you're not used to it.

There was a running back on our team named Tony Leone, who hailed from somewhere in New York. He was a fantastic athlete, but he was also one of the *cockiest* smartasses you could ever meet. Unconcerned that anyone other than his teammates would hear what he was saying, Tony sat at the cafeteria table and boasted very loudly about how we were going to manhandle Gallaudet's football team.

"There's no way these guys can beat us!" sneered Tony. "We're gonna *kill* them! They're gonna get so many penalties for piling on because they can't hear the whistle. How can they even snap the ball on time?"

By that point, I was praying that one of the guys from Gallaudet would knock Tony's dick in the dirt during the game. I didn't appreciate how Tony was so joyfully making fun of people with clear disabilities, let alone doing it while he was sitting right next to them in their own safe haven.

Gallaudet had a drum on the sidelines that they would hit either one time or four, and the number of drumbeats determined whether the offense got the play off on the count of one, or on the count of four. Even though the Gallaudet players couldn't hear the drum, they could feel its vibration, and they could get off the ball just as quickly as we could. If being able to hear gave us some sort of advantage over them, I certainly wasn't able to tell on that day.

Tony was always good for 100 rushing yards a game, but Gallaudet *totally* shut him down. In the end, we lost by two touchdowns. Everybody gave Tony the business throughout the entire trip from D.C. back to Florida. Usually, I was downright dejected if we lost. I was always concerned about why I missed blocks and tackles, and I would review everything in my head. Never once had I ever been happy about losing a game; this was the sole time I wasn't seriously upset about taking a loss. If I had to lose a game, I was glad the loss came at the hands of Gallaudet, and I'm glad we got the chance to make Tony miserable for having been so cocky.

The loss at Gallaudet was a humbling experience, and it taught me a lot to see these athletes from Gallaudet simultaneously overcome both their physical disabilities and their on-field opponents. It was a big feather in their caps, and they deserved all the credit in the world.

Unfortunately, I also suffered one of the worst injuries of my life while playing for St. Leo. While I was playing nose guard on the defensive side of the ball during our game against Duke, the Blue Devils ran a fullback dive through the I-hole, and I was shooting the gap on that play. As usual, I was quick off the ball as soon as it was snapped.

When I shot the gap, I had my arms up because I was splitting the center and the left guard. As I raised my arms, it lifted my chest protector up, and the fullback hit me dead in the middle of my chest with his helmet. I went down like a ton of bricks, and was in the most excruciating pain I'd ever experienced. In addition to the physical agony at the point of impact, I also couldn't breathe. Everything expands when you breathe, so as I panicked and tried to draw in air, it only served to enhance the pain. Every time I took a breath, it felt like someone was plunging a *knife* further and further between my ribs and into my heart. That sternum fracture was far and away the worst injury I ever sustained on a football field.

I was thrilled to finally get to the University of Louisville; I had really enjoyed my recruiting trip there. During that trip, I was

B. Brian Blair: Truth Bee Told

taken to the home of a guy named Otto Knopp Sr. He was a very wealthy man who owned a place called the Breckenridge Inn. There were five recruits and five football players who were already at Otto's house when I arrived, including Mark Pongonis and Jim Embry, who I became very good friends with. We all sat down at the dining room table to eat a meal that was going to be very memorable for me because it appeared as if we would be having steak. My family *never* had enough money to buy steak; liver was typically the best substitute for steak that we could afford.

With Louisville teammates Jim Embry and Mark Pongonis

After grace was said, I wasted no time before sinking my teeth into the steak on the plate before me. It was incredibly tender and tasty, even though it didn't quite taste like any steak I'd ever had before, not that I was in any position to pose as a steak connoisseur.

"Hey, is this venison?" someone asked while I was chewing.

"Yes," Otto said.

I'd never had deer meat before, but this meal made me an *instant* fan of it.

My career as a Louisville Cardinal wasn't particularly memorable. I was certainly never a football superstar in college. By that point, I was infinitely more interested in wrestling; I had already been training to wrestle for two years, and had a guaranteed job awaiting me with Championship Wrestling from Florida whenever I decided I was ready to return home and claim it. Even though I was a

B. Brian Blair: Truth Bee Told

college football player and student, the only thing I was concerned with was the next time wrestling would be shown on TV.

All of the decorations in my college dormitory were wrestling related. One time, I even dragged a large segment of the Louisville football team along with me to the Louisville Gardens. I'll never forget it, because my teammates were always saying to me, "Awww, come on! Wrestling is fake!" and I would defend the sport and say, "No, it's not!" All of it was good-natured ribbing, and no serious heat ever developed between myself or any of my teammates.

We arrived at the Louisville Gardens in time to watch a card that featured tremendous wrestlers like Phil Hickerson and Dennis Condrey. The main thing that I remember is that all of the guys from my football team were thoroughly and surprisingly enthralled with the action. It was like everyone on the entire football squad had a simultaneous change of heart about wrestling as the evening progressed. I began to hear them say things like, "Man, this wrestling is *tough!*"

The main event of the show featured Plowboy Frazier against George Gulas, and it was a stipulation match where George Gulas had to slam Plowboy. If Gulas couldn't slam Plowboy within the 30-minute time limit, Gulas would be forced to leave the territory. Unfortunately, the people in the arena could see through the match, meaning that you could plainly see that the wrestlers were cooperating, and the moves weren't as tight and crisp as they should have been.

Then, when it was time for the finish to the bout, you could see that George couldn't summon the strength or leverage required to lift Plowboy on his own without considerable help. Plowboy had to go out of his way to try to hop up and assist George with the slamming effort. Even with Plowboy supplying him with so much assistance, Gulas *still* couldn't get him off the mat even after attempting the bodyslam five separate times.

At long last, Plowboy just fell over onto his back after Gulas had barely lifted him six inches off the mat during his sixth effort. The referee officially ruled it a bodyslam and awarded the match to Gulas. People in the crowd were pissed off by how phony the ending to the main-event match had looked. According to the stipulation of the match, Plowboy would now have to leave the Kentucky region, and it seemed unfair that he should have to suffer such an injustice since he hadn't even been truly slammed.

When that abomination of a match concluded, my teammates started heckling me, saying things like, "You *can't* tell me that's real! That's *clearly* fake!"

B. Brian Blair: Truth Bee Told

I had to admit to them that they were right.

"I'm not gonna tell you *that* was real," I conceded. "That looked fake to me, too."

I started trying to come up with excuses for why that particular match might not have appeared to be genuine, but I didn't have a good explanation to give them. It didn't matter so much, because those guys were really nice about it afterwards. Even if they still thought wrestling was all phony, they never mentioned it to me ever again because all of the other matches had been great, and all of them had obviously enjoyed the action that evening at the Louisville Gardens.

For the rest of the guys, it had all been entertainment, but for me it was an opportunity to get a personal look at the wrestling action in a territory outside of Florida, and to fantasize about what it would be like to finally get a chance to compete inside of a professional wrestling ring. I would have my chance sooner than I realized.

Things were quite different for me at Louisville compared with how they had been at St. Leo's College. I'd commuted to St. Leo's on a daily basis, but at Louisville I was fully immersed in the campus lifestyle of a college athlete. I stayed in two different dormitories during my time at Louisville – Threlkeld Hall and Johnny Unitas Tower. It was preferred that football players stayed in Johnny Unitas Tower, but I made a special request to stay in Threlkeld Hall along with Mark Pongonis, one of the offensive tackles.

Across from Threlkeld Hall was a place called The Red Barn. Everyone loved to go there for the cheap beer and hot dogs. I even participated in a hot-dog-eating contest there once, and I'm pretty sure I finished in last place. The same was true of my finish in the beer-drinking contest. It was something I'd do just to be social and to be involved, but I wasn't a heavy drinker and couldn't compete with the true super heavyweights of the team.

It wasn't like I went about the competitions in a casual fashion either; I starved myself for two days before I competed in the hot-dog-eating contest, and I *still* felt totally stuffed after eating only six of them. Meanwhile, we had guys on our team who could eat in excess of 20 hot dogs at once! When it came to the beer, I could drink a full pitcher of beer in what seemed like a short period of time.

To me, a pitcher held a *lot* of beer. Of course, we had guys on our team that could drink *six* or *seven* pitchers of beer in one sitting. That's a lethal quantity of alcohol for some people. In the meantime, guys would be falling off of their barstools and girls would be stripping their clothes off and dancing around. It was a wild and unruly

B. Brian Blair: Truth Bee Told

environment. We were granted a lot of leeway at college-campus restaurants in the 1970s that probably wouldn't be given to students today.

The season I joined Louisville's football program, our team had just transitioned over from the Missouri Valley Conference into Conference USA. Our record was 2-9 my first year, and 5-6 my second year. I wore a few different jersey numbers at Louisville: 57, 63 and 65. I played as a dutiful backup on the second and third team during my first two seasons with the potential to start in my junior year. My priority was on receiving a great education, and the scholarship covered my expenses. I already had my post-football career path lined up in the form of a wrestling career, so I was really just biding my time until Eddie Graham and I both felt fully comfortable with the idea of sticking me inside of a Florida wrestling ring.

One of the stars of our Cardinals team was Otis Wilson, who transferred in from Syracuse and was an absolute stud at the outside linebacker position. He rightfully played on the 'A' team during our scrimmages, and I had to face off against him on the 'B' team. He was such a beast that most guys on the team were afraid to hit him, but I *loved* to challenge myself by targeting him during our practice sessions.

Otis had incredible power and agility, but his big weapon was his "flipper" – a forearm shiver that could stop a Mack Truck. The psychology you had to employ against Otis was to not let him know whether you were coming at him high, low, left or right. It was like a mental chess game. Linebackers needed to possess the ability to shed blocks, and Otis could shed a block better than anybody.

Despite his block-shedding ability, there were a few times when I absolutely flattened Otis during practice and left him wheezing on the field. No one *ever* knocked Otis around like that, so being able to do so was certainly a highlight of my collegiate football career, even if no one outside of our practice sessions ever got to watch it happen.

Since the University of Louisville's football team was a typical NCAA program, players had the ability to eat meals at the training table, which is where we could all eat planned meals consistent with our performance goals. Thursday night was a particularly popular night for the athletes, because it was always steak night. There were two Knopp brothers who were on the football team at the same time I was, including Otto Knopp Jr., who would go around bumming the leftover fat off of everyone who didn't eat the fat from their steak. Once Otto had collected the giant plate full of steak fat, he would sit down and eat the *entire* load. It was one of the most disgusting sights I had ever beheld in my young life.

B. Brian Blair: Truth Bee Told

The basketball players were also present at the training table, which provided me with plenty of opportunities to sit with basketball coach Denny Crum. There were several times I would be sitting by myself, and he would just come sit by me, even though I was an inconsequential player in the grand scheme of things. Every time Denny spoke, he always said something motivational to the players who were seated around him. He was so poised and inspirational that everything he said resonated as if it had been divinely inspired. It's no surprise to me that his teams at Louisville were so successful for so long, because his players would have *literally* run through walls for him.

I would have been obligated to see plenty of Denny Crum whether I'd wanted to or not; first-year football players were required to sell t-shirts and other items at Freedom Hall, which is where the Cardinals basketball team played.

Every night, whether it was in Threlkeld Hall or Johnny Unitas Towers, several members of the football team would all gather around a deck of cards and play Hearts. Six people would be actively playing cards, and another five would be spitting tobacco residue into the community dip receptacle. Between that and going to the Red Barn, those were the two most exciting things available for us to do. Louisville generally had a very dull, boring campus life. In a way it was good, because we couldn't do much else other than study.

I had an unfortunate experience at the University of Louisville when I returned to campus following our winter break. I had no idea that there was a devastating snowstorm approaching the Louisville area. When the storm arrived, people had to pull their cars over all along the highway, there were wrecks *all over* the roads, and it was about as nasty a traffic situation as you could ever imagine. Somehow, I steered my powder-blue 1972 Lincoln Continental through all of the turmoil. I was fortunate enough just to arrive at the Louisville campus in one piece!

I quickly ran to my room and switched the radio on, and that's when I learned that the entire campus had been shut down due to the snowstorm. Everything was closed up and emptied out. No one had given me any warning about what was going on there. My immediate thought was, "I need to call Jim Embry."

I ran down to the payphone to call Jim, but the phone had stopped working as a result of the storm, and that meant I would be stuck there all by myself. I returned to my empty room and sat down on my bed. The only thing I had with me that was of any entertainment value was my radio, so I turned it back on to listen to

B. Brian Blair: Truth Bee Told

some music. The sound of Aerosmith's "Dream On" filled the air, and I sat back and tried to brainstorm a plan for survival.

The only thought in my mind, at that moment, was that I was going to have to survive for a full week without food, and I *honestly* believed I was going to starve to death. The other thing that dawned on me in that moment was exactly how much I *loved* the song "Dream On." The instant the song ended, I spun the dial over to one of Louisville's other two rock 'n roll stations, and "Dream On" was just starting on the other channel. It was inspirational. I lied back down and strategized my next move.

As a carefree college kid

During that stormy night in Louisville, I went 24 hours without receiving any communication from the outside world. When service finally returned to the payphones the next day, I was able to reach Jim Embry and effectuate my rescue. Being the good friend that he was, Jim invited me to stay at his house until classes resumed. To

B. Brian Blair: Truth Bee Told

this day, if I hear "Dream On" playing anywhere, I think back to the time I spent in my Louisville dorm room wondering where everyone was and how I was going to find my next meal.

Since the University of Louisville emptied out around the time of the Kentucky Derby, I came up with a scheme to make some extra spending money after seeing the rates hotels were charging for rooms during the weekend of the Derby. I asked the resident assistant if it was okay for me to rent out some of the rooms in the dormitory, and then I would split the money with him. Just like everyone else in college, he also needed money, so he loved the idea and gave me the keys to five dorm rooms in addition to my own. I'd arranged to stay at the home of my friend, Jim Embry, who was one of the linebackers on our team.

I advertised the six rooms for $100 a night for up to four nights, and expected to walk away from my master plan with an extra $1,200 in my pocket. That amount of money would sustain me for a long time.

I drove over to Churchill Downs and took up a position right in the middle of the race-day crowd.

"Anyone looking for a room?!" I would repeat, over and over again. It was a lot like hawking sodas in the bleachers of the University of Tampa.

I didn't waste my time trying to pitch a night in a college dormitory to the well-dressed couples, because I was certain they wouldn't be even remotely interested in the idea. After all, none of the rooms had showers of their own, but they offered access to the student showers located further down the hallway.

Eventually, I smartened up and wrote "Room for Rent" on a sign in large letters. That made it far easier for the folks in search of rooms to find me amidst the large, bustling crowd. Whenever someone approached me with a room inquiry, my standard spiel was, "I'm a member of the University of Louisville football team, and we don't have much money. We need book money for next semester, so we're renting our rooms out for $100 a night. The rooms have TVs, and there are showers in the hallway."

It was a very easy sell; *all* of the rooms were rented out in no time at all. I stayed close by to keep my promise to the RA and to ensure that things ran smoothly. I was able to pull this off for two consecutive summers, and it was some of the easiest money I ever made in my life.

One of my most memorable instructors at Louisville was a professor who was very knowledgeable about nutrition and really got

B. Brian Blair: Truth Bee Told

me interested in it. She was a firm believer in the benefits of nutritional supplements. She inculcated in all of her students that if we could live on the sustenance provided by only one food source, pizza would be the best thing we could consume because it has carbohydrates, protein, fat and fiber, along with vitamin C in the tomato sauce. That was a concept that really appealed to me as a young man, because I was enamored with the idea of pizza actually being healthy for me. She also advised all of us to take a multivitamin as an insurance policy, because most people would never eat all of the required servings of food necessary to hit all of the recommended nutritional benchmarks.

This professor also said if you were lacking a particular vitamin, it might inhibit the ability of other vitamins to do their jobs. The example she provided was that vitamin E works better if selenium is also present in the body. As soon as she imparted that information to us, I went out in search of a daily multivitamin. I still take one *every* morning, like clockwork.

That same instructor told us that world starvation could be solved for as little as $1.00 a day, in 1970s money. Her formula was a multivitamin, two cups of uncooked rice, and 16 ounces of milk. Back in the '70s, these items were cheap, particularly in underdeveloped countries. It sounded so brilliant to me back then that I thought she should have gotten an award.

Simple strategies for solving problems often seem to go overlooked. I was about to be faced with a complex problem of my own, but the solution was easy to find. All I had to do was follow the money.

Then and now: Wearing two of my Louisville football jerseys

FIVE – *Ribs to go*

Right after my third semester at Louisville, one of the CWF referees told Eddie Graham that he couldn't make it to an event promoted by Don Curtis in Jacksonville, Florida. Eddie allowed me to fly over to Jacksonville with him on his plane so that I could get involved in the show as the replacement referee.

"You're going to be refereeing the match between Angelo Poffo and Butcher Vachon," announced Eddie after we arrived at the building. "You know how to do that, right?"

I honestly had *no clue* how to be a referee, and I still hadn't been officially smartened up to the fact that wrestling wasn't real.

"Actually, I'm not really sure what I'm supposed to do in there," I responded.

"How many wrestling matches have you had?" Eddie inquired.

"No *professional* matches, sir," I replied.

"*Wrestling* matches!" he yelled. "How many *wrestling* matches have you had?"

"Many, many, *many*, sir!" I answered.

"Okay… So, what does the referee do during the match?" Eddie asked me.

"He awards or takes away points and counts the pinfall," I stated.

"Right," Eddie nodded. "It's the same thing in pro wrestling. Except you forget the points and just count the pinfall. Count at an even cadence. One… two… three. If they're outside the ring longer than a 10 count, they get counted out. For that, you should count like this: One… Hey, wait a minute…"

Eddie paused to wave Don Curtis over.

"Hey, Don… Show the kid how to count," Eddie instructed.

As Don Curtis advised me on how I should go about the task of officiating a match, a bunch of wrestlers wandered over to monitor my instruction session. This included both Angelo Poffo and Butcher Vachon, the participants in the match I was going to be refereeing.

When the instructional session concluded, Eddie pulled me aside just before I stepped through the door and out in front of the crowd.

"Angelo is going over by pinfall," Eddie said. "Just count like normal. Butcher will keep his shoulders down."

B. Brian Blair: Truth Bee Told

This is how I finally learned that wrestling results were predetermined. Eddie had waited to tell me until the very last instant before I strode through the curtain to referee my first match.

As I stepped into the ring for the opening match of the night, I was overcome with nervousness. Even as a fully-clothed referee that no one had paid money to see, I was still overrun with fear.

Of course, everything in pro wrestling has to be a rib – or a practical joke. Knowing full well that I was paranoid about refereeing my very first match, Angelo and Butcher did everything they could to make me as uncomfortable as they could. Several times during the bout, they pulled me in between the two of them as they pretended to struggle to get in and out of holds. At my expense, they turned the opening bout of the night into a comedic affair.

At the conclusion of the match, Angelo held Butcher Vachon's shoulders to the mat just as I'd been told he would, and I dutifully slapped the mat three times while Butcher was lying on his back. Satisfied with my actions, I signaled for the timekeeper to ring the bell.

Instantly, Butcher shot up from the mat like a rocket, and both he and Angelo abruptly backed me into a corner of the ring.

"*I* was supposed to go over, you dummy!" Butcher roared. "*I* was supposed to go over!"

"What were you thinking, kid?!" Angelo yelled directly into my face. "*Butcher* was booked to win this!"

I was immediately panic stricken.

"Oh my gosh!" I yelled. "What can we do?!"

"Nothing!" Butcher screamed. "We're *ruined* in this town!"

Angelo turned away from us with his hands on his hips and hung his head dejectedly.

"We can *never* come back here," Angelo lamented. "It's all over. Don Curtis will have to sell his house and leave Florida."

I felt so low. I wanted to jump off a bridge.

There was no relief awaiting me when I walked back into the locker room either.

"What did you *do*, kid?!" Eddie screamed at me. "I told you *Butcher* was supposed to go over with a pin!"

I apologized until tears welled up in my eyes and were ready to stream down my face. I thought I'd done irreparable damage to my heroes with my poor officiating. I sulked off to the corner and hung my head in shame. In my mind, I'd just committed an unpardonable sin.

B. Brian Blair: Truth Bee Told

I guess the sight of me sitting alone in the corner of the locker room looking forlorn was all Jack Brisco could stand.

"Brian, come on!" Jack said with a smile. "They were just ribbin' you! You did fine!"

One by one, everyone who was in on the rib came up and congratulated me on the fine job I'd done as a rookie referee. From that point on, it was a great evening. I could bask in my accomplishment of having survived my first experience in a professional wrestling ring and enjoy the rest of the show. From there, we had a 350-mile trip to Miami, the next city on the agenda. You could either drive to Miami, or you could fly there if you had $75 to spare for a plane ticket.

It was after my very first week in the wrestling business that I made the decision to leave the University of Louisville. I simply couldn't justify *not* wrestling in my mind. Eddie paid me $750 at the conclusion of that week, and he even flew me in his personal Twin Beach – with the call letters 69 Echo Gulf – at no extra charge to me.

By comparison, I had been practically starving while I was living the college lifestyle. The university cut costs, which limited what they could spend on student-athletes. They even took away our laundry check, which resulted in my mom sending me an envelope in the mail each and every week, containing a very loving letter and a $10 bill.

I was forced to find creative ways just to acquire enough money to eat. My friend Jerry Ward was the right offensive guard on the football team. He and I would save up money until we both had $20, and then we would run off to play pool together. Jerry was a *sensational* pool player, and he used to hustle people as a means for the two of us to make some extra cash. He was so reliable that it wasn't really much of a risk, even though we each only put up about 50 percent of our money anyway. We'd use his winnings to help us afford meals at White Castle.

Academically, I had been decent at Louisville. I majored in Political Science and minored in Business, and I would have carried a 3.1 grade point average into my junior year. Although I already had it in my mind that I was going to be a professional wrestler, I thought I might want to become an attorney someday as my fallback plan.

I was driving down the road with Buddy Colt and King Curtis in May of 1977, about a week before I had my first official match as a wrestler. Buddy was at the wheel, King Curtis was in the passenger seat, and I was in the back seat trying to listen to those two and absorb every shred of information about the wrestling business that I could.

B. Brian Blair: Truth Bee Told

In the middle of their discussion, Buddy cast me a pondering gaze through the rearview mirror and said, "I'm trying to think up a ring name for Brian. I'm thinking 'Buck Board.' But you don't really look like a cowboy."

"Brian Blair..." Curtis replied, as if he was saying it for the first time. "Brian Blair..."

The words hung in the air for a second, and then Curtis spoke again and punctuated his words with that thick Hawaiian accent of his.

"Buddy... Bruddah..." Curtis began. "I don't think you should change his name. 'Brian Blair' has a catch to it. It's got a good ring. Why you want him to be a 'Buck Board'?"

"Well, it's always good to have a gimmick," argued Buddy.

The two went back and forth for a while without reaching an agreement, but in that moment, I knew King Curtis was clearly right. No matter how much I respected Buddy, I shouldn't allow him to label me with a gimmicky name.

Thankfully, Eddie Graham agreed with that view.

"You're Brian Blair," affirmed Eddie. "It's catchy. It has alliteration. It's a *good* name."

Whether my ring name was the same as my given name or not, it would have no bearing on what the boys called me behind the scenes thanks to a fortuitous faux pas my mother would commit shortly thereafter.

My mom and I were still living at the same Waterford Village apartment complex while I was in the final stages of my training. Mom called Charlie Lay at the CWF office at 106 N. Albany and asked him to put Buddy on the phone. Once Buddy had picked up the receiver, my mom said, "Buddy, whatever you do, don't let those guys hurt my Beeber today!"

The name "Beeber" was bestowed upon me during my childhood by my sister Sheryl. Of course, Buddy exited the office and *immediately* told Dusty Rhodes, the Briscos, and everyone else within earshot that he had just gotten off the phone with Mrs. Blair, and that no one was supposed to hurt her "Beeber."

Dusty *never* let me hear the end of that.

"Damn, man... don't be hurtin' Beepah!" he said the next time I came in. "Beepah... I can't believe ya mama's callin' here!"

At that stage of the game, none of those guys would ever call me by my real name no matter what happened. Thanks to my mom letting my childhood nickname slip during a phone call, I was destined to be referred to as either "Beeber," "Beeper," "B" or "Beep," but almost *never* as Brian.

B. Brian Blair: Truth Bee Told

I eventually bladed hundreds of times in my career, but the first time I was asked to blade, I became as skittish about the idea of cutting my own forehead as you can possibly imagine. After all, it's basically self-mutilation. We were all gathered together at the Sportatorium in Tampa, and the practice of learning how to blade was more or less established as my final exam prior to my first match.

It all started when Buddy walked up to me with a look of concern on his face.

"Eddie wants to make sure you know how to get color," he stated.

"What do you mean?" I asked him.

"You've got to get *juice*," Buddy said. "I'll show you how to make a blade."

I was aghast and had no idea what to think. Until then, I wasn't really sure how the wrestlers succeeded in making themselves so bloody. In training, Terry Bollea had mentioned to me that he thought it was from a razor blade, but he hadn't been sure about it either.

I followed Buddy over to some chairs, and he produced a medicine bag from underneath one of the chairs and took a seat on the chair itself. As I sat down next to him, Buddy unzipped the bag and began to pull out alcohol swabs, razor blades, scissors, bandages and an antibiotic cream. Buddy took the razor blade and began to instruct me on how I was supposed to go about cutting the blade down to a smaller size. As Buddy talked, I grew increasingly more nervous. The thought of getting my forehead sliced open with a razor blade was not appealing to me at all.

"We can do this one of two ways," Buddy advised me. "*I* can cut you, or you can cut yourself. Take your pick. Eddie is gonna come down and watch you get juice to make sure you do a good job. Remember, no one in the crowd should be able to see you cutting yourself."

I tried to mask my horror as I asked my next question.

"How am I supposed to hide the blade when I cut myself?" I asked.

"I like to carry mine in my mouth," said Buddy.

"*What?!*" I exclaimed in total disbelief.

"Yep," Buddy said. "In my mouth, right under my tongue. Easiest place to hide it."

"Have you ever *swallowed* it?!" I asked. I was finished with my attempts to mask how terrified I was by this subject matter.

"Just once," smiled Buddy. "But nothing happened."

B. Brian Blair: Truth Bee Told

I couldn't envision being so nonchalant about having a razor blade pass through my entire digestive system. With every day of training that passed, the wrestling business just seemed to be getting weirder and weirder.

After cutting the blade, Buddy prepped it further by showing me where to apply the tape to it. The tape was a precautionary step to ensure that the blade could only be inserted so far into my skin. To see the razor blade being prepped with the knowledge that it would soon end up in my scalp was very unsettling.

"Don't you think you should add more tape and move it up just a bit?" I asked Buddy, nervously. "That's too much. There's still a bit too much of the blade still sticking out, don't you think?"

"No, it's good," laughed Buddy. "You've got to get enough color to make Eddie happy. This will *guarantee* you get enough color."

"That's *a lot!*" I said, with my voice betraying the obvious panic that was now swirling through my brain. "That's a *lot* of blade!"

Buddy refused to budge on the length of blade that was exposed from the tape. He handed the blade over to me once he was satisfied that he had suitably prepared it.

"How do I do it?" I asked, as I stared at the blade and turned it over in my hand. "Do I just stick it in?"

"No, man!" answered Buddy. "You've got to *rip* it across your head!"

"Oh, *God!*" I said in horror.

"When you're down on the ground, just spit the blade into your hand," Buddy explained while miming the motions he wanted me to replicate. "Then put your opposite hand over your head to sell like you're hurt. Cut yourself quick, and then stick the blade back in your mouth. *Don't* leave the blade out in the open! That's *really* important to remember."

"Okay," I said, "Don't leave the blade. I got it."

"No, listen!" Buddy said, sternly. "Never *ever* leave the blade! You hear me? You leave the blade, you get *fired. Period.*"

"Yes, sir!" I said. "I got it!"

As I sat there nervously awaiting my juicing trial, I could see Hiro Matsuda – my opponent for my blading exhibition – waiting in the corner of the ring talking with Duke Keomuka. Then Dusty came down from the office with Gordon Solie hot on his heels. Then, when everyone was gathered together, Buddy went up to the office to retrieve Eddie, who descended the steps like a monarch.

Heeding Buddy's advice, I put the blade in my mouth and underneath the tongue. From there, I got in the ring with Matsuda and

B. Brian Blair: Truth Bee Told

worked a quick three-minute match with him. The entire time, I was inescapably paranoid about the idea that I was going to cut my tongue and several other parts of my mouth with the razor blade that was concealed therein. The whole presentation was a test to see if I could absorb the pounding, get fired outside of the ring, and then juice myself without anyone detecting the blade in my hand.

As we wrestled, Matsuda slammed me to the mat and dropped a knee on my head. From there, he scooped me up, threw me out to the floor, then picked me up and smashed my head into the ring post. I collapsed to the ground.

I could hear and feel everyone gathering close to me and hovering over me. They were so close, I could practically feel their breath. As I'd been advised, I spat the blade into my hand, fumbled around with it, and then jammed it into my scalp. I felt my forehead and looked at my hands, but I didn't see blood. I repeated the jabbing move with the blade, yet came up empty once again.

In absolute panic that I was failing the test, I jammed the blade deep into my forehead and twisted it, which sent a stream of crimson-colored blood gushing out all over my hands. Reluctantly, I stuck the bloody blade back into my mouth, and then began selling the damage to my bloody face, which now looked like I'd been shot in the forehead.

A mixture of applause and laughter arose from the assembled spectators.

"Not bad for your first time, Beepah!" Dusty commended me. "Now go put somethin' on that, kid."

I wound up having a couple cat scratches across my head from my first two attempts at blading, but the jab that successfully penetrated my skin was bleeding like crazy. I went over to a mirror with Buddy Colt accompanying me, chuckling behind me the entire way.

As it turned out, there was *no* hard-and-fast requirement in place for wrestlers to blade prior to their first match; the whole thing had been a rib on me. In fact, they had tried to get Orndorff to do it prior to him leaving to go on the road for the first time, but he had totally refused to do it.

One thing that Eddie and Buddy *did* emphasize to me as an absolute requirement was that I learn to speak "Carny." It seemed like an odd skill for a wrestler to be required to possess, but Steve Keirn explained to me why smooth communication was absolutely essential for in-ring success.

B. Brian Blair: Truth Bee Told

"You'd *better* make sure you understand everything being said in there," affirmed Steve Keirn. "Let me tell you what happened to *me.*"

Keirn then proceeded to describe a match he and Mike Graham had with Bob Orton Jr. and Bob Roop in Dade City.

"Orton draped me over the ropes while I was facing the crowd,'" explained Keirn. "He said 'Don't move,' but I thought he told me to move. Then he hit the ropes, and when I turned around he was already in midair with his knee up. He caught me dead in the face with his knee and knocked my teeth through my bottom lip."

"That's terrible!" I remarked.

"Yeah!" continued Keirn. "You see *this?*"

Steve pointed to the left side of his mouth, which was noticeably crooked.

"That's from Orton," said Keirn. "I had to pull my bottom lip back up and over my teeth, and then I finished the match. They sewed me up at the hospital and told me I needed plastic surgery. Like I said, make sure you can understand *everything* going on in there!"

I got the message loud and clear.

When it was time for my premiere as a professional wrestler, the first thing I did was walk into the Sportatorium with my bag and the purple jacket that Pat Patterson had given me. There was an "X" that had been taped onto the paneled walls of the locker room with electrical tape. Dusty Rhodes was sitting at the office desk, and about 15 of the boys were huddled around him. On the desk in the middle of the huddle sat a big pile of money.

Gerald Brisco was wearing a blindfold. He'd been reaching for the X on the wall, but he'd missed it by about two inches. Dusty Rhodes called out to me and said, "Hey, Beepah! Ya got a dolla?"

"Yes, sir, Mr. Dream!" I responded. "I've got a dollar! I think I can do this!"

"Well then put ya dolla on the table and see if ya can do it!" encouraged Dusty.

I put my dollar on the table, and then I took my position at the starting point. I made sure I lined my hand up perfectly with the X on the wall, and then I let Jerry place the blindfold over my eyes. I stayed as still as I possibly could to make sure I didn't move a single muscle. Slowly, I crept toward where I was certain the X would be with my right hand extended straight out in front of me. That was one *massive* mountain of cash sitting on the desk over by Dusty, and it was as good as mine.

B. Brian Blair: Truth Bee Told

Suddenly, my finger struck something, but it sure wasn't the X; it was *much* too soft. I ripped the blindfold off to see Pat Patterson bent over in front of me with his pants pulled down to his knees. My fingers had struck him right in his butthole. The room *erupted* in laughter.

This sort of treatment was simply something that I was going to have to get used to. The wrestling business was fraught with wrestlers who would take advantage of any opportunity to draw a laugh from the boys at another wrestler's expense. As the newest and youngest inductee into the wrestling fraternity, I was an attractive target for hazing, and all sorts of practical jokes and ribs.

Receiving a reverse chinlock from the great Pat Patterson

My first match ever was in a tag team match with Skip Young – the super-athletic Black babyface known as "Sweet Brown Sugar" – as my partner. He and I faced off against Pat Patterson and Ivan Koloff. Skip and Pat were already very familiar in-ring adversaries to one another. They had a match in Tampa before I broke into the

B. Brian Blair: Truth Bee Told

business that made such an impression on me that I was left excited by it well after I'd left the arena.

They started the match with Pat pantomiming to the crowd that he was going to break Skip's leg. Then he got in Skip's face and called him "boy" in a clear display of racial insensitivity designed to get the fans thoroughly pissed off. You have to have a coach in the ring, and Pat was a ring general and a half. He knew a million different tactics to get a crowd riled up.

When Pat saw that the people were buying what he was doing, he kept it up and told Skip to be patient with him. From there, he did nothing other than yell and gesticulate, using all sorts of motions to explain to the crowd exactly what he intended to do to Skip. Then he walked over to one side of the ring and yelled at the audience, before slowly walking over to the other side of the ring and riling up the crowd on the other side of the ring. The entire building began to buzz and boil.

At that point, Pat rushed over to Skip, kicked him in the stomach and fired him into the ropes. Skip reversed the Irish whip attempt, leapfrogged over Pat, and then tagged him with three of the most beautiful dropkicks you could ever see. Pat rolled out of the ring and sold those dropkicks like they'd fractured his jaw while Skip pounded on his chest to the approving roar of the crowd. Skip was *so* over with the audience, and with me, too. I couldn't believe what an incredible athlete he was.

"You're going to get shitcanned during the match," Eddie informed me. "They're going to throw you out to the floor, and you just stay down and sell. Pat is going over on Skip."

Skip was taking the fall and putting Pat over since he was about to leave the Florida territory to wrestle in Texas. Eddie was being very generous to me by not making me eat a loss during my very first match, which is customary in the wrestling business. Naturally, he wasn't going to let me beat one of his superstars during my first bout either.

Behind the scenes, Skip was a real loner. He would drive down the road with his beautiful Mexican wife "Senorita" alongside him, and he would travel to some of our stops along the way even if he wasn't working at those shows. Obviously, that drove up his expenses. It quickly became evident to me that bringing your wife on the road with you could be a major mistake, because it was a rapid way to decrease the profit margin from your appearances.

On the way to one of my next matches, which was in West Palm Beach at the Auditorium, I fell asleep in the back of the car only

B. Brian Blair: Truth Bee Told

to be rudely awakened by the commotion caused by Gerald Brisco and Steve Keirn.

"Beeper! Beeper!" yelled Gerald. "God dang! Get up! You gotta get dressed! We're late!"

I was due to wrestle first, so this was a total nightmare scenario for me.

"Oh no!" I cried out in a panic. "How are we late?! Why'd you guys let me sleep this long?! I *can't* be late! This is my *first* week!"

"You better hurry up and get dressed!" repeated Gerald. "You might be in trouble!"

Just starting out as a rookie

I scrambled to change clothes and to get into my ring gear as quickly as I could while squirming around in the back seat of the car. Gerald and Steve weren't helping matters at all with their commentary. As I hurriedly changed into my ring attire, the pair of them assured me that I would be harshly punished if I wasn't prepared to wrestle as soon as we arrived at the building.

B. Brian Blair: Truth Bee Told

At the West Palm Beach Auditorium, the wrestlers had to drive their cars beneath a bridge that the fans would walk across in order to get into the building. Jack and Jerry stopped the car, honked the horn a few times, and let me out so that I could rush into the building as rapidly as I could. With my sparkly ring jacket on, I sprinted past the fans who were all attempting to politely greet me since they'd just seen me on television for the first time during my match with Skip against Ivan and Pat.

Thanks to my unadulterated panic, I wasn't immediately tipped off by the fact that so many people were still standing *outside* of the building. I raced right up to the front door only to discover that it was still locked. Frantically, I started pulling on all of the different door handles until I finally found one that would open. I surged through the entranceway only to be met by a janitor whose face wore an expression of deep annoyance.

"Take it easy, kid!" he cautioned me. "We're still about 10 minutes from opening up the building! Settle down!"

Gerald and Steve had moved the car's clock one hour ahead after I'd dozed off in the backseat. I'd been freaking out over absolutely nothing. Just a few short days later, they got me *much* worse.

This time, I was riding back from that night's matches with both Jack and Gerald Brisco, and I sat dutifully in the back like a good wrestling rookie. We'd already purchased our beer, and we were on the highway about 60 miles from Yeehaw Junction, which was a point in the journey where we had to pay a toll and make a right turn, but we could also use that opportunity to get fuel, or grab something to eat.

Pat Patterson was behind the wheel of his brand new, gold Lincoln Continental, and he was driving with his boyfriend, Louis Dondero, and "The Great Mephisto" Frankie Cain as his passengers. As we progressed down the road, Pat abruptly pulled past us while Louie mooned us from out of the moonroof of Pat's Continental.

"Goddammit!" yelled Jack. "Pat is always fuckin' with you! We've got to come up with something to do to get him back!"

"Yeah!" I chimed in. "Let's get him back! What should we do?"

"*Here's* what we'll do," Jerry suggested to me. "We'll pass them and pull over, and you act like we have to pee. After they pass us back up, you get in the trunk and pull your pants down. When we get to the Yeehaw Junction, I'll make sure nobody is around us, and then when I count to three, you pop up out of the trunk and *moon* them."

"But you have to moon them *real* good," Jack added. "You have to spread your cheeks and *really* give it to them! Moon the hell out of them!"

B. Brian Blair: Truth Bee Told

"That's a *great* idea!" I said. "They'll never see it comin'."

Sure enough, we stopped, Pat and Louie passed us up, and I hopped in the trunk of the Briscos' car.

"Are you okay?" Jack asked as the car rolled along. "Can you breathe in there?"

"I'm fine!" I answered.

Eventually, I felt the car come to a halt.

"What's going on?" I shouted. "Are they behind us?"

"Not yet, Beeper," Jerry said. "They stopped and they're peein'."

Suddenly, the car's radio cranked up and I couldn't hear anything aside from the customary country music.

The car sprang back to life and started moving again. A short time later it stopped once more.

"Okay! We're here at the tollbooth," said Jerry. "They're right behind us and we're the only ones here! On the count of three, moon 'em good!"

"Yeah, Beeper!" Jack said. "Spread your ass! Moon the hell out of 'em!"

"Don't worry! I'll get 'em good!" I promised him.

I readied myself for my big moment as Gerald counted it off.

"One... two... *three*!"

The trunk of the car popped open, and as I remained face down in the trunk, I elevated my hips and poked my ass out with one hand on each of my butt cheeks. I spread my cheeks open and shook my ass as aggressively as I could. Instead of hearing the appalled reactions of wrestlers, the next thing I heard was a loud "Honnnnnnnnnkkkkkk" from our car. I couldn't figure out why Gerald was on the horn and wouldn't lay off of it. I stopped mooning people for a moment and turned around to sneak a peek at their reactions. That's when I realized that the joke was on *me*.

The Briscos had backed the car all the way up to the picture window of the Stuckey's Restaurant. The diner just happened to be in the middle of its nightly dinner rush, and it was *packed* full of people. The Briscos had set me up beautifully.

Surprised and crushingly embarrassed, I ducked down as far as I could inside the trunk of the car.

"Go! Go! Go!" I screamed to the Brisco brothers.

They responded by continuing to lay on the horn.

"If you want us to go, you have to get back in the car!" Jack laughed.

B. Brian Blair: Truth Bee Told

I had no idea how I was supposed to do that. My pants and underwear were all the way down to my ankles, so I had to turn around and climb out of the trunk. I stumbled my way out of the vehicle, fell to the ground, and then rose to my feet. My pants and underwear were still down around my ankles, so the folks inside Stuckey's saw far more than a moon while I was trying to regain my bearings.

I looked back inside the restaurant and saw a grey-haired lady sitting right by the window with a black gentleman. They both had huge, wonderful smiles on their faces as I made eye contact with them. I'll *never* forget it. I'd never felt so embarrassed in my life.

I waddled my way around to the car door, but as soon as the door handle was within my reach, Gerald pulled the car slightly ahead. In sheer desperation, I waddled some more, and Gerald pulled ahead once again. I chased the car all the way down to Highway 60 with my pants around my ankles before the Briscos peeled out and left me standing there looking like an idiot. I turned toward the gas station to see Frankie Kane, Pat Patterson and Louie Dondero all sitting in Pat's Lincoln, laughing their heads off. Another man at the station had dropped his gas pump from laughing so hard.

At the next airing of CWF television, Gordon Solie added to the rib and said, "The people at Yeehaw Junction would like to thank Brian Blair for his public appearance last week."

I was embarrassed, but I took it all in stride. What's more, I'd learned that ribbing was a cherished art form in the wrestling industry. It wouldn't be long before I began doling out a healthy serving of ribs as well.

SIX – *Maui Owie*

My first paycheck from Eddie Graham was around $800, and that was after only working for four days. At that point, I just couldn't justify to myself that going back to school was worthwhile if I had the ability to make that much money. As I mentioned, my father always stressed to me that I should get an education, but he also instilled in me that I should take advantage of opportunities and strike while the iron was hot. My worst-case scenario would be that I would spend some time making more money than I had ever made in my life, save as much of it as I could, and then I could return to school and finish earning a degree if the money ever dried up.

Also, I'd learned that there were different ways to accumulate understanding, knowledge and wisdom, and that they're all *very* different things. You gain knowledge from books and experiences, and you gain understanding from overcoming challenges, accepting things you can't change and developing the courage to overcome that. Wisdom comes from accumulating *both* of those things.

The booker in Florida at the time – my very first booker in the wrestling business – was Johnny Valentine. Johnny was a tall, strong, rugged wrestler who had been an absolute legend in the business until a 1975 plane crash in North Carolina had robbed him of his career and left him partially paralyzed. Even though he was hobbling around on crutches and could no longer wrestle in matches, Johnny still had the full respect of everyone in the locker room. He would regularly gather all of the boys around him and remind us to make our punches and strikes look as realistic as possible.

"I want you boys to really lay 'em in," Johnny said, before raising his hand up and motioning for me. "Blair... come here."

As ordered, I walked right over to him and stood in front of the hobbled legend.

"Bend over," Johnny said.

That request stunned me a little.

"What?" I asked him, fearing that I was about to experience a crueler version of the rib Pat Patterson had pulled on me with the blindfold. "How do you want me to bend over?"

"*Backwards*," answered Valentine. "I'm going to show these boys how to lay 'em in."

I was terrified at the thought of being clubbed by Johnny Valentine. Despite being held up by crutches, Johnny was still close to

6'5" and weighed about 280 pounds. He was a *big* man. Little did I know, this was yet another rib for the benefit of the rest of the boys.

Johnny bent me backwards, raised his arm high over his head, and clubbed me so hard in the chest with his forearm that I dropped straight down like a ton of bricks and took a back bump on the concrete floor. Everybody laughed at my expense. It was a rib, but only to the extent that Johnny had convinced the new kid to willfully allow pain to be administered to him. There wasn't anything truly funny or creative about it. This was just another part of my initiation.

Johnny didn't last much longer as Florida's booker after I started out. The Great Mephisto took over as the booker after Johnny was finished. Even though Mephisto was the booker, he was still willing to put me over and let me beat him just to give me the experience and to see firsthand how the crowd would react to a new talent being presented as a successful wrestler.

One of the wrestlers I gravitated towards straight out of the gate was Don Muraco. He was absolutely *huge*, with one of the greatest sets of shoulders I'd ever seen on anyone. His deltoids were positively massive. On top of that, Don was very symmetrical with strong legs that provided him with a sturdy base. He was blessed with that natural, big-boned structure that a lot of his fellow Hawaiians possessed. Needless to say, he also had an *excellent* tan.

I first met Don in Tampa during my training sessions before I had even broken into the business. On top of being an incredible performer in the wrestling ring, Don was also an amazing surfer. It was a part of Don's wrestling gimmick was that he was an avid surfer from Hawaii, but it was also true of Don in real life. His surfboard was his most frequent travel companion. He once tried very patiently to teach me how to surf over by Cocoa Beach on the east coast of Florida. He drove me over there in his brown El Camino and advised me on how to stand up on the board and catch a wave, but I just didn't have the necessary balance to stay up on the board for more than a second before I went crashing into the water.

I officially started in the business about six weeks before Terry Bollea was cleared to wrestle as well. They put him under a hood as a masked wrestler known as "Super Destroyer." Eddie decreed that Chiefland would be the ideal place for Terry to face me, in August, in his first serious match. Up until then, he'd worked in a match with Hiro Matsuda that was about five minutes long, but this was going to be his first true test as a pro wrestler.

Terry and I were notified that we would be working together two days ahead of time, and we prepared some highspots together in the ring prior to the match. Rehearsals were rare back then, but since we were both extremely green, we thought it was best to prepare together for our 15-minute broadway. I was *really* nervous since I was the veteran in the ring after only six weeks of experience on the road. Terry was also sweating nervous bullets backstage, and the building hadn't even opened yet. After both of us climbed into the ring and faced off, the referee gave us our official instructions while the announcer made the call: "One fall; 15-minute time limit!"

Our actual match got off to a decent enough start. For the first five minutes, we engaged in some chain wrestling. From there we transitioned into some strongman stuff to get over Terry's size and strength with the audience. After about eight minutes had elapsed, we knew it was time for Terry to start drawing as much heat from the crowd as he could. As I held Terry in a rear chinlock and waited for him to rise to his feet and overpower me, I heard him whisper, "Brian... Look! We're having a heck of a match. All the boys are watching!"

I glanced upward, and I was surprised to see that Terry was right. Sure enough, the locker room had completely emptied out, and all the boys were standing in the entranceway and admiring our match. I took it as a reassuring sign. In that brief moment, I felt pretty awesome.

"Let's do it right, brother!" I whispered back to Terry.

Terry started getting the heat on me with some punches and other illegal moves before securing a hold on me. Finally, the referee informed us that 10 minutes of match time had gone by. We were two thirds of the way done.

We continued with our match, but the referee stopped giving us any sort of minute-by-minute time cues. That's when I began timing things out in my head and figuring out what else we needed to squeeze into the match before the full 15-minute time limit expired. That's when I became somewhat frantic, realizing that we probably only had two minutes remaining in our bout before it was over with.

Terry went to hit me with a shoulder thrust into the corner, but I ducked out of the way and began to unload on him. I bombarded Terry with punches, then bounced off the ropes and threw dropkicks at him. Terry sold everything as hard as he possibly could. Neither one of us wanted to look like we weren't putting all of our effort into making the match look good, because all of the boys were standing directly outside of the ring and scrutinizing every move we made.

Terry "Super Destroyer" Bollea clamps a headlock on me

Once the exertion had gotten me as blown up as I could possibly be, and I could see that Terry had also been gassed into immobility, I secured a sleeper hold on him for the second time during the match. Admittedly, I put the sleeper on Terry for the second time because I didn't know of any other moves that would allow me to convincingly stall the match until the bell rang. Both of us sat there in the center of the ring, sweating profusely, exhausted to a point nearing death, and waiting for the bell to ring and signal the time-limit draw.

"Fifteen minutes gone!" came the announcement from the timekeeper. "*Fifteen* minutes to go!"

B. Brian Blair: Truth Bee Told

Dropping a big knee on Terry Bollea

My eyes visibly widened in disbelief, and I immediately swung my head over to look toward the boys. *Everyone* was laughing hysterically. At Muraco's behest, the Briscos had changed the length of the match without smartening up Terry and I. As a result, the match went from being a fantastic early-career match between two green wrestlers to being what was probably one of the worst matches of all time. We rolled around like two beached whales trying to apply rest holds to one another until we got our wind back. From there, we had to try to recreate some tension in the match even though we'd already used every move we knew how to perform safely. It was *awful*.

In those days, the fans were polite enough not to start calling everything "boring," but the second half of the bout was *definitely* boring. The boys thought it was the funniest thing that ever happened; especially Don Muraco.

On the way back home, Don doled out some of his expensive Maui Wowie – his high-quality marijuana from Hawaii – to Jack, Jerry and me. I was flabbergasted by what was going on, and by how brazen some of the boys in the business could be with their illegal activities. The car quickly became all smoked out, and then everyone cracked open a post-match beer. All of this was fairly routine for the tail end of a wrestling road trip, where guys would pass beer and marijuana around in the cars to dull the pain and liven up the conversations.

Back in those days, if you were to head south from Chiefland on U.S. 301, you would run into a lot of speed traps. We were all in our own little marijuana-soaked world, sailing along and listening to Gerald's amazing country music tape. Our revelry was interrupted by the flash of red-and-blue police lights that materialized right behind us and illuminated the interior of our car. To me, those lights signaled imminent *doom* for us all. I assumed my wrestling career was over since those cops were bound to notice the powerful scent of Maui Wowie and the bewildered antics of four sky-high wrestlers.

This was going to be front-page news. I was about to be hauled off to some small-town jail before my career even got off the ground, and my parents were going to be so horribly embarrassed and disappointed in me. I *couldn't* imagine anything worse.

Everyone inside of the car began scrambling, as if there was anything we could have done to rid the vehicle of the scent of weed and conceal the illegal acts we had been engaged in. As I was pondering our fate, something landed in my lap. Don had tossed his huge bag of Maui Wowie into my lap because I was sitting behind Gerald's passenger seat and was positioned closest to the shoulder of the road.

"Get rid of it, Beeber!" yelled Don. "*Throw* it out the window!"

"Dump that *shit* out!" yelled Gerald. "Hurry up!"

As Jack pulled his blue-and-tan Bill Blass Lincoln off the road and deep into the tall grass, I flung the bag of pot out of my window as deftly as I could. Then Jack parked the car, and we all sat in silence. The local cop walked up to the driver's side door and wrapped on the glass. As Jack rolled his window down, a thick plume of smoke drifted through the window and directly into the cop's face.

The officer coughed, but then his harsh features softened, and a smile spread slowly across his face and then grew frighteningly wide.

B. Brian Blair: Truth Bee Told

"Jack Brisco!" the policeman announced. "You're my *favorite* wrestler! I can't believe it's you! Goddamn! *The* Jack Brisco!"

"Uhhh… yeah?" Jack said. "Hiiiii…?"

"Ya know… I pulled Pat Patterson over just a little while ago," the officer continued. "I told him you were my favorite wrestler, so he told me you'd be behind him in a little bit and what kind of car you drive! You got an 8x10 I can have?!"

I couldn't believe what I was hearing, but it obviously meant that things were looking up once again for my career prospects. This officer didn't say a single word about the marijuana, the alcohol, or any other sort of malfeasance that he might have a reasonable suspicion of. Jack spoke with that cop for a full five minutes, signed whatever autographs the officer requested that he sign, and *probably* even taught him the secret to the figure-four leglock. The cop spoke about how closely he'd followed Jack beginning with his collegiate career at Oklahoma State, and Jack obliged him by answering whatever questions he could.

On the one hand, we were fortunate that this cop happened to be the biggest Jack Brisco fan on the planet. On the other hand, we probably wouldn't have been pulled over at all if Pat Patterson hadn't stooged on us and told the policeman to be on the lookout for Jack's Lincoln Continental.

Once the cop took off, Muraco dove into the grass and said, "Beeper! Get out there and help me find my pot!"

It was the middle of the night, and none of us had any form of a flashlight. Jack had to back his car up and shine his brights on the tall grass for us even to have prayer of finding Don's weed.

"The cop is gonna come back, man!" I whined as I frantically searched through the grass for the bag of Maui Wowie.

Apparently unsatisfied with the work I was doing on my own, both Don and Gerald waded out into the tall grass to assist me. By the time it was all over with, we had only recovered one-fifth of Muraco's marijuana at the most.

"That was a $400 bag of pot, goddammit!" growled Don as he climbed back into the backseat of the Continental.

Drugs and alcohol aside, the most fun thing about those Florida road trips was all of the singing we did. I had never been a fan of country music before, but I got a quick indoctrination when I started riding with the Briscos. Gerald made a mixtape with the greatest hits of Hank Williams Jr., Waylon Jennings and David Alan Coe, and we all took turns stealing it from one another. It was the dumbest in-group rib of all time, because we were all riding in the same car anyway, so the culprit would always pull the tape out before too long and pop it into Gerald's tape deck.

Once we'd all gotten a little bit snookered from the beer, we were more inclined to sing along loudly to the music. I quickly discovered that drinking all that beer every night caused me to gain weight rapidly, and it was awful for my physique. That's when I made the switch from beer over to red wine. A single bottle of wine would last me two days, so I wound up consuming way fewer calories that way.

One of the rare times we were going to have a Saturday off, Don and I took a trip out to West Palm Beach.

"Why don't we go down there and spend the night; I've got a girl I want you to meet," Don announced with a smile.

"Sounds good to me!" I said.

"The lady I'm seeing has a daughter that's the perfect age for you," Don continued. "They already know to meet us at the hotel."

"How much is the hotel?" I asked him. "Is it expensive?"

"We're going to a nice hotel, and it's *all* on me," Don assured me.

When we got to the hotel, it was a classy, four-star facility. Just as he'd promised, Don paid for everything. He was making main-event money, and he knew I was a struggling rookie wrestler.

My mission was to keep the 20-year-old daughter of Don's 38-year-old lady friend occupied while he had his fun. The two of us spent two consecutive nights with this pair, and it was one of the wildest and most bizarre experiences of my life. It was definitely the first time I ever had sex with a woman while another couple was present in the room. What made it doubly awkward was the fact that the two women in the room were a mother and daughter. Eventually, the awkwardness of the incident gave way to excitement.

"How cool is *this*!" I thought to myself. "I'm living like a rock star, and this is Don Muraco, of all people, with a woman on the bed right next to me! And this girl I'm with is absolutely beautiful!"

The mother and daughter acted like best friends throughout the entire experience, which was a strange dynamic to see in that setting. You'd think the girl's mom would have had a huge problem with watching her own daughter have sex with a young wrestler on the bed right next to her, and I can't imagine it was any *less* awkward for the daughter to watch her mother engaging in sexual acts on the bed across from her.

Seriously, though, my top priority at that moment was impressing Muraco, *not* satisfying the girl. My reputation was definitely on the line in that scenario. If I was a one-minute wonder in bed with that girl, Don would have told everyone in the locker room, and I *never* would have lived it down. He would have been telling stories in every wrestling territory he ever visited about how Beeber couldn't get the job done when a beautiful girl was served up for him on a silver platter. I did everything I could to make him proud of me!

Back in the ring, I was learning something new every night. Ed Wiskowski provided me with one of the best learning experiences of my career during a 20-minute broadway we wrestled in Orlando at the Eddie Graham Sports Center. Ed held me in a front facelock for a full 18 minutes. Every time I would work my way out of the front facelock, he would either grab my hair or sneak in a quick heel spot to pull me right back into it. Early in the match, the crowd was showering us with chants of "boring."

"Hey, is everything okay, Ed?" I asked Ed while my mouth was obscured by the facelock. "Are you *sure* we should be doing this?"

"Shut up, kid," Ed replied. "Just shut up and listen. It's *fine*."

This is when I learned the true art of ring generalship. Ed kept using his cheating tactics to illegally maintain his front facelock on me. By the 18-minute mark the crowd was absolutely incensed at what they were watching. I was thinking this was going to be the worst match of my young career. Yet, as the match progressed and Ed kept me grounded, I quickly realized this was rapidly becoming one of the best matches of my young career. Finally, Ed released the front facelock and missed a big move like an elbow drop. That's when I channeled Jack Brisco's fiery babyface comeback routine and started beating the crap out of him. The crowd *erupted* for all of it.

Ed gave me a full two-minute comeback in that match, which is a *very* long comeback, but it was also an appropriate length under the circumstances. It allows the babyface to pay the heel back for all the punishment that was inflicted on him while the crowd goes along for the entire ride. I like to have comebacks where the heel will cut me off just for a second with some sort of reversal where it looks like the tide is going to turn, but it really doesn't. It was Ed's psychology and Ed's bumping that got that match as over with the audience as it became. After that match, whoever followed us had a very hard time capturing the crowd again. Ed taught me that wrestlers who know what they're doing can maintain control over the audience, and they can't allow the audience to control them.

I didn't have anything else to compare it to at the time, but in retrospect, Florida was a *perfect* wrestling territory to get your start in. All of your training came at the hands of the best wrestlers in the business, and all of the top stars came through Florida at one point or another during the year. When you started working at the shows, you could drive home and sleep in your own bed every night if you really wanted to. The road trips weren't all that bad even if we had double shots on Sundays.

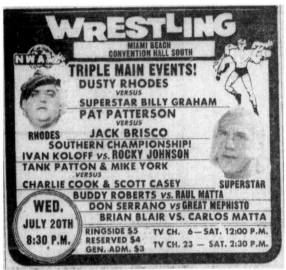

One of the first advertisements that included my name

During those Sunday double shots, we'd wrestle in Ocala at 1:00 p.m. in the afternoon at their jai alai fronton, and then go to the Eddie Graham Sports Center in Orlando on Sunday night. On Wednesdays we would wrestle two shots in the morning before heading to Miami for the night. All in all, we would often wrestle 11 matches in a week's time and only have a few days off every year.

While wrestlers in Verne Gagne's AWA territory in Minneapolis would wrestle four or five times a week in a very stretched-out territory, we could easily have more than twice as many matches over the course of a month of working in Florida. All of us acquired a ton of experience in a short period of time.

On top of all of that, Florida had no State tax, so that minimized our ability to get into tax trouble, and maximized the amount of money that remained in our pockets. Florida wrestlers could make very good money *and* save it. I averaged $1,500 per week during my time wrestling there. This means I probably spent $300 on the road each week and returned home with $1,200 in my pockets.

B. Brian Blair: Truth Bee Told

Wrestlers in the territory also had huge write-offs, like our miles and our outfits, which were business expenses.

However, most wrestlers simply didn't pay their taxes, and a lot of them unnecessarily suffered because of it. To my credit, I always tried to pay at least a little bit of the taxes on my income, even early on. My dad told me that someday I'd be on social security, and if I didn't pay into it, I wouldn't have any money to live on once I got older. That was valuable advice that I kept in the back of my mind.

I divulged very little about my wrestling lifestyle to the people around me that weren't involved in the business. In those days, it was usually in a wrestler's best interest to move to a part of the country where people weren't familiar with them, and to change their name so that no one could possibly find out who they were. Yet, here I was, remaining in my home state, living in my hometown, and wrestling under my real name.

It worked out in my favor, because it prevented anyone from saddling me with a silly gimmick that no one would have believed, and that would have been discredited immediately. If I'd tried to come out as a tobacco-chewing cowboy, everyone would have recognized me and said, "That's Brian Blair! I know him! He's nothing like how he portrays himself on TV!" I might have been able to get away with that in some parts of the state, but enough people knew me in Tampa that it never would have worked close to home.

On the other hand, wrestling under my real name enabled me to develop an immediate and natural fan following, because I was a clean-cut local kid. In fact, I was concerned that I was a little *too* clean-cut. I looked at my first promotional picture of myself as a pro wrestler, and I thought, "Geez... I look like a little kid!"

I desperately wanted to look older and immediately set out to grow a moustache. It *instantly* made me look like an older, more mature wrestler. In my experience, when you're younger you want to look older, and when you're older you want to look younger. Those are simply the rules of life.

Other rules of life can only be learned by experience, and there were plenty of experiences awaiting me outside of Florida.

SEVEN – *Double blackballed*

Following the advice of Eddie Graham about the first territory I should work in after my initial run in Florida, I drove my baby blue Lincoln Continental all the way to Shreveport, Louisiana in December of 1977 to meet up with Bill Watts and Leroy McGuirk – the promoters of the Mid South territory – along with the wrestlers working for them.

The first time I ever met Bill Watts, he greeted me with, "Hey, Beeper!"

To say Watts learned everything he knew from Eddie Graham was no understatement. Aside from knowledge about ring psychology and booking mastery, the knowledge that passed between them included details about my childhood nickname. There would be no escaping it.

In addition to his long-lasting friendship with Eddie Graham, Watts also had a strong relationship with the Briscos due to the ties all of them had with the state of Oklahoma. Their interactions were also seasoned by a healthy friendly rivalry owing to the fact that the Briscos wrestled and won championships for Oklahoma State University, while Bill Watts played football for the University of Oklahoma in the late 1950s.

"I watched a lot of your matches on tape," said Watts. "I love the way you wrestle. It says 'wrestling' on the marquee, and that's what I like. I like wrestlers, and I like *tough* wrestlers… and I heard you were a tough guy."

"Well, I certainly wouldn't want to mess with *you*, sir."

Bill chuckled at that response. He had a reputation for being a tall, strong and intimidating man, and he appreciated my respectful recognition of that reputation. From that point on, he treated me very well and took me under his wing. Despite the relatively long stint of training I'd endured, Watts knew I was still in the early stages of learning how to perform in the ring, and that all areas of my performance could be improved with some refining and polishing.

The owners of the official wrestling territories of the National Wrestling Alliance had long ago carved up the United States into different regions. There were very real lines drawn behind the scenes that dictated precisely which promoters had the rights to run shows in assorted locales. For example, if Eddie Graham ran a CWF show north of the Florida state line, he would run afoul of Jim Barnett, the owner of Georgia Championship Wrestling. Likewise, if Jim held a wrestling event in South Carolina, he would have violated the claim to the Carolinas held by the Crockett family.

The territory of Watts and McGuirk stretched from Oklahoma to Arkansas, and then south into Louisiana and Mississippi. It also included parts of southern Missouri. Wrestling for them would allow me to gain experience by plying my trade in front of fresh audiences in five different states, and also enable me to make the majority of my rookie mistakes in places far from home.

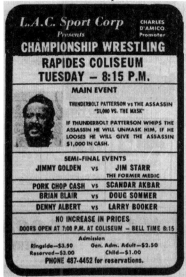

My second stop within the Mid South territory was at the Western Hills Hotel in Bossier City, which is where I was told that all the boys stayed during Mid South events there. During my check-in process, I was handed a note by the clerk at the front desk; it bore the name and phone number of a lady along with a suggestion to call her. I did exactly what the note said and called the woman up out of pure curiosity. She answered and then promptly asked me if I would like to meet her for dinner. I immediately accepted her invitation.

We met up for dinner, then went back to my room and wound up spending the night together. It wasn't until two weeks later, after I'd already revealed to this woman that I really liked her, that she finally informed me that she was *married*. It was a startling dose of reality. Here I was, just a young 21-year-old kid, and it was a huge shock to me that I'd just been seduced into several romantic rendezvous with another man's wife.

Aside from the uncomfortable education in grownup problems that I received from that woman, the most unappealing lesson I learned was that working in the Mid South territory required substantially more driving than Florida did. Driving across five states was very taxing; the average mileage in Mid South was 2,700 miles a week. Somehow, we all still managed to squeeze in everything we needed to accomplish over the course of a day.

During a typical day in Mid South, wrestlers would wake up in the morning, eat breakfast, hit the gym, and then head back to our hotels to shower. After all of that, we would hop into our cars and drive to whatever town we were wrestling in that night. The smartest wrestlers put agendas together and figured out who they would be riding with and how much time they'd be spending together out on the road. Fortunately, all the old timers would tell the new guys where we should eat, which hotels we should stay at, and also which gyms charged wrestlers a fee to train, and which didn't.

For some of my earliest Mid South matches, Watts put me in the ring with guys like Ali Bey, Gary Young, Don Kodiak and Bobby Jaggers. Len Denton became my first regular tag team partner there, and I also got to be friends with Thunderbolt Patterson.

The adventure of being in Mid South was really all about finding my way through my first territory away from home. It was a special treat to me that Paul Orndorff was already working for Watts after beginning his pro wrestling career the summer before I had. Watts had already provided Paul with a solid education in the wrestling business, and he was putting on incredible matches and eliciting powerful reactions from the crowd.

Since I'd idolized Paul so much from when I was just a kid selling sodas in the stands at University of Tampa football games, hanging out with him out on the road was like hanging out with the coolest older brother you could ever imagine. This also meant that whenever Paul suggested that we should do something that might land us in hot water, I was always standing right alongside him, often as the one who wound up getting burned.

One of my earliest road trips through the territory involved Paul and I spending an eternity seated in the back of Dick Murdoch's Bonneville, with Killer Karl Kox riding shotgun. Murdoch and Kox couldn't have cared any less that there were two human beings crammed into the seats behind them. They shifted their seats all the way back and forced Paul and I to suffer through an entire one-way, 300-mile road trip with our knees practically pulled up into our throats because the veterans wanted to maximize their leg room.

"Hey, Murdoch... do you mind moving your seat up?" Paul asked a few minutes into one of our first rides with him. "We have *no* room back here!"

"I got gout," Dick said, matter of factly. "Need the leg space."

That was the end of the discussion. On account of Murdoch's ever-present gout, Paul and I were constantly sore and miserable from having to endure long trips without even enough space to wiggle our toes

Despite Bill Watts' adamant rule that heels and faces were never to be seen riding together, it seemed like there was a special exception made for Killer Karl Kox and Dick Murdoch. The two of them were constantly switching their on-screen roles to the point where you couldn't keep their heel-face alignment straight. They were also drawing a ton of money for Watts in Louisiana, so it was probably to the benefit of everyone involved with Mid South that Watts didn't enforce his traveling restriction with the two of them.

During one of our trips, we pulled up to a convenience store, and Paul and I embraced the opportunity to climb out from the back of the Bonneville and stretch our legs. Dick and Karl went into the store, and as Paul and I stood around, two young Black kids rode their bikes up to us.

"Are you guys wrestlers?" one of the kids asked politely. "You've got such *big* muscles!"

"Yeah, we are," Paul smiled. "Do you watch wrestling?"

The boys both nodded and grinned.

"Can you do like *this*?" one of the boys asked us while making a double-bicep flexing motion.

Paul treated the boys to one of his classic double-bicep poses; their jaws dropped open in amazement.

"Wow!" the boys said. "Can we *feel* them?"

Paul leaned down and allowed the children to touch his arms and feel how powerful his biceps were. As the boys were admiring Paul's physique, Murdoch and Kox exited the convenience store and walked toward the car.

"Dick Murdoch!" yelled the first kid.

"Killer Karl Kox!" called out the second kid.

There was an awkward silence, and then the second kid asked, "Don't you guys *hate* each other?!"

Kox glanced over at Murdoch, smirked, and then looked back over at the children.

"Well, we're trying to make up, kid," said Karl.

"That's good!" the boy exclaimed. "And you have nice guys riding with you! They're really nice!"

"These guys?" said Kox, gesturing toward Paul and I. "They're just *punks*."

"No, they're *not*!" the first young man said. "They're *good* guys!"

"Don't worry about it," I told them. "We're gonna work it out right now."

"Be careful," they warned me. "Killer Karl is really mean! He's a *dirty* man!"

B. Brian Blair: Truth Bee Told

Young Orndorff and Blair

Paul may have managed to bypass the blading rib that the boys pulled on me before my first match in Florida, but he couldn't go forever without blading. I was present when Orndorff finally got juice for the first time, in Tulsa, Oklahoma. He was preparing to have a cage match with Ernie Ladd, and I had to walk Paul through the process of discretely blading just like Buddy Colt had patiently explained it to me.

"So, I'm supposed to put it *back* in my mouth *after* I cut myself with it?" Paul asked disgustedly.

"Yeah, but the most important things are to hide what you're doing, and then make sure you take the blade with you," I advised him.

Like a true ring veteran, Ernie expertly got juice first during the bout, and then it was Orndorff's turn. As I watched Paul, he went down to the ground, and he couldn't have been any more obvious about spitting the blade into his hand, or about the fact that he was attempting to slice himself with it. Blood *did* materialize on Paul's body, but it wasn't on his forehead. Instead, it was on his leg. I looked

B. Brian Blair: Truth Bee Told

back up at his forehead, saw nothing once again, and then it dawned on me what had happened: Paul had accidentally cut his *hand* with the blade, and he was forced to finish the match with blood dripping from his fingers.

This initial mishap with a blade soured Paul on the blading experience so much that I honestly don't recall him ever attempting to get juice again in his career.

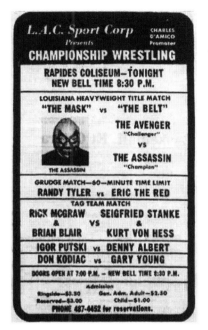

Paul and I saw a commercial for *Saturday Night Fever* starring John Travolta while we were hanging out in our hotel room, and we decided to go see it together. It was a rarity for us to have the sort of downtime required to have an evening to ourselves and watch a film in a movie theater. Just the experience of being able to relax inside of a dark theater without having to worry about being slammed to a mat was a treat.

While we were at the theater, Paul was clearly vibing to the music. His legs were bouncing up and down every time one of the signature songs from the film played, like "Night Fever" or "More Than a Woman." Despite his rugged exterior, Paul allowed himself to get completely engrossed in the spirit of the film.

"You know what, Beeper?" Paul gushed after the film. "We should go disco dancing!"

That was a *horrible* idea. Paul couldn't dance to save his life, and I'm not exactly Fred Astaire either. Going dancing would have only resulted in Paul feeling self-conscious about himself if people pointed over in his direction and laughed at him. Paul was very exacting about his appearance. Everything had to be *perfect*. If he wore jeans, they couldn't have a single wrinkle in them. Placing him in a situation where he might be ridiculed would only result in him getting his feelings hurt, and then possibly getting into a confrontation with whomever made the mistake of mocking him.

We didn't go disco dancing, but the music being played in the car during our long road trips changed quickly and conspicuously from country western to disco for quite some time. The conversations were always great as well, because we rapidly grew to become very close friends. Paul's upbringing was in circumstances that were even more dire than mine had been. He grew up impoverished in Brandon, Florida, and was raised in a converted chicken coop. I think growing up poor had imbued both of us with the desire to make the most out of our opportunities and not to take anything for granted. I think the rigors of our similar upbringings also prepared us for the discomforts of life on the road.

Speaking of discomfort, Paul began to feel unbearably constipated during one of our road trips. In the early stages of his duress, Paul had tried taking Ex-Lax to remediate the problem. When four days of Ex-Lax doses failed to provide Paul with any sort of relief, Paul had us stop at a pharmacy so that he could buy a quart of prune juice. After we'd arrived at our hotel and we were getting ready for bed, Paul seized upon that moment as the ideal time to down the *entire* bottle of prune juice.

In the middle of the night, the combination of four days of Ex-Lax combined with an entire quart of prune juice mingled in Paul's intestines and finally did its intended thing. The best analogy would be to say that if the Ex-Lax had been a bottle of soda, adding the prune juice had been the equivalent of dropping a Mentos tablet into it. Fecal matter erupted from Paul's backside and sprayed his bed. Holding his rear end, Paul sprinted to the toilet and sat there for hours, while I was forced to suffer in an acrid-smelling room that Paul had just decorated with shit.

It was a crappy situation, to be sure.

Not willing to let his bout with explosive diarrhea go to waste, Paul spoke to me in the locker room a day or so later and said, "Hey, Beep... how do you like *this* for a promo?"

Paul then stood up proudly as if he was giving an interview on television and said, "You know, when it comes to being inside of this ring, I've got more moves than a quart of *prune juice*!"

I nearly *died* from laughter.

Paul went on to use this line repeatedly during promos and interviews throughout his career. What most people would never have known is that this creative line sprang from a real-life situation in which a quart of prune juice had given Paul several hours' worth of movements all over our hotel room.

Other creative lines of Paul's were designed to help him accomplish his goals outside of the wrestling ring as well.

"I got a *great* idea, Beep!" Paul announced during a car trip.

B. Brian Blair: Truth Bee Told

"What's that?" I asked him.

"I'm going to start introducing myself to the ladies as 'Coffee,'" he replied, smiling proudly.

"Coffee?" I repeated. "That's *stupid*."

"Wouldn't you ask '*why*'?" Paul responded, annoyed that I hadn't already done so.

"Okay... *Why*?" I asked, still concentrating on the road.

"Because I grind so fine!" Paul said, laughing hysterically.

I looked at him and smirked.

"*Seriously*?" I asked.

"Oh yeah!" Paul said. "The ladies are gonna *love* that!"

From that point on, the "coffee" introduction became one of Paul's standard pickup lines. I can't say that it didn't work, either, but that would be like Larry Bird thinking he would be less accurate if he shot layups with his left hand instead of his right hand. When it came to the ladies, Paul couldn't miss. There was something about that redneck from Brandon that made him irresistibly charming to young women.

It didn't hurt that Paul was also handsome with perfectly blow-dried hair, or that he was unbelievably well built during an era where there truly weren't many human beings on Earth as physically impressive as he was, let alone wrestlers. Women *definitely* took notice whenever Paul was around.

The thing is, girls were *always* around. Wherever wrestlers went, the ladies followed. However, there were certainly occasions where we would deliberately go looking for female companionship. There was a particular bar in Shreveport that the wrestlers would frequently visit. The bar had two sides to it: a country bar for most of the visitors, and a topless bar for those interested in more prurient forms of entertainment.

One of the dancers working at the bar caught the attention of Harley Race. She made sure Harley did what the NWA World Heavyweight Champion was expected to do, which was to buy drinks for all of the other wrestlers, and everyone else who was partying with them. In the process, Harley kept buying drinks for the attractive dancer, clearly hoping to impress her and get lucky with her later that night.

Harley rapidly racked up quite a sizeable bar tab in his attempts to appeal to this young lady, but he became suspicious when she didn't seem to be behaving in an inebriated manner despite downing several of the drinks that Harley was footing the bill for.

B. Brian Blair: Truth Bee Told

At a key point in the night, Harley tasted the girl's drink while her back was turned to him. It immediately became crystal clear to him that there was no alcohol in her drink. She had been drinking ginger ale with nothing else in it.

Three different things occurred to Harley at that moment: First, the girl was charging him for premium alcohol and wasn't consuming any of it. Second, she was flirting with him solely to get him to drop a lot of money in the establishment, but probably had no intentions of privately entertaining him afterward. Third, since the girl wasn't getting intoxicated at all, his odds of coaxing her into a sexual encounter would be very poor.

Harley was *furious* about the whole thing.

"I'll teach this bitch not to fuck with *me!*" he growled.

Harley then reached into the pocket of his sport coat and pulled out a bottle of Visine. Then, when the girl wasn't looking, he dumped about half of the bottle into her drink. From there, he began goading her into dancing for him.

"Come on, honey!" said Harley, flashing some dollar bills in front of the dancer's eyes. "Get up on stage! I've been waiting all night for you to dance for me!"

The girl smiled and shook her head in the negative as she returned to nursing her ginger ale, which unbeknownst to her was now laced with Visine. Ten minutes later, after the girl had finished her drink, she decided to humor Harley and dance for the champ.

The girl climbed onto the stage and began to writhe and twirl along the metal pole at the stage's center. Harley began to call out to the rest of the boys and waved us over to him to make sure we all witnessed what he unmistakably knew was about to happen.

The longer the girl danced, the more the smile on her face gradually faded, replaced by a look of growing discomfort and duress. All at once, the girl suddenly stopped dancing, withdrew her hands from the pole and placed them on her stomach. Then she bent over and let out a groan. Through her bright blue, G-string panties burst a steady brown stream of diarrhea. It made a disgusting noise as it splashed all over the hardwood flooring of the stage. Then she bent over and vomited clear liquid out of the other end. It was a *repulsive* scene.

Other dancers materialized on the stage and helped to whisk the afflicted dancer away. All the while, Harley laughed uproariously, as if it was the funniest incident his eyes had ever beheld.

I can't imagine that girl ever returned to working there at the topless bar. It would be hard to imagine a topless dancer's sexual appeal being harmed by a single incident any more than by having a public attack of uncontrollable vomiting and diarrhea in front of her paying customers.

Harley Race wasn't the only wrestling legend who occasionally visited the Mid South territory. Andre the Giant was always a special attraction wherever he went. Vince McMahon Sr. handled Andre's bookings out of the World Wide Wrestling Federation's office in New York City, so Andre made a lot of money by touring the different territories, squashing his opponents everywhere he went, and then departing and moving on to receive another massive payday in the next territory he traveled to. In that respect, Andre was a lot like the NWA World Heavyweight Champion, except Andre was always more famous than the NWA champion and made a *lot* more money.

My very first promotional photo

Similar to Andre, "The American Dream" Dusty Rhodes was a special attraction in other NWA territories despite also being the most popular regular main-event wrestler for Eddie Graham in Florida. Much like the Giant, he almost always wrestled as a babyface when he was booked in other territories. This also stood in contrast to the NWA champions of the time, who usually wrestled as heels, and took it upon themselves to make the territorial main-event babyfaces look like world beaters who were capable of competing admirably against the most elite wrestlers in the world.

Because of their similar roles as special-attraction babyfaces, Dusty Rhodes and Andre the Giant often tagged together on shows around the United States. Andre's transient nature – combined with the fact that no one was ever supposed to be seen getting a clean victory over him – meant that he almost never held any championships during his career. However, holding a tag team championship meant that someone else could take the loss for the team, and Dusty didn't mind doing the honors if it meant he got to be on the same team as Andre. This is why Dusty is the only man to be a tag team champion with Andre in multiple classic territories.

When the Giant and the Dream were together, they were inseparable. The pair absolutely adored one another. Since I'd become friends with both of them under different circumstances, I got roped into chauffeuring the duo around when they visited the Mid South territory, and hilarity always ensued.

Veterans typically called the shots during wrestling road trips, so you can only imagine what it was like for me as a relative rookie wrestler traveling with two true veteran *superstars*. Dusty called me in my hotel room when we were all staying in Jackson, Mississippi, and instructed me to meet him outside because he needed me to get some things for him before we began our two-hour trip to Greenville, Mississippi, right on the Arkansas border.

"Listen here, Beepah!" began Dusty, sounding just like he was cutting a pre-match promotional interview during a wrestling broadcast. "You're gonna be doin' all the drivin', kid. You know me and Andre like to drink a lot when we're on the road."

Everybody knew this. The stories of Andre's drinking were legendary, and Dusty could more than hold his own when it came to alcohol consumption. An honest depiction of our road trips would capture Andre leaning all the way back in the roomy passenger seat of my Lincoln with a smile on his face and a whisky bottle in his hand, while Dusty sat dead in the middle of the back seat, breathing right in Andre's face with his beer-soaked breath, drunkenly telling road stories to us both.

"I need you to go down to the store and get Andre a case of Budweiser and two large bottles of Crown Royal," said the Dream.

I figured Dusty had made a mistake.

B. Brian Blair: Truth Bee Told

"*Two... large* bottles of Crown Royal?" I asked, emphasizing both key words and expecting some form of a correction from Dusty.

"*And* the case of Budweiser," affirmed Dusty. "And get me a case of Lone Star, too."

Dusty handed me about $200 in tens and twenties.

"And get yourself a six pack or somethin', but don't go *crazy* with it now!" said Dusty. "Remember... you're drivin'. And bring me back my change, kid."

I began to pull off in my car when I heard Dusty yell, "Hold on, kid!"

I hit the brakes and rolled the window down as the Dream approached.

"Get us *two* coolers, too," added Dusty. "A big one and a little one. We'll keep the beer cold in the big one and pee in the little one. It's cold out, and I don't wanna have to get out of the car to pee."

The heater of my car was broken, and it had picked a very inconvenient time to misbehave. It was January, in the dead of winter, and the temperature was only about 40 degrees outside during the daytime. Dusty's request wasn't all that odd, though. It was actually quite common for us to save time on road trips by bringing along bottles and other receptacles to urinate in as we traveled.

We settled into the car and got underway. Dusty had played both baseball and football at West Texas State, and on this day he was wearing a travel-appropriate West Texas State football jersey during our road trip. Andre was wearing one of his guayabera shirts – a short-sleeved, button-up shirt common in Caribbean countries – along with a white t-shirt underneath it. Neither one of them complained about the lack of heat in the car, probably because their bodies were quickly warmed by the influx of alcohol. By the time we reached Greenville, Andre had already dispensed with a full bottle of Crown Royal, and he and Dusty had emptied an entire case of beer.

I pulled into the parking lot of the building we were wrestling in, and Dusty barked out a special set of instructions to me.

"Beepah, you're goin' on early and we're on last," he said. "We ain't takin' no showers. It's too fuckin' cold out here, and it's gonna be cold in there, too. You betta have the car warmed up by the time we get done. We're gonna come right out to the car, put in some Willie Nelson and pop us a beer. You got that?"

"Yes, sir!" I said. "I got it!"

I'd been instructed early in my training that I shouldn't act like too much of a mark – or an extreme wrestling fan that believed or acted like it was all real – for guys that were technically my peers. Yet, it was so hard not to be at least a little bit markish when you were hanging out with guys who were probably two of the three biggest wrestling stars on the planet at the time.

I was so determined to make them happy that I missed the last two matches of the night and sat in my running car for 25 minutes just to make sure it was adequately warmed up for them by the time they finished their match. I even grabbed a few extra guys to sit in the car with me to try to generate a little extra body heat and raise the car's toastiness. Then I dumped the urine out of the smaller cooler and waited. Sure enough, Andre and Dusty exited the building wearing sopping wet towels around their necks.

We got back underway, and the alcohol began to flow freely once again. Dusty dispensed beer from the backseat like a bartender. As soon as I finished one beer, he was right there to slap another can of beer into my hand. Over in the passenger seat, Andre was two-fisting his drinks; he had a Budweiser in his left hand and the *second* bottle of Crown Royal in his right hand.

Dusty said something that Andre considered to be profoundly funny, and the Giant leaned forward in his seat and unleashed a deafening peal of laughter. His head was touching the dashboard. I started laughing at the sight of Andre laughing so intensely, but my laughter came to a sudden stop when Andre slammed his body back into my passenger seat with enough force to break it. It snapped like a twig beneath Andre's mammoth frame.

The destruction of my passenger seat was bad enough, but Andre's momentum carried his head and left shoulder straight down onto the Styrofoam cooler that had been resting over to the right side of Dusty. The cooler burst into several fragments under the weight of the Giant, unleashing a fresh batch of urine that splashed *all over* the American Dream.

Dusty was *incensed*, but to my great surprise he directed 100 percent of his ire toward me instead of aiming at The Eighth Wonder of the World, who was the true culprit behind the calamity.

"Dammit, Beepah!" wailed Dusty. "It's *cold* in here! You turn that goddamn heater on! Dammit, Beepah! You just got piss all ova the greatest supastar in the wrasslin' business! And the second greatest supastar in the wrasslin' business is just sittin' there lettin' it happen! You pissed all over the American Dream! I can't believe it! You about to be blackballed, Beepah! You'll *never* wrassle again!"

It was impossible to take Dusty seriously when he was sitting there drenched in urine and sounding like he was cutting a wrestling promo. Andre and I continued laughing for at least another 10 minutes.

Three days later we arrived in New Orleans. We had a show scheduled at the Superdome the following day, so we were enjoying having a rare evening of freedom. We found a restaurant named Felix's over on Bourbon Street, and Dusty and I both ordered oysters. Andre usually only ate one gigantic meal every morning, so he ordered a side of shrimp to go with the endless series of beers he guzzled. As we all ate and drank, Andre noticed sets of motorized ladies' mannequin legs that twirled in and out of some of the Bourbon Street display windows. Andre assumed it to be a gentlemen's club and asked us to accompany him there.

"If that's where the Boss want to go, that's where we're goin'!" answered Dusty, gleefully.

"I need to go to the bathroom real quick," I told them. Hanging out with those two had definitely caused the level of my beer intake to skyrocket.

"Dammit, Beepah!" said Dusty. "We ain't got time to be waitin' on you. Just hold it 'til we get in there."

We entered the gentlemen's club of Andre's choosing and immediately walked up a flight of stairs. There was a second set of stairs we were expected to climb in order to reach the level where the live entertainment was, but the lights went out as soon as we reached the top of the first flight of stairs. Just like that, we were cloaked in darkness. It was a blackout on Bourbon Street. I couldn't even see my own hand in front of my face.

"Hold on to your *poke*!" Andre yelled.

It was the Giant's way of advising us to hang on to our wallets. Frankly, I was more concerned about holding on to my *life*. We could hear rustling all around us, but we couldn't see anything at all. For around five minutes, the three of us stood there in a strange configuration. Andre held the rail and his wallet. Dusty held on to Andre's waist, and I kept a hand on Dusty's shoulder. It was a very unnerving situation. I wasn't certain of anything going on in our surroundings. The only thing I *was* certain of was the fact that my bladder was preparing to *burst*.

My eyes adjusted to the darkness just enough over that five-minute period that I was able to make out a plastic palm tree standing just over to the side of me on the platform.

"Look, guys," I began, "I've got to pee like a racehorse, and I can't hold it anymore!"

B. Brian Blair: Truth Bee Told

I unzipped my pants, held on to a branch of the palm tree and relieved myself all over it. When I finished, I zipped up my pants, satisfied that I could now continue standing in the darkness without the fear of wetting myself.

Right at that moment, the lights in the building abruptly began working once again.

"God damn!" yelled Dusty. "What the hell happened to my *pants*?!"

What I thought had been the trunk of the palm tree had actually been Dusty Rhodes' right leg. To make matters worse, the Dream always tucked his jeans into his cowboy boots, so my warm urine had flowed right down Dusty's leg and into his boot.

"*Beepah!*" roared Dusty, as his face flushed red with rage.

Dusty removed his right boot, turned it upside down and dumped the urine right out onto the floor. Andre and I were doubled over in laughter, and Andre had to take the additional step of sitting down on the top step of the staircase so that he wouldn't stumble over.

"God dammit, Beepah!" Dusty ranted. "I already told you once that you was gonna be blackballed! Now you 'bout to be *doubly* blackballed! You just embarrassed me in front of the second greatest supastar in the wrasslin' industry! *I'm* the greatest! The Giant is the *second* greatest! You ain't *nothin'* in this industry, and you done pissed on the American Dream *twice*! I can't believe it!"

Dusty continued to curse me out for a solid five minutes while Andre's low-pitched laughter resonated throughout the building.

As hysterically funny as the episode had been, Dusty's threats sounded sincere. I had no idea what repercussions might befall my career as a result of that one innocent act. I would soon learn that I would have to stand up for myself if I wanted to take control of my own destiny within the world of wrestling.

EIGHT – *Hard Decisions*

In the ring, things didn't always go smoothly for me during my first stint outside of Florida, and the fallout occasionally reverberated into awkward situations, both in and out of the locker room. For example, I refused to sell Larry Booker's headlocks during one of our matches because he applied them so sloppily. Eddie Graham had taught me to make every bit of contact look as realistic as possible and also to only sell contact if it looked real. If I sold Larry's headlocks, I would have been exposing that the business was phony.

"Why weren't you selling?" Larry angrily asked me after we'd returned to the locker room.

"Because I couldn't feel it," I told him. "When you had a headlock on me, there was a six-inch gap in there. I had to keep pulling your arm down. *Tighten up* next time!"

Larry didn't take too kindly to receiving pointers from me. He was very new to wrestling in his own right, but his training hadn't been nearly as strict as mine. The ill feelings gradually escalated between us over the course of several matches until we found ourselves back at the Western Hills Hotel in Bossier City. This time Larry was incensed at me because he thought I'd been working too stiff. In reality, we'd had a really good match that evening *precisely* because I had gone out of my way to make everything look as authentic as possible. What I knew to be appropriately snug wrestling was interpreted by Larry as being much too stiff.

A group of us, including Karl Kox and Dick Murdoch, had just met outside on a sidewalk adjacent to the exterior brick wall of the hotel. As we were trying to decide where to go out to eat and grab a beer that evening, Larry decided to challenge me to a fight right then and there.

"It seems to me like this punk wants to *shoot* with me!" Larry proclaimed.

"Are you talking about *me*?" I asked him, as I glanced around to see if there was someone else around that he might have been directing his threats toward.

"I'm talking to *you*, Brian!" Larry said. "If you ever want to shoot with me, go ahead and try it. No one can outshoot 'The Book!'"

I started laughing. Larry was really starting to antagonize me, and I wasn't about to back down.

"Okay, Larry," I said, raising my fists to indicate that I was ready to do battle. "Let's do it! Right *now!*"

B. Brian Blair: Truth Bee Told

Gaining the advantage over Larry Booker

Larry quickly put his hands up, and as soon as he did, I kicked him hard in his exposed stomach. That got him to drop his hands, so I wound up and clubbed him in the face with a sweeping left hook. Larry spun into the wall back first, and while he was leaning against the wall, I hit him in the face several times in quick succession, even as his body began to slide toward the ground. By the time Larry's unconscious form came to a rest at the base of the wall, he was out like a light.

Dick walked over and leaned over to assess the damage. Then he whistled.

"I'll tell you what…" said Dick. "Whoever taught Larry how to shoot should have his license taken away!"

I totally understand that I may have looked like I was milquetoast and clean-cut to some of the boys, but after spending more than three summers in the Dungeon with guys like Hiro Matsuda, Karl Gotch and Gordon Nelson teaching me the art of hooking – which to them included what would now be referred to as ground-and-pound in the mixed martial arts world – I could hold my own in a fight better than most other wrestlers might have thought at first blush.

One of the things I learned from my teachers is that most people don't really want to fight. They're waiting for you to posture up in the beginning without fully committing to fighting; that's usually the best time to strike if you're serious about throwing blows.

Despite my very brief outdoor scuffle with Larry, Watts still booked me in a match with him the following week. I was concerned that lingering resentment between the two of us might bubble over inside of the ring, so I shared my concerns with Bill.

"If Larry messes with me, I'll have to kick his ass *again*, except this time it will be in the ring in front of fans," I told Bill. "Do you *still* think we should have this match?"

Watts just chuckled at me.

"I'm serious, Bill!" I continued. "What if I have to defend myself and we get into a shoot?"

"How could a *shoot* hurt the business, Beeper?" Bill asked in a very direct manner.

I pondered Watts' question for a moment before I looked him in the eyes and said, "I guess it can't!"

Bill's message was clear; a spontaneous fight that spilled real blood couldn't possibly cause a decline in the fans' entertainment level. However, it never came to that. Larry always worked his ass off with me in the ring from that moment onward, and he always made sure his execution was as tight as it should have been all along.

Larry was a rookie like me, but veterans were more likely to take liberties with you in the ring and then dare you to challenge them afterwards. I learned this lesson firsthand in Jackson, Mississippi, which was the city that George Caulkin promoted in for Bill Watts.

Before my match that night, Watts sat me down alongside Ox Baker, who was a well-known, main-event brawler with a thick, black, handlebar moustache. Ox was definitely booked to get his hand raised in victory that night, but that didn't mean I needed to look feeble and helpless in the process of losing to him.

"Ox, I want you to go over, but I want Beeper to slip on a banana peel and for you to make him look good because we have plans for him," Watts explained.

"You got it," Ox said. "No problem, Bill."

As soon as the bell rang to start the match, Ox swooped in on me, rained forearms upon me, and took total control of the bout. He kept pounding on me and beating me without giving me any room to fire back. After absorbing far too much of that abuse, I started trying to communicate with Ox to figure out when he wanted me to make my comeback. Instead, Ox decided to pretend as if he couldn't hear a word I was saying and continued his assault in the form of clubbing forearms and elbows.

I knew Watts wanted me to get a comeback in, so I started firing on Ox with worked punches, meaning the punches weren't intended to do any actual damage. Ox refused to sell any of the punches, so I opted to throw in a few knees to see if he would sell those. Again, Ox wasn't interested in selling *any* of my offense.

Finally, Ox started going into the sequence that we'd established as the setup to the finish of the match, despite the fact that he hadn't allocated any portion of the match for me to get my comeback in. When Ox's infamous Heart Punch connected with my chest, I stayed down, but I put my foot on the rope while Ox held the rope to gain illegal leverage on the pin. The referee counted three anyway, having not seen either of us making contact with the ropes.

As you might imagine, I was absolutely *enraged* about what had just happened.

When I saw Watts after the bout, I said, "I can't believe what Ox just did to me!"

"I know, Brian," acknowledged Watts. "I saw it. I'll talk to him about it right now. You should just go somewhere and cool off."

"Well, what if I'd tried to take care of it *myself?*" I asked. "What the hell would've happened if I'd shot on him in the ring?"

"You have to do what's best for the business, Brian," Watts answered. "How can a shoot hurt the business?"

Watts' redelivery of the same message he gave me following my scrap with Larry Booker was enough reassurance that I wasn't going to get fired in the event that a fight ensued between Ox and me.

"Well, the next time I see him, I'm *gonna* shoot on him!" I vowed.

I stormed into the dressing room, and that's where I found Ox. He was sitting in a chair looking quite pleased with himself.

"What do you think you're doing, Ox?!" I yelled at him. "You heard Bill tell you to give me a good match! *Why* did you just eat me up like that?!"

"Don't worry about it, kid," Ox said, coolly. "You're young. *Nobody* knows you here. You've got plenty of time to get over in this business. I need to look strong in this town."

I'd seen Ox squash guys for Watts on television before, but this was just a local house show. It wasn't even being taped for

B. Brian Blair: Truth Bee Told

television, which meant there was no need for him to go into business for himself like that other than to simply be a jerk.

I wasn't about to let Ox get away with that response. I took a step forward and hovered directly over him.

"Yeah, I may be young," I began, "but…"

Instead of ending my sentence with words, I punctuated my anger by slapping Ox as hard as I could across his face. His bushy moustache swayed even further to the right than the rest of his head. The force of the slap nearly knocked him loose from his seat.

"Get your old ass up and show me how tough you *really* are!" I challenged him.

Our little exchange now had the full attention of all the boys in the dressing room. Rather than getting up and facing my challenge directly, Ox simply sat there with a red mark on his face from where my open palm had struck him. He absolutely refused to get up from his chair.

Now *I* was the one who was worried about looking like a jerk. Ox was about 44 years old, and he moved like he was *at least* 20 years older than that. Feeling how awkward it was that I now appeared to be the bully in that situation, I threw my hands up in disgust and walked away.

To my relief, Jerry Oates came up to me afterwards and said, "All the boys will have a lot of respect for you for doing that."

No one in the Mid South territory ever took liberties like that in the ring with me ever again.

There were other things I learned in Mid South aside from how to take care of myself when things got dicey with other wrestlers. One of the things I learned was how to take advantage of some of the raw deals that life had dealt me and use them to get over in the wrestling business.

Grizzly Smith was serving as one of Watts' bookers at the time, and he booked me in a match with Eric the Red in Jackson, Mississippi. Eric's heel tactics got the crowd so hot that night that he started a riot. The following evening, Eric and I were sitting around in the locker room in New Orleans and making preparations to wrestle one another for the second time. As Grizzly was laying out the finish to the match for us – which was set to involve three different false finishes – he noticed me favoring my right hand.

"What's wrong with your hand?" asked Grizzly.

I explained to Grizzly and Eric how a broken Budweiser bottle had penetrated my right hand when I was with my grandparents in Arkansas as a child, and how the doctor had botched the initial surgery to repair it.

"Let me see your hand," demanded Eric.

I offered my hand over to Eric, and he evaluated it and saw where the marks from the assorted incisions and stitches had irreversibly blemished my skin.

"Wow, man... that's terrible!" remarked Eric, in his deep, husky voice. "It looks like somebody *stabbed* you during a fight!"

When Eric said this, Grizzly's eyes grew wide with excitement.

"You should say *Eric the Red* stabbed you!" said Grizzly.

Eric's face lit up like a Christmas tree at Grizzly's suggestion.

"Yeah, man!" he exclaimed. "*I* stabbed you! I'd get heat with that! Tell everyone I stabbed you with a bottle!"

The conversation continued, and we discussed the heat for the finish to our match. With three false finishes, we were guaranteed to incense everyone in the building, even though I was booked to eventually win the match with a schoolboy rollup. Given the intensity of the riot we'd had during the prior evening, I was surprised Eric hadn't been killed, and I was even more surprised that he was so excited about the idea of accumulating even *more* heat for himself.

"Look, I *am* going to get stabbed *for real* if we do this finish that we're talking about!" I said.

Eric and Grizzly just laughed it off.

B. Brian Blair: Truth Bee Told

"Your match will get great heat from it," insisted Grizzly. "Just make sure you tell people that Eric stabbed you with a bottle whenever anyone asks you about your hand. It will be great for both of you."

At Grizzly's urging, from that moment forward I told anyone who asked me about the state of my right hand that Eric the Red stabbed me with a beer bottle during a fight. The sad thing is that Eric didn't live long enough to benefit from any of the heat my story generated for him. He died one year later when he was hit by a car while working in Tampa. Out of deference to him, for the rest of my career, I continued to tell everyone the imaginary tale of how Eric the Red had stabbed my hand with a bottle during a fight.

Another thing I learned in Mid South was the lengths to which some wrestlers would go to improve and maintain their muscular physiques. During one of our long car trips to Shreveport, I was regaling Paul with a story about the incredible strength of Ron Olejack, the center on our Louisville football team who'd had thickly muscled arms. From there, the topic shifted to Steve Keirn and the tremendous physical improvements Steve had been able to make in terms of his appearance. I naively attributed all of it to diligent dieting and arduous training at the gym.

To Paul, this all sounded like the gullibility of a child who probably still believed in Santa Claus.

"Don't be a fool, man!" Orndorff interjected. "Yeah, they might be eatin' right, but they're also takin' anabolic steroids. That's what *you* should be doin', man! *You* need to start takin' some steroids!"

Until that very moment, I'd had no idea how prevalent steroids had already become within the wrestling business. Also, if Paul Orndorff of all people was personally advising me to take steroids, you could bet that I would soon be taking them.

"What are they gonna do to me if I take them?" I asked.

"Nothin', man!" Orndorff said. "Shit... I've been takin' them for years. Nothin' has happened to me at all besides gettin' big muscles!"

Paul promptly set me up with a bottle of Dianabol, which set me back about $100. I had a very hard time parting with that $100. It's not like I was in horrible shape to begin with, and $100 seemed like a steep price tag for something that I wasn't sure I needed. This was a clear-cut case of peer pressure winning out.

I must say, Paul was my favorite guy to work out with, ever. He had been a gym rat for his entire life, and he had vast knowledge when it came to weight training. Paul liked to incorporate some powerlifting moves into his training, but he also added a lot of strict, slow bodybuilding repetitions where he would individually train each muscle in his body by forcing as much blood into it as he possibly could. All of the guesswork was eliminated from training as long as I was with Paul. He would determine our workout regimen for each week, and I just followed along with him.

Under Paul's tutelage, I took one blue, 10-milligram Dianabol pill every day for a week, and then I started taking two pills each day during the second week. During the third week, I was supposed to up the dosage to three pills per day. I didn't make it to the third week, because I had an unforeseen reaction to the unprecedented level of testosterone that was now coursing through my body.

Right in the middle of my second week on Dianabol, I experienced a sudden erection that absolutely wouldn't go down. It *really* hurt! Nothing I did could make the erection go away. I actually had to see a doctor who gave me medicine to reduce the blood flow and finally get the erection to subside.

That was a rough introduction to the world of steroids. Of course, that surge of testosterone did have its uses, although some of those scenarios involved behaviors that I'm no longer particularly proud of.

The presence of women was so thick in the Mid South territory; it was like a young man's fantasy come to life. If you were a decent-looking wrestler with a sexual urge, you *never* had any trouble finding an attractive young woman willing to help you satisfy it.

One night in Oklahoma City, Paul had a rather crude suggestion.

"Let's see who can bang the most girls tonight!" Paul said.

"You mean like a *contest?*" I asked.

"Yeah, man!" Paul said.

I didn't see what possible harm could come from engaging in this contest with Paul, so I quickly agreed.

"Sure!" I said with a smile. "So what are the rules?"

"We've got three hours from the time the doors open until we have to leave, right?" asked Paul.

"That's true," I agreed.

"Okay; it's simple," concluded Paul. "Whoever has sex with the most girls in three hours wins!"

The wrestlers were on very good terms with the building's janitor, and he left us the key to his office. The office had a couch in there, and we had easy access to the room, so we were all set.

B. Brian Blair: Truth Bee Told

I can't remember who won the contest, which probably means that I lost. What I do remember vividly is that one of us was with six girls that evening... and *still* lost the contest. The winner of our contest had relations with *seven* girls in three hours. This isn't an event that I'm particularly proud of now that I'm older, but there is no better example I can give that would do justice to how easy it was for wrestlers to gain sexual access to their female fans.

It wasn't like we needed to aggressively pursue the women either. They would wait for us to arrive at the buildings, call on us individually, and would occasionally get violently upset when we didn't give them what they wanted. More than one wrestler had his car spray-painted and *keyed* for refusing the advances of a wrestling groupie.

It's difficult for most men to fathom an environment where women would literally line up for you and would become angry enough to spray paint your car if you wouldn't sleep with them, but those types of situations transpired regularly. The girls would walk straight over to wrestlers and openly proposition us for sex, and if we flirted with the girls and then didn't put out, the girls would get *very* upset. It was akin to a ludicrous reversal of gender stereotypes!

Not too long after our sexual competition, I was driving down the road with Orndorff. My hands were on the steering wheel of my 1972 powder-blue Lincoln, but out of the corner of my eye, I noticed Paul scratching away at his crotch. I didn't want to say anything about it to avoid having an uncomfortable talk with him, even as his scratching became increasingly more vigorous. Finally, Orndorff broke the silence and addressed the issue, probably because he realized the abundance of scratching he was doing was both obvious and awkward.

"Beep... Goddammit, man!" Paul said

"What's wrong?" I asked him.

"I don't know, man. I just don't feel right."

Paul unzipped his pants and yanked his penis out into plain view. He pulled it upward, and some white puss oozed out of the sores that decorated it.

"Paul, man!" I yelled. "You've got *gonorrhea!*"

"What?! No way!" he shouted.

"Yeah, you do, bro!" I exclaimed. "That's the *clap*, man! I guarantee it!"

The next day after we woke up, I drove Paul to see a doctor that could treat his genital malady.

We didn't have AIDS to worry about back then, or any of the sexually transmitted diseases that might have been considered lethal.

B. Brian Blair: Truth Bee Told

The scariest thing most of the guys dealt with usually came in the form of crabs, herpes or gonorrhea. I was very fortunate when it came to avoiding STDs during my wrestling career. I almost always wore condoms, so I didn't have any problems like that.

Many other wrestlers weren't nearly as careful as I was. Pregnancy scares and STDs were *prevalent* in the locker rooms. Some of the other guys were either too cheap to purchase condoms, or they were simply far too eager to get down to business. Buddy Colt is one of the wrestlers I knew who sired more than one child with a wrestling fan during his career.

Not everything was about sex. Sometimes there were girls that we'd spend entire nights with because we actually liked them. In several cases, the women had their own apartments and would cook meals for us, which was great because then we didn't have to spend any of our own money on hotel rooms or dinner.

Some of the girls were special to the wrestlers, which usually meant a wrestler had identified them as an exclusive girlfriend in some form or another. That didn't mean that a girl was your sole girlfriend, or even that you were in any sort of dedicated relationship with her. What it *did* mean was that none of the other wrestlers were allowed to mess around with her or sleep with her. This also meant that if a wrestler was working in Florida, for example, he could have one special girl reserved for him in Miami, another in Tampa, and still another in Fort Lauderdale, and no one else was permitted to touch her.

That was one of the unspoken road rules amongst wrestlers; you don't mess with another guy's wife or his girlfriend… *ever*.

When we wrestled in Florida, most of the cities were close enough to Tampa that we were home every night. It was especially true that if you traveled with the boys, you had to pile back in the car and leave after the matches, so you couldn't spend much time with your favorite girl in that particular city. This meant that if you saw your special girl, you usually didn't stay with her very long because you needed to get home.

In the Mid South territory, the notion that we could even attempt to establish any semblance of a true home was essentially out of the question. We would stay in a different city every night, with very few exceptions. I had a regular room in Shreveport that I might have stayed in three nights out of the week, but the other four nights it could be in your best financial interest to have a regular girlfriend in each of the standard towns to help you cut down on expenses.

B. Brian Blair: Truth Bee Told

During that same tour of Mid South, I met a dark-haired, pale-skinned Canadian guy named Bob Marcus. He was constantly poked fun of by the other wrestlers for being so pale, and everyone used to tell him he was in desperate need of a tan. Despite being so hopelessly pasty-looking, Bob was a handsome guy, and very affable.

Bob wound up scoring an *exquisite-looking* girlfriend that he'd bring around the matches. This girl was *so* beautiful that I really had no choice but to compliment Bob on landing such a gorgeous woman.

"Your girlfriend is *really* pretty, Bob," I told him in the dressing room one day. "Nice work."

"Thanks," he replied as he continued getting changed. "There's just *one* problem."

"Oh yeah?" I asked. "What's that?"

"She's married," Bob said, staring into my eyes to drive the point home.

"Really?" I asked. "Like are they separated or is she about to get a divorce?"

Bob shook his head.

"Nope," Bob answered. "She and her husband own a country-and-western store. I met her when I was buying cowboy boots."

Bob always wore a lot of western-themed attire, including boots, hats and bolo ties, so it wasn't surprising that he would have been sniffing around town for cowboy apparel.

As the weeks and months wore on, Bob continued to date this woman in a rather brazen fashion. He also persisted with showing off whatever new cowboy products he had actively acquired during the affair. He once opened up the trunk of his car to display his cowboy boot collection to Paul Orndorff and me. There must have been at least 30 pairs of brand-new cowboy boots stashed in that trunk. He even sorted through them and listed off the names of each pair of boots.

"This one is called 'Galapava,'" Bob said, lifting up one of his favorite sets of boots.

"What the heck is Galapava?" I asked him.

"It's made out of turkey skin," replied Bob with a grin.

Bob also had boots made out of snake skin, alligator skin and elephant skin. He had boots from just about any animal that you could reasonably make a boot from. They were in all types of colors, all in his size, and all perfectly molded to fit his feet. He also had belts stashed in his trunk, along with three new cowboy hats displayed by the rear windshield.

B. Brian Blair: Truth Bee Told

Realistically, we didn't know if Bob's interest in the woman had more to do with the fact that she was so attractive, or because she was providing him with such easy access to rare and exotic cowboy garments. I'd hate to even imagine being the woman's husband in that situation, thinking about how his wife was probably bleeding him dry and giving the store away to her wrestler boyfriend behind her husband's back.

"Don't you feel guilty at all about this girl giving you all this stuff from her husband's store?" I asked Bob.

"Not at all," Bob responded. "I met him. He's a really nice guy. He likes me a lot."

I didn't ask any further questions. I don't think the husband knew the full scope of the relationship that was going on between his wife and Bob, so even if he liked Bob, I don't really suspect he knew about the affair, or how much of his shop's inventory was ending up in the trunk of Bob's car.

One night, Paul and I were riding around looking for a place to eat with Phil Mercado, one of the other wrestlers in the territory who was going by "El Mongol." On the way to the restaurant, we were all talking about the differences between natural babyfaces and natural heels, and what character traits needed to exist deep down inside of a wrestler in order for him to become a standout performer in each role.

"You could *never* be a good heel, Beeper!" sneered Orndorff. "You're just too nice!"

"I *can* be a heel!" I retorted. There's no doubt about it!"

"What a joke!" Orndorff said. "You don't even know how to act like one!"

"He's right," said Phil. "You're just too nice, Brian. To be a good heel, you have to have the heel lurking inside of you somewhere. You're just *too* wholesome!"

It sounded like they were just harmlessly busting my chops, but when you think about it, it's rather insulting. If another wrestler is labeling you as someone that can only ever be a babyface, they're really saying you're an incomplete performer. After all, half of the roster is made up of heels, and if you can't play the heel role, and the promoters never have the option of turning you into a heel, that can be extremely limiting to your career prospects.

We continued the argument right up until we reached the restaurant, and then Phil had an idea.

"Here's what you need to do, Mr. Heel," he said, mockingly. "Pretend like you're deaf and dumb while we're eating. Paul and I are going to act pissed off at you that we're stuck with someone who can't hear or talk, and you have to speak in sign language."

"You're on!" I laughed. "Let's do it!"

"Good idea!" Paul chimed in. "But if it works and they start feeling sorry for you, you have to say 'Thank you!' to them at the end. Then they'll know you understood what was happening the whole time."

A close-up of me as a clean-shaven young wrestler

It would be a nasty rib to pull on an unsuspecting civilian, but I felt like my honor as a performer was on the line. If I could prove I could be a villain in real life, my peers would have a greater level of respect for me.

We walked through the entrance of the restaurant and seated ourselves at one of the booths. Soon after, we were joined by a waitress who strolled up with a smile on her face and asked, "What'll it be boys?"

B. Brian Blair: Truth Bee Told

"Just a minute, ma'am," Paul said. "We don't know what we want just yet."

The waitress looked at me and repeatedly asked me if I knew what I wanted to order. Sticking to the rules of the rib we were attempting to execute, I instead turned toward Paul and Phil and began to approximate sign language as best I could.

Paul shook his head disgustedly, and if my mere existence was some sort of personal affront to him.

"You know, we could have been here with some chicks tonight if it weren't for us having to drag this dumb son of a bitch along with us!" Paul blurted. "He's like a damn anchor, man. Nobody likes to be around his ass because he can't even talk or hear! Deaf, dumb *bastard!*"

I acted as if I was completely oblivious to what Paul was saying about me, but the jaw of our waitress dropped open in absolute horror.

"How *dare* you!" she said, immediately coming to my defense. "It's not his fault he has this condition! How can you say that about him?!"

"I don't care if it's his fault or not!" Paul responded. "Why should we have to go without getting any tonight just because *he* has a problem hearing?"

"I can't believe you would say something like that!" the waitress remarked.

After reluctantly taking the orders of Paul and Phil, the waitress quickly returned with a platter of appetizers that she plopped down directly in front of me. Then she rubbed my back. This pattern continued throughout the night. Every time she would return to the table and deliver food, she would rub my back to let me know how much she sympathized with me, and regretted the abuse she imagined I must have been receiving on a regular basis from the evil pair of companions that accompanied me.

Of course, Paul and Phil were having a field day. During each of the return visits made by the waitress, the two of them would have these incendiary, off-the-cuff exchanges that were so unrelentingly rude, I almost broke character a few times to laugh at them.

"What are you rubbing *his* back for?" Phil said. "You know you're the only woman who's touched him in years, right? He's too stupid and ugly for anyone else to want to touch him. This guy just kills all our action!"

Then Phil shifted gears, turned to Paul and said, "He's *your* brother; can't you just send him back to your parents?"

B. Brian Blair: Truth Bee Told

"What do you want me to do?" Paul shrugged. "I'm stuck with the idiot."

"You two are *unbelievable!*" the waitress exclaimed. She soon returned with an extra plate of chocolate cake for me.

When the time came for all of us to pay, the waitress slammed bills down in front of Paul and Phil, but simply turned and smiled at me. Then she gestured to herself to make it clear that she had paid for all of my food that evening.

I immediately stood up and pantomimed to her that I insisted on paying for my own food, but she shook her head stubbornly and gave me a passionate hug. She was *incredibly* sympathetic toward me. She had such a wonderful disposition that I was truly dreading what I knew I was going to have to do next.

As we turned to walk toward the door, the waitress went on the offensive. She stuck her finger directly in Paul's chest and glared up into his eyes.

"You two *better* be nice to him!" she yelled. "You shouldn't be mistreatin' him like that!"

I moved a little bit closer to the door, and then I turned once more toward the woman and very loudly said, "Ma'am... I really appreciate everything you did for me. Thank you so *very* much!"

The silence in the room was deafening, and the crestfallen look on the face of the waitress was truly heart wrenching.

I stepped outside, but I only made it a few strides into the parking lot before I heard the irate voice of the waitress coming from behind me.

"You no good son of a *bitch!*" she screamed after me at the top of her lungs. "You guys are all *bastards*! You're so terrible! I can't believe you did that to me!"

The three of us then sprinted to the car and took off. It was funny to us at the time, and I felt that I'd proven I could be as dastardly as the most vile heel in the territory. When I think back on what that night must have meant to that poor waitress, it's all far less humorous for me to think about than it was at the time. This is not one of the times when I look back on the actions of my youth and I'm proud of what I did. I suppose most people get their idiotic, immature actions out of their systems when they're young, and the important thing is not to continue to do stupid things when you're older.

As a case in point, the worst and perhaps the most inappropriate rib I ever personally witnessed also occurred during this stage of my career. I was driving a rented van and shuttling Andre the Giant, J.J. Dillon, Terry Garvin and Koko Ware from Mississippi back

B. Brian Blair: Truth Bee Told

to Tulsa. Koko sat in the seat next to me and bobbed his head up and down to the music that was emanating from the van's speakers. Behind me, Andre and Terry – a Frenchman and a French-Canadian, respectively – conversed in French, which no one else in the vehicle understood.

Andre laughed heartily at something Terry said that had been unintelligible to me. Then Andre turned his attention to Koko in the front seat.

"Hey, Koko!" Andre yelled.

Koko couldn't hear the Giant over the deafening music, so Andre persisted.

"Hey, Boss... Come here," ordered Andre. "I want to tell you something."

Koko replied to Andre by saying, "What is it, Boss?" It was a compulsory show of respect to the gargantuan man who had begun the practice of referring to everyone around him as "Boss."

Andre gestured with his hand for Koko to lean in closer, which Koko managed to accomplish only after unfastening his seatbelt.

"I have a secret to tell you," Andre said. "Don't tell this to anyone else, but..."

Suddenly, Andre latched his meaty paws around Koko's head and shoulders, pulled the much smaller man clean out of the front passenger seat and into the back of the van, and secured a front facelock on him.

"Hey, Boss, what are you doing?!" screamed Koko. "I can't breathe!"

It was widely known that Terry Garvin was bisexual, and when I looked into the backseat through the rearview mirror, I could see to my great horror that Terry had removed his pants and was attempting to remove Koko's while Andre restrained him. As I continued to drive the van down the freeway at 70 miles per hour, Terry began to taunt Koko with the threat of sodomizing him. With Andre restraining him, there was nothing Koko could have done to defend himself against it. He eventually began to cry.

When I saw all of this happening behind me, I screamed for them to let Koko go. They didn't listen, so I swerved the van onto the shoulder of the road and brought it to a screeching halt. I wasn't about to be an accessory or accomplice to a rape. As I climbed out of the van, everyone else did as well, and that's when Koko escaped from the scene and began walking down the shoulder of the road all by himself, holding up his pants which Garvin had ripped in his forceful efforts to remove them from Koko's backside.

Everyone seemed to realize how excessive the rib had been, because no one was laughing anymore. The rest of us all got back in the van, and then I pulled the van alongside Koko as he walked along the road. I then pleaded with him through the window to get back in the van.

"This is terrible!" remarked Koko. "Look at my pants, man!"

"We were just playing, Boss!" insisted Andre. "We're sorry. We won't do it again."

"Sorry, Koko," said Terry. "I drank too much. I got a little carried away."

After what seemed like ages, Koko climbed back into the van, and we continued to drive the rest of the way back to Tulsa in silence. As far as I'm concerned, when a rib takes the form of physically hurting someone, or sexually threatening someone, it has gone *much* too far.

Terry got Koko's pants the next day in Tulsa and had his wife sew Koko's pants back together for him. Terry should have counted his blessings that Koko was in a forgiving mood, because I've seen Koko shoot on people before, and he could really dish it out. If Terry had actually gone through with what he was suggesting he would have done to Koko, I'm sure Koko would have *killed* him.

NINE – *Life lessons learned*

One thing about my career that I was always grateful for was that I never had to sit idly at home unless I wanted to. There was always a promoter somewhere who wished to bring me in as a wrestling asset. Even while I had been working in Mid South, Eddie and the Briscos had been singing my praises to other promoters around the country. Bob Geigel, the owner of the Kansas City territory, was interested in bringing me in during the late summer of 1978, and he contacted Eddie to arrange for me to spend some time wrestling for him once my initial foray into Mid South reached its eventual conclusion.

Once it was firmly established that I would be going to wrestle in the Central States territory, Jack Brisco pulled me aside to give me some advice on how to get in everyone's good graces.

"Beeper... Listen... Pat O'Connor is the booker, and he owns a piece of the promotion along with Harley Race," whispered Jack. "He and Bob Geigel are really excited about you coming in. Pat told me you're going to need a *special* finishing move, and he's going to ask you what it is when you get there. I was thinking you should use 'The Brisco Rollup.'"

"The Brisco Rollup?" I asked. "What's that?"

I'd been following Jack Brisco's career forever, and I'd *never* once heard of the Brisco Rollup before.

"You've seen me do it 100 times!" Jack said. "It's where someone picks you up for a slam, except you drop behind them, push them into the ropes and then roll them up in the middle."

Jack then spent the next 15 minutes or so showing me a variety of ways to apply the Brisco Rollup to my opponents during my matches. We worked on it until I was an expert who could apply it to an opponent from virtually any position in the ring.

When I ultimately arrived in Kansas City, I met with Bob Geigel, Harley Race and Pat O'Connor at the same time. All of them affirmed that they were very happy to have me working in their territory. Huge grins adorned each of their faces.

"So, kid... what's your finishing move?" asked Pat with the smile still on his face.

"Well, sir, I've been working very hard with Jack Brisco," I began.

"I know that!" Pat said, excitedly. "So, what did the two of you come up with?"

B. Brian Blair: Truth Bee Told

"Well, thanks to Jack, I've got the Brisco Rollup down pat," I said proudly.

Pat O'Connor stared blankly at me.

"The Brisco Rollup?" he muttered. "I've never heard of it. What's the *Brisco* Rollup?"

"Oh, you know the move," I said, and then I started gesticulating to him. "You know like when someone goes to slam you, and you drop behind him, push him into the ropes, and then roll him up for the pin from behind."

Pat's face flushed a bright shade of red, while Geigel and Race both burst into laughter.

"That son of a bitch!" Pat yelled. "That's the *O'Connor* Rollup!"

This was a *tremendous* long-term rib by Jack. I had just described Pat O'Connor's legendary finishing move right to his face, and then attributed its origin to Jack Brisco. Fortunately, Pat thought it was funny too once he took a moment to cool off.

"The *Brisco* Rollup!" Pat laughed. "That bastard…"

Harley was in Kansas City when I arrived, but he was off defending the NWA World Heavyweight Championship for the majority of the time I was working in the Central States territory. Whenever he *was* around, it was amazing. I got the privilege riding shotgun in Harley's white Porsche on a few occasions. The upside to it was I got to listen to his stories about working in matches all over the globe, and defending the championship in Japan in Giant Baba's All Japan Pro Wrestling company. Harley made Japan sound like a fascinating place to work.

The downside to riding with Harley stemmed from the fact that I was always somewhat leery about speeding through traffic, and was terrified at the thought of dying in an automobile accident. From that standpoint, riding with Harley was the *worst* conceivable place for me to be. When you rode with Harley, you were at the mercy of a wild man. He would swerve and weave in and out of traffic along two-lane roads at 110 miles per hour, all the while acting as disinterested as if he was plodding along at 25 miles per hour through a school zone.

During one of our trips, I saw a jackrabbit that we were approaching on my side of the road, so I pointed to it and yelled out to Harley, "Hey! Look at that jackrabbit!"

Harley pressed the brake and the Porsche rapidly decelerated. As we were slowing down, Harley reached under his seat, fumbled around for a second, and then produced a huge .357 Magnum revolver from beneath it. Harley aimed his *Dirty Harry* handgun at the jackrabbit and fired off two deafening shots from inside the car. He missed the rabbit, but scared the hell out of me and nearly broke my eardrums, which I'm sure was his objective.

Even though the actual promotion was formally referred to as Central States Wrestling, most people referred to it informally as the Kansas City territory because everything was headquartered in Kansas City, and that's also where nearly all of the wrestlers stayed. I quickly moved into an apartment in Kansas City, and Jesse "The Body" Ventura lived in the adjoining apartment. Jesse was magnificent with a microphone in his hand, and he had a physique worthy of his nickname.

Jesse and I were both very young, green, inexperienced wrestlers at the time, but our youth was seen as a strength. There weren't many young wrestlers in Kansas City when we arrived, and we were tasked with increasing the excitement level in the area and helping to eventually sell out the Kansas City Municipal Auditorium. This was the signature arena in the Central States territory, but they hadn't sold it out in over a year.

During one of my interview segments, Jesse attacked me and left me quivering in a pool of blood. This unprovoked and brutal attack, combined with our youthful energy, generated enough fan interest throughout the greater Kansas City area that our main event match at the Municipal Auditorium managed to break the non-sellout streak. Harley, Bob and Pat were so thrilled to have finally sold out that building that they hugged us and thanked us profusely.

Jesse and I made our way to the ring in front of a packed house, and that's when Jesse asked me a critical question as we received our instructions from the referee.

"What's the finish, Brian?" asked Jesse.

"Oh, shit… I don't know!" I told him.

Neither of us knew. The three owners of the territory were so excited and distracted by the novelty of having a packed arena on their hands that none of them bothered to tell Jesse or I what the finish to our match was intended to be.

"I'll get the crowd worked up, and then you can chase me out to the floor," suggested Jesse.

"Okay... and I'll chase you back inside and then you do the thing where you beg for mercy," I said.

We did exactly that. Jesse worked the crowd to the point where they were frothing at the mouth. After I chased him around the ring and then back into the ring, Jesse hit the ropes, jumped over me after I dropped to the mat, and then bounced off of the other rope only to see me standing there on both feet, with my fist cocked back, prepared to knock his teeth out. Jesse dropped to his knees and cowered in fear, and the crowd erupted and begged for me to kick him in the face. I allowed Jesse to rise to his feet as the referee stepped in to try to separate us. At that point, Jesse attempted to sucker punch me. I dodged his errant swing and began to rain fists upon his head.

The audience screamed at the sight of me exacting my revenge upon the man who had left me lying on the floor in a crumpled heap only a week prior. Without knowing what the intended booking plans had been, we eventually decided that I should pound Jesse into oblivion to the delight of the crowd, and then chase Jesse out of the ring and back through the curtain as the match ended in a double count out. It was the most logical and satisfying ending we were able to come up with in a spur-of-the-moment situation like that. For me, it was definitely a trial by fire, and at that moment I was proud of both of us for being able to think on our feet.

Once Jesse and I got back through the curtain, we realized just how tumultuous things had become in the locker room. Pat, Harley and Geigel had gotten into a huge argument over who was supposed to tell Jesse and I about the finish to the match. What's more, Jesse and I had been *far too successful* in giving the audience exactly what they'd wanted to see.

Ideally, Jesse would have won the match due to cheating from his friend Buck Robley, and then we could have returned to the Municipal Auditorium with a cage match or a similar match that would have prevented outside interference. Instead, by beating Jesse down so convincingly and forcing him to publicly flee from me, I'd effectively satisfied the bloodlust of the audience, and we'd killed off some of our momentum and the demand to see future matches between the two of us. Either way, it had been a valuable learning experience.

The Central States territory was also where I captured my first championship: The Central States Tag Team Championship, which I

B. Brian Blair: Truth Bee Told

held with "Bulldog" Bob Brown. Unfortunately, these highlights didn't prevent Kansas City from becoming the worst of the traditional territories that I would ever work in. There was no nightlife to speak of in Kansas City, and the road trips were depressingly long and tedious. Our tours of the region took us all through Missouri, Kansas, Iowa and Southern Illinois. It was far more taxing than traveling through the Mid South territory, and to top it off, it was *much* colder and we were making far less money.

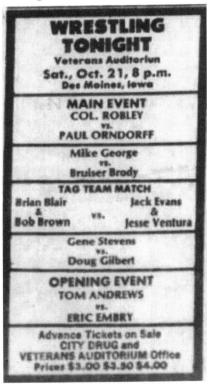

The average payoff there was only about $600 to $750 a week, for six nights of traveling and wrestling. This meant the maximum I could make in a week was half of what I'd made in Florida. Plus, we didn't have the same luxury we had in Florida of driving home every night. This meant we were paying for food, fuel and lodgings on the road out of our own paychecks every week.

All things considered, these were the worst payoffs I ever received once I factored in the abundance of traveling attached to them. This swing through the Central States wasn't about personal comfort for me, though; this was all about gaining in-ring experience while learning how to work different styles and read different crowds.

To help conserve our money, many of the boys would pile into the same wrestler's van. With five or six wrestlers in the same vehicle, the amount of time each of us was forced to spend behind the wheel was minimized. It also maximized the number of interesting personalities and events that could unfold while we traveled.

Eddie, Jack and Buddy drilled it into my head before I left Florida that I was always to pay "trans," which referred to the one-nickel-per-mile fee that was charged for riding in another wrestler's car during that era.

B. Brian Blair: Truth Bee Told

"You should always pay it right away, and no one should *ever* have to ask you for it," advised Buddy.

"Quickdraw" Rick McGraw was a very innovative guy outside of the ring, and was one of the first wrestlers I knew who developed a scheme for extracting large sums of trans money from the rest of the guys that he worked with. He also made it a point to call me "Triple B," even though I was still simply known as Brian Blair at the time. He heard everyone calling me "B," and heard Paul Orndorff calling me "Beeper," so he decided to take it to another level.

"Triple B, what do you think about this?" asked Rick in his rural North Carolinian drawl. "I'm gettin' a new car. I was thinkin' about gettin' a van, though."

From there he told me that it would cost him about a nickel per mile to own the van.

"And if everyone agrees to ride with me, I'm gonna get this van," Rick continued, "because then I'll be able to afford it with all the trans people are payin' me."

"You're right," I nodded. "That sounds like a great idea."

A short time later, Rick arrived at a show driving a beautiful new van that could comfortably seat about eight people. It was a brilliant move; that van became a trans *factory*. Everyone wanted to ride with Rick McGraw, and what he pocketed from trans money every week was more than enough to cover his payment on the van and put extra money in his pocket. As a matter of fact, he was also able to cover the cost of his insurance and his hotel rooms with the money he charged for shuttling everyone else from town to town.

The funny thing about it was how Rick would also ask other people to drive his van for him half the time. So, while it was true that he owned the van and was always in it, there were usually seven other people who could rotate in and out of the driver's seat while he hopped into the back and drank beer, which was a common occurrence during the rides home from the matches. Wrestling in matches and then drinking beer in the cars afterwards went hand in hand. How we managed to get away with it for all those years without any truly disastrous accidents happening on the road, I'll never know.

During one of our trips in Rick's van, Bobby Jaggers kept droning on and on to all of us about the nearby horse ranch that he owned.

"We're going to pass by my ranch today," announced Jaggers, proudly. "Might as well stop in and let me check on my horses. I've got some nice cattle that you guys can see, too."

"That sounds really cool, Bobby," I replied.

B. Brian Blair: Truth Bee Told

That wasn't sarcasm, either. I was honestly very excited to check out Bobby's ranch, and so were several of the other guys in the van with us. As we progressed, Bobby directed Rick to pull off of the highway and turn down a long, dirt road. A sprawling, fenced-in ranch property with cattle and horses came into view.

"Pull over right here!" Bobby yelled.

When Rick pulled the van over and brought it to a halt, Bobby opened up the door, climbed out of the van, and propped himself up on the fence. A huge grin split Bobby's face as some horses actually began making their way over to him.

All of a sudden, a red pickup truck roared up the road and veered in front of us. A rugged-looking man wearing a baseball cap and some filthy bib overalls hopped out of the driver's side of the truck. He took two steps forward and cocked the double-barreled shotgun that rested menacingly in his palms.

"Hey!" the man yelled, aiming the working end of the shotgun at Bobby's chest. "What the hell are you guys doin' on *my* property?!"

"We just wanted to see your horses, sir!" Bobby replied, raising his hands up. "We weren't gonna do anything to 'em!"

"Get in your van and get your asses outta here!" the farmer yelled.

When a man levels a shotgun at your chest, you do *exactly* as you're told. We got our asses out of there.

As we drove a little further down the road, and the farmer's shotgun disappeared from the view of Quickdraw's rearview mirror, Rick broke the silence by saying, "Bobby... what the *fuck* was that?!"

Bobby was clearly embarrassed, but he forced a grin onto his face and said, "Oh, come on, Rick! I was just ribbin' you guys! I wanted to see if I could get one of the horses to kick you!"

I always respected Bobby for his work ethic, but he was the biggest liar in the world. *Everybody* knew he was full of shit.

Touring the Kansas City territory accomplished its intended purpose; I became more comfortable in the ring. When that happened, I also became comfortable enough to make suggestions prior to matches, and even to innovate new spots.

I was talking to the Brisco brothers at the Kiel Auditorium one night, right before Spike Hubert and I went out to wrestle against a heel team. The plan was for the heels to get the heat on me by battering me for a while, and then I would give Spike the hot tag and let him unload on them.

B. Brian Blair: Truth Bee Told

I said to Jack, "What if I had the heels grab hands like they were going to clothesline me, except then I duck under it, come off the other rope and double clothesline both of them?"

Jack thought it through for a couple of seconds before saying, "Wow! I like that! That sounds great!"

During the match, we executed that spot exactly as I had laid it out in the locker room, and the crowd went *ballistic*. Then I sold my fatigue in the ring until the fresher of the two heels had reestablished himself on the ring apron, and I waited until he was tagged in before I leaped over and made the hot tag to Spike. As expected, the fans erupted for the tag after all of the tension we'd built up.

To the best of our knowledge, *that* is how the first double-clothesline counter to an attempted double clothesline was performed inside of a wrestling ring. I know it has been executed thousands of times since then and has become a staple of tag team matches, but the first time it ever happened in a wrestling ring was when I executed the move against the Briscos at the Kiel Auditorium.

I wasn't the only one attempting to innovate things in the territory at the time. Buck Robley was the booker in the territory, and he decided to test out a new variety of match in Ottumwa, Iowa: a blindfold battle royal. It was a match type I'd *never* heard of before, and I *still* haven't seen it presented anywhere else.

All of the wrestlers in the ring wore blindfolds. Even though we could see through the blindfolds, we'd still do cartoonish spots during the match. One example would be a spot where we'd throw a guy into the ropes and act like we were going to backdrop him when he rebounded off of the ropes. Instead, the guy would run past us, or end up falling either through or over the ropes and out of the ring. We would also swing wildly and miss with all of our punches by a mile while the crowd howled with laughter.

One of the most entertaining spots to pull off would be when you'd also grab another babyface wrestler and get ready to punch him in the mouth, only to be interrupted by the fans screaming at you, "No! No! No! That's the wrong guy! That's your *friend!*"

After finishing up in Kansas City at the end of 1978, I resumed wrestling in Mid South. My return to Oklahoma coincided with the termination of the partnership between Bill Watts and Leroy McGuirk. While I certainly wasn't the cause of their falling out, I may have played an inadvertent role in driving the final wedge in between the two of them. It wasn't due to any direct, behind-the-scenes politicking on my part. Rather, it more than likely involved my romance and eventual marriage to Leroy's daughter, Michael Kathleen McGuirk.

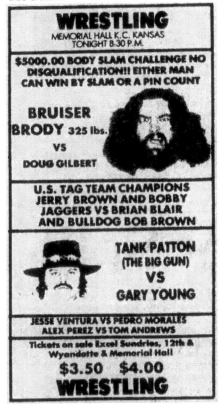

I knew that Mike had once been romantically involved with Ted Dibiase, but by the time I returned to Mid South, she was single and ready to mingle. What began as casual flirting rapidly escalated into a full-blown courtship between two lovestruck kids in their early 20s.

Our romance and subsequent engagement were common knowledge to all of the boys, and I was so madly in love at the tender age of 21 that I couldn't see any downside to the relationship. After all, Mike was young and beautiful, and she had an intimate knowledge of the wrestling business, having been raised in it by an accomplished promoter and former wrestler. This meant she was one of the only girls in the world of an appropriate dating age who was interested in wrestling, knew it was all a work, and who I wouldn't have to lie to about its true nature. In my young mind, this made her *perfect* marriage material.

While I had my love-induced blinders firmly fastened to my eye sockets, Ted Dibiase pulled me aside one day to offer me a bit of prophetic advice.

"I heard you and Mike are getting married," began Ted.

"We are," I responded, "and things are going great."

"I'm happy for you," nodded Ted, "but I just want you to remember one thing… and I'm telling you this as a friend: Mike is really possessive. Really possessive. Just be careful and think it over before you make a big mistake."

"I appreciate it, Ted," I lied. "Thanks for that."

B. Brian Blair: Truth Bee Told

I didn't really care what Mike's ex-boyfriend had to say, because as far as I was concerned, he was merely attempting to sow the seeds of discontent between my future wife and I before we had even walked down the aisle. I would never have guessed how wise Ted's advice had been, nor how much heartbreak I would have been spared if I'd heeded it.

Learning to accommodate a wife when your position as a wrestler allows you to easily sleep with a different girl every night requires a dramatic shift in decision making. Against all evidence to the contrary, even at the very young age of 21, I thought I was mature enough to handle that type of transition.

Leroy McGuirk was no fan of the idea of his daughter dating the wrestlers who worked for him, let alone marrying one. Fortunately, he grew to tolerate me, and eventually to like me. Part of what prompted Leroy to accept me was probably the announcement of my formal engagement to Mike. Once I became an official part of the McGuirk family, Leroy would have an obvious heir in place that could carry his territory for the next 20 years or more. Also, Leroy was 70 years old, so having me marry his 22-year-old daughter also ensured that she would be provided for after he retired.

Spending time around Leroy was made even more interesting due to the fact that he was *completely* blind. Two separate events, including a car accident, had robbed him of his eyesight when he was in the prime of his career. How he managed to run a wrestling promotion so effectively without the benefit of his sight completely escapes me, especially considering the vast amount of alcohol he drank. Honestly, between the drinking and cigar smoking that Leroy constantly engaged in, you could usually *smell* him coming long before you ever saw him.

I recall a time early in my relationship with Mike when I was standing in the kitchen of Leroy's house. Mike left me there while she went to grab something from another room, and she said she would be right back. As I stood there, the stench of cigars and booze wafted into my nostrils and prompted me to turn my head to search for the source of the scent. When I glanced over to my right, there was Leroy, moving hurriedly in my direction with his arms straight out and his palms facing down.

Instinctively, I backed up against the wall and assumed a defensive posture. My heart was racing a mile a minute. It took me a moment before I remembered that Leroy was blind and had no idea I was standing there in front of him, let alone who I was. Ordinarily, Leroy's arms would have been sliding off in different directions to provide him with a sense of what was around him, but in this case he knew the layout of his house so well that he'd neglected to do so.

As I remained as silent as I possibly could, Leroy stumbled right past me, never suspecting there was a living, breathing human being standing within three inches of him. It was an uneasy moment for me to say the least, but it also made me very sympathetic toward Leroy. Being blind made him extremely vulnerable, and if someone in that setting had wanted to inflict considerable harm upon him, they could easily have done it, and Leroy would have had no clue whom it had been.

After only six short months of dating, Mike and I got married in Tampa. Steve Keirn and Jimmy Garvin were the two best men in our wedding.

Shortly after our wedding is when the final split between Bill and Leroy occurred. Watts took Mississippi and Louisiana, while Leroy took control of Oklahoma, Missouri and Arkansas. Without question, this resulted in monumental animosity between the two longtime business partners, and I'm sure Watts was none too pleased to have to forego promoting wrestling in his beloved home state.

Inarguably, the true bone of contention between the two men stemmed from the handling of money. Leroy's wife, Dorothy, would handle the northern box offices for the company, and Bill would always handle the box offices from the shows that took place further south. This resulted in many arguments over the handling of the cash, including accusations of underreporting attendance figures in order to facilitate the misappropriation of funds without the other stakeholders having any knowledge of it.

Unsurprisingly, Watts was thoroughly pissed at me and made it clear that he held me at least somewhat responsible for the final split. Frankly, I'd done nothing to directly fan the flames of resentment that Bill and Leroy felt for one another, but I'll concede that having a wrestler marry into his family probably left Leroy feeling empowered enough to allow the partnership to be permanently dissolved.

In the ring, I began working in a high-profile feud with Ron Starr over the NWA World Junior Heavyweight Championship, which I won from him in Springfield and held for two weeks before dropping it back to him in Joplin. The NWA prohibited its territories from promoting any of their own wrestlers as a "world heavyweight champion," but the use of just about any other championship name was fair game within the individual territories. This included world tag team championships, and world titles in other weight classes.

B. Brian Blair: Truth Bee Told

I don't care what any other wrestlers say; it's rewarding to win championships and have them on your resume. Winning titles is something I'd dreamt of doing ever since I was a child watching Championship Wrestling from Florida in my living room, so winning a championship of any kind was an honor, even if it was a scripted accomplishment.

At the same time, I knew I had to be extremely wary of how I was being presented in the ring, and how I was being perceived by the rest of the boys. Leroy had granted me a spot as Art Nelson's assistant booker, which meant the opportunity was there for me to exert an inappropriate and questionable level of control over the results of my own matches if I'd wanted to. Art was a great guy, but he was never really able to get things clicking in the territory; Skandor Akbar was soon brought in to take Art's place.

To avoid being branded as a guy who was only out for himself, I tried to make it crystal clear through my actions that I was always interested in improving our business outcomes and ensuring that everyone working in the territory knew that as well. I figured it was a sound strategy to be perceived as a worker that wanted to help others and wouldn't use booking control to artificially lift himself up to a higher spot in the pecking order, like so many other wrestling bookers had done.

The way I saw it, the rest of the boys had goals they wanted to achieve in the wrestling business as well, and I couldn't make it all about me. The worst thing I could have done would have been to give the impression to my fellow wrestlers that they were coming to one of those territories where the booker was just going to put himself over all the time.

In my experience, wrestlers preferred to work for guys like George Scott; he controlled the book for a long time in the Mid

Atlantic area, but didn't work in matches himself. That meant no one had to be concerned that George might book himself to win all of his matches, or to arrange for the championship belts to be distributed amongst all the wrestlers in his circle of friends.

In fact, one of the things that made our northern segment of the Mid South territory so attractive to incoming talent at the time was precisely the fact that there wasn't an owner monopolizing one half of the main-event positions every night, and thereby soaking up half of the main-event *money*. This way, more wrestlers could be confident that they would have a fair shot at earning a very healthy living, and potentially being elevated into the main events.

Clamping a headlock on Jimmy Garvin

Just a few of the guys who were attracted to our territory included Hector Guerrero, Koko Ware, Jerry Brown, Buddy Roberts, Doctor X, Doug Somers, Tom Prichard, "Sugar Bear" Harris and Jimmy Garvin. I was primarily interested in bringing in young guys that I got along with, and who I thought would be loyal to our territory.

B. Brian Blair: Truth Bee Told

In the ring, Jimmy Garvin was already one of my favorite opponents. As great as the matches were that I had with him in Florida as a rookie, our matches improved markedly while we worked together in Mid South and gained increasingly greater levels of familiarity with one another as our overall skills also improved.

Outside of the ring, Jimmy Garvin quickly became one of my best friends and favorite people. We got along so well that he moved onto the ranch owned by Leroy and Dorothy. Mike and I also lived there most of the time even though we owned a house together in Tulsa.

When Jimmy moved in, he was accompanied by his wife, Patti, and his mother, Geneva. He was always on hand to help me enjoy some of the toys that I'd purchased and kept on the ranch, like my two motorcycles: a Suzuki 125 and a Suzuki 175. During one of the occasions when we were out riding on the ranch, Jimmy somehow convinced his mother to ride on the back of one of the motorcycles while he was commandeering it.

"I'm a *great* driver, Mom!" Jimmy said in his attempts to persuade her to ride with him. "I promise you: Nothing bad is going to happen to you."

Geneva relented, climbed aboard the motorcycle, and wrapped her arms tightly around her son's waist. The instant Jimmy took off on the bike, he lost control of it and inadvertently popped a wheelie. This resulted in Geneva sliding awkwardly off the back of the bike and breaking her tailbone on a rock. I'm quite certain she never allowed Jimmy to hear the end of it.

Several of the guys began to see me as an extension of Leroy, which meant they would come to me with their problems. I appreciated the level of trust they showed in me, but I was so conditioned to look for opportunities to rib people that I often let that temptation get the better of me.

As a case in point, Hector Guerrero approached me to help him work through an ongoing problem he was having with his blonde girlfriend, Judy, who was an absolute *witch*, and with whom he engaged in screaming matches on a daily basis.

Hector made sure there was no one else around when he presented me with his problem in the Tulsa locker room.

"Amigo..." Hector whispered. "I have these little blisters on my *penis*. Do you know what they are?"

"Ummm... no," I replied, stifling a laugh. "Show me."

B. Brian Blair: Truth Bee Told

Hector looked around and made sure the coast was clear before quickly pulling his pants down, lifting up his private parts and displaying the cluster of little blisters near the head of his penis.

"You've got *herpes*, brother," I informed him.

"*What?!*" he exclaimed.

"Yeah, man," I reiterated. "That's herpes. There's only one cure for that."

"What is it?!" Hector asked desperately. He was no longer whispering.

"Oh, man…" I said, shaking my head. "It *really* hurts, though."

"What is it?! Tell me!" Hector insisted.

"Okay, Hector…" I whispered. "You've got to do it for two weeks straight, and you've got to do it *now* while the blisters are still broken out. If they aren't broken out, it won't work."

"Okay, okay, Amigo!" Hector said. "Tell me what to do! What is it?!"

"You've got to run straight to the store and get a bag of lemons," I advised him. "Then you cut the lemons in half so that it curves a little bit. Then you have to rub the lemons on your dick hard so that all the juice gets in there. You've got to do it for about five minutes, twice a day. If you can't do it for five minutes, do it for as long as you can stand it."

The next day, Hector slid up alongside me in the locker room.

"Amigo!" he wailed. "That hurts *so* bad! Are you *sure* this is gonna work?"

"It will," I assured him. "It takes two weeks though. You have to keep going."

For the next two weeks, I watched as Hector toted a bag of fresh lemons into the locker room at every show we attended. Each night, he explained to me in painstaking detail how he would vigorously scrub lemons over his afflicted penis. This included descriptions of the scabs and what they looked like. It took every bit of restraint I could muster not to burst out laughing at how well my rib was working.

To my amazement, Hector actually toughed it out for the full two weeks. What's more, he was extremely pleased with himself when it was all over with.

"I'm done, amigo!" Hector informed me. "How long does it take to heal now?"

B. Brian Blair: Truth Bee Told

"It might take a few weeks," I told him. "You just can't have sex until the herpes fully clears up."

"That no good *bitch* probably gave them to me!" spat Hector, angrily.

To this day, Hector thinks lemon-scrubbing therapy helped him to recover from his herpes outbreak. Yet, to my credit, I may have accidentally stumbled upon an *authentic* cure for herpes; Hector later told me that he only had one herpes outbreak after that, and then never had another one.

I have no idea how I managed to make it through that entire two-week episode with a straight face, but I suppose it was something of an acquired skill. The more ribs you pull off, the more accustomed you get to maintaining a poker face despite every compulsion you might feel to explode into laughter.

Sometimes my penchant for ribbing my coworkers managed to manifest itself in the wrestling ring in front of live audiences. Skandor Akbar was the head booker, but since neither he nor Leroy was at the show one night, this meant all of the booking responsibility fell to me, and that was a scenario that guaranteed a rib was going to be pulled off.

There was a wrestler working on the show named Doctor X, and he had a loaded-boot gimmick. One of his boots supposedly had a special toe on it, and when he tapped the boot on the mat, the fans were led to believe that some sort of heavy object slid into the toe position of the boot. Then Doctor X could kick his opponent, administering tremendous damage to them, and pin them to win the bout.

Because this gimmick was so hot, I booked a battle royal specifically with this gimmick in mind. Moreover, I singled out Tom

Prichard as the target for the rib. The participants in the battle royal would enter the ring one at a time, alternating between heels and babyfaces. Tom was intentionally scheduled to enter last.

Before Tom arrived at the show, I smartened up everyone else in the locker room about what I wanted to see happen. Then I wrote "One-Boot Battle Royal" at the top of the booking sheet.

When Tom finally arrived in the building and studied the booking sheet, he was perplexed.

"What's a one-boot battle royal?" Tom asked me.

"It's pretty self-explanatory," I replied to him. "You're only allowed to wear one boot, and it has to be your left boot, because Doctor X always loads his right boot. We're telling the crowd that the athletic commissioner said if Doctor X is going to be in the battle royal, he's prohibited from wearing the boot that people think is loaded."

Everyone in the dressing room was already sitting around with one boot on, so Tom followed suit and took his right boot off as well. Just before the ring entrances started, I had Oni Wiki Wiki get Tom's attention to distract him. When Tom walked out of our line of sight, I had everyone hurry up to put their boots on, and then they rushed out of the locker room and out to the ring.

When Tom returned, I was standing by the door with one boot laced, and the other laced only halfway.

"Aren't you gonna take *your* boot off?" asked Tom.

"I'm going to wear it out to the ring to help get the match over," I assured Tom. "The referee is going to argue with me and then ask me to take it off."

"Good idea!" nodded Tom.

The announcer called for me, and I quickly sprinted out into the arena and joined my fellow babyfaces on their side of the floor outside of the ring.

When the announcer called Tom Prichard's name, he emerged from the locker room like a proper babyface, energetically shaking hands with all of the fans he encountered during his walk to the ring, all while wearing only one of his boots.

"Where's your shoe?" politely asked one of the lady fans as Tom approached the ringside area.

Tom remained completely oblivious to the fact that he was being ribbed. Then, when Tom got close enough, the babyfaces and heels all climbed into the ring. It was at that point that Tom glanced down at everyone's feet, realized what was happening, and blushed a dark shade of red. Rather than hustling back to the dressing room to get his other boot, Tom simply stood there as several of the fans began to laugh.

The referee went through the motions of explaining to Tom that he was supposed to have two boots on. Tom was so embarrassed, but his problems were only just beginning. Once the battle royal got underway, all of the other wrestlers went out of their way to make sure they stepped on Tom's exposed foot. He had to fight for his life in the ring that night.

That was Tom's initiation into our wrestling territory, and he was good-natured about it and accepted his ribbing like a man. To this day, if Tom and I are ever in the same room, the first thing he'll say after he sees me is "One-boot battle royal."

Even though I usually preferred working with guys the size of Jimmy Garvin, one of my favorite memories was working with James "Sugar Bear" Harris. He was such an imposing specimen of a man who stood 6'6" and weighed more than 300 pounds. I was presented to the fans as being the epitome of a clean-cut kid, and I was one of the hottest babyface wrestlers in the territory at the time. Sending me out there to wrestle against a giant who towered over me and outweighed me by 100 pounds was an altogether simple story to present to the crowd.

When James and I wrestled one another in Joplin and Springfield, the place rumbled so loudly when I made my comeback, only for it to go *dead silent* when he jumped up and dropkicked me right in the face. Then things would progress further to where he would miss a move or get knocked off balance, and I would hoist his giant frame up into the air and slam him to the mat. The crowds in those buildings would erupt. Even after all that, Jim cut me off and splashed me from the top turnbuckle, and the fans thought he had *killed* me. It was perfect. I could tell that Jimmy Harris was eventually going to be a big deal in the wrestling business.

It was right around that time period that Haystacks Calhoun asked me if I wanted to ride to the shows with him. I was very reluctant to travel with him for several reasons. First, I'd heard several stories about how he talked a lot and emitted a foul odor that could be overpowering in close quarters. Second, he rode around in a dilapidated, blue Suburban that he'd put about half a million miles on. Most importantly, Haystacks typically traveled with two vicious Doberman Pinschers. When I relented and agreed to travel with Haystacks, it took me more than two minutes just to get into his Suburban because I was terrified that I was going to get eaten by the two dogs that growled at me and eyed me hungrily.

B. Brian Blair: Truth Bee Told

The filthy, red interior of Haystacks' car was littered with around 20 empty packs of Red Man chewing tobacco. Once we settled in and began our journey, Haystacks stuffed some tobacco into his cheek, and sure enough he began to gab away. It was one of the longest, most unbearable road trips of my life. Not only was Haystacks talking every bit as incessantly as I'd been led to believe he would, but the stories of his *rancid* stench were true as well. To make matters even worse, Haystacks kept a giant thermos jammed into his center console, and that's what he spat into. Within an hour of our departure, the thermos was *overflowing* with tobacco-saturated saliva, and every time the Suburban hit a bump, the spit would splash all over the vehicle.

"Haystacks, don't you think you should dump that spit out in case you hit a bump?" I suggested. "It's getting all over your car!"

"No way!" Haystacks responded. "If I ever run out of Red Man, I can just use this!"

"What do you mean?" I asked.

"If I run out of Red Man, I can just suck on the spit," Haystacks said. "After all, it's *my* spit. I can just stick it between my cheek and gum, and it'll get me by until I can get some more."

As if I needed any more of a reason to be repulsed by Haystacks, that comment certainly put things over the top. I should have counted my blessings; Haystacks *hadn't* made me sit in the back seat. Any time I turned around to so much as sneak a peek at the dogs behind me, they lifted their lips slightly to bare their teeth. They would have gladly torn me to shreds if Haystacks wasn't sitting right beside me.

As awful as it would have been to be chewed up by Haystacks' dogs, that sort of physical agony would have been nothing compared to the emotional trauma that was awaiting my life just beyond the horizon.

B. Brian Blair: Truth Bee Told
TEN – *Leaving the North of Mid South*

There was a guy on our territory's talent roster named Herb Calvert, and he was one of the cockiest guys you could ever meet in your life. He was even greener than I was, but he was also a *tremendous* amateur wrestler at the University of Oklahoma. He'd even won the Gorriaran Award for recording the most pins in the least amount of time in the 1976 NCAA Wrestling Championships, even though he hadn't successfully captured the championship.

Herb was very nice to me because I was the assistant booker and represented the ownership of the territory, but he was abrasive to anyone he thought he could take advantage of in the ring. He didn't treat the guys working preliminary matches with much respect, even though nearly all of those guys had vastly more ring experience than he did. Herb had the mindset that he was a budding main eventer on the fast track to superstardom, and he only needed to be polite to the main event guys. This led him to believe he had a license to take physical advantage of anyone that he didn't regard as a top-tier talent.

The cockiness of Herb made me desperate to dream up the perfect rib to victimize him with. Once Andre the Giant scheduled a visit to our Mid South territory, I knew I finally had the resources at my disposal to unleash a giant-sized rib on Herb.

Andre and I already had a great relationship by that point. Aside from the road trips we had been on in both Florida and Mid South, I had also chauffeured him around a few times to see his various girlfriends. It was unusual for the Giant to entertain a lady while he was around the boys. More often than not, he preferred to keep those two worlds separate. Andre's regular girlfriend was 6'3", but chiseled and beautiful like a volleyball player. I distinctly remember the first time I saw her; I pulled my car into the hotel parking lot to deliver Andre to her, and she emerged from her own car, ran over to Andre and greeted him with a huge embrace and a long kiss.

Armed with the full knowledge that Andre would be on the card that evening, along with the fact that his lovely girlfriend would be in attendance, I devised a special finish to that night's pole battle royal. A bag containing $10,000 was going to be suspended from a pole in one corner of the ring, and Andre was booked to fight off all challengers, retrieve the bag, and emerge victorious.

"Andre brought his girlfriend to the show with him tonight," I told Herb, after I'd cornered him in the locker room. "I think you should use this as a chance to get on his good side and score some points with him."

B. Brian Blair: Truth Bee Told

Herb's eyes lit up. He loved to ingratiate himself with the stars, and there was no greater wrestling star in the world at that time than Andre the Giant.

"Oh yeah?" Herb smiled. "How do I do that?"

"When Andre goes up the pole the second time, right before he's ready to grab the bag of money, I want you to jerk his tights down," I advised him. "His girlfriend will get to see his ass, and she'll *really* get a kick out of that."

The smile dissolved away from Herb's face and was replaced by an unmistakable look of fear.

"Are you for real?" Herb asked, raising a questioning eyebrow at me.

"Absolutely, man," I lied. "She'll *love* it!"

"Okay, then," Herb said, smiling once more. "I can do that. That sounds great!"

I walked away from Herb, but a few minutes later, he approached me again.

"Hey, B..." began Herb, clearly having second thoughts. "Are you *sure* Andre won't get mad?"

"No, no, no!" I insisted. "In fact, he told me he wanted to do something like that. Can you do it for him?"

"Yeah, I'll do it," Herb said.

"Great!" I responded. "I'll go tell Andre."

I *didn't* tell Andre.

Pole battle royals were already among the epicenters for infamous wrestling ribs. We'd do things like slather Vaseline all over the pole to make it practically impossible for the person who was supposed to win the match to climb up and retrieve the bag. None of this ever bothered the Giant, though. At seven-feet tall, all Andre had to do was hold the pole and stand on the second turnbuckle to reach the money. In that respect, Andre was rib proof, and most people were far too frightened of him to *ever* attempt to rib him.

Once the match got underway, everything proceeded as planned. Andre made his initial attempt to secure the bag of cash, and we all piled on top of him in the corner to weigh him down. Minutes later, Andre had effectively dispensed with all of us and scattered us outside of the ring, which provided him with an easy opportunity to grab the cash. Slowly and deliberately, Andre started climbing the turnbuckles in the corner for the second time in pursuit of the bag. That's when Herb glanced over to where I was lying on the mat, and I nodded to him that it was now the ideal opportunity for him to expose Andre's giant ass to his girlfriend, along with the rest of the audience.

B. Brian Blair: Truth Bee Told

Andre extended his arm up toward the bag to the point where he was right at the cusp of grasping the money and winning the match. That's precisely when Herb scrambled over to Andre from behind, snatched each side of Andre's baby-blue tights, and jerked them down.

Talk about a full moon over Tulsa! Andre's butt had more dimples on it than a golf ball. His entire backside was laid bare before the crowd, and I saw his face turn as red as a radish from the embarrassment. I had *never* seen Andre like that; no one would ever have dared to rib him in that fashion. When I saw that, I knew someone was about to get *murdered*. Andre descended from the pole and pulled his tights up, and then he whirled around to set his bulging eyes on Herb.

All the while, Herb was standing there smiling as if he'd somehow done Andre a huge favor by so effectively unveiling the Giant's rear end to his lady friend. Andre reached out, snatched Herb up by the head, and then readjusted his hands to get a firm grip on Herb's hair. Then he dug a hand way down into the back of Herb's tights, spun around like he was preparing to throw the discus, and *launched* Herb over the top rope as hard as he could.

Herb weighed about 270 pounds, yet Andre was able to heave him into the *third* row of the ringside crowd. Herb never made contact with any of the ropes during his brief flight through the air and into the sea of people in the audience. That was the last match that Herb had during that run in Mid South. He went straight to the locker room, grabbed his things, and disappeared without a trace.

I couldn't believe my rib had almost gotten Herb killed. I was merely trying to teach him a lesson.

As well as things may have been going for me professionally, my marriage was in dire straits. Ted Dibiase's words had proven to be prophetic; Mike was every bit as jealous and paranoid as he had predicted she would be. Things at home were steadily becoming more contentious with each passing day.

The breaking point in our marriage was reached one night after Jimmy Garvin and I returned from the Shrine Mosque in Springfield. Mike was well aware that I was with Jimmy the entire time. More significantly, Mike *also* knew what the Shrine Mosque was all about: Everyone went downstairs to the basement of the building to enjoy cocktails after the shows, and no women were permitted to be there, *ever*, with the sole exception being Mike herself.

B. Brian Blair: Truth Bee Told

Even though she was in possession of all of this knowledge, Mike was still incensed when Jimmy and I returned to the ranch in Claremore, Oklahoma about half an hour later than we usually would have been expected to arrive. Without asking any questions, she launched into a tirade.

"So who were *you* fuckin'?!" Mike sneered venomously.

"Nobody, and you know it!" I replied, as I strode past her.

"I know you were!" she said as she followed behind me. "I should have known better than to marry *you*!"

"I didn't *do* anything!" I said, as I continued to defend myself. "I can't take this anymore! I'm leaving!"

"You're not goin' anywhere, you son of a bitch!" Mike screamed.

With that, Mike reached out, latched onto the back of my shirt, and tugged it so violently that all of its buttons popped loose and clattered onto the floor. Mike was right; I *wasn't* going anywhere. Not with my shirt looking like that, anyway. However, we had a show in Tulsa the very next day, and with 30 miles now separating me from Mike, I had the space I needed to file for a divorce.

It was a sad end to what had begun as a promising marriage. Jealousy kills more relationships than just about anything else, with the possible exception of financial problems. If I'm being honest, though, it's impossible to place too much blame on Mike for her wariness of being in a serious relationship with a wrestler. Few women could have had a better understanding of the sorts of temptations wrestlers yielded to on a nightly basis than Mike. I just thank God that we hadn't had any kids together, because that would have made things even more disastrous during our split.

Fortunately, our company had some forays into North Texas, and that allowed me to make the acquaintance of David, Kevin and Kerry Von Erich. Their family ran a thriving territory that encompassed much of Texas, including the Dallas market. On the occasions when I had some nights off, I had even made a few appearances at some of the Von Erichs' shows for some extra money.

The Von Erichs had expressed interest in me before, but I obviously couldn't work out of Dallas full time; I had to look out for Leroy's business interests. That familial connection had clearly taken precedence. It's not like I was getting rich in Oklahoma, but I had been making a comfortable living at $1,200 a week, and I was married. Now that the dissolution of my marriage was finalized – except for the certificate of divorce, which was due to arrive in the mail – there was no longer anything binding me to Oklahoma or the rest of the Mid South territory.

I made a call to David to explain how quickly things had spiraled out of control in Oklahoma, and how my situation there was now untenable. Plans were hastily put in place to allow me to finish out my term in Mid South and then promptly begin wrestling full time in Dallas in the fall of 1980.

Throughout the remainder of the time I had in Oklahoma, Mike and I negotiated a truce that would permit us to coexist with one another, and I agreed to finish out my dates amicably before moving down to Dallas. In the midst of this, Doug Somers found out I was getting a divorce from Mike, so he started putting the moves on her.

I began to suspect the worst when I saw Doug and Mike riding to the shows together. A little later, the awful truth of the situation was confirmed for me by Hector Guerrero while we were in Tulsa.

"Hey, amigo," Hector said. "I hate to be the one to tell you, but Doug and Mike are…"

Rather than completing that sentence, Hector made a circle with the thumb and index finger from his left hand, and then repeatedly shoved his right index finger through the hole. This was a classic case of a picture being worth a thousand words.

"I thought so, Hector," I said, as I stared vacantly into his eyes. "Thank you for confirming it for me."

In my eyes, and in the eyes of the courts, Mike and I were *still* married until the divorce was finalized. Even if Mike and I were technically separated and heading toward an imminent divorce, Doug was *still* sleeping with my wife in full view of the boys, and he was breaking one of the cardinal rules of the wrestling business: You don't mess around with another wrestler's wife or girlfriend… *ever*.

What made it worse was that Doug and I had actually been pretty good friends up until that point. Even though Doug was a heel and I was a babyface, I'd been letting him ride along with me in the babyface car. For him to turn around and do that to me was especially hurtful, and he should have known better.

When I finally caught up with Doug, it was right after my final match against Ron Starr in Tulsa for the World Junior Heavyweight Championship. I returned to Leroy's office while I was still in my ring gear, only to find Doug standing there. As soon as I saw him, I became overwhelmed by the uncontrollable urge to punch his lights out.

"Hey, you motherfucker!" I screamed. "Mike and I are still married! I let you ride with me, and then you *fuck* my old lady?!"

Somers started stammering, but he never got a coherent word out of his mouth; I didn't give him the chance. I smacked him hard in the face, and he stumbled backwards. Then I shoved Doug toward the wall. He fell to the ground with his upper body slightly elevated by the wall, and I began to stomp his head as hard as I could. In the process, I broke his nose and his orbital socket, and also shattered his cheekbone.

Oni Wiki Wiki and Skandor Akbar heard the commotion, burst into the office and pulled me off of Doug. If they hadn't, there isn't a doubt in my mind that I would have beaten Doug to death.

After rearranging Doug's face, I drove straight back to the house that I'd been living in with Mike, grabbed whatever things I had that would fit into my Continental, and secured the trailer holding my 17-foot Caravelle speedboat right behind it. I called my Great Dane over to the car and got him to sit beside me in the passenger seat. From there, I pulled off and left our house in my rearview mirror. All of the money that I'd put into the house would be staying behind in Oklahoma.

I wanted to make sure I said a proper goodbye to Mike before I made my final departure for Dallas. It was probably a mistake, but in my mind, it seemed like the honorable thing to. I drove over to Leroy's house in Tulsa since I knew Mike was staying there until she was certain that I was gone for good.

When I finally made it to Leroy's place, I ambled past Leroy's Lincoln Continental, which was parked on the grass rather than in the driveway. The house was made of brick and had a recessed front door, and I walked right up and rapped my knuckles on it.

Through the door, I heard Leroy's voice asking, "Who is it?"

"It's Brian," I announced, raising my voice a little more than usual so that I could be clearly heard through the door. "Can I talk to Michael for a minute?"

B. Brian Blair: Truth Bee Told

"I heard you tore my office up!" Leroy screamed. "Goddammit! I *can't* believe you! You broke my pictures and everything! You son of a bitch! Get the *fuck* out of here! Mike doesn't want to see you around here anymore, and *neither do I!*"

Sadly, I turned and walked back over to my own Lincoln Continental. I sat inside the car for a few moments, petting my dog, and recognizing that this was probably going to be my final opportunity to talk to my wife before our divorce was finalized. Ultimately, I decided that I wouldn't be able to live with myself if I didn't make every effort to speak with her one last time. Instead of simply driving away like I probably should have, I got out of the car and walked right back to the front door of the ranch.

I knocked on the door once again, and this time Leroy *did* open the door. Unfortunately, he also had a .38 revolver in his right hand.

"I *told* you not to come back!" Leroy screamed at me through the screen door. "If you don't get outta here I'm gonna shoot your ass!"

"Shit!" I yelled, scared out of my wits.

I sprinted away and sought cover behind the brick siding of the house. That way Leroy wouldn't be able to reach me if he started firing. That would turn out to be the wisest decision I ever made in my life, because Leroy let loose a volley of shots that exited through the open door.

BLAM! BLAM! BLAM!

From where I was standing, I could see the grass in front of Leroy's car being torn up by the .38-caliber bullets. In his attempts to shoot me, Leroy came perilously close to damaging his very own Lincoln. Evidently, Leroy didn't mind if he *murdered* me that night. However, he *had* successfully scared the piss out of me.

When the coast was clear, I walked cautiously back to my car. I was literally trembling with fear, but I was also in tears. I really had been in love with Mike, and I couldn't believe things had deteriorated to such an absurd extent that my own father-in-law was content to kill me. Between the jealousy that drove us apart, to Mike's liaison with one of the wrestlers that I'd befriended, to my father-in-law trying to unload his revolver into my face, things had devolved well beyond the point of dysfunction.

The thing was, I just didn't know when to leave well enough alone. I knew Mike was somewhere in the house because her car was there in the driveway. Against all logic and common sense, I decided to get back out of my car, and I crept through the darkness and around to the rear of the house. From there, I tiptoed up to the rear window of the house and peered inside.

The first thing I saw was what appeared to be a mummy seated on the living room couch. As I watched, I saw Mike approach the mummy with a metal tray in her hands. She set the tray on the table, sat down on the couch, took the bowl from the tray, and began to spoon feed the mummy. That's when I realized the "mummy" was Doug Somers. Mike was nursing him back to health after the thrashing I had given him roughly four hours prior.

Over and above everything else, the image of my wife consoling Doug Somers was too much for me. My heart was well and truly broken. Feeling completely defeated, I dragged myself back to my car and finally hit the road for Dallas. It was a long trip, and I cried at least half of the way there.

Aside from the added in-ring experience I'd acquired, the only things I left Mid South with were my car, my clothes, my boat, my Great Dane, $500 cash, and a broken heart.

I arrived in Dallas at around 6:00 a.m. and drove straight to David Von Erich's house. It was still dark outside when I knocked on the door to his place, and the last thing in the world I was expecting was for a young, *naked* girl to open the door with a smile on her face, and to usher me straight into the living room.

The girl politely introduced herself, and then got down on her knees and started unzipping my pants.

"This is a welcome-home present from David," the girl said.

About 10 minutes later, David casually strolled into the room wearing a robe, told the girl to take a hike, and then gave me a huge hug.

"Welcome to Dallas, Beeber!" he said.

David then walked into the kitchen where he started pulling eggs out of the refrigerator to make himself an omelet with picante sauce.

"You hungry?" David asked me while he cracked the eggs into a bowl.

"Yeah, I could definitely eat something," I told him.

David got some omelets going on the stovetop, threw some bread in the toaster, and then returned to the omelets and ladled some picante sauce on top of them. They tasted *amazing*. To this day, whenever I think of preparing myself a David Von Erich omelet, it means I'm going to use three eggs, I'm going to layer lots of shredded cheese in the middle, and then I'm going to top it off with picante sauce.

B. Brian Blair: Truth Bee Told

We sat there eating breakfast while David stared out of the back window and out onto his massive property. The skies were much brighter than they had been when I'd arrived, and you could see for quite a way into the distance. Simply being in the presence of a friend with my marital problems 250 miles behind me had already immeasurably improved my sanity.

David walked into the kitchen and placed his dish in the sink, but as he began to walk in the direction of his room, he casually glanced toward his front yard. Something unexpected had clearly caught David's eye, because he came to an abrupt halt.

"Beeber!" David yelled suddenly.

"What?" I replied.

"Look!" he said. "Over *there*!"

David still wasn't wearing anything aside from his robe and his underwear, yet he sprang up out of his chair and made a beeline for the front door. Just before he reached the door, David yanked open one of the kitchen drawers and extracted a long, silver revolver from it. Then he opened the door and ran out into the wooded area right near the front of the house.

I watched through the front window as a white cat looked toward the house and tensed itself. Suddenly, the cat exploded into a crimson mist as a massive bang rang through the air and shook the kitchen where I was seated. David returned to the house with the smoking gun in his hand and said, "I *hate* cats, man! We've got so many fuckin' cats around here! I can't stand 'em!"

That was my early-morning welcome to Dallas, and it perfectly set the tone for what it was going to be like working in the Von Erichs' territory. It only got more fun from there.

B. Brian Blair: Truth Bee Told
ELEVEN – *Getting stronger and growing up*

In Dallas, I hit the ground running. The Von Erichs – led by their legendary patriarch, Fritz Von Erich – controlled all of the area surrounding Dallas, and also extended their sphere of influence into southern Oklahoma. The Blanchard family operated Southwest Championship Wrestling to the south of the Von Erichs in San Antonio, and the Funk family owned the Western States territory in Amarillo. In Houston, promoter Paul Boesch collaborated with everyone to provide his fellow Houstonians with the highest caliber of wrestling action that he could muster. Texas was a veritable *dreamland* if you were a professional wrestler *or* a wrestling fan; there were so many options to choose from.

By then I had discovered myself as a worker and realized that I could get in the ring and adapt to any style of wrestling. I had also been involved in matches with wrestlers of all shapes and sizes and delivered great matches against seemingly impossible odds.

The Von Erichs had a roster full of young wrestlers during that era, and I fit right in. They quickly booked Al Madrill and I to win a tournament for the NWA American Tag Team Championship. Outside of Florida, I had now won a championship in every territory I had performed in, and it definitely meant something to me.

Again, it wasn't so much about winning championships for their own sake. In my eyes, if a promoter put a championship belt on you, it was a sign that you were viewed as a key contributor to the success of the territory, and that your efforts were appreciated. Title belts could go a long way toward making you feel secure about your standing in a wrestling territory, or with an individual wrestling promoter.

Al was a great guy, but he was singularly obsessed with big-breasted women. He didn't care how skinny or fat the girls were, how pretty they were, or even how attractive any of their other body parts might have looked. He was laser focused on girls' breasts, and as far as he was concerned, the bigger they were, the *better* they were.

In that sense, Al epitomized the guys who had an unabashed fascination with pornographic magazines. If you were on a road trip with Al and you were behind the wheel, you could expect your view of the road to be intermittently obstructed by a pair of large, bare breasts, because Al would make it a point to shove them under your nose even if doing so might cause an accident on the freeway.

"Take a look at *these* boobaloogas, Beep!" Al would say. "Pretty good, right?"

B. Brian Blair: Truth Bee Told

"Yeah, those are nice," I'd shrug. "Really nice, Al."

Ten seconds later, Al would shove another page from the magazine in my face and say, "Now how about *these*, man!"

A little bit of nudity could go a long way. I wanted to dismissively say, "It's just a pair of boobs, Al. It's not that big a deal." However, Al probably would have considered such words to be very hurtful.

Al may have had an ulterior motive in establishing himself as the big-breasts guy. He was a handsome man that a lot of the girls found attractive, and I think that was his way of preemptively letting everyone on the roster know that any big-breasted women who were in an amorous mood should be brought to his attention and reserved exclusively for him.

Fortunately for Al, he usually had plenty of women to choose from. The crowds in Dallas were nearly always 40 percent female at a minimum, and sometimes the percentage of ladies in attendance made up well over 50 percent of the crowd. World Class outperformed the other territories in that regard because the young women of Dallas had been conditioned to expect that the wrestling cards would be filled with good-looking young men. Without question, Kevin, David and Kerry were all good-looking guys, and once they were featured on local Dallas television, the attractive women followed them to the wrestling shows, or to *any* of the other places they were advertised to appear.

If you lived in Dallas during that era and wanted to meet an attractive girl, your safest bet might have been to attend a World Class show and simply search through the crowd. The ladies were *everywhere*.

At one of our television tapings I was wrestling against a very odd wrestler known as the Monk. He stood about 6'2", and he was also baldheaded and pale-skinned with a round belly. During our match I called for a crisscross, and the two of us began the process of hitting opposite sets of ropes while narrowly avoiding one another. In the process, I hit one set of ropes really hard, and the top rope snapped. The Monk noticed this while running across the ring the other way, and as he ran by me, he said to me, "Your rope broke!"

For a reason that eludes me, it never dawned on him that the ropes are *all* connected, which meant if *my* top rope was broken, the *entire* top rope was broken all the way around the ring.

The Monk continued to point toward my side of the ring ropes while continuing to run toward his set of ropes. Instead of putting a halt to his run, he charged straight into the ropes with a full head of steam. Since there was no longer any tension in the top rope, the Monk took an unbelievable, face-first spill out onto the concrete floor and broke his nose.

The fans gasped as the Monk unexpectedly descended out of their line of sight. It was one of the most *devastating* falls I'd ever seen in the vicinity of a wrestling ring. From most angles, it would have looked like the Monk had just *died*. Yet, the Monk was so green and inexperienced as a performer, he didn't have the good sense to sell the damage from the fall. Instead, he popped right up to his feet as if nothing had happened.

Either the Monk was so shaken by the mishap that he forgot to sell his tumble, or he thought he would look tougher and less clumsy if he sprang to his feet. Either way, there was no worked damage that I could administer to him during the remainder of the match that could compete with the *real* damage that fall should have inflicted upon him. It didn't look good from a presentation standpoint for the Monk to suffer noticeably from all of the typical in-ring punishment he received, only to rise swiftly from a hellacious fall to the floor as if he had been completely unhurt.

After the match, everyone got on the Monk's case for potentially exposing the business.

"The *next* time you fall like that, you need to stay down and *sell* it!" Fritz told him.

One of the things that David and I shared was a fondness for ribbing the other wrestlers, and the Monk's spur-of-the-moment decision to not sell that fall out to the floor planted him squarely in David's crosshairs.

We were in the city of Lawton, Oklahoma, which is very close to the Texas border, and the building we were wrestling in featured a prominent stage. Located behind the stage were dressing rooms, along with showers on each side. There was also a big curtain at the front of the stage that we could look through, just like bands or other performers might have done if they were performing at the venue. From that staging area, we had the space to sit, talk and monitor the show, and then we could walk down either side of the stage and out toward the ring. It was an ideal arrangement for a small-town wrestling event.

Taking David Von Erich for a ride with the airplane spin

The show was well underway, and things were progressing into the later stages of the night. That's when the Monk opted to take a shower, and David had been waiting longingly for that opportunity. Once the Monk was thoroughly distracted by his shower-taking ritual, David took the Monk's towel, climbed a 20-foot ladder, and hung it over an air conditioning duct. He made it a point to leave the ladder conspicuously in place.

When the Monk got out of his shower, he performed a quick search for his towel, and soon spotted it at the top of the air conditioning duct with the ladder propped just beneath it. Putting two and two together and realizing someone had moved it up there, the Monk gamely pulled himself up to the top of the ladder to retrieve his towel despite the fact that he was stark naked.

Just as the Monk reached the ladder's apex and was about to recover his towel, the timekeeper rang the bell to signal to everyone that the next match would be starting. This led everyone in the audience to turn their heads back toward the stage to watch as a new set of wrestlers made their way to the ring. As soon as all eyes were trained on the stage, David jerked the curtain open, and the Monk's pale, white, naked body was *fully* exposed to the world.

The audience gasped in horror, and the Monk's pale skin abruptly turned cherry red. The embarrassed grappler practically leaped from the ladder and dashed away, covering as much of his private area as he could. That was *easily* one of David's best ribs.

Drug use was prevalent in the Dallas territory, and I got to see a lot of it firsthand during the year I spent living in David's house. One of David's drugs of choice was what he referred to as "pickles," which were actually 750 mg Placidyls. They were intended to be used as sleeping pills, but a lot of wrestlers liked to take them because of the euphoric effect the drugs could have on their bodies.

Because I was always within arm's reach of David, it only made sense that he would offer me drugs on a routine basis.

"Here, Beeber! Take one of these!" David said, handing me one of his bottles of pickles.

"No, man... I'm good!" I replied.

I was honestly really afraid to take them. I'd seen how spaced out and daring David became when he was on those pills, and they weren't something I wanted anything to do with.

"It won't hurt you," David assured me. "I promise."

I acceded to David's wishes and took one on the Placidyls. What resulted was the highest high I'd ever felt in my life; it was *not* a feeling I relished. To be honest, it was rather disturbing.

Once both of us were sky high, David had the bright idea for the two of us to go outside, and then he found a creek with a log that served as a makeshift bridge for the two of us to cross. When you're high, *everything* sounds like a brilliant idea. This means when David decided we should both walk across the log, I agreed to it like an idiot. Within seconds, both of us had fallen off the log and into the creek, and we had to swim for our lives while we were high out of our minds. That was the first and *last* time I ever took one of David's pickles.

The Von Erichs epitomized what it meant to be Texans, and there were plenty of fun outdoor activities to engage in on their adjoining properties. The Von Erichs were quite fond of horses, and Kevin, Kerry, David and I regularly went out riding together. During one of those excursions, Kerry said, "Let's all go up to the top of Cemetery Hill."

From the crest of Cemetery Hill, I could plainly see how the hill received its name: Someone's name was chiseled into a cement block at the top of the hill, above what was presumably a grave. While we were up there, all four of the horses began to freak out at the exact same time. They all started bucking like crazy, and one of the Von Erich boys fell off of his horse. It was almost as if the horses had felt the presence of some type of spirit, all at the same time. Something about that hilltop had really spooked them. This was highly irregular behavior for tame riding horses that had always been very calm every other time they'd been ridden.

With David Von Erich learning what it takes to be a Texan

There were great times to be had in every place we gathered. We often took my Caravelle boat out onto Lake Dallas to go water skiing. One of the most memorable days of my life was spent with David, Kevin and Kerry, along with Brian Arias, who was a lifelong friend of Kerry's. We took turns double slaloming out on the lake, and only concluded our excursion when the sun began to dip. As we steered the boat toward the dock, we beheld the picturesque sunset that hung in front of our eyes. The Texas sky became suffused with a coral shade, and we all agreed that we had just enjoyed one of the best days of our lives.

The fact that the Dallas territory was filled with young wrestlers often meant we would get involved in some reckless behaviors and throw around insane ideas. I certainly got caught up in my fair share of questionable activities as well. One day, David, Kerry and I were all sitting around at David's house, and the idea was suggested that if we could grow our own marijuana, we could make some money off of it, and also have a steady supply of it to smoke ourselves.

B. Brian Blair: Truth Bee Told

"I'm pretty good at gardening," I offered. "I learned a lot from my grandfather in Arkansas when I helped him tend to his property. All I'd need is a book on how to grow pot."

"This might work," said David.

"But *where* would we put it?" Kerry asked.

The Von Erichs owned a sprawling property that stretched for hundreds of acres, so there were plenty of potential weed-growing locations we could choose. Each of the boys owned a separate house somewhere on the property. Next to Kevin's house was a corner acre of barren land that was obscured from view by trees. Smack in the middle of it was an unobstructed quarter acre upon which some pot could be grown, so we decided this would be the best place to grow our marijuana. That quarter of an acre was more than adequate for our purposes.

I researched a host of books about botany in order to learn how to grow marijuana, and Kerry went and secured the seeds for us to start our gardening project. It was a true team effort. Al Madrill even went so far as to secure some potential buyers for our weed who were willing to pay between $800 to $1,000 per pound depending on how high the quality was. We had no desire to become the drug kingpins of Dallas or anything like that. This was just one of those asinine stunts that kids dream up when they have too much free time on their hands.

We went about the process of growing the marijuana like true professionals, including prepping the soil, and making sure we maintained and monitored its pH balance. Then we planted corn all along the perimeter of the plot where we wished to grow the marijuana to further obscure detection of the *true* cash crop being grown in the plot's center. It took three 100-foot garden hoses to transport the water down to where it could be administered to the plants. David and I were primarily responsible for doing the watering and the gardening. It didn't take much time before we owned more than 100 healthy marijuana plants that had all grown to a size of about six feet tall and four feet wide. They were robust and beautiful.

The plan was to allow the plants to grow throughout the entire summer, and then to harvest them around October, which seemed to be the optimal time. David and I specifically told Kevin that under no circumstances was he to water the marijuana anymore, because the plants were required to dry out before being harvested.

Still, Kevin decided he should water the plants at least one more time. In and of itself, I guess that was fine. However, he neglected to roll up the bright yellow garden hose and carry it back to the house. When Fritz's gardener and caretaker, Brock, saw the garden hose trailing away from the house, he followed it the full 100 yards from the house straight through the trees, and directly into our marijuana patch. After we'd successfully operated in secrecy for so long, Kevin had inadvertently led Brock *straight* to our weed-growing operation.

I was sitting around the house with David when the fateful phone call came in. Even though he wasn't talking to me, I could hear Fritz's voice booming through the receiver of the phone while he spoke with David, and it was clear that Fritz wasn't pleased. David hung up the phone, and his forehead broke into a spontaneous sweat.

"Oh shit; I'm in trouble," David stated. "I don't know how much trouble, but Dad is really pissed."

David hastily left the house without me, and then he came back about half an hour later and told me what had transpired. When David arrived at his parents' house, Brock was holding a branch in his hand from one of the marijuana plants. He asked David point blank if he knew anything about the pot in the field.

"I told him I didn't know anything about it," said David. "So then he said if I didn't know anything about it, then I shouldn't mind if he *destroyed* it all."

It was at that point that Fritz asked Brock to mow the marijuana field. Brock got on the Bush Hog and sheared *everything* in that field to tiny little pieces, including the corn.

We were just three guys who thought we had a nice payoff coming our way after a summer full of hard work, only to have our plans dashed by Kevin's absent-mindedness. Thousands of dollars' worth of weed was chewed to worthless shreds by Fritz's lawnmower because Kevin had left a bright yellow garden hose out in plain view. The only way he could have made it more obvious would have been to post a sign with an arrow that read, "This way to the *secret* marijuana patch."

Fritz may have had a gruff, demanding demeanor that intimidated a lot of people in the wrestling business, but on the inside, he had a warm, tender heart. He put a $100 bill inside my pay envelope every week as a cash bonus, and he always had something positive to say to me about my matches.

Not to be outdone, Fritz's wife Doris was an incredibly sweet woman. She always kept food on top of the counter by the stove for anyone who was hungry. She also had conversations with me about God, and she helped to deepen my religious faith with her kind, Christian conduct.

B. Brian Blair: Truth Bee Told

One of the *best* credits to Texas-based wrestling was the conduct of Paul Boesch, the promoter over in Houston. If a wrestler developed a reputation for reliability in any of the neighboring territories that bordered Houston, they might receive an opportunity to slip into Southeast Texas to work a few dates for Paul.

After wrestling in my first show in Houston against one of the Twin Devils, Paul came through the locker room and distributed envelopes with checks inside of them.

"Thank you, Mr. Boesch!" I said, as I accepted the envelope.

"Please, call me Paul," he replied, before continuing on his way.

Once Paul had walked far enough away from me, I opened up the envelope and saw a *huge* payoff amount. I had heard that Paul was a good payoff guy, but never in my life had I ever received *double* the payoff amount that I'd expected. If anything, wrestlers are accustomed to being shorted on payoffs by promoters. Very seldom would you ever receive *more* than you'd been promised, let alone twice what had been promised. It was no wonder that everyone raved about working for Paul. I would spend the rest of my career wondering why more wrestling promoters couldn't have followed the stellar example set by Paul Boesch.

My impression of Paul was that he received plenty of money from his ventures outside of wrestling, and he wasn't dependent upon the Houston shows to earn any sort of a living. As long as he broke even on his shows, he was satisfied enough with the idea of simply presenting quality shows to wrestling fans in hometown and sending them all home happy.

Although I was bound to World Class, I was still able to leave for Hawaii with Kevin Von Erich to work on two different six-week tours for Lord James Blears. We only made about $600 a week during the tour, while generally working five nights a week on the different islands, but the Ambassador Hotel was only charging us $350 to stay there for the entire month. It was an *incredible* deal.

Working in Hawaii was more of a working vacation than anything else. The priority was to enjoy the sights in Hawaii and to have a great time, not to actually make money.

One of the mainstays of the Hawaii territory that I worked with was Ripper Collins, a pudgy, bleach-blond heel in his late 40s. He had this odd quirk about him, inasmuch as every time I would take him over onto the mat, he would *bite* my nipple. It hurt a lot, and I had to tell him in no uncertain terms that he needed to stop that B.S.

B. Brian Blair: Truth Bee Told

I wasn't sure if that was his own bizarre form of ribbing me, but I'd heard from some of the boys that Ripper was bisexual. That knowledge led me to believe the nipple biting was just one of Ripper's personal kinks. What people like to do behind closed doors is their business, but I certainly didn't want rumors spreading that I had somehow *enjoyed* it, and I certainly didn't want *Ripper* thinking that either.

When Ripper bit me a third time, I cinched a tight hold on his arm and told him, "*Quit* doing that!"

Well, Ripper *didn't* quit doing it. He bit my nipple a fourth time, and I snapped and decided to turn him into a pretzel. I tied him in knots and made him holler so loudly that all of the boys could hear him in the back. Once I knew I had gotten Ripper's attention, I snatched him in a double wristlock.

"Holler *louder!*" I ordered him as I applied more pressure. "Holler louder, or I'm going to *break* your arm!"

"Please! Please let me go!" Ripper begged.

"Then don't you fuckin' bite my nipple again!" I threatened him. "Do you understand me?!"

"I won't! I *promise!* I won't!" he screamed.

That was the end of the nipple biting in Hawaii. Shockingly, it wouldn't be the last time he would ever bite one of my nipples in the ring, though.

Much of my downtime during my two tours of Hawaii was spent hanging out with Kevin Von Erich and Mando Guerrero. On one occasion, Mando and I had just finished wrestling at the Blaisdell Center in Oahu, and we stopped off at a liquor store to get some beer to take back to the hotel. I pulled our $15.95-per-day rental car into the liquor store's parking area, and as I stopped the car and turned off the engine, two Hawaiian guys pulled up alongside us on our right side. The driver of the other car carelessly swung his door open, and it banged loudly into Mando's passenger-side door.

With zero hesitation, Mando leaped out of our car in a seething rage.

"Hey, man!" Mando screamed. "What the fuck is your problem?! Are you fuckin' *blind*?!"

The two large Hawaiian men both walked menacingly toward Mando. Sensing that a confrontation was imminent, I opened my door and climbed out of the car. It was a foregone conclusion that we were about to get into a fight, and I didn't like our odds if the fight stayed fair. Instead of posturing, engaging in a conversation with the two men, or giving them any other sort of opportunity to prepare themselves, I faced off with the driver on the sidewalk in front of our parked cars and swiftly kicked him in the balls as hard as I could.

"Ahhh!" the driver screamed as he crumbled to the ground. "My *balls*!"

Then, as the passenger instinctively looked over toward his fallen buddy, I sucker punched him in the jaw with a perfect right hook.

The element of surprise had paid off *perfectly*. It may not have been a very honorable set of tactics to use in a fight, but I was taught that there is no honor code in a street fight. Ivan Koloff had explained to me very early in my career that if you're fighting with another wrestler, you're not allowed to go after the guy's eyes, nor can you go after his balls. In a two-on-two Oahu street fight with two non-wrestlers, *everything* was fair game.

Mando kept kicking the defenseless driver while he was clutching his testicles, and I jumped on top of the other man and began clubbing away at his head while he tried desperately to protect his face. Everything was going well for us until about 10 more Hawaiian men emerged from within the liquor store, incensed that two non-natives were wailing away at their fellow Hawaiians.

"Mando!" I yelled. "Let's go!"

Mando was very slow to leave his guy alone, and that gave the Hawaiian newcomers a chance to encircle us. It was *over*. These men were going to kill us, and there was nothing left for us to do but to go down swinging.

Just as the men were about to converge on us and rip us to shreds, Don Muraco pulled into the parking lot. His timing could not have been any more perfect. Don leapt out of his car wearing a tank top and looking like a Hawaiian Hercules. He inserted himself right into the middle of the fray and began speaking with our adversaries in a mixture of Hawaiian and English.

"Those are *my* friends!" declared Don in what was the only part of his diatribe I was able to clearly understand.

Don exchanged words with his fellow natives for a few moments before the leader of the Hawaiian contingent held up his hands in a gesture of appeasement and took a couple backward steps.

"Okay, Don..." the man said. "I'm sorry. We'll get our friends."

Suddenly, Don whirled around and redirected his anger toward Mando and I.

"And *you*!" he screamed. "You guys get the fuck out of here right now! Don't you *ever* mess with these guys again! You hear me?!"

B. Brian Blair: Truth Bee Told

Thankful that our lives had been spared, Mando and I did exactly what Don asked of us: We got out of there.

Posing for a fan alongside Bam Bam Bigelow and Don Muraco

"Mando, you almost got us *killed*, brother!" I accused him.

"I couldn't help it!" he said. "I couldn't just let that guy hit our car!"

"It's a freakin' *rental* car!" I said. "It's not even our car! *And* we bought the insurance on it! You can't do that shit here in Hawaii!"

It was true; we had opted to pay the additional $6.00 per day for insurance on the rental car, so Mando almost got us murdered over absolutely nothing.

Without a doubt, Don Muraco saved both of our lives from a brutal ass whipping. If he hadn't pulled up when he did, Lord Blears would have been shipping me back home to Tampa in a box. Don pretty much owned Hawaii. Hanging out with him in Honolulu was like being in the company of the mayor.

Don helped Mando and I to preserve our lives on that day; back in Dallas, I was in the midst of a master class from a wrestling legend who taught me how to preserve both my time *and* my money.

TWELVE – *Hangin' and bangin'*

Frank "Bruiser Brody" Goodish was in and out of Dallas constantly while I was down there. He was a native Midwesterner like I was, having spent the bulk of his formative years living in Metro Detroit, and he had become one of the top headliners and true road warriors of the wrestling industry. Being able to travel with him was one of the true godsends of my wrestling career, because just one week spent with him was all it took for a wrestler to master the art of stretching a penny so far that it *screamed*.

The word that comes to mind when I think of Frank is "optimization." Frank had learned how to optimize everything about his life, from his money to his diet, to his training methods, to the mannerisms of his performance. Frank had *everything* in his life down to a science that maximized his success in and out of the ring.

Even among main event wrestlers, Frank was a high earner, but he always lived and ate like he was staving off homelessness. He had mastered the art of "heeling" a room, which first involved learning which hotels offered rooms that contained two double beds. When you reached the hotel, one person would check in and agree to be charged the single-occupant rate, and then a second person could stay there unbeknownst to the hotel's staff. This would help you save about $10, which was key to the second phase of Frank's money-saving scheme.

Everyone who knows Frank knows that he was a giant man who stood about 6'8" and weighed more than 300 pounds. Yet he had mastered the art of fueling his mammoth figure – while eating something every two hours – for less than $10 per day. Therefore, Frank could take the $10 we'd saved from heeling the room, and turn it into an all-day feast.

In 1981, Frank could turn a $5 bill into five cans of tuna fish, a carton of eggs, baby carrots, broccoli, and a loaf of bread. He would also bring a portable grill into the hotel rooms with him, so when we woke up in the mornings, he would quickly whip up two dozen egg whites for our breakfast, along with a side of rye toast.

"This isn't the best-tasting breakfast in the world," I complained to Frank after the fourth or fifth straight time eating tasteless egg whites for breakfast.

"But now you're *full* and your body has the protein you need to build muscle!" laughed Frank. "You couldn't eat anything else now if you wanted to, no matter how it tastes. That's the whole point. Eat

B. Brian Blair: Truth Bee Told

something healthy and cheap that will do the trick, and then be *done* with it."

It was impossible to argue with Frank's logic. I was undeniably full, and I'd saved plenty of money simply by not running off to a breakfast diner every morning. By the time I was done riding around with Frank, he had informally inducted me into "The Noble Order of the Tuna Fish Kings."

When it came to working out, Frank taught me a totally different style of training than Paul Orndorff had. Under no circumstances would anyone have caught Frank doing bicep curls while he was on the road; he would have dismissed them as a huge waste of training time. Instead, Frank would do powerful movements like squats, deadlifts, bench presses and heavy shoulder presses. *Everything* he did was about training for raw power.

Frank's theory of training was that we were adequately training the smaller muscle groups – or secondary muscles – while we were targeting the larger muscle groups. In his view, heavy back training worked the biceps, heavy chest training worked the triceps, and squats worked the entire body, so there was no need to train the arms separately since they received sufficient attention when we trained our largest muscle groups.

I wound up leaving Texas just before the Von Erichs' syndicated shows became viewable everywhere. Although I missed out on the beginning of the explosion in popularity for World Class, my career definitely benefited from my being there as long as I had been.

Even in the absence of circulating match footage, if you were in the hunt for a championship in a major territory, you would still end up getting written about in all of the wrestling magazines, or even in Dave Meltzer's *Wrestling Observer Newsletter*. Publications like that were legitimately helpful to guys' careers, because they helped promoters all over the world to get a sense of who mattered in the industry, who knew how to get over, who might look good on camera, and who might be a solid attraction in their wrestling territory.

The other major benefit to working in Dallas was being able to refine my style in a relaxed environment. The Von Erichs had been like family to me, and David Von Erich in particular had gone above and beyond to make me feel like one of his own brothers. By the time I departed from Dallas, in September of 1981, I was about halfway to becoming the ring general that I would eventually become. A truly polished wrestler can *work* with anyone, but it takes a *long* time to develop into a true ring general who is capable of having a *great* match with anyone.

Unfortunately, there was one key piece of advice from David that I didn't follow: The Von Erichs bought gold for themselves every single year as a stable form of investment.

"Beeber… you should buy a gold Krugerrand every year!" David would tell me. "You'll make a fortune if you buy it and save it!"

David was right; if I'd done that, I'd have so much more money in the bank than I do now!

On my way out of Dallas, I contacted Eddie Graham to let him know that I was wrapping things up with the Von Erichs. That's when I learned that Don Owen had called Eddie and asked him if he thought I'd like to come out to Portland and wrestle for him.

Don Owen was a well-respected promoter in the Pacific Northwest territory, and it sounded like an ideal situation for me to garner experience in a region thousands of miles away from the Southern stretch of territories that I'd been traveling through up to that point. Still, I had already received an offer to work in Atlanta for a couple of months, and that's where I had been planning to work next.

"Working in Portland sounds great," I replied to Eddie. "Do you think I should go?"

No matter where my employment offers came from, I always asked Eddie what I should do, because he was the advisor that I trusted the most to steer the trajectory of my career toward long-term success.

"I think Portland will be open for you anytime you want to go there," Eddie said, "but I think it will help your *career* more if you go to Atlanta."

On the rare occasions when I might have questioned Eddie's advice, I would then turn to either the Briscos or Buddy Colt. In this case, Eddie was wrong about Portland being open for me anytime I wanted to go there, but he would have had no way of knowing that in

B. Brian Blair: Truth Bee Told

1981. However, Eddie was absolutely correct about working in Atlanta being good for my overall wrestling career.

The Georgia territory had been broadcasting a nationally syndicated show since 1976, which made it easy for wrestlers based in Atlanta to promote themselves to wrestling fans all over the country. Simply by wrestling a few times at the WTCG studio in Midtown Atlanta, I would ensure that exponentially more people would get to see me wrestle during that short span of time than had ever seen me wrestle live during the first four years of my career combined. I was anxiously looking forward to that opportunity.

One of the unique aspects of working in Atlanta that you were constantly aware of as a young wrestler involved the lingering rumors that encircled promoter Jim Barnett. As a wrestling promoter, Jim was an absolute legend. He had made a name for himself promoting shows in my birth state of Indiana before relocating to Australia and enjoying tremendous success there with his World Championship Wrestling promotion. I had heard many stories about Jim from some of the veterans in Florida, including King Curtis Iaukea and Mark Lewin, both of whom had headlined shows as Barnett's local IWA World Heavyweight Champion during several long tours of Australia.

Naturally, those stories were also punctuated with excerpts from Jim's social life. He was an open, practicing homosexual, who was rumored to have been embroiled in a 1962 prostitution scandal involving athletes from the University of Kentucky's football team. Youthful wrestlers were advised to be very wary whenever they were around Jim.

"He *really* loves young wrestlers," King Curtis warned me. "You just don't wanna be alone with him. As long as you have *other* people with you, you're fine."

Fortunately, I didn't have any unsettling interactions with Jim Barnett while I was in Atlanta, but it would only be a matter of time before our paths would cross in an awkward setting.

It was during my stay in Atlanta that my brother Kevin first chose to tag along with me on the road. He was around 17 or 18 years old at the time., and he was a virgin who was on a mission not to remain one any longer than he absolutely had to. He'd heard enough stories from me by that point that he thought he could rid himself of his virginity fairly quickly if he hung out with me after a wrestling event.

When Michael Hayes saw my brother hanging out with me, he pulled me to the side and asked me in the traditional fashion if Kevin was "smart" to the business.

B. Brian Blair: Truth Bee Told

"Is he kayfabe?" queried Michael.

"Kind of, but not really," I answered. "I never exactly told him about the business, and he doesn't watch it closely enough that it's going to make any difference."

That seemed like it was good enough for Michael.

"He should ride with us to Macon," Michael said.

Kevin and I took our positions in the van right behind Michael Hayes and Terry Gordy – collectively known as The Fabulous Freebirds. Gordy was driving the van while Michael kept him entertained from the passenger's seat. Kevin and I sat in the captain's chairs in the back and had the responsibility of doling out the beer from the giant cooler that was stationed between us, just as I'd done for Andre and Dusty years prior.

During our road trip to Macon, the term "kayfabe" was used in the van quite a few times.

"What's 'kayfabe'?" asked Kevin.

"Kayfabe is code for when you get laid," I told him. "If someone says 'kayfabe,' it means they're about to go get laid."

"Makes sense," nodded Kevin.

That wasn't true, of course. 'Kayfabe' was a way for wrestling's insiders to reference the fact that wrestling was a work. It also served to identify others who knew wrestling was a work, and who were sworn to protect wrestling's secrets from outsiders.

I never drank prior to the wrestling matches. It just didn't seem like the most responsible thing to be doing right before another man's life was placed in your hands. Hayes and Gordy had no such reservations about drinking before they wrestled, and they pounded down several beers along the way.

The further south we drove, the darker the skies grew, and it seemed inevitable that rain would soon descend from the clouds above us.

"Pull over, Terry!" said Michael. "I need to take a piss!"

"Yeah, I've got to piss, too!" said Terry.

Terry pulled the van over and we all climbed out and selected a spot along the roadside upon which to relieve ourselves. As the urine was exiting my body, I began to feel droplets of rain striking me on the head.

"Hey, guys, it's starting to rain!" I warned them. "Let's go!"

I heard a loud burst of laughter from behind me, and I turned my head to see what was so funny. As I did, I was splashed in the face by a putrid-smelling liquid. When I stepped over to one side of the downpour, I could see that a long, golden stream of urine was cascading down upon me from over the top of the van. It was Michael Hayes. His urine stream was sufficiently *powerful* that he could project a steady, stable stream of urine from one side of Gordy's van all the way over to the other side.

"Oh man!" I shrieked. "You son of a bitch!"

I said it good naturedly, but I had been embarrassed in front of my little brother, and I knew I needed to get instant revenge on Michael.

The four of us climbed back into the vehicle, and every time I worked up the urge to urinate, I took the opportunity to expel my urine into an empty can of beer that had been lying on the floor of the van. Once I'd filled the can to the brim with fresh urine, I stashed it securely inside of the icy cooler.

Hayes and Gordy were growing tipsier with every subsequent sip of alcohol, and they were relatively oblivious to everything that was happening around them. Before too long, Michael Hayes made the request that I'd been dying for him to make.

"Give me another beer, Brian!" requested Hayes. "It's beer time!"

I gleefully reached into the cooler, flipped open the top of a new can of beer so as not to arouse any suspicions, and then handed Michael the urine-filled beer can.

Just as Hayes was getting ready to take a deep sip of my urine, Terry Gordy said, "Give *me* a beer, too!"

As I watched helplessly, Hayes handed Gordy the can full of urine. All I could do at that point was to hand Michael a legitimate can of beer from the cooler. Once Michael had a full can of beer in his hand, the two Freebirds smashed their beer cans together and began to chug deeply. In the blink of an eye, Terry jerked his head violently in Michael's direction with a look in his eyes that communicated both betrayal and alarm. Then he spewed a huge mouthful of urine *directly* into Michael's face.

"You son of a bitch, Michael!" Gordy said.

It was a moment Michael Hayes would never forget, but he had absolutely brought it on himself.

One of the notorious stops for wrestlers in Georgia was the Falcon's Rest Hotel. It had a reputation as a place where every wrestler stayed while working out of Atlanta, and all sorts of inauspicious events unfolded there. Over the course of my career, I wound up staying there for several cumulative months.

I was returning to the Falcon's Rest after a brief stop at my place in Tampa, and I lifted up the center console of my Continental so that my harlequin Great Dane Bo could put his head on my lap. As I proceeded to cruise along at around 75 miles per hour, Bo abruptly raised his head and banged it into my shifter, knocking it into "park." The wheels of the car instantly locked up and caused the car to swerve violently, resulting in the Continental coming within mere inches of colliding with the vehicle next to it.

Relaxing by the pool

I managed to pull the car over onto the road's shoulder, and then I got out to check on the engine. Thick smoke swirled out from beneath the car's hood. I assumed that was the end of my beloved Continental, but there was fortunately no damage to the car that couldn't be easily fixed by an experienced auto mechanic.

Upon arriving at the Falcon's Rest, I met the redheaded manager, Miss T, who directed me to my room. Miss T was known for being a very kind woman, and the room fee at the Falcon's Rest was dirt cheap – around $95 per week. With so many wrestlers regularly staying there, crazy incidents were virtually assured, and on nearly a nightly basis.

People never remained in their rooms for too long when they stayed at the Falcon's Rest, which meant that you always became acquainted with the people who occupied the rooms next to yours before too long. On this occasion, the couple in the room across from mine was both memorable and bizarre. The woman was very good looking, with long, dark hair and a lovely body, but her husband was a mortician who was as odd as you can imagine.

B. Brian Blair: Truth Bee Told

For those familiar with Percy Pringle's stint as Paul Bearer in the WWE, this guy's appearance resembled Percy's a great deal, except *no* part of it was an act. He seemed like he was in a constant trance and didn't say much of anything, but his wife ran her mouth relentlessly.

During our discussion in their room, the woman's husband excused himself to go to the bathroom. Once he left the room, the woman's demeanor changed drastically.

"You know… it's sad…" the woman began. "My husband has this condition where he can't have sex anymore."

"Oh, yeah?" I replied. "That's tough. Did something bad happen to him?"

Ignoring my perfectly logical follow-up question, the woman stood up, walked over to me, and leaned in closely. She stared into my eyes and began rubbing my leg.

"We have an *arrangement*," she said suggestively. "He knows I still need to get my needs met, and he doesn't mind."

I've had my moments of questionable behavior, but something about knowingly having sex with another guy's wife made it out of the question for me, especially after my experience as a rookie in Shreveport, Louisiana. It was an area I refused to dabble in.

"You know what…" I said as I wriggled free from her grasp. "I think I should get going."

"No, please *stay!*" the woman said. "I promise it's fine!"

"Sorry… I can't do it," I said, and I departed from the room.

Now, the person who *could* do it was David Sammartino. Like many of the young, single wrestlers in the business, David was an unabashed skirt chaser who relished the opportunity to have as many sexual experiences as he could with as many different women as he could. I had *almost* grown up at this point, and I was starting to phase the partying out of my lifestyle. By contrast, David was just beginning to grasp everything that the lifestyle of a popular professional wrestler could entail.

We were supposed to leave for a show at 2:00 p.m., and I told David I would meet him in his room, which was right down the hallway from mine. I also assured him that I would be driving, which was non-negotiable. If David and I were booked on the same show, I always drove, because David was an *atrocious* driver.

One week before I'd arrived, David's room had been broken into while we were out of town. As a result of the break-in, the backdoor to his room would barely close. This created a very scary situation. A railroad ran directly behind the inn, and a lot of vagrants would walk along the tracks. Even from the rear of the Falcon's Rest, you could see that the door was broken and ajar, and that the hotel could be easily entered without having to pass through the lobby.

I knocked on the door to David's room, but he didn't answer. I tested the knob, and discovered that the door was unlocked, so I let myself in and then locked the door behind me. I figured it would be a mild rib to make David walk all the way around the inn to the back door, and then I could do something to startle him once he finally regained access to his room.

Before too long, I heard David's voice coming from the other side of the door. He was yelling, "Brian! Brian!"

I didn't respond. Instead, I opted to stand in the room and wait him out. A few minutes later, I heard someone try to open the door, which wouldn't open because I'd locked it. Then I heard a pair of frantic voices.

"Shit! I know I left the door open!" David said. "Come on; we've got to hurry!"

"What time is he supposed to be here?" a woman asked him.

"Any minute!"

"Well hurry up!" she said. "I'm gonna fuck your *brains* out!"

I quickly realized I was listening to David and the mortician's wife, and I knew they were going to be sprinting through the back door of the room in an attempt to complete the fastest quickie they could muster before I showed up. I dashed over to the bedroom closet and concealed myself behind the see-through bamboo door. Then I grabbed one of David's white shirts and threw it over my head to further camouflage myself. As expected, David and the woman burst into the room, and she began to give him *very* graphic sexual instructions as they became intimate.

Right at the opportune moment, when it became clear that their tryst was about to reach an aggressive climax, I burst out of the closet with a shirt over my head and screamed, "AAARRGGHH!!"

Scared senseless, David darted through the back door of the room and down the steps. He thought I was the same burglar who had ransacked his room a week prior, and that I'd returned to murder him. The woman remained there, curled up in a helpless ball on David's bed, but she didn't say a word.

A short time later, David re-entered The Falcon's Rest wearing a box around his midsection that he'd found in a nearby trash can. He frantically informed Miss T that someone had broken into his room and tried to kill him. Miss T was freaking out, and I had to quickly run down the hall to intervene before she summoned the police. All the while, David was standing there wearing the box.

B. Brian Blair: Truth Bee Told

"There's a guy trying to kill me!" yelled David when he saw me. "Call the police!"

"It was *me*!" I told him. "Please *don't* call the police!"

Once she realized what had happened, Miss T thought it was the funniest thing she'd ever seen. David didn't think it was nearly as humorous.

"That shit *isn't* funny!" he said.

David had deserted the woman he was having sex with and left her to be murdered by some maniacal vagrant. It *wasn't* the most heroic moment of his life.

After I'd finished my very brief run in Atlanta, Bill Watts was gracious enough to allow me to return to Mid South for the next few months. In the ring, this trip meant that I would be working with Ed Wiskowski almost every night, which meant I would enjoy working even if it meant I was booked to lose the majority of those matches. Outside of the ring, this resulted in a reunion between Paul Orndorff and I, and we picked up right where we'd left off just a couple years prior.

We wrestled in Oklahoma City every Friday night, and the women of Oklahoma City were still just as ravenous as I'd remembered. To top it off, I was no longer a married man.

There was a hole in the locker room wall that the wrestlers would take turns looking through so that they could watch the matches while they were in progress. Paul came over to me and said, "Hey Beep… go gather some of the girls down there. I'm gonna get a woody, and I'm gonna stick my dick out through the hole. Be on the lookout for it, and when you see it, tell all the girls to look up here!"

I just stared at him in disbelief.

"Are you *serious*?" I asked him.

"Serious as a heart attack," he nodded. "Let's do it!"

"Wow," I said to him. "You must be *really* bored."

I walked downstairs and did exactly as Paul instructed. When I showed my face at the back of the building, a lot of girls came rushing over to chat with me and have me sign some autographs for them. Every few seconds, I would look up over my shoulder to see if the promised object was protruding from the hole in the wall.

Sure enough, I eventually looked up and saw an erect penis sticking through the hole in the wall.

"Look!" I pointed. "What is *that*?!"

All of the girls started screaming.

"It's a *dick*!" said one of the girls.

"Oh my god!" said another girl. "It *is* a dick!"

B. Brian Blair: Truth Bee Told

There was about a four-second pause, before another female fan broke the silence with, "It's *Paul Orndorff's* dick!"

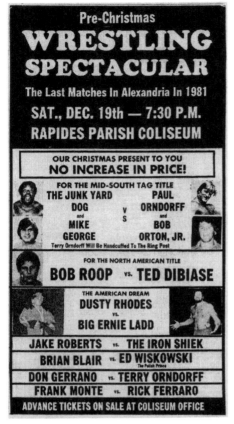

Apparently, Paul's penis was so prolific and memorable in Oklahoma City that at least one of the girls was able to recognize it on sight, even if the rest of Paul wasn't clearly attached to it.

During the same show, Nelson Royal saw that Paul and I were goofing off and having a good time. He walked down to the ring after the matches were over wearing a cowboy-themed, white leather jacket with frills running down from the sleeves. He was also carrying the World Junior Heavyweight Championship belt over his shoulder as he waved me over.

"I know you and Paul have been chasin' a lot of tail around here," Nelson said. "I'm gonna let you two in on the *real* secret."

I was all ears.

"What is it?" I asked him. "What's the big secret?"

"Go to the drug store," he advised us. "Y'all need to find this stuff in a blue-and-white tube. It's called 'Nupercainal.'"

"What does it do?" I asked him.

"It's for hemorrhoids," he said. "It's like Preparation H, except it's a lot better. You've gotta rub it on the head of your dick and leave it on for about 30 minutes. Make *sure* you wash it off after 30 minutes. Use soap and water and scrub it off. If you don't, you won't be able to feel anything at all, and then there won't be any point. Besides, you'll get *her* numb, too, and your whole night will be ruined."

All of this made total sense to me, and at that point of my life I wanted to make sure I did whatever I could to make sure I was a memorable lover for whomever I was with. You never wanted rumors swirling around that you were inadequate in the bedroom, or all of the girls around town would endlessly make fun of you. So would the boys in the locker room, for that matter.

There were these two girls who Paul and I saw quite a bit in Little Rock, Arkansas: Cynthia and Veronica. Those two girls always went out of their way to see us whenever we wrestled anywhere near them. During our very next trip to Little Rock, Paul and I stopped off at a pharmacy and scooped up some Nupercainal. We knew we could stay with Cynthia and Veronica in their one-bedroom apartment without having to rent a room of our own, and they would also cook for us.

The two ladies had a narrow couch in their living room, so the worst-case scenario involved me either sleeping on the couch, or sleeping on the floor with a couple of pillows underneath me while Paul stayed in the bedroom with Veronica.

We knew in advance that Cynthia and Veronica were planning to cook us an Italian-themed meal, including spaghetti and salad. Both of them were pretty, but Cynthia was absolutely *gorgeous*. She had long hair that went down past her butt, and was as beautiful as could be. I'd already been on several dates with Cynthia but had never had sex with her. I was convinced that this night was finally going to be the night.

As the evening unfolded, Paul said, "You know... we should have some wine to go with this meal. Do you think you girls could go get us some wine?"

"Yeah, we can do that," nodded Veronica.

"Cool," Paul said, reaching into his pocket and pulling out his wallet. "Here's 20 bucks."

Paul handed the money to Veronica, then paused and thought to himself for a moment.

"Hey, while you're out, do you think you could grab me some Preparation H?" he asked. "My hemorrhoids have been killin' me!"

I had no idea why Paul would so willingly and casually suggest that he had a hemorrhoid problem, but everyone laughed at the remark.

As soon as the ladies left to collect the wine for the meal, *and* the Preparation H for Paul's backside, Orndorff and I ran into the apartment's sole bathroom and applied the Nupercainal so that we would be fully prepared for later in the evening.

When the girls returned, we enjoyed a lovely meal. I excused myself to go to the bathroom, and I washed the Nupercainal off as Nelson Royal had advised me to do. Then I returned to the table as if

B. Brian Blair: Truth Bee Told

I'd made a run-of-the-mill bathroom trip. Once the meal was over, Paul and Veronica retreated into the bedroom.

After a few minutes, I excused myself from Cynthia to go to the bathroom again. Through the door on the opposite side of the bathroom, I could see directly into the bedroom. Paul was in the process of receiving oral sex from Veronica, and when he saw me peering into the bedroom, he pointed down toward Veronica's head, then looked at me and pantomimed as if he was laughing.

Just then, the phone rang, and Veronica stopped what she was doing so that she could answer the phone. I quickly closed the door slightly so that Veronica wouldn't see me. From behind the door, I could hear Veronica's end of the conversation.

"Hello? Hey, Mom! Yeah, Mom. Okay. I'll see you tomorrow. Hey, Mom... I have to go; my mouth is getting numb."

When I heard that, I almost started laughing right there in the bathroom. Paul had forgotten to wash the Nupercainal off, and now Veronica was losing all sensation in her mouth.

Veronica hung up the phone, and said, "Damn it, Paul! You got carried away with that Preparation H!"

Hanging with Paul Orndorff was always eventful. As outlandish and wacky as our times together had already been, we were only getting started.

THIRTEEN – *Honing my craft*

During one of our many swings through North Little Rock, Paul Orndorff and I visited Shakey's Pizza Parlor after a show one night. It was a frequent eating spot for the boys whenever we visited the area, and it was typically *packed* with diners. The two of us grabbed some plates and snagged several slices of pizza from the buffet before finding a table and taking our seats.

As we ate, I noticed that Paul and I had caught the attention of a large gentleman who resembled a lumberjack, except he was the *biggest* country boy I'd ever seen who wasn't *also* a professional wrestler. This guy was about 6'8" and looked like he weighed more than 350 pounds. He was wearing a set of garden-variety bib overalls, and was going to town on a massive hunk of chewing tobacco.

"Hey, Paul… Do you see that big guy over there looking at us?" I asked.

"Who? Him?" Paul answered.

"Yeah. Do you know him?" I continued.

"Never seen him before in my life," said Paul.

"Do you think maybe you messed with his girlfriend or something?" I asked.

"Don't think so," Paul replied.

"Do you think he was at the show tonight?" I pressed.

"Hell if I know," said Paul. "I wasn't lookin' out into the crowd."

"Well, you pissed off a lot of people during your match tonight," I warned him. "He might try to take a shot at you."

"He can if he *wants* to," Paul shrugged. "You know *I* don't give a shit."

Paul kept right on eating and made several return trips to restock his plate at the buffet counter. The benefit to eating at a buffet was that we could stay there and eat as much food as we wanted. The two of us were notorious for spending as little on the road as we could. As we ate, the Aces High pinball machine at the far end of the restaurant caught my attention. I *loved* that game.

"Hey, I'm about to go play Aces High real quick," I told Paul. "Can you watch that guy and make sure he doesn't do anything stupid while I'm playing?"

"Yeah, okay," answered Paul through a mouthful of pizza.

I popped a quarter into Aces High and began to slap away at the controls. I was still decent at the game, and patrons of the restaurant soon began to gather close and monitor my pinball skills.

B. Brian Blair: Truth Bee Told

BAM!

I instinctively ducked when I heard the noise; it sounded like someone had smashed a watermelon with a baseball bat right behind my head. I turned around to see Paul hovering menacingly over the unconscious body of the giant lumberjack.

"What happened?!" I asked Paul.

"I watched him like you told me to," answered Paul, matter of factly. "He made a move toward you, so I had to take him out."

As Paul and I were engaged in this discussion, the mammoth man remained motionless on the floor in front of us. His body hadn't even twitched.

"Geez, Paul... I think you *killed* him," I observed. "He hit his head pretty hard on the floor. We should make sure he's okay."

Paul would hear none of it.

"Let's get out of here quick, Beep," he said. The two of us bolted for the door and made an abrupt departure from Shakey's.

Of all the friends you could have in the wrestling business, Paul was one of the very best. In his efforts to defend me, he'd knocked out that gargantuan lumberjack with just one shot to the chin.

I sustained a knee injury during one of my matches, but there was no way for me to receive any meaningful medical care for it until our road trip was over with. That meant Paul had to assume all of the driving responsibilities while I was stretched out in the back of our green Pontiac rental car, attempting to elevate my knee. Surprisingly, Paul hadn't complained about having to do all of the driving. In fact, he was being uncharacteristically kind to me. When we stopped at a gas station on the way to our motel room in Tulsa, Paul purchased a bag of ice for my knee without being asked to do so, and even helped me wrap it in an ACE bandage.

Paul was generally a considerate person, but this over-the-top display of sympathy was making me highly suspicious. I knew he was hiding some ulterior motive for his kindness.

We arrived at the motel a little while later, and Paul parked the car for us.

"I'll get us checked in, Beeper," he said. "Just stay there and I'll help you out when we get to the room."

My B.S. antenna shot right up. Paul was taking it *way* too far. We checked in, and Paul drove us right up close to the staircase that led to our second-floor room. Paul got out first, walked around to the passenger side of the car, and reached in to help me out. Sure enough, Paul *goosed* me as I was in the process of rising to my feet. The surprise caused me to jump, and I slammed my head hard against the Pontiac's door jamb. I *nearly* knocked myself unconscious. Paul cackled gleefully in response.

I was thoroughly pissed off that Paul had set me up that way, and I grew even angrier when I felt my head beginning to swell up in the spot where it had struck the door jamb.

"That was *really* wrong, Paul!" I yelled at him. "I'm *hurt!* I don't need you trying to *rib* me when I can barely walk!"

Paul just kept right on laughing away.

"Oh, whatever," he said dismissively. "Hey, let's go to the gym. I mean… *you'll* probably just have to watch me get a pump while you sit there and get *smaller*. Shit… you're *already* gettin' smaller. I can see you shrinking from here!"

While I was seething over on my bed, Paul went through his process of getting ready to hit the gym. He began his odd custom of taking his jeans off without first taking his shoes off. This was one of Paul's odd quirks, right up there with the fact that he hated to wear underwear; he never took his shoes off unless he absolutely needed to. I chalked it up to the fact that Paul was raised in a chicken coop and never wanted his feet to be exposed to the floor.

Paul put his hand on the wall for balance as he struggled to remove his pants while keeping his shoes on. His bare posterior was pointed right at me while he hopped up and down trying to yank his pant legs off of his feet. My eyes panned down from Paul's behind and over to the unsharpened No. 2 pencil that sat on the nightstand. I saw an immediate opportunity to exact some instant vengeance on Paul for daring to rib me while I was injured. I grabbed the pencil, licked the eraser end, aimed for Paul's rectum, and jabbed the pencil forward.

"*Ahhhhh!*" screamed Paul as he reached for his rear end.

As Paul rose up and continued his screams, the pencil was sucked way up into his rectum. The lead of the pencil was barely sticking out, and Paul began frantically attempting to secure the narrow, sharpened tip of the pencil with his fat fingers.

The pencil now protruded from Paul's backside without any involvement from me. It had been a one-in-a-million attempt, and I had struck the bullseye. Paul hopped away from me and tried in vain to extract the pencil from between his butt cheeks.

"You mother*fucker!*" yelled Paul. "Son of a *bitch!* I'm gonna *kill* you!"

Paul started to move toward me, but I rolled off of the bed and hopped toward the door. I stood there prepared to open it and run outside, but Paul thought better of attempting to attack me.

"Help me get it out!" he commanded me.

B. Brian Blair: Truth Bee Told

I just shook my head.

"I ain't helping you take a pencil out of your *ass*, Paul!" I laughed at him.

Incensed, Paul started toward me again, so I opened the door and scampered outside. Paul followed me, and the door slammed shut behind him and locked itself. Paul turned around and tugged at the door handle to our second-floor motel room with his pants around his ankles and his ass cheeks squeezed tight. It was an *unforgettable* moment.

I looked around to see if anyone else was there to view Paul's embarrassment. Sure enough, a rather rotund Black lady who worked at the hotel was standing there staring at us with wide-eyed bewilderment all over her face. All three of us froze for a moment.

"My, oh, my..." she said, breaking the silence with her heavy Southern accent. "My, my, my... *What* is going on *here*?!"

I started chuckling. I couldn't imagine what must have been going through this poor woman's mind. She kindly walked over and unlocked the door for Paul, and he disappeared back into the motel room without permitting me to follow behind him. He emerged a few moments later. He'd changed into his gym clothes, but the pencil was conspicuously absent from his backside. We silently walked down the steps, got into the car, and drove off to the gym. It was a while before Paul decided to speak to me again, and I never asked him exactly what he had done to get that pencil out of his ass.

It wasn't that long into 1982 before Eddie Graham invited me to return to Florida. He made it crystal clear to me that I was going to be groomed to become his own homegrown version of Jack Brisco.

"You've learned a lot, Brian," Eddie told me. "Now you're ready to be a *star* here."

What that meant was that I would be winning my matches more often than not, wrestling all of the top heels up and down the CWF roster, and even wrestling some of the other young babyfaces on occasion. This meant participating in a ton of matches against Dory Funk Jr., Kendo Nagasaki, Jimmy Garvin and Ed Wiskowski, who was now officially working under the name of Derek "The Mongoose" Draper."

It was during this run in Florida that I truly began to establish variations of the sleeper hold as my preferred finishing move, including a cobra-clutch version, which Gordon Solie liked to refer to as a "Japanese sleeper" to make it sound more exotic. I liked to use the sleeper because you could use it to create different angles, or you could build drama if you were going to have outside interference to prevent the recipient from passing out or submitting.

B. Brian Blair: Truth Bee Told

The other thing I liked about the sleeper was its realism. If you secured a sleeper hold on someone in a real fight – as mixed martial artists famously apply it to one another in the form of a rear naked choke – you can render them unconscious very quickly if you know what you're doing.

Locking in my dreaded Japanese sleeper

Other than that, I liked the idea of having several finishers so that when I did false finishes, people would believe that it might actually be the end of the match. What I mean by this is if the fans didn't have a firm idea in their mind that I could only beat my opponents with a single move, they would still be on pins and needles for every attempt at a pinfall or submission, even if my opponents had survived one of my favorite attacks.

B. Brian Blair: Truth Bee Told

To establish my feud with Ed, he was booked to attack me right after I scored a quick pinfall victory on television over "Golden Boy" Jerry Grey. As Jerry and I brawled after the bell, Ed climbed into the ring wearing a mask, tied up my neck in the ring ropes and began to pummel me. During his follow-up interview segment, Ed explained that I'd assaulted him with a chair in a Mid South locker room – which *hadn't* actually happened – and that he was on a quest to finally see who the better man was.

Putting away Kevin Sullivan with the sleeper

As always, working with Ed was like a night off, and that angle lasted about three months. All across the state, we fought in every sort of gimmick match you can imagine, including steel cage matches, Texas death matches, and anything-goes street fights. It was also during these bouts that I perfected the art of blading my own forehead to get juice. Whenever one of my matches required me to bleed, I would swallow three 500-milligram baby aspirin, and then chase it down with four ounces of red wine and a glass of water. That mixture would thin my blood so thoroughly that it wouldn't take much of a cut to make it look like I'd been launched through a car's windshield in a head-on collision.

Eddie Graham used my feud with Ed to establish me as a wrestler who had grown up quite a bit since he was last in Florida, and who was now able to fend off heels under any circumstances. This was all reinforced further by my next feud with Kendo Nagasaki.

Bloodied and firing away at Kendo Nagasaki

Kendo was a strange individual, and I'm not just saying that because of his bizarre appearance, which was punctuated by a partially painted face to go with his pronounced, U-shaped hairline and long, dark hair. Kendo would walk around the locker room while looking under things in an arbitrary fashion. If a piece of furniture had legs – like a drawer or a cabinet – he'd be looking inside of it, around it or underneath it. He always seemed to be wandering around on a constant quest to find something that he could never quite seem to locate.

Two major incidents set up the angles to my matches with Kendo. The first involved him spitting his mystical, poisonous green mist into my eyes, seemingly blinding me. Fans believed I was on the verge of losing my eyesight and were justifiably outraged. The other incident put the whole thing *way* over the top. During a televised match, Kendo and J.J. Dillon tied my neck in the ropes and began clobbering me. That's when *Eddie Graham* himself came out to the ring to intervene, only to be brutally thrashed by Kendo. In the process, Kendo even went so far as to break Eddie's glasses while Eddie sold his ass off. When I worked with Kendo in the ring to seek revenge on Eddie's behalf, our matches drew plenty of spectators to the arenas and led to fantastic paydays for both of us.

Eddie wasn't afraid to advertise a few babyface-versus-babyface matches from time to time if he thought there would be a benefit to it. I had a match against Terry Allen in Lakeland where we absolutely tore the house down. When the match started, the fans in Lakeland were about 50-50 in their support for both of us. At the onset of the match, Terry and I did some chain wrestling, which was something people tended to enjoy because is deepened the connection between amateur and professional wrestling. Terry had been a state champion wrestler in Virginia, and he didn't mind getting down on the mat and doing some true wrestling.

From there we did the traditional lockup, and I backed Terry into the ropes and began pounding him with uppercut forearms similar to those of Dory Funk Jr.'s. Then I followed that up by giving him a few suplexes. Since I was the first one to break from the purity of amateur wrestling, the fans began to perceive me as the heel and lent more of their support to Terry. Despite this, the fans still expressed their fondness for me once Terry and I shook hands after battling to a time-limit draw.

Babyface matches can be quite difficult to execute effectively because you have two good guys going against each other, and one of them will invariably end up assuming the role of the heel whether he wants to or not. However, the wrestler playing the heel role has to be *very* careful not to advance too far into heelish territory, or else he runs the risk of becoming a total heel. You have to strike a *very* delicate balance.

The object of a babyface match is to entertain the crowd, but the crowd *still* needs to view both competitors as babyfaces by the end of the contest. This is why babyface-versus-babyface matches were always less enjoyable for me: It takes much more psychology to have a successful babyface-versus-babyface match than to have a traditional face-versus-heel match.

The best babyface-versus-babyface match I ever remember seeing was when Jack Brisco wrestled Mr. Wrestling #2 at the Tampa Armory. Jack went to whip Two into the corner, and Two flipped and found himself dangling upside down in the corner with his leg hooked underneath the rod between the turnbuckle and the ring post.

The referee was trying to assist Two out of his predicament, and everyone in the crowd was screaming for Jack to help Two as well. Jack walked around the referee, went to the other turnbuckle, walked slowly toward the middle of the ring, and looked out at the people for a moment. Then he swiftly bolted forward, jumped into the air and delivered a flying knee to Two's abdomen. The crowd went *molten* hot with rage and rained disapproving boos down upon Jack. Ignoring the reaction from the fans, Jack then followed up by repeatedly kicking Two in the chest.

Jack turned heel so suddenly and violently during that match. He'd been my hero and my favorite wrestler for so many years, but even *I* got upset with Jack on that day. To balance things out, Two wound up retaliating against Jack with some heelish tactics of his own. Jack ultimately won the match, and when the two shook hands afterward, everyone in the audience gave them a standing ovation.

If Two hadn't retaliated with heel tactics, and if both wrestlers hadn't openly made amends after the bout, Jack Brisco might have been *permanently* branded as a heel. This example just underscores why dabbling in heelish tactics without turning into a full-blown heel is risky to attempt if you don't fully know what you're doing.

Once my first two feuds had proven to Eddie that the fans would embrace me as a homegrown babyface competitor who was both clean-cut *and* capable of exhibiting toughness, he finally had me wrestle the Florida Heavyweight Championship away from Jimmy Garvin. Unmistakably, it was the greatest accomplishment of my career at that point, and I didn't really know that I would ever need to ascend any higher to feel like I'd succeeded in the wrestling business.

When I was growing up, the Florida Heavyweight Championship was even more meaningful in Florida than the Southern Heavyweight Championship. Florida was like its own universe, and being the Florida Heavyweight Champion meant more to me than it would have meant to have been the World Wrestling Federation Heavyweight Champion at the time.

B. Brian Blair: Truth Bee Told

After all, I had watched all of the CWF's programming that I could stomach from the time I was 11 years old. My wrestling idol Jack Brisco had proudly held the Florida title, so it's impossible to overstate how overwhelmed I was to carry the same title that he'd once held.

The Florida Heavyweight Champion

The thing is, Eddie Graham informed me that I would be winning the Florida championship while *simultaneously* presenting me with a question that I'd always dreamed of receiving.

"Are you ready to work for the *world* title?" he asked me with a grin.

"Yes, sir!" I answered.

The world heavyweight champion only came through the territory so many times. That meant the promoter was making a major investment in you by sticking you in the ring with the world champion. He was assuming that you would help draw some money, he was assuming you would put on a great match, and he was also assuming that you were going to be even *more* valuable to him as an attraction after you'd worked with the world champion. It really did mean a lot to me.

B. Brian Blair: Truth Bee Told

"Ric Flair is going to be here in about two weeks," explained Eddie. "You're going to win the belt from Jimmy, and then it's going to be you and Flair in the Armory."

Eddie smiled for a moment before adding: "You're ready for this."

One of the things that helped me feel prepared to wrestle Flair was the fact that I'd already had countless matches with Dory Funk Jr., who was booking the territory at the time, and who had previously been the longest reigning NWA world champion ever next to Lou Thesz. The man I patterned myself after, Jack Brisco, had also been a reputable world champion for the NWA, so I assumed my wrestling style would blend well in a match with any traditionally styled NWA titleholder.

If you were the NWA World Heavyweight Champion for a substantial length of time, you needed to be able to wrestle a very specific type of match. Your job as the world champion was to travel to every NWA territory and make the headliners of those territories look like world-title material. In practice, this meant you would absorb a lot of punishment, you would make your opponents look as if they had pushed you to the brink of losing your championship, and then you would escape with your belt by the *skin* of your teeth.

In other words, it took a lot more than simply being a box-office attraction to be the NWA champion. Yes, you still needed to be an above average box-office attraction, but you also needed to be able to make *everyone* you worked with look spectacular in the ring for the sake of their future marketability in their home territories. Guys like Flair, Brisco and Funk could work with a broomstick and make the match entertaining, whereas Dusty was more of a blood-and-guts wrestler who also had some very exciting spots thrown in that were built around his unique charisma. This made Dusty a massive attraction, who was one of the greatest wrestling superstars of all time, and perhaps the most emulated. At the same time, that didn't necessarily mean he was capable of pulling a great match out of absolutely anyone the way Flair and a few others could.

I never spoke with Flair until he got to the building in Tampa on the night of the match. To me, it was a career-defining moment, but to Flair, it was just another day at the office. By that point in my career, I was definitely experienced and polished enough to have a great match with the world champion, and the match went off without a hitch.

Then again, *how* do you have a bad match with Ric Flair? Ric treated me like any other opponent that he ever worked with, which is

B. Brian Blair: Truth Bee Told

to say that I exited the match looking like a Florida Heavyweight Champion who was capable of winning the world title one day. For me, it was like my graduation day, because Flair had helped me to conclusively solidify my position as a main event wrestler in Florida.

The night was made even better by Flair's compliments to me in the locker room after the bout.

"Great match, Brian!" said Flair, extending a hand for me to shake. "God... you're *so* over here!"

I grasped the world champion's hand in a show of my great respect and appreciation for him.

"Thanks, Champ!" I told him. "I really appreciate the opportunity!"

"I'll ask Eddie if I can work with you some more the next time I'm down here," Flair said.

Flair had to work with wrestlers of all different sizes and ability levels, like Ernie Ladd, Dusty Rhodes, Billy Jack Haynes and Abdullah the Butcher. Compared to working with certain guys, wrestling me was probably like a night off for Flair. I was over with the crowd in my home state, which meant he didn't have to do outlandish things – like shove the referee – to get the crowd invested in the match. I was also in the size range that permitted him to call for just about any move short of a press slam, and I would be capable of executing the move and making it look real. Flair could spend more time working *with* me, and less time working *around* me. All in all, I would end up wrestling Flair five different times in my career, and all of those matches were tremendous, in my humble opinion.

Now that my standing as a newly minted Florida champion had been bolstered by a stellar performance against the world champion, the next phase of my breakout run in Florida would be to defend my championship against Bruiser Brody.

B. Brian Blair: Truth Bee Told

Brody was a box-office attraction at the same level as Flair, although the styles of the two were polar opposites. Frank was one of the greatest brawlers in the history of the wrestling business, so his presentation was far closer to that of a street fighter than it was to that of a classic wrestler. Also, Frank was a giant man who stood 6'8", and the expectation was that he would tear straight through everyone he faced. This was especially true when he faced dyed-in-the-wool babyfaces like me.

Getting a police escort out to the ring

Fortunately for me, I had already spent a ton of time with Frank in Texas and Louisiana, and we were on very good terms. When we wrestled in Tampa, Frank was prepared to be as generous toward me as he could possibly be. The match was billed as a non-title affair, with Brody scheduled to finish me off cleanly in the middle of the ring.

B. Brian Blair: Truth Bee Told

The only thing Eddie requested of Frank was that he make me look good in the process of beating me, and not to simply bulldoze me, like Ox Baker had done years before.

"We're taking care of this kid," Eddie explained to Frank. "He's gonna be a star for us. Please make him look like a threat."

In that area, Frank exceeded our wildest expectations.

During the match, Frank surprised me when we locked up and he said, "Listen to me: I'm *not* gonna beat you. Just follow me."

"Okay!" I replied.

Granted, I was going to listen to Frank anyway, because he was the senior wrestler, he was a huge star, and he was also *much* larger than me.

Frank led the match outside of the ring and into the crowd at the packed Tampa Armory. Once we were fighting out in the stands, he rammed me headfirst into the concrete wall. After soaking up the sounds of displeasure from the crowd and taunting them by yelling "Huss! Huss!" over and over again, Frank lifted me off the ground and whispered into my ear.

"Block it," he said.

This time, I blocked Frank's attempt to slam my head into the wall, and instead I drove *his* head into it. The crowd went bananas. The next time I looked at Frank's face, there was blood spurting from a fresh wound in his forehead. He had *bladed* for me.

Frank carried me through one of his classic brawls as if I had been one of his seasoned brawling opponents, like Dick Murdoch or Fritz Von Erich. In the process, he had further raised my stock and made me look like one of the toughest wrestlers in Florida. To top it off, Frank changed the ending of the bout to a double count-out, so instead of pinning me in the middle of the ring, Frank permitted me to claim a visual victory by battling one of wrestling's most legendary monsters to a standstill.

By arranging for me to emerge victorious in so many gimmick matches with Ed Wiskowski, to booking me to win the Florida title, to having me hold my own against Ric Flair, and then having me look respectable against Bruiser Brody, Eddie Graham had engineered the perfect stretch of matches to catapult me to main-event status in just a few short months… with the help of Dory Funk Jr.'s booking, of course.

It was during my surge to prominence that Ripper Collins arrived in Florida for a very short stay, and we were booked to have a match together in Jacksonville. This was my first time interacting with Ripper since the infamous nipple-biting incident in Hawaii where my retaliation had been sufficient enough to cause him to scream for mercy. I was prepared to put all of that behind me and have a garden-variety match with him, but those plans quickly fell by the wayside since Ripper couldn't manage to behave himself.

We had just locked up to start the match, and as I took Ripper over in a headlock, he *bit* my nipple once again. I immediately pulled away and shot him a death stare; he recognized the danger and began scooting away from me along the mat.

"Oh, I'm sorry!" Ripper said, as if he had forgotten how I'd nearly tried to break his arm in Oahu. "I'm so sorry! I forgot! I *forgot!* I was just playin' around!"

All it took was one look from me for Ripper to know that he'd made a critical mistake. We resumed that match, and he never bit me again, but I wasn't prepared to let that transgression slide. I couldn't imagine that Ripper had somehow forgotten that he wasn't supposed to bite my nipple, or that maybe he just wanted to see if I had grown to be accepting of it after a year had passed. Either way, I was going to make sure that he regretted his decision.

A day or so later, I pulled into the arena parking lot in Fort Myers, and I saw Bubba Douglas fishing. During his lifetime, Bubba Douglas was probably one of the nicest people on Earth. He was always so happy and full of life, and could put a smile on anyone's face. He was also a great worker in the ring who was adored by everybody.

People often referred to Bubba as "The Unofficial Mayor of Lakeland, Florida." One of the reasons the two of us got along so well with one another was because we both had a deep fondness for fishing.

"Hey, Bubba!" I greeted him. "Have you reeled anything in yet?"

Proudly, Bubba opened up his cooler to show me the five bass that he'd already caught. Each of them probably weighed at least one-and-a-half pounds.

"You want to cast?" Bubba asked me. "I have another rod."

I took Bubba up on his offer, and I was fortunate enough to catch a bass of my own during my very first cast.

As I held my newly-landed fish in my hands, I looked toward the arena. In Fort Myers, the distance between where the babyfaces parked on the right and where the heels parked on the left was about 200 feet. Each group of wrestlers also had their own separate entrances. Despite this, a lot of wrestlers preferred to pull their cars onto a grassy area that sat adjacent to the parking lot instead of leaving their cars in the parking lot itself.

At that particular moment, the grassy area just happened to be occupied by Ripper Collins' shiny, black Pontiac GTO. I stared at it for a while and hatched a magnificent plan to rib the nipple biter.

"Hey, Bubba… I'll be right back," I said.

"Sure thing, brother," Bubba said.

I walked straight over to the GTO and soon noticed that the windows were cracked. I also noticed that Ripper's car had the round door lock knobs that were very easy to pick. I retrieved a clothes hanger from my car, and then I went back over to Bubba, who was still engrossed in his fishing.

"Do you think I could have one of those bass, like a small one?" I asked politely. "I don't want to take anything you plan to eat."

"Sure, man, sure," Bubba said. "No problem, brother."

Bubba opened up his cooler, extracted the smallest bass and handed it over to me. I wasn't ready to take possession of it quite yet.

"Do you think you could get it all bloody for me?" I asked. "You can take the fillet if you want. I just need the carcass and the head."

Without saying a word, Bubba plopped the bass down on the picnic table, got a knife from his supplies, and filleted the bass with blinding speed before handing its remnants over to me.

"Can you get the head a little bloodier for me?" I requested.

Bubba laughed and plopped the carcass of the bass back down on the table and stabbed the head a few times.

"Whatcha gonna do with it?" Bubba asked through a grin.

"Just watch, brother," I told him. "Ripper has been messing with me for way too long."

"Okay! Okay!" Bubba said, and then he found some newspaper and wrapped the cadaver of the fish in it.

It wasn't much newspaper, but it was just enough for me to keep myself relatively clean while I did what I needed to do.

With Bubba watching my every move, I slinked over to Ripper's beautiful GTO, which he kept in immaculate condition. The passenger-side window of the GTO was not rolled all the way up, which left me with just enough room to maneuver the hanger around one of his golf-tee style locks. It was a piece of cake to open it.

Once I had opened up the GTO and seated myself within the car's all-black interior, I took the fish corpse that was concealed in the newspaper and shoved it up inside a piece of cloth that was held in place by the springs beneath the seats. Encased within the cloth, the fish would be *very* difficult to detect.

Three days later, it was Sunday, and we had to do the double shot: First we wrestled at Ocala at the Jai Alai fronton at 1:00 p.m., and then at the Eddie Graham Sports Arena in Orlando. We would park at the Days Inn at Fletcher Avenue off of the interstate. It was a great meeting place because it was centrally located, and the owners of the hotel didn't mind us stashing our cars there.

Ripper liked to pull his GTO into spots that were relatively secluded so that it couldn't get scratched by other cars. This was midsummer in Florida, which meant it was as hot and humid as it gets. We all reconnected at the Days Inn around midnight, and my assumption was that the fish in Ripper's GTO would have been reeking *unbearably* by that point, having spent all day boiling in the hot sun.

As the group of us divided ourselves up into different vehicles for the trip home, Ed Wiskowski, Rick Rude and a couple other heels decided to leave the parking lot with Ripper. Ed walked around to the passenger side of the GTO, opened the door, and immediately recoiled at the stench that struck his nostrils.

"Oh my god!" Ed spewed. "It smells like a fish market in there! That's terrible!"

"I know; I'm so sorry!" Ripper apologized. "I already cleaned it, and it still smells! I don't know what to do!"

The next night in the locker room, everybody was standing around talking about how awful Ripper's car smelled. Ripper was both embarrassed and mightily pissed off.

"*Who* did that to my car?!" he snarled. "I've taken it to four different cleaning places and no one can get rid of that smell!"

Bubba Douglas knew *exactly* who had done that to Ripper's car, but he didn't say a word. Instead, he stood behind Ripper and continued his animated chuckling.

After examining the faces of everyone else in the room, Ripper marched right up to me.

"Did *you* put a fish in my car?" he asked, accusingly.

"No, Ripper," I lied, in as innocent a voice as I could muster. "*Why* would I do that?"

"I don't know!" Ripper said. "I've done everything I can and now my wife is making me sell my fucking GTO!"

Ripper turned and walked away, but he called out over his shoulder to say, "If I ever find out who put that fish in my car, I'll fucking *kill* him!"

B. Brian Blair: Truth Bee Told

In the end, Ripper never found out who put the fish in the GTO, and his wife *did* make him sell his prized possession. I never knew a rib could ever go so far that it could make a guy sell his favorite car, but that's what he gets for biting my nipple one time too many. That's also what he gets for not marrying a more sympathetic woman.

Sadly, I was only a short time away from learning what it was like to work for an unsympathetic *booker*.

FOURTEEN – *Never grow up*

By late 1982, Ernie Ladd had been booking the Florida territory along with Jack and Jerry Brisco, but the trio wasn't getting along very well. In the midst of the looming discontent, Ernie decided to leave Florida, but he also didn't want to lose any televised matches on his way out.

This didn't sit well with the Briscos at all, who owned a piece of CWF. During a live event, the company tried to capture footage of a match Ernie had been booked to lose, but Ernie looked up during the match and noticed that the bright red light of the hard camera had been turned on. Incensed at the idea of a double cross, Ernie simply left the ring and refused to finish his bout.

I was riding with the Briscos afterwards, and I couldn't decipher much of what they were saying from my position in the back seat of Gerald's Lincoln Versailles, partially owing to the country music that was blaring through the car's speakers. Among the words I could clearly make out were "Ernie" and "son of a bitch."

When we arrived back at 106 N. Albany Street at about 3:00 a.m., Gerald brought the Versailles to an abrupt stop when he noticed Ernie's car parked in front of the building.

"We've got to talk to Ernie for a little bit, Beeber," Jack said. "You should take off, and we'll see you tomorrow."

I did as I was told and drove off without giving it a second thought. The next day, I met with the Briscos, and both of them looked very much the worse for wear. Gerald described how the two of them had gotten into a fight with Ernie when they confronted him in the parking lot. During the ensuing argument, Ernie rummaged through the trunk of his car, produced a tire iron, and *waylaid* them. Both of the Briscos required stitches afterwards.

I loved Ernie, but I had a much closer friendship with the Briscos, and Ernie knew it. For the short remainder of Ernie's time in Florida, he seemed to shy away from me.

Right after Christmas of that year, I went over to the Briscos' Christmas party adorned in all of the new trinkets I'd scored during the holiday season. My attire consisted of my new sweatsuit and Timex watch, both of which I was very proud to show off.

I walked along the side of Jack Brisco and made the mistake of placing an arm around his shoulder.

"Hey, Jack!" I greeted him.

In a flash, Jack stuck his leg and hip out in front of me, applied pressure underneath my arm, and hip tossed me onto the hard ground. It wasn't pleasant to eat a hip toss onto a hard surface, but I'll admit that it was *very* funny. It's very easy to hip toss someone if you know what you're doing and they're not expecting it. All you have to do is position yourself one step ahead of the guy who has his arm around your shoulder, step across the front of him, and then hoist him up and over your hip.

Clothing ad for Mr. Man clothing at Tampa Bay Center Mall

The thing is, I was a very slow learner when it came to catching on to their ribs. Later on in the evening, Jack managed to do the exact same thing to me once again. He just couldn't help himself. It was all in fun, though. Jack and I had a terrific bond, as mentor and mentee. From that point on, I went out of my way to never place my arm anywhere near Jack Brisco's shoulders.

A while later, I was conversing with the Briscos in the backyard when two kids returned from swimming in the lake and announced that they had spotted an alligator nest on the opposite side. Nestled in the nest were a mother alligator and several babies.

"Hey, you two probably shouldn't be swimming in there with alligators in the water," I scolded them.

"Naw... it's okay!" Jack said. "In fact, why don't you two show *Beeber* the alligators."

"I'm *not* going over there," I objected.

I wasn't excited about the idea of being close to alligators to begin with, let alone while I was all decked out in my fresh, new Christmas attire. None of that mattered to the Briscos, who were masters at applying peer pressure.

B. Brian Blair: Truth Bee Told

"Don't be a *pussy!*" Jack said. "Go see the gators!"

Gerald overheard Jack mocking me, so he decided to wander over and get in on the taunting.

"Yeah, go see the gators, you wuss!" said Gerald. "All you have to do is get in the canoe and go see 'em. These little kids were *swimming* in that water, and you're not man enough to go see some gators from a canoe?!"

It was about 60 yards across the lake to where the kids said they had seen the alligators. I sized up the lake and asked myself, "Is the reward of being considered one of the boys worth the risks involved with paddling over to see those alligators?"

The answer to that question was always "yes," and I alway suffered for it, one way or another.

Like a dummy, I decided to climb into the center of the canoe while these two young children began paddling us over to the other side of the lake to view the alligators. As we neared the other side, I saw movement around me. I was convinced the swirling action in the water was the result of alligators' tails sliding past us, and I was terrified that we were all about to fall in and get gobbled up. The canoe we were riding in wasn't particularly steady, and it could easily have been tipped into the water.

The kids stopped paddling and let momentum bring the canoe closer to the bank.

"Do you see them?" one of the kids asked. "They were right over here!"

"Quiet!" I whispered sharply. "Look out for them! Watch the *water!*"

We could see a bunch of little alligators on the land once we crept within about 15 feet of the bank. I don't know if it was out of fear, or because they were going to attack what they perceived to be a threat, but those little alligators slid into the water and appeared to be headed straight for the canoe.

"Let's get out of here!" I screamed. "Let's go!"

I'm so happy no one carried a video camera to Jack's house that day, or I would have been called a "sissy" for the rest of my life. I couldn't have been any more scared. It wasn't the baby alligators I was scared of, though; I was afraid of their *mother*. I didn't want *anything* to do with her.

Heeding my commands, the children immediately turned the canoe around and began to paddle forcefully back toward Jack's house. Suddenly, there was a big splash next to the boat as if something had landed in the lake, and the water leapt up to strike me in the face.

B. Brian Blair: Truth Bee Told

My eyes darted around to see where the splash had come from as similar explosions of water began to occur all around me. I lifted my eyes toward Jack's house, and I could see both of the Brisco brothers were standing at the water's edge next to an entire wheelbarrow full of oranges and grapefruits. It was clear that I'd been double crossed. Once I had climbed into the canoe and departed with the kids over to the opposite side of the lake, Jack and Gerald collected as many oranges as they could find so that they could hurl them at me during our return voyage. I was a sitting duck.

In an effort to protect themselves, the kids began swinging at the citrus fruit with their oars to protect themselves by knocking away the airborne fruit before it reached them. As they did, the fruit caromed off the oars in unpredictable directions. I quickly realized what was likely to happen and tried in vain to prevent it.

"Stop!" I pleaded with the children. "Just hold your hands up to block it! Don't swing the oars at it!"

Of course, one of the children intercepted the very next inbound grapefruit; it was deflected upward at a perfect angle and smacked me in the face. With my weight thrown to one side, the whole canoe tipped over, sending myself, the children, my new Timex watch, *and* my brand-new sweatsuit straight into the murky lake water.

Like a coward, I frantically swam right over the tops of the children without giving it a second thought, desperately attempting to escape from the alligators that I'd imagined were nipping at my heels. Upon reaching the shore, I looked down at my new sweatpants, the legs of which had been stretched so far by the water that they now extended two full feet past my shoes. Then I looked at my new watch, which was full of water and ruined.

While world-title contender Brian Blair anxiously collected himself at the water's edge, the two small children who had been swimming in the water with the alligators earlier in the episode calmly took their time retrieving the canoe and the paddles, and then guided the items back to the shore.

Incidents like this were by no means out of the ordinary. In fact, similar events tended to happen whenever groups of Florida wrestlers got together. Even a respected veteran in his 40s, like Jack Brisco, would act like an overgrown teenager every chance he got.

At a different get together at Gerald's house – which was on Lake Calm, right across the street from Crescent Lake, where the alligators thrived – the Briscos were present along with Don Muraco, Steve Keirn, Jimmy Garvin, and a few of the other guys from the roster. Just like Jack, Gerald had a ton of citrus fruit growing on his own property. Just about anything can sound like a stellar idea after a few drinks, and someone suggested that we engage in a citrus fruit fight. All of us agreed to it, but Gerald wanted to lay down some ground rules for us before the food fight ensued.

"Only take the stuff off the ground," Gerald said. "Leave the fruit in the trees alone."

The thing is, *all* the fruit on the ground was overripe, rotten and nasty. No one would leave this fruit fight smelling fresh.

The food fight commenced, and we all ran around the yard like children, chucking fruit at one another as hard as we could. Even as the rules of engagement for the food fight were being hashed out, I began thinking about what Jack had done to me when I went to examine the alligators, and I went out of my way to find the nastiest, most putrid orange that I could find. After I'd found an orange of sufficient rancidness, I crept to within 15 feet of Jack, wound up my arm and yelled out, "Hey, Jack!"

I let loose with my most wicked lightning bolt of a fastball throw, and I caught Jack right between the eyes with that disgusting orange. It was *perfect*. It exploded when it made contact with his face, and all of the rotten juices splashed into his eyes and mouth.

The boys all reacted in unison with a loud, "*Ohhhhhhh!*"

To Jack's credit, he sold that shot from the orange like he'd been blinded and poisoned by Kendo Nagasaki's mist.

Hearing the commotion, Gerald's petite, blond wife walked out through the rear door of the house to assess the damage we were causing to her backyard. She took a long, judgmental look around at the scene of grown men in her yard who were behaving like absolute children – and primarily her brother-in-law, Jack. The former NWA champ was absolutely *drenched* with putrid orange juice.

After she had taken it all in, she glared at her husband with her arms akimbo.

"You guys will *never* grow up!" she scolded us in her thick, South Carolinian accent.

From there, she turned and walked back into the house.

"How do you feel about going up to Charlotte and working with Greg Valentine?" Eddie asked me early in 1983.

"I'm supposed to be going to *Atlanta* in a month," I replied. "I can't go to Charlotte right now."

"They only need you for a couple weeks," clarified Eddie. "Somebody got injured and they need a new babyface to fill in for a few dates. You'd be doing me a favor."

B. Brian Blair: Truth Bee Told

Far be it from me not to help out Eddie Graham if he was asking me to do him a favor.

"Okay, that's fine," I said. "I'll do it."

"There's just *one* other thing," smiled Eddie. "They want you to wear a *mask*."

When Eddie said *that*, you could have knocked me over with a feather.

As "The Champ" preparing to suplex Greg Valentine

Slugging it out with Valentine in the center of the ring

B. Brian Blair: Truth Bee Told

Eddie brought me over to Gordon Solie who pulled up some footage of Mr. Wrestling #2, who had been one of the most popular masked wrestlers in the South. I could see that I was going to have to communicate all of my excitement and emotions with my body, because I wouldn't be able to rely on my face to express to the audience how much pain I was in, or how enraged I was.

It was arranged for me to spend my full two-week stint with Roddy Piper and his wife Kitty, who treated me like a member of their family during my short stay. As Piper and I traveled together and got to know each other, I told him stories about my upbringing, including how my family had been on food stamps, and how I'd been forced to help provide for them at such a young age.

"You know that song by Clarence Carter?" Piper asked me as he drove.

"Which one?" I asked.

"The one where he says the rains came and washed all the crops away?" he said. "I think it's called 'Patches.' That's what your upbringing reminds me of."

From that point on, Piper called me "Patches" whenever he saw me.

During my *very* brief period of wrestling under that blue and silver mask as "The Champ," my version of overselling with my body looked less like Mr. Wrestling #2, and far more like a bit of Jack Brisco mixed with Dusty Rhodes. I wiggled and gyrated my body more during those matches than I ever had before.

Under normal circumstances I would try to fire up just like Jack Brisco, which involved slapping my head or pulling on my hair while glowering at the heel or seeking support from the fans. With the mask stripping me of my most reliable means for expressing myself, I resorted to shaking my butt and waving my finger in the direction of the heels. Dusty would have been *very* proud of me if he could have seen it.

With that brief bit of business concluded in the Mid Atlantic, I headed off to Atlanta as scheduled. It remained Eddie's fervent belief that I would become an even larger national star if I went there, and it was difficult to argue that point with him. The power of cable television had allowed Georgia Championship Wrestling to stretch its boundaries well outside the state of Georgia.

While it didn't compete directly against other established NWA territories, GCW was willing to follow its television signal into areas where there was no defined NWA presence. This meant leapfrogging the Mid Atlantic states where the Crockett family ran shows, and hosting events in West Virginia, along with Ohio and Michigan – states that had been left unserviced following the disintegration of the Sheik's wrestling promotion that had once been headquartered in Detroit and stretched well into Ohio.

On the surface, wrestling for GCW was a no brainer in terms of the logic behind it, but that was if you were under the assumption that I was going to be booked to look strong following my stellar run in Florida. Unfortunately, Ole Anderson was booking for GCW at the time, and he simply *refused* to showcase me in a positive light. Moreover, since GCW's shows aired nationally, this had the potential to compound the problem. The same Florida wrestling fans who saw me win 90 percent of my matches on Florida television in 1982 might have seen me lose 90 percent of my matches under GCW's banner in 1983. Fortunately, I rarely lost a bout on television even though I did lose the bulk of my matches that took place at house shows.

One bright side to being with GCW was that I was once again reunited with Paul Orndorff. I also made the acquaintance of a fresh crop of wrestlers, including Tony Atlas, Tommy Rich, Arn Anderson, Matt Borne, Tito Santana and The Iron Sheik.

Wrestling in GCW allowed me to fulfill a personal dream by working against Paul Orndorff in a singles match at Atlanta's Omni Coliseum. However, that dream ultimately deteriorated into one of the most *embarrassing* nights of my career.

Paul was already standing in the ring as I began to make my entrance. I was smiling, jogging and waving to the fans just as I had done more than 1,000 times before. However, a problem quickly emerged when my stomach began gurgling and rumbling uncharacteristically, and then that digestive discomfort rapidly descended even deeper into my abdomen. It was immediately apparent to me that I needed to use the restroom, but it was much too late for that. I was already halfway down the aisle headed for the ring, I was in *clear* view of the fans, and they were already screaming in anticipation for the match. I was stuck with no other alternative but to go forward with the match.

While the referee gave us our instructions in the center of the ring, I maintained a look of intensity on my face, but I used that as an opportunity to advise Paul, "Hey, man... whatever you do, *don't* slam me. My stomach is *killin'* me."

Paul just couldn't help himself. Being the way he is, that joker immediately whisked me off the mat and slammed me as hard as he could as soon as we performed our lockup. When that happened, fecal matter oozed forth from my bowels and into my baby-blue tights. There wasn't a thing that I could do to stop it.

Paul laughed about it, thinking that he'd just played a minor rib on me by furthering my internal discomfort with the slam. He had no idea that he'd just caused me to literally shit myself. Instead of getting up, I decided to sell the pain in my back like the slam had caused a herniated disc or something. I writhed in agony, but refused to stand up or roll over.

When I wouldn't get up after about 30 seconds, Paul curiously walked a bit closer to me.

"Pin me!" I begged him, as quietly as I could say it.

"What?!" Paul replied. "Man, I just gave you *one* move; I can't pin you."

"Pin me!" I repeated. "I just shit my pants! *Pin* me!"

Paul simply stood there motionless. He had no idea what to do. But there was no way I was going to stand up and expose to the audience what I had just done. No amount of money could have urged me to stand up at that moment in time.

Eventually, Paul realized that I wasn't going to stand up and engage with him any further. He hit the ropes, dropped a big elbow on me, and covered me.

As the referee administered the three count, Paul sniffed the air above me.

"Did you *shit* yourself?!" he asked.

"Yeah, you idiot!" I moaned. "I told you *not* to slam me!"

To the fans it probably looked like Paul was chuckling because he'd crippled me and beaten me with a single bodyslam. In reality, Paul was laughing hysterically because he'd caused his best friend to publicly shame himself.

Paul made his departure from the ring, and I had to figure out how to get out of the ring without everyone noticing that I'd soiled my own trunks. I decided to continue writhing around in agony as if I'd been mortally injured, and the fans were *totally* buying into it. Everyone in the arena thought they were witnessing the end of Brian Blair's promising wrestling career.

Eventually, a couple people came out from the locker room to help me. To their credit, they did a decent job of keeping straight faces since Paul had probably smartened them up to what had happened to me before they climbed into the ring.

If I'd been a tad bit smarter, I would have stayed there and requested that they bring in a stretcher. Instead, I rolled out of the ring with their assistance. Once my legs were fully extended and my feet reached the arena floor, gravity did its thing, and diarrhea residue began to drip down my legs.

My baby-blue trunks did absolutely nothing to conceal what had happened to me. Some smartass at ringside quickly recognized this, pointed to the brown stain on my trunks, and cried out, "Look! He shit his pants!"

The murmurs and the laughter grew with each second that passed, as more and more fans were able to confirm that I had, in fact, defecated all over myself in the middle of the arena.

"Guys, get behind me!" I instructed the attendants who were supposed to be simultaneously helping me to the back *and* helping me to conceal the source of my shame from the crowd.

It was too late. A few of the young kids in the front row took it upon themselves to start chanting, "He shit his pants! He shit his pants!" It was like something you would have expected to hear years later coming from the mouths of the hardcore fans of Extreme Championship Wrestling.

Nothing else that happened in the ring during the remainder of wrestling career would ever be that personally embarrassing. I learned in the worst possible way that I should *never* eat so closely to the beginning of a match, and that I should try to use the restroom as early and often as I could.

If I'd been smarter and surer of myself, I would have stopped and pantomimed to the fans that I'd be right back, walked back through the curtain, sprinted to the restroom, relieved myself as quickly as possible, and then returned from the locker room with a chair, a stick, or some other gimmick that would have made my departure look like it had a purpose. Instead, the situation deteriorated into the most humiliating night of my professional life.

The unique arrangement of the GCW territory meant that we had to endure an unorthodox set of travel arrangements. GCW's extended, atypical territory sometimes required that we fly into a Mid Michigan airport, wrestle in Saginaw or Lansing, and then descend via rental car through Ohio and West Virginia. From there we would continue all the way back to Atlanta, wrestling at shows all along the way.

The combination of the long hours spent traveling, the general combativeness of the wrestlers in the territory, and the competitive nature of our business resulted in more than a few fights amongst the wrestlers on the GCW roster. I was an eventual, unwilling participant in one of the most legendary of those altercations, but I insist that it wasn't my fault.

B. Brian Blair: Truth Bee Told

We were in Wheeling, West Virginia, and Tony Atlas was being even more aggressive than usual in the locker room after finding out he would have to take a loss against Ric Flair that night. He repeatedly slammed the locker room's doors and railed on about how he was the most authentic tough guy in all of wrestling.

Training hard in the weight room

His bad temperament may have been somewhat enhanced by chemicals. That same night in the locker room, Tony had pulled two different 3cc syringes out of his gym bag and inserted one into each of his ass cheeks in an open and proud demonstration of the abundance of steroids he was taking. One 3cc syringe was full of Deca-Durobilin, while the other syringe was filled with straight testosterone.

Tony had a prominent scar on his backside that resembled a crater. He once told me the story about how Rocky Johnson injected him with a steroid-filled needle that was too short, and the injection site became infected.

B. Brian Blair: Truth Bee Told

"How do they expect *me* to lose?!" Tony continued to yell to no one in particular. "The only person in this business who could kick my ass for real is Andre, and I don't think *he* could whup me neither!"

Tony's foul mood persisted during the car ride back to Atlanta, and he sulked in the passenger seat next to me while I drove. From his position behind "Mr. USA" Tony Atlas, Paul Orndorff decided to phrase a request in the form of a joke.

"Hey, Murdoch!" Paul exclaimed. "Move your seat up; you're crunchin' my legs!"

Tony wasn't at all in the mood for it, and responded with, "Don't call *me* Murdoch! That redneck son of a bitch!"

Paul laughed, but Tony was so wound up that he wasn't in the mood for any good-natured attempts at humor.

"If you call me that again, I'll kick *your* ass," Tony threatened.

"You ain't gonna kick *my* ass," Paul laughed.

"Bullshit!" Tony said, before turning his attention to me. "Brian, pull this car over so I can show your boy he's not the man he thinks he is."

Tommy Rich started trying to play peacemaker at this point, and piped in with, "Guys! Come on! *Please* don't fight!"

He almost sounded like he was ready to cry.

"We don't have time for this," I told them. "It's too late; I'm tired. Work it out later."

"Beep…" Paul began. "If you don't pull over, I'll beat *your* ass, too."

I glanced at Paul in the rearview mirror to see if he was serious, and the look in his eyes implied that he wasn't joking around in the slightest.

"Okay, I'll find a place," I said.

I wasn't about to fight Paul Orndorff for all the money in the world. It's not that I think he really would have attacked me, but he was certainly pissed off, and I wasn't willing to take that chance.

As I looked around for a place to stop, I saw the glowing lights of a well-lit bowling alley up the road. It had grass, asphalt and trailers adjacent to it.

"*This* should work," I said. "Plenty of space for you two to fight."

"No!" Tommy cried. "You guys shouldn't be doing this!"

I parked the rental car, and everyone climbed out. Orndorff walked over to me and said, "Hold this."

He had removed the gold crucifix from his neck and was handing it to me for safekeeping.

B. Brian Blair: Truth Bee Told

Without looking back, Tony walked all the way over to the asphalt and the rest of us followed his lead. Tommy continued pleading in vain for everyone to stop what they were doing, but it was to no avail. Tony selected an acceptable spot for the sparring session, turned toward Paul, and then the two lunged toward one another like two bulls.

In the midst of the struggle, Paul got behind Tony and they both toppled to the ground while Paul maintained his grip around Tony's waist. Then the two of them rolled over on top of one another a few times along the asphalt, with neither truly gaining an advantage. I couldn't make out much of what was happening as they struggled because of how little light there was in our vicinity. Out of nowhere, I heard Tony let loose an ear-piercing scream.

"*Ahhhhh!*" he cried. "You cheated! *Ahhhhh!* You cheated!"

Tony clutched his ear and blood spurted through his fingers. Behind him, Paul spat a meaty chunk of ear out of his mouth.

"Oh my god!" screamed Tommy. "It's an *ear*! He bit his ear off!"

Tommy ran over to retrieve the ear remnant, and continued sobbing as he carefully collected the fleshy nugget and held it up.

"My ear's been bit off!" Tony yelled. "I quit! I quit! You *cheated!*"

"You had enough?" Paul asked him, with blood settling on his chin.

"You cheated!" repeated Tony.

Paul let go of Tony and both men rose to their feet.

"So, you had enough?" Paul asked again.

"Fuck you, man!" Tony said, as he walked toward Tommy to collect his lower ear.

We all returned to the car after agreeing that an impromptu trip to a local hospital was in order. The car was a lot quieter now, with no one wanting to converse anymore. Finally, Tony decided to break the silence.

"Brian, find another spot," Tony said. "We need to do that shit again. Paul cheated."

"Okay," Paul said. "Fuck it. Let's do it again."

After about 10 seconds, Tony thought better of it, and said, "Naw... Just take me to the hospital."

We dropped Tony off at a local hospital and then continued our drive to Atlanta. That would be the last time we would see him during our run with Georgia Championship Wrestling. Paul was willing to fight absolutely anyone at the drop of a hat. This included people that he'd otherwise been on good terms with, like Tony. You can safely guess how little mercy he would extend to people he didn't even know.

My typical look during the 1980s

Paul and I once drove through a dangerous blizzard after a show while some guy aggressively tailgated the two of us. The tailgater's presence only exacerbated my problems as I attempted to navigate my Lincoln through the icy terrain. For mile after mile, the rude motorist remained an unrelenting fixture on my rear bumper.

"What is this guy's problem?" I said to Paul. It was more of a statement than a question.

We approached a red light at an intersection, and I knew I was going to have to bring the vehicle to a halt.

B. Brian Blair: Truth Bee Told

"Get ready," I warned Paul. "This guy is not a happy camper. He might get out of the car and come after us."

"If he's lookin' for trouble, he's about to find it," Paul said.

"He might have a gun," I replied. "If he has one, just be really nice."

Once I brought the car to a stop, I looked into my rearview mirror. Just as I'd predicted, the man stopped behind us and climbed out of his car.

"Does he have a gun?" Paul asked me.

Although the combination of the snow-filled air and the dark night sky greatly obscured my vision, the man's headlights were trained on our car. Because of this, I was able to examine the man's hands and determine that they were both empty.

"No gun," I confirmed.

"Good!" Paul said.

I rolled my window down and opened my door a crack. There's no way the man could have noticed it because of all the snow filling the air around us. He was screaming loudly enough that we could make out a few muffled obscenities as he drew nearer. It was only when he reached a spot within swinging range of my driver's side door that I shoved the door open as hard as I could.

Maintaining his footing on that slippery pavement had been difficult enough for the man, and getting whacked by a car door hadn't done any favors for his balance. He fell right over and onto the snow-covered ground. I jumped right up out of the car and kicked him hard in the face as he was trying to regain his footing. He fell face first into the snow and groaned. Just like that, he was out of commission.

While this was going on, Paul had gotten out of the passenger side seat and had been stalking his way around to the front of the car.

"He's done!" I told Paul.

Instead of returning to his seat, Paul closed the rest of the distance between himself and the man and began stomping the guy's back and ribs.

"That's *enough*, Paul!" I yelled.

"Don't you *ever* fuck with us again!" Paul said to the guy, before walking back around the front of the car to his seat.

Paul just absolutely *had* to get his shot in, even on a guy who had already been rendered defenseless. We left that tailgater lying in the snow, freezing, with his car still sitting idle in the middle of the road.

Our impression was that this guy had followed us after that night's matches and wanted to take a shot at us. Because I was always a babyface wrestler, it was very rare for fans to want to take any shots at me in the streets or elsewhere in public. Heel wrestlers had far more issues with vengeful fans that wanted to pay them back for the injustices they committed against babyfaces on a nightly basis.

Unbeknownst to me, I would soon be targeted by a vengeful fellow wrestler, and the repercussions of that conflict would be felt half a world away.

FIFTEEN - *Sayonara*

My time performing for Georgia Championship Wrestling was cut well short by events that transpired at a bar following a show in Charleston, West Virginia. What was notable about this night was that Ric Flair was in attendance, which guaranteed that everyone present would be entertained; Ric always made sure of it.

At a different bar in Wheeling around the same time period, Flair had just finished purchasing a round of drinks for all 50 people who were at the bar. When music began blasting through the jukebox, Flair decided to climb on top of the bar and start dancing. The girls nearest to the bar begged Ric to continue his display, so he upped the ante of his performance by stripping off his pants and swiveling his hips while wearing only boxer shorts.

"Take those boxers off, Ric!" one of the girls screamed.

Ric grinned and then immediately obliged. He tore his boxers off, and then did a particularly animated Ric Flair strut along the bar top with his penis flopping along as he went. The whole bar erupted. Ric could get away with *anything*. Who could climb up on a bar top, strip naked, and then strut around without facing any repercussions whatsoever? Only Ric Flair.

However, this occasion was far different. The energy in the bar on this particular night became palpably violent in short order. I was at the bar minding my own business, talking with Karl Kox, Dick Murdoch and Arn Anderson, when a livid Matt Borne stormed up to me.

"Why are you fucking my girlfriend?" Matt huffed.

"What are you talking about, Matt?" I replied. "I don't have a girlfriend here."

"Yeah, I know; you're fucking with *my* girlfriend!" Matt insisted.

"*What* girl am I messing around with, Matt?" I asked him.

I made a sweeping gesture with my arm and looked all around the bar to emphasize the point. I seriously had not been screwing around with any girls in the area, and I had no earthly idea what Matt was talking about.

"Show me a girl," I challenged him. "*Who* am I messing with?"

When I turned around again to take a gander around the room, Matt sucker punched me in the back of the head. It was a stiff, brutal shot that knocked me totally off balance. I staggered forward and felt Matt's arms lock themselves tightly around my waist and lift me as if he was going to give me a German suplex and drive my neck into the hardwood floor. Fortunately, I was able to spin in midair, and we both went crashing awkwardly onto the floor.

I wound up in a dominant position on top of Matt, so he grabbed the sides of my hair and yanked my face toward his. His mouth was wide open with his teeth exposed, and it was evident that he intended to bite my nose clean off. Seeing what Matt's intent was, I shifted the angle of my own face, and allowed him to pull me close. From there, I bit down extremely hard on Matt's lip until I felt blood bursting forth, and then I jerked my head backwards. A huge chunk of Matt's lip came loose in my mouth. I spat the bloody hunk of flesh out onto the floor and climbed off of Matt.

"*Aaaaaahhhh!*" Matt screamed as both of his hands clutched where his lower lip had once been just a moment ago. "You son of a bitch! You motherfucker!"

Matt continued to scream. Then he climbed up off the ground and took a swing at me with his right hand, all the while clamping down on his bloody mouth with his left hand. His clumsy swing missed, and I was able to catch him clean in eye socket with a stiff, left-handed blow. Matt crashed straight to the floor with a thud.

I kicked Matt once in the ribs, but he began to turtle up to protect himself. Meanwhile, all of the boys were standing around us and cheering us on, and no one had any interest in stopping the melee. I backed away from Matt, and someone managed to get him to his feet and usher him away.

In the immediate aftermath of the skirmish, a lot of the boys congratulated me, including Ric Flair, who was ecstatic!

"Holy shit, Brian!" Flair hollered. "I didn't know you were *that* tough, brother! That was beautiful!"

Flair then began to reenact the whole thing, starting with how I twisted in the air and wound up on top of Matt.

I was feeling pretty proud of myself at that moment. I'd given a good physical accounting of myself in front of all the boys, and they all knew I hadn't started the fight, so everything that happened after Matt's sucker punch to the back of my skull had been justified. Matt was known as a shooter, a tough guy, and a bit of a redneck bully. For me to take him out like that had placed a major feather in my cap.

As I was reveling in the plaudits from my compatriots, I felt something heavy strike me from behind. Matt had somehow managed to break free from whomever had pulled him away, and he was intent on redeeming himself. Once again, we fell to the ground. I was able to hook Matt's arm on the way down, so I wound up in what could best be referred to as a side-mount position. I started punching Matt directly in the face, and he did his best to cover up once again. From there, I punched and elbowed him in the ribs to get him to expose his face once again. Once he lowered his guard, I caught him in the center of his face with one more solid shot that broke his nose.

With blood now streaming from Matt's mouth *and* nose, I climbed off of him once again, and more wrestlers came to carry him away. Matt appeared to have been thoroughly vanquished. Everyone that remained behind insisted upon buying me a drink. They put more drinks in front of me than I could ever drink, and within 10 minutes, I was absolutely plastered.

Just as I was polishing off what would be my final drink, I felt something sharp strike me in the back. Fortunately, the sharp object *wasn't* a knife. Instead, it was Matt Borne's knee. Now with his head completely wrapped with bandages that were sopping wet with blood, Matt had returned once again in the pursuit of payback.

Matt capitalized on the surprise and shoved me forward into some chairs. From there, Matt utilized a classic heel wrestling tactic in a real-world setting; he removed part of the bandage from his head and wrapped the bloody rag around my neck in an attempt to choke me. Once again, I managed to spin around and face Matt. With both of his hands clutching the bandage, his face was fully exposed. I managed to shove him back slightly and then clobber him with a right hand to the jaw. Matt crumbled to the floor. This time, I was *sure* he was out cold.

Ivan Koloff was seated at the end of the walkway smiling away and taking it all in. The grin on Ivan's face distracted me, and then suddenly I felt myself being pulled off balance. Matt Borne simply *refused* to die! I fell straight forward onto my face. Matt climbed on top of me and began gouging at my eye sockets.

Ivan wasn't having any of it. He reached his foot out, kicked Matt's hand away, and punctuated the kick by stoically stating, "*No eyeballs.*"

Thanks to Ivan's kick, Matt was jolted away from my back, providing me with just enough space to leap to my feet and soccer kick him in the head as hard as I could. Matt's eyes went blank as he crashed onto his back. Finally, Matt Borne was well and truly unconscious. He was hauled away, and *that* was the end of it.

I don't know what sort of substances Matt was taking that night, but I must assume he was under the influence of one or more drugs. Later on, I would find out that Matt made a habit out of doing a lot of cocaine. *Whatever* it was that Matt was on that night, he was completely unrelenting. His resilience was otherworldly. He'd aggressively pursued a fight with me four different times, and three of those attacks came after he had already gotten his lip bitten off. Any other person would have been knocked out and finished off long before our fight reached its ultimate climax.

Matt had plastic surgery after that fight, and then returned to the ring a few months later in his primary stomping grounds in the Pacific Northwest. Despite the surgery, Matt's mouth remained scarred for the rest of his life. In my case, I promptly gave my notice and went back to Florida.

Eddie Graham thought it was still far too early to bring me back to Championship Wrestling from Florida on a full-time basis, so he called up his good friend in New York City, Vincent J. McMahon.

Vince had developed his collection of lucrative, large cities in the Northeast United States into the World Wide Wrestling Federation. It was a regional wrestling company and a member of the National Wrestling Alliance, but it often operated as if it was an independent, national company. As a case in point, when the name of the company was applied to its top championship, it was impossible not to think of the World Wide Wrestling Federation Heavyweight Championship as a world title in the same vein as the NWA title. To top it off, the promotion had exclusive access to the most famous arena in the world, and the most prominent battleground for legendary boxing bouts, Madison Square Garden.

Just a year prior, in the summer of 1982, Vince Sr. had completed the sale of his company to Vincent Kennedy McMahon, better known as Vince Jr. The younger McMahon promptly rebranded his promotion as the World Wrestling Federation. To my eternal benefit, Vince Sr. still had some leverage and influence when it came to his son's talent acquisition decisions.

"Vince says you can come up to New York, but he wants to try you out in Japan for a few months first," said Eddie.

That statement was completely out of left field as far as I was concerned, but I was absolutely thrilled by it.

"*Japan*?!" I exclaimed. "That's incredible! How did he set that up?"

"Vince has an arrangement with New Japan Pro Wrestling – that's Antonio Inoki's company," said Eddie.

"Inoki is the guy that fought Ali at Madison Square Garden, right?" I answered.

"That's right," said Eddie. "Vince rotates talent in and out of New Japan to give them some time to cool off, and then he brings them back and gets them over again. If things work out in Japan,

B. Brian Blair: Truth Bee Told

Vince says he can bring you into New York when it's time to rotate his talent back in again."

All of that sounded better than sitting at home doing nothing. It was too quick for me to wrestle in Florida or Mid South again. I had just left Georgia, and I *couldn't* go to the Pacific Northwest after what had just happened with Matt Borne. The only other high-profile place it would have made sense for me to go would have been to the American Wrestling Association owned by Verne Gagne, but living in Minneapolis didn't sound all that appealing to me.

In the meantime, going to Japan would provide me with an opportunity to learn another style of wrestling, and also to earn good money without having to worry about paying any taxes on it. New Japan paid 25% of the wrestlers' payoffs directly to the U.S. Treasury, and still gave us 100% of the money we had agreed upon. I quickly accepted the offer and packed my bags for a six-week tour of Japan. Little did I know that I would eventually spend more than two years of my life in Japan, touring the nation as a wrestler.

To say Japan was very different from the United States in terms of its treatment of wrestlers would be an understatement. From the moment I touched down at the airport in Tokyo, I knew I was in a totally different environment from what I was used to in my home country. A representative from the New Japan Pro Wrestling office greeted me at the airport and handed me a customized, gold-colored Samsonite suitcase along with a bouquet of flowers. Even in the way they picked me up from the airport, there was an air of refinement to my handling that was absent from American promotions at the time.

During the van ride from the airport to my hotel room, I took in the surroundings and was surprised by how different things appeared to be compared with the U.S. Every street corner seemed to feature a vending machine that sold Japanese beer brands like Kirin and Asahi. Despite the public availability of the beer, the minors were still respectful enough of the law not to go anywhere near those vending machines.

I simply couldn't believe the quality of the accommodations that had been reserved for me. All of the wrestlers stayed at the Keio Plaza Hotel in Shinjuku, which is a main hub of Tokyo. The hotel itself had two elevators, one of which went up to around the 25th floor, and the other elevator climbed all the way up to the 47th floor. Each wrestler received his own king-sized, American-style room with all of the bells and whistles. We were also given yukatas to wear, which were light Japanese bathrobes, and we were permitted to take them back home with us when we left.

B. Brian Blair: Truth Bee Told

The owner of New Japan Pro Wrestling, Antonio Inoki, had developed the in-ring presentation of New Japan around his preferred style of wrestling. He employed a hybrid style of pro wrestling mixed with other martial arts disciplines. In the ring, this meant he engaged in a ton of mat-based wrestling, and then implemented plenty of kicks, punches and other realistic-looking strikes. Combined with an atmosphere that treated every component of its presentation like it was a true-to-life sport, Inoki's matches made the Japanese fans believe they were watching the greatest professional fighter on planet Earth.

Then again, it hadn't hurt Inoki's reputation at all when he had publicly competed against legitimate fighters like Everett Eddy and Willie Williams, and paid them to let him beat them.

Receiving an abdominal stretch from Antonio Inoki

The net effect of Inoki's rise to prominence was that New Japan's contests gained a reputation for being exceedingly stiff at times, with primarily the young Japanese wrestlers trying to take liberties in the ring with their foreign competitors. It was never an issue I had to deal with on a regular basis, but it was a possibility that I always had to be mindful of.

B. Brian Blair: Truth Bee Told

Almost immediately, I was thrust into main-event matches with Abdullah the Butcher as my tag team partner. Although he was billed as "The Madman from the Sudan," Abdullah's name was actually Larry Shreeve, and he had grown up in Windsor, Ontario, Canada in what is more or less the Metro Detroit area. Without question, Abby's wrestling style replicated many of the features of Ed "The Sheik" Farhat's matches at Detroit's Cobo Arena, which was less than three miles from the house Abby grew up in.

Abdullah's over-the-top, violent wrestling style was one of the reasons I was paired with him. He was morbidly obese, and relied heavily on theatrics, bloodletting, and the conspicuous use of a fork during his matches. He was a massive box office attraction to the Japanese fans, but he couldn't be relied upon to do any serious wrestling, nor could he do much bumping inside of the ring. The responsibility to carry both of those elements of our matches fell to me, and the two of us had several contests against Kengo Kimura and Seiji Sakaguchi.

Teaming with Abdullah was challenging at first, because our styles were worlds apart. I was a wrestler, and he was a havoc maker. Even to refer to Abby as a brawler doesn't paint an accurate portrait of him. The scar tissue on his forehead was so prominent due to the deep grooves that had been etched into his head by repeated blading. If he was struck in the head enough times, he would bleed easily, so it wasn't even necessary to cut him in order for him to get juice.

Getting juice was part of the basic package with Abdullah, and he bled in almost every match he was ever involved in. He also bladed his opponents' foreheads in nearly every match, so most of the bouts he was booked in deteriorated into bloodbaths and mayhem.

Seiji Sakaguchi had all of the combat-sports legitimacy that you would ever want a professional wrestler to possess, having won a bronze medal at the 1965 World Judo Championships. He was also uncharacteristically large for a Japanese man, standing 6'5" and weighing close to 300 pounds.

In spite of his popularity, Sakaguchi was the polar opposite of Inoki inside of the wrestling ring, at least in terms of his activity level. Sakaguchi's idea of having a good match consisted of applying an armbar to his opponent and then lying on the mat for 15 straight minutes. Occasionally, he would throw in a snapmare and pound on your chest, or put you in a reverse chinlock and hope that you wouldn't reverse out of it and force him to expend more effort than he'd planned on exerting that evening

B. Brian Blair: Truth Bee Told

No matter how hard Sakaguchi tried to control the pace of our matches, I kept moving and kept fighting to make sure I injected as much action into our matches as I could. After all, I needed to make sure I impressed the *McMahons* back in the U.S. with the quality of my performances, and not just the Japanese audiences. When it was all over with, I think Sakaguchi respected me even more for having forced him out of his routine and raising his activity level, because he complimented my effort.

"Good match," he said. "I like the way you fight."

It was nice to get direct praise from one of the top guys in the New Japan front office, who also happened to be the booker of the company. Impressing Sakaguchi would help to ensure lucrative paydays for me in Japan for several tours down the line.

American wrestlers enjoyed a 300-to-1 exchange rate of yen to dollars at the time, and with all of our food, travel and other accommodations taken care of, anyone who could cope with the language barrier and unfamiliar surroundings could enjoy a *huge* financial boon as long as they saved their earnings from the tours. I was handed $1,250 in cash each week during the first tour, and they quickly bumped my weekly pay to $1,500 for my next round of tours, which almost immediately followed my first Japanese tour.

The traveling arrangements in Japan certainly took some getting used to. Instead of dividing ourselves up into different vehicles and driving ourselves to shows, we piled into buses and were chauffeured all over the country. One bus was reserved for the gaijin wrestlers – which is another way of identifying us as foreigners to Japan – and the other bus was reserved for the native Japanese wrestlers.

The buses were always well stocked with beer and snacks so that we could eat and drink in comfort throughout our travels. This made traveling through the country very relaxing, and it allowed all of us to settle in and take in the sights of the Japanese countryside.

One day on the way up to Sapporo on the northern Japanese island of Hokkaido, Akasaka the bus driver even pulled the bus over by a beautiful stream so that we could watch the bears catch salmon in the river. The entire scene was backdropped by an arrangement of gorgeous cherry blossom trees. It was breathtakingly *beautiful*, and I purchased a hand-carved bear holding a salmon in its mouth to help myself remember the scene.

Even though we had food on the buses, we still made frequent stops for food at rest areas along our touring route. Ordering food from the restaurants and vendors in the small Japanese towns was a struggle at first, because the photos of Japanese dishes weren't accompanied by any writing that might clue me in as to the correct pronunciations of the food items; everything was written in Japanese. Akasaka, the long-time New Japan bus driver, taught me how to order my favorite item, which was tamago – a raw egg served atop steaming hot noodles. It was absolutely delicious, and is a dish I still have frequent cravings for.

In the midst of an unusually long bus trip through Japan, Abby kept himself entertained from his typical seat at the front of the bus by ceaselessly heckling one of New Japan's referees, whose last name was Shibata.

"Hey, Shit-bata!" Abby repeated, over and over again.

Shibata didn't appreciate this treatment at all. Despite the clear language barrier, *all* of the Japanese wrestlers and officials understood the meaning of the word "shit."

Abby persisted with the name calling for hours, and when we finally stopped in a town famous for its wooden dolls, that's when Shibata let Abby know that he'd had enough of his mouth. As we pulled into our parking space, Abby called Shibata "Shit-bata" one time too many, and Shibata decided to let the Butcher know that he had crossed the line, whether he was a wrestling legend or not.

Shibata marched straight up to Abby, physically blocked his exit from the bus, and figuratively slapped the *piss* out of him. The sound of the slap echoed all through the bus, and it got the attention of everyone. We *all* froze. Shibata began to vocalize his grievances to Abdullah in loud Japanese, which no one else on our gaijin bus could understand except for the bus driver, Akasaka.

I hopped up in case there was a fight, because I wanted to make sure Abby could at least get out of his seat so that the fight would be a fair one. Shibata saw me approach, but he only glanced at me, then turned his attention back to the Butcher and continued berating him. When he was finished, Shibata got off the bus, and then the rest of the wrestlers began to file out behind him. I remained behind with Abby because he was my friend and regular tag team partner.

"Abby... what the hell happened, man?" I asked him.

"If he would've made another move toward me, I'd have taken his *jugular* out," Abdullah said, seething.

Abby held out his right hand and produced a sharpened can opener, which I guess he kept for protection just in case he was ever physically threatened in a real-life setting. His hands were trembling. I sat with him until he calmed down, and then we both joined the others outside of the bus. Nothing more happened during that incident, but I never again heard Abby taunt Shibata by calling him "Shit-bata."

Abdullah took enough of a liking to me that he started requesting that I hang out with him when we had time to kill, which is something that happened quite a bit in Japan. During one such occasion, Abby asked me, "Hey, do you want to go to the movies?"

With Abdullah the Butcher

"I've never been to the movies here, Abby," I responded. "Do they just put up English subtitles or something?"

"Some of them are *in* English," the Butcher replied. "We can try to find one that has subtitles. I was looking at one that looks good. It looks like a great scary movie. I *love* scary movies."

I *can't stand* scary movies. I saw *The Exorcist* once when I was a kid, and it scared the crap out of me. I took my high school girlfriend to see it with me. After I dropped her off at home after the movie was over, I stared through my rearview mirror into the backseat of my car for the full eight miles of the trip home. I was convinced a demon was going to materialize in the backseat and grab me. To this day, I have *zero* interest in watching any scary films.

"I'm not a fan of scary movies, Abby," I admitted. "I can't handle that stuff. It gives me nightmares."

"Oh, come on!" he said. "Don't be a baby. I'm telling you, this one looks good. It's called *Cannibal Holocaust*."

B. Brian Blair: Truth Bee Told

"We're seriously about to watch people getting eaten?" I asked him. "There *has* to be something better than that."

"No, man!" Abby said. "I'm Abdullah the Butcher! You've got to work your gimmick. It's good for people to see me watching movies like that. If we go together, someone will see us together and they'll take pictures of us there together. It will be good publicity for us as tag team partners."

After about half an hour of prodding on Abdullah's part, I finally relented and agreed to accompany him to see *Cannibal Holocaust*. I didn't want him telling all of the boys on the bus that I was too scared to go watch a horror flick with him.

I don't know how the producers of *Cannibal Holocaust* put that film together, but everything in it looked 100 percent legitimate... or at least it did by the standards of the very early 1980s. The plot involved two groups of Pygmy headhunters: ground headhunters and tree headhunters. The archeologists in the film were hoping to build a relationship with this dangerous group of cannibals. As the film progressed, there was a scene depicting two corpses that had been impaled on spears that were plunged into their groin areas and exited through their mouths. They were surrounded by flies, and the camera captured every grotesque detail.

Undeniably, the movie was grossing me out, and I was going out of my mind with fear. The tree headhunters had all of these reels of film that they confiscated from the documentarians before they killed them, and then they strung them up with the film like they were decorations. Later, as one of the ground cannibals brandished a spear and came running around a corner, two of the tree cannibals jumped down from the branches and started stabbing him to death, and then began eating his raw, fresh corpse. It was *sickening*, and I squirmed uncomfortably in my chair.

It was right at *that* moment when Abdullah the Butcher threw up. He projectile vomited all over the movie theater, and the vomit *erupted* to a distance that I didn't know vomit was capable of traveling. At a minimum, his vomit struck filmgoers at least four rows ahead of us.

Here we were, the infamous "Madman from the Sudan" who could barely complete a match without somehow smearing blood everywhere, and Brian Blair, the clean-cut babyface who was too squeamish to sit through a horror film. Yet, between the two of us, it was wrestling's most infamous bloodletter who wound up losing his lunch at the sight of the film's barbarity. Granted, I was *plenty* scared, but at least I hadn't gotten *sick*.

B. Brian Blair: Truth Bee Told

Abdullah's display of projectile vomiting disrupted the entire theater. Several Japanese moviegoers stood up and pointed over at him. Meanwhile, I couldn't help but to laugh at the spectacle. The people in front of us fled to the bathrooms to clean themselves up, and a few attendants soon arrived to assist Abby so that he could get cleaned up and make his way back to the hotel.

I never did get to see the end of the film. I still have every detail of the film seared into my brain, so if I watched it today, I could probably stomach it and suffer through to the ending.

When Abby saw me the next day in the lobby, he said, "Brian... don't tell anyone about what happened at the theater, okay?"

"No problem, Abby," I told him. "I won't say anything."

Aside from telling a few friends much later on, I hadn't told that story to anyone. I don't think the Butcher would mind me telling that story now.

Within a few weeks of my debut in Japan, I was delighted to welcome Paul Orndorff to the country. His arrival occurred just as Abdullah was preparing to take some time off. As a departure gift to me, Abby invited Paul and I to a Tokyo bathhouse, along with Adrian Adonis. We were accompanied by Abdullah's Japanese sponsor, who had prepared everything for us. As far as I could tell, we were the only four patrons in the bathhouse at the time.

Adrian was clearly looking forward to this excursion the most. He always carried a bag full of sex toys with him, so this venture was right up his alley. That dog collar that he wore around his neck during some of his matches was more than just a wrestling gimmick; he liked to use it in his private life as well.

There were four girls already standing there waiting for us when we entered through the door of the bathhouse. Abdullah already had the best-looking girl set aside for himself, which left three girls for the rest of us to choose from.

Of the three remaining girls, one of them had no teeth, so she wasn't someone I was interested in becoming acquainted with. I quickly selected the most attractive of the three girls that were reserved for us. Orndorff saw the same thing that I saw and also chose quickly, which resulted in Adrian getting stuck with the toothless girl. Abby was long gone with his girl by the time the rest of us got situated. The bathhouse had a bar where we could grab a few drinks before things got serious, or we could opt to take a hot bath or a cold bath. They also had a sauna.

When we'd finally had enough of the amenities and were ready to get down to business with the girls, we were escorted down a hallway with rooms. One of the rooms sounded like it already had some activity going on behind its door, so I slid the door open to take a gander at what was going on. Hilariously, Abby's girl was attempting to service him, but she was having unbelievable difficulty doing anything with him as a result of the vast quantities of fat that layered his frame. Her tiny hands worked hard to shove his protruding belly out of the way.

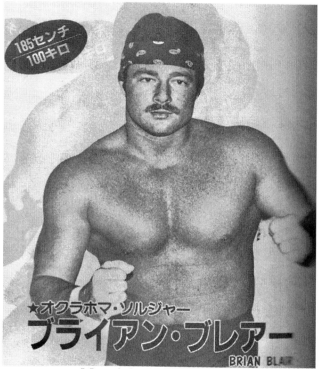

My original look in Japan

Abdullah hadn't initially heard us open the door, but he did hear us laughing at the sight of this poor girl doing her damnedest to pleasure him orally. He was livid when he saw that we'd been secretly watching him.

"What are you doing?!" the Butcher erupted. "Get the *fuck* out of here!"

Shortly after arriving in my own room, I found myself lying on my stomach getting a shoulder-and-back massage. I was really enjoying myself when I heard one of the other girls screaming at the top of her lungs.

"*Itai! Itai!*" she screamed, signifying that she was in tremendous pain.

The source of the interruption was coming from Paul's room. "Itai" translates to English as "it hurts," and Paul was pounding this tiny girl so hard that she was practically crying.

Suddenly, there was a commotion in the hallway, followed by a different type of screaming. I hopped up out of my spot and slid the door open to see what was happening. The toothless Japanese girl ran by me, naked, followed by Adrian Adonis. Adrian was also naked, and he was hunched over on all fours, chasing this girl down the hallway with his favorite dog collar around his neck. Between his clenched teeth he held a condom that looked like it had already been used. Lord knows what Adrian wanted the girl to do for him, let alone what she had *already* done for him. He continued chasing the girl on all fours while he growled like a dog, and the girl retreated all the way to the front desk to try to hide from him.

To this day, I have no idea what Adrian intended to do with that condom, and I *don't* want to know. I refused to ask him.

As crazy as that story was, that wasn't even the most memorable experience I had with Adrian Adonis in Japan. *That* incident happened when NJPW referee Peter Takahashi invited us to dine with him at one of the two mamushi snake restaurants that he owned.

Early in the tour, I told Peter that my grandfather was killed during World War II, which was a total lie on my part. The reason I lied to him was because he hated Americans so vehemently. Peter had built up a lot of resentment toward Americans because of the defeat Japan suffered during the war, and I assumed if I told him my grandfather had been killed during the war, he would be sympathetic toward me. It worked.

In truth, the lie was only a minor one; my great uncle truly *was* killed at Pearl Harbor during World War II. I assumed it would sound more personal if the person who died had been my grandfather, and Peter did seem to empathize with me more when I told him that.

As the three of us entered Peter's restaurant, we saw reading material on the walls, including testimonials about how venom and blood is supposed to kill stomach cancer along with all sorts of intestinal ailments. Adrian and I sat down, and we beheld several clear, half-gallon sake jars containing tiger penises, walrus penises, and a bevy of other exotic animal penises. Once consumed, all of these penises were supposed to endow those who drank the penis-enhanced sake with inestimable sexual potency.

With the bottle of snake sake in 1983

The bottle of snake sake, nearly 40 years later

"That sounds awesome!" Adrian exclaimed. "I need to get some of *that* sake."

B. Brian Blair: Truth Bee Told

I didn't like sake anyway, but I also saw another problem looming.

"Why do we want to drink this and then go home with woodies already in our pants?" I asked him. "Does that make *any* sense to you?"

"Come on, man!" Adrian said. "We have to try it at least!"

"Yes!" Peter chimed in. "You try!"

With Adrian cheering him on, Peter began to order a selection of fine penis wines for the table. We imbibed each of them in turn as we watched the chef prepare the mamushi snake – a member of the pit viper family – for consumption right before our eyes. The process involved using a long set of tongs to capture the live snake and pin it to the wall. From there, the chef secured the tail and held a glass beneath the snake while draining its blood and venom into the glass. The blood and venom mixture was further mixed with sake, and then we chugged it all down.

While we drank the exotic sake mixture, the chef cleaned the snake and prepared its meat in the form of what resembled a small hamburger patty. The snake is eaten with seaweed, vegetables and rice. Adrian, Peter and I did exactly as we'd been advised: We got hammered from penis wine, ate the snake and drank the poison. Peter deposited Adrian and I back at the Keio Hotel after dinner concluded, and we quickly went to our rooms and slept. I knew I should prepare myself for a massive hangover; I was already nursing a *huge* headache. I had *no idea* what was coming.

At about 4:00 a.m. I awoke from the most vivid nightmare of my entire life. In this nightmare, I was standing on top of my king-sized hotel bed, attempting in vain to fend off snakes. No matter how much I defended myself, the snakes kept biting me over and over again. I screamed my lungs out, both in my dream and in my sleep. My screams were so loud and blood-curdling that members of the hotel staff entered my room and hauled me downstairs. When I awoke in the hotel's infirmary, every part of my body was sore, and I could barely move my legs.

Twenty minutes later, Adrian was carted into the infirmary by two other hotel workers who plopped him down right beside me.

"I just had the craziest dream..." Adrian said.

Adrian had been having a dream that was *identical* to mine, and his screaming had been just as intrusive to the hotel's guests. Both of us had needed to be removed from our rooms to bring us out of our venom-induced, penis-inspired hallucinogenic states. As crazy as that coincidence sounds, I guess that's just the brain's reaction to being administered a voluntary dose of non-lethal snake venom. That was also the first and last time I ever ate at a mamushi steak restaurant.

As absurd as these experiences sound, they were all part and parcel to life as a gaijin wrestler. I just needed to make sure I kept the snake-poison drinking to a minimum so that I could survive long enough to make my debut in the World Wrestling Federation.

SIXTEEN – *The Most Underrated*

We usually had a decent amount of time off in between our tours for New Japan Pro Wrestling, so I flew back and forth between the U.S. and Japan quite a few times in 1983. New Japan always provided us with business-class accommodations on our flights into Tokyo, which was a very comfortable way to travel. During one of my return flights to Japan, I flew with Orndorff on a big 747. It had a second deck set aside for first-class and business-class passengers to ride in.

After Paul and I were comfortably situated in our business-class seats, one of the flight attendants approached us.

"Are you Paul Orndorff?" she asked.

"Yeah, that's me," Paul replied.

"There's a woman in first class who wants to meet you," smiled the flight attendant.

At the mention of a woman, Paul perked right up.

"*Really*?" he asked with a smile.

"Yeah… it's Phyllis Diller," grinned the flight attendant.

By that point, Phyllis Diller was well into her 60s. She used to crack me up with her humor and her stand-up antics. Paul disappeared into the first-class section of the plane, and I didn't see him again until well after we took off.

Long after our flight was underway, Paul emerged from the first-class section of the aircraft just one time to visit me in business class.

"Man, I'm havin' a blast up there!" Paul said, as he dove into his bag to look for an 8x10 photo to sign for Phyllis. "They're giving me whatever I want! It's *great*!"

Once Paul had found his 8x10 photo and a black Sharpie marker, he disappeared back into the first-class section of the aircraft and rode the entire way from JFK Airport to Narita International Airport alongside Phyllis Diller. I was definitely a little bit jealous that Phyllis hadn't invited *me* to come along, too.

Paul was constantly complaining about things everywhere we went in Japan, and Big John Studd came up with a special nickname for Paul while we were riding on the bus one day.

"My children watch a show called *Sesame Street* back home," said Studd. "There's this green character on the show named 'Oscar the Grouch' who lives in a garbage can. You sound just like him, Paul… always complaining about *everything*!"

B. Brian Blair: Truth Bee Told

From that point on, Studd called Paul "Oscar," and so did a lot of other people.

During that tour, Paul slipped a few Tuinal sleeping pills into Tiger Hattori's drink while we were riding on the bus. Tuinal typically does its thing within 15 minutes, and it wasn't long before Tiger was having considerable difficulty maneuvering around the bus. In fact, it caused quite an entertaining scene to unfold.

Tiger tried his best to navigate up and down the center aisle of the bus while walking on wobbly legs. Every time the bus would slow down, Tiger would stagger up toward the front of the bus, nearly ending up in the lap of the bus driver, Akasaka. When the bus would speed back up, Tiger would stumble all the way to the back of the bus where we were sitting.

"What's wrong with me?" Tiger wondered aloud, before realization suddenly registered on his face. "One of *you* guys gimmick me! *Who* gimmick me?!"

It was Paul who had gimmicked Tiger, and he proudly leaned over to me and proclaimed, "I slipped Tuinals in his beer."

I found it all very humorous at the time, but I found it far less humorous when Paul gimmicked *me* in a similar fashion.

We were staying at a hotel in a small town, and Paul managed to slip Tuinals into my drink just as he'd done with Tiger's.

"You dickhead!" I said, after realizing that I'd been drugged. "How could you do this to me?!"

I was so tired from the Tuinals that I retreated to my room to try to sleep off the discombobulation and fatigue. The rooms of this hotel were all stocked with several mats that could be laid out on the ground to accommodate large groups of people. If necessary, there were enough mats for at least ten people to sleep in the same hotel room.

Thanks to the Tuinals, I barely had enough energy to lie down on one of the mats, and I didn't even bother to try to locate my covers. Instead, I pulled another mat on top of me to shield myself from the icy fury of the unrelenting air conditioning. Because of Paul's childhood origin inside of the converted chicken coop, he considered air conditioning to be a luxury, and exploited its availability whenever it was offered. On top of that, Paul preferred his rooms to be as dark as possible, and he would tape the curtains with athletic tape so that not even a hint of light could seep into the darkness. Whenever I bunked with Paul, I had to be prepared to sleep in a frosty, pitch-black room.

日本で暴れることを宣言するブレアーとオーンドーフ

Blair & Orndorff – Gaijin Heels in Japan in 1983

Going head-to-head for the Japanese wrestling photographers

B. Brian Blair: Truth Bee Told

In my drug-influenced nightmares that evening, I had the uncomfortable feeling of being unable to move. Waking up from my nightmare introduced me to the startling reality that I couldn't move in *real life*, either.

While I had been unconscious and vulnerable on the floor, Paul had collected every mat he could find in the hotel - at least 30 mats – and neatly laid them all on top of me. The combined weight of the mats felt like about 100 pounds, which was more than enough to keep me pinned to the ground in my intoxicated state. I could barely breathe.

"Help!" I shouted as I tried to wriggle myself free of the mats. "Somebody *help* me!"

Paul eventually entered the room and chuckled heartily as he began to pull the mats off of me.

"Dammit, Paul!" I yelled. "Why would you do that to me? That wasn't funny!"

Paul honestly thought that was one of the funniest ribs he had ever pulled on a fellow wrestler, but getting somebody inebriated and then smothering them is actually quite dangerous. That episode just gave me all the more incentive to come up with creative ways to pay him back.

We went to one very old town during our tour, and the hotel that NJPW booked us into seemed to be as ancient as the town. It always seemed like New Japan rented rooms for us in the finest hotels in every city we visited. If that was truly the case, then the quality of this hotel was a clear indication that this town wasn't a bustling tourist mecca.

Studd had been working with an injured back during the tour, which caused him to act like a very cranky giant at times. He became even crankier when it was time for all of us to go to sleep and he couldn't find the light switch in his room.

"Hey guys, where the fuck is the light switch?!" yelled Studd. "My back is hurt and I really need to lie down!"

"It's *under* your bed!" I yelled back to him, jokingly.

For the next few moments there was relative silence, save for the sounds of the doors to wrestlers' hotel rooms closing as we each turned in for the night.

"*Aaaaarrrggh!*"

A deep, ear-splitting yell cut through the silence. I climbed out of bed, opened my door, and followed the sounds of the agony to Big John Studd's room. His door was wide open, and two large, long legs extended from beneath Studd's bed and into the center of the room.

B. Brian Blair: Truth Bee Told

"I can't get out!" bellowed Studd. "My back hurts too much! I can't move! Help me!"

I couldn't believe it; Studd had actually *believed* me when I told him the light switch was underneath his bed. Now this 6'8" mountain of a man was completely helpless beneath a tiny bed in a small, Japanese town. It was a hilarious sight to behold.

One by one, the boys entered the room to see the unenviable position that Studd had worked himself into. Eventually we pulled him out from beneath the bed and helped him up.

"That was a terrible rib, Blair!" said Studd.

We all had a good laugh over it, and it certainly had the same outcome as a rib. I suppose I could classify it as the best accidental rib I ever pulled off.

Paul was constantly by my side as we traveled throughout Japan. We visited the Amami Islands of Japan, which are a very popular tourist destination even amongst the Japanese citizens. In particular, they're known for the fights that are staged there between cobras and mongooses. A substantial gambling enterprise had been developed around the outcomes of those fights. Paul and I took our seats and watched everything unfold before us.

The mongoose was placed on one side of a square box and the cobra was positioned on the opposing side. A plexiglass partition separated the two combatants. As soon as the partition was raised, there was an instant standoff between the cobra and the mongoose. The cobra stared coldly at the mongoose, while the mongoose paced back and forth without ever removing its eyes from the snake. The initial attack between the creatures nearly resembled the opening of a wrestling match; one of them made the first move, and the other jumped right in to meet the aggressor and tie him up. The cobra tried to bite the mongoose, and the mongoose attempted to apply a firm grip on the cobra's neck. It was a rather gruesome spectacle.

Paul and I were told that the mongoose wins about eight out of ten times, so the smart money is always on the mongoose. We watched three different snake-versus-mongoose contests before we'd had enough; the cobra actually won one of the three fights we witnessed.

When the fights were all over, Paul and I hit the souvenir counter, and we each bought a posed cobra-and-mongoose diorama set composed of real cobras and mongooses that had been preserved and stuffed. The pairs of animals were posed as if they were engaging in life-or-death combat, even though all of the animals used in the dioramas had *obviously* already lost a fight in real life. The mongoose was in a hissing pose, and the cobra was hovering over it. It set us each back about 10,000 yen, which converted into about $150 at the time. Paul was *really* proud of his.

It was rare for Paul to want to spend money on things like that, because he was usually as frugal as I was. That was something that was bred into everyone that trained with Hiro in Florida: Save your money; it's not how much you make, it's how much you *save*.

We got on the airplane to fly to another city in Japan, which was a rarity since most of the travel was by train or bus. Back then, they didn't care what we carried onto the planes. As long as it fit into the overhead carrying compartment, they allowed us to bring on whatever we wanted. We carried our cobra and mongoose sets in bags. Mine was pretty well covered, but Paul left the head of his snake exposed so that you could see its head and exposed fangs protruding out from the top of the bag.

Paul was one of those guys with the magic ability to fall asleep in any location, and under just about any circumstances. I was always envious of that ability, because if you could fall asleep whenever you wanted, you could more or less guarantee that you'd always accumulate the necessary rest. As soon as we sat down in our seats and prepared for takeoff, Paul fell dead asleep.

When we reached our destination, Paul was still hopelessly unconscious. Seizing the opportunity to pay Paul back for the Tuinal rib, I snagged the snake-and-mongoose set from Paul's overhead storage compartment and made a beeline for the front of the plane. Standing by the exit door was a cute, tiny Japanese flight attendant who was issuing her customary farewell to everyone that departed from the plane.

In Japan, it is very rare not to accept gifts if someone hands you one and says "Presento." On my way off the plane, I marched straight up to the flight attendant, extended Paul's cobra and mongoose diorama set to her and said, "Presento!"

"Ohhhh!" the girl shrieked with excitement, followed by some words in Japanese.

The rest of the flight attendants gathered around the set of combative figures I held in my hand and examined them while speaking in their native tongue. Soon after, one of the pilots emerged from the cockpit of the plane and seemed very surprised and impressed by the sight of the stuffed cobra and mongoose.

"Sank you very much!" the flight attendant said in the best English she could muster, before formally accepting the gift, and then treating me to a full 90-degree bow.

B. Brian Blair: Truth Bee Told

I stepped out onto the portable steps and then down to the ground below. From there, we were expected to walk over to the concourse, but I lingered on the airport apron about 30 yards from the plane to see what would happen. The flight attendants emerged from the plane and stood next to the stairs. Shortly thereafter, a bewildered Paul burst forth from the door of the plane and pointed an accusatory finger in the direction of the flight attendants.

"That's *my* snake!" Paul yelled. "That's *my* mongoose!"

Paul ran down the stairs and reiterated to the flight attendant that the cobra and mongoose cradled in her arms actually belonged to him.

"No no no!" she cried. "Presento! Wrestlah *give* to me!"

The pilot of the aircraft joined in the discussion, which went on for at least five minutes. When it was all over with, the dejected flight attendant handed the cobra-and-mongoose set back over to Paul after clearly being advised to do so by the pilot.

With his literal stuffed animals now in hand, Paul stormed toward me. You could practically see the steam emanating from his ears.

"What the hell, Beeper?!" Paul said. "*Why* would you do that?!"

"*Me?*" I said with a smile. "*You're* the one that broke that poor flight attendant's heart!"

"You've got a *big* one coming your way," Paul threatened. "I'm gonna get you back for that!"

Paul wouldn't let up about the whole thing even as we moved into the concourse. This meant that other wrestlers we were with began to hear about it. Before long, everyone in our contingent was laughing at Paul.

Even after everything that had just gone down, Paul decided to leave his cobra and mongoose sitting out in the open while he went to collect his luggage from the conveyor belt in the baggage claim area. Naturally, I picked up the diorama behind Paul's back, ran them over to the side of the baggage claim on the opposite side of Paul and dropped them off so that they would travel around the belt. Shortly thereafter, Paul collected his luggage and walked back over to us, only to discover that his cobra and mongoose had once again mysteriously gone missing.

"Where's my snake and mongoose?!" Paul said.

Immediately, he whirled toward me.

"Goddammit, Beeper!" Paul yelled. "*You* did this, didn't you?!"

B. Brian Blair: Truth Bee Told

"No, man," I responded through my poker face. "What are you talking about?"

The rest of the boys piped up and said, "Come on, Paul! Hurry up! We're going to be late!"

Of course, that just pissed Paul off even more.

"I'm *serious*, Beeper!" Paul yelled. "Give me back my snake and mongoose!"

Paul followed the eyes of the wrestlers back over to the conveyor belt, and he was able to spot his cobra-and-mongoose diorama set having just completed its second full lap around the baggage claim area. Paul was very tanned back then, but even through his deep, brown tan, we could still see the rage-induced redness seeping into his skin tone as he ran off to collect his prized possession.

That was the best part of pulling ribs on Paul; he would convey his displeasure over the pranks to a cartoonish degree. He was almost like a real-life Yosemite Sam.

A short time before I was set to make my long-awaited debut in the WWF, I had a very unfortunate incident occur in Hiroshima. I was on a team with Studd and Paul against Antonio Inoki, Tatsumi Fujinami and Osamu Kido. We got so much heat from beating on the national heroes that night that the fans actually swarmed the area around the ring and began taking wild swings at our legs.

I was in one corner of the ring working over Kido while the rest of the guys were involved in a melee in the opposite corner. From there, I transitioned to choking Kido with my left hand while pulling on the back of his black tights. I felt the hands of fans at ringside as they began to grab at my legs while screaming insults in Japanese. Kido was so startled by this that he made a sudden leap into the corner while my right hand was still pulling on the back of his tights.

When Kido made his panicked, impromptu leap, the two tendons of my right hand's middle finger and ring finger were snapped in half. This was the *exact* same hand that was punctured by a shard of glass from a Budweiser bottle when I was only nine years old.

Out of necessity, I worked the next two weeks of the tour with my hands wrapped. When the tour concluded, I traveled to Tampa and visited Dr. Thomas Green, who is probably the best hand surgeon in the history of Florida. He attached tendons of the middle finger and ring finger of my right hand to my pinky, so ever since then all three of those fingers have been obligated to move simultaneously. None of those fingers can move independently of the other two. I was truly forced to become an ambidextrous wrestler thanks to that injury, and to this day I still have no feeling in my right hand.

B. Brian Blair: Truth Bee Told

The New Japan office wired cash directly to Dr. Green to cover the cost of the operation, which was very kind of them. They always took care of your injuries. My journey to New York was delayed by a couple of months, but it was nice to get the extra time at home.

I received rave reviews for the quality of wrestling I displayed in New Japan, and the WWF welcomed me with open arms. Vince McMahon Sr. greeted me with a career-defining suggestion shortly after I arrived in New York.

In the early stages of my time in the WWF

"There are a lot of Brian Blairs in the phone book, but I've never met a 'B. Brian Blair,'" explained Vince. "So... why don't you go by 'B. Brian Blair'? That will help to set you apart from everyone else."

Even after six years in the wrestling business, I still hadn't been given a gimmick name yet, and Vince Sr.'s suggestion made plenty of sense. Also, I was honored to have such a legendary promoter taking such an interest in my name, especially when he was basically retired by that point.

B. Brian Blair: Truth Bee Told

"Oh, I *really* like that!" I told him. "I appreciate that, sir. Very much."

From that point forward, I was always introduced to fans in the United States as some version of B. Brian Blair.

The WWF had an eclectic mix of talent when I arrived. It seemed like Vince Jr. was attempting to blend in some of the young but well-traveled talent – like myself, Eddie Gilbert, Roddy Piper and Tito Santana – with the mainstays of the territory like Mr. Fuji, Tony Garea and Ivan Putski.

Ivan Putski was an established veteran in the Northeast, and he was very picky about who he chose to ride with. He correctly identified me as someone who wasn't a big party animal and asked me if I would ride with him. I accepted his offer, thinking it would be wise for me to ingratiate myself with one of the WWF's most recognizable wrestlers. The move *quickly* backfired when I discovered Ivan's penchant for eating raw onions.

Ivan carried a sack full of onions with him everywhere he went. On top of that, he would request extra onions with his food every time we ate out, and sometimes he'd even go so far as to ask for an *entire plate* full of onions. I'd never seen anyone eat so many onions. The axiom that you are what you eat is very relevant here, because Ivan straight up smelled like an onion most of the time.

This discovery of Ivan's onion-eating habit was a rather jarring experience to me. We were driving along when Ivan reached into the bag on his lap and pulled something out. This was followed by a loud crunching sound. I looked over, fully expecting to see an apple in Ivan's hand. Instead, he was holding a whitish-colored onion. As I looked on in horror, Ivan continued to chomp away at the onion.

"How can you eat *onions* like that?!" I gasped. "That's *disgusting!*"

"No, it isn't!" Ivan replied through a mouthful of onion. "It's a sweet onion from Georgia. It's a Vidalia onion."

"I've had those, and I like onions." I told him. "But I could *never* eat an onion like that!"

"It's good for you!" Ivan said. "Make you live for a long time."

Then Ivan flexed his right bicep.

"Make your *dick* hard, too!" Ivan said.

"Ummmm... thanks, Ivan," I replied. "I don't need help in that area, but I appreciate the advice."

Ivan's fondness for onions might have been a little off-putting, but he was still a solid guy to travel with.

B. Brian Blair: Truth Bee Told

By this point, my buddy Terry Bollea had become a true megastar in professional wrestling. The McMahons had scooped him up in 1979 and renamed him "Hulk Hogan" due to their fondness for all things Irish. A few years later, he had managed to score a feature role in the film *Rocky III*, which sent his marketability through the roof. Everyone thought Sylvester Stallone was a big guy, and Terry made him look downright *puny* by comparison.

Right when I arrived in the WWF, Terry defeated the Iron Sheik to win the World Wrestling Federation Heavyweight Championship. With Hulk Hogan's name at the top of the marquee, the WWF was officially the hottest wrestling territory in the world.

Terry had come a long way from being a young South Tampa kid who grew up two blocks south of Gandy Boulevard and had to share a tiny bedroom with his brother Allan. Not content to be a local rock legend who entertained teenagers in night clubs, now Terry was a certified wrestling legend with an *international* fan following. I couldn't have been any prouder of him.

My role was to be one of the workhorses of the WWF, and to add some youthful excitement to the matches. I wrestled against a wide variety of opponents at the time like Roddy Piper, Mr. Fuji, Greg Valentine and Bob Orton, all while doing my best to showcase myself as an active, scrappy and competitive babyface.

After one of our shows at Madison Square Garden, I found myself riding around New York City in the company of Andre the Giant and French-Canadian star Rene Goulet, who was affectionately known as "Sarge" to his close friends. Andre loved opportunities to converse in his native language, so it was common to find him in the company of his fellow French speakers.

Rene had his car, but we were planning to go out drinking, so we parked his car and found ourselves a cab instead. It was a relatively small cab as far as cabs go, but it was far too cold outside for us to be choosy. We were in the midst of a classic New York winter, and it was *excruciatingly* chilly outside. Rather than wait for another cab, Andre squeezed himself into the first cab that became available to us.

The cab driver seemed to be from somewhere in the Far East, and the headpiece he wore made me think he was likely from the region of India and Pakistan. Andre took a seat in the front of the cab while Rene and I slid into the back seat, where there was a plastic partition between us.

Andre wanted to go to a specific bar in New York's downtown area. As we toured Broadway, all of us were spellbound by the sparkling lights of downtown New York. It was while we were all under the enchantment of the lights that Andre spoiled the atmosphere and the mood by unleashing a *deafening* fart in the cramped confines of the cab.

The driver of the cab turned his head and fired off a look of pure disgust in the Giant's direction. Andre responded to the driver's look of protest by bellowing with laughter as only he could. A putrid stench filled the air, and the cab driver frantically cranked away at the handle to roll down his window as quickly as he could. He then adjusted his posture and angled his head, sticking as much of his cranium out of the window as he possibly could to free himself from the funk of Andre's flatulence.

The cab driver's panic was understandable, except that he kept the window down for several minutes, and the frigid winter air surged into the backseat of the cab.

"It's *really* cold back here!" I protested. "Can you *please* roll up the window?"

"Yeah!" echoed Rene. "Roll the window up! Roll the window up!"

The cab driver shook his head adamantly, absolutely refusing to acquiesce to our wishes.

"No!" he said.

In the mind of the cab driver, it was better to freeze to death that to be subjected to one of Andre's farts. I can't say I blame him.

After visiting the bar, downing a few drinks and returning to Rene's Bonneville, the three of us tried to navigate our way back to our hotel, but quickly found ourselves lost in one of Manhattan's residential neighborhoods. In front of every cramped, narrow residence sat a variety of trash cans in different colors, shapes and styles. They had been set out on the street in the expectation of a visit from the garbage collector in the morning.

"Hit the trash cans," commanded Andre out of the blue.

Whatever the Boss wanted, he tended to get. Rene steered his Bonneville directly into the very next trash can he encountered. Debris went flying everywhere, and Andre roared with laughter. Seeing his friend so jubilant provided Rene with the incentive to replicate the feat, so he proceeded to plow straight through every trash can in the neighborhood.

Both men started laughing and exchanging French comments that were totally incomprehensible to me. I may not have known what they were saying, but I certainly knew I didn't want to be sitting in the backseat while they were engaged in such obvious vandalism. The idyllic snowscape of the neighborhood had now been desecrated, and the streets were fraught with garbage.

When it was all over with, I'm certain Rene had knocked over at least 20 trash cans. I was absolutely convinced we were going to get arrested, but we managed to get off scot-free. Honestly, I can't even imagine what a police officer would have done if he stopped our car to investigate the neighborhood carnage, only to find himself staring into the face of Andre the Giant.

Teaming with Tony Garea as referee Dick Worley looks on

One of my most memorable WWF matches was against Randy "Moondog Rex" Colley at the Cap Center in Washington, D.C. We had a tremendous match in progress, and the crowd was on its feet the entire time. However, I was *dying* to go to the bathroom. As soon as I won and the match ended, I had to get out of there as quickly as I could. Every person in that arena was eating out of the palm of my hands. They were captivated because Randy had performed his role as a heel perfectly and we had taken the audience on an incredible ride.

B. Brian Blair: Truth Bee Told

The choice before me was a simple one: I could grab the microphone and risk crapping in my tights in order to cut a promo asking the crowd for their continued support, or I could head to the bathroom for some intestinal relief. I split the difference. I took the microphone and said, "Thank you!" really quickly, and then I made a beeline to the locker room in search of a toilet. I'd learned my lesson from my humiliating episode with Orndorff at the Omni.

If I'd been smart and gone to the bathroom before the match, I could have gotten on the microphone and said, "I couldn't have done this without your support. I know that together, we *will* win the Intercontinental title. I could win that belt right here in the Cap Center, and I would dedicate that belt to each and every one of you. Will you come back next month and help me win the belt? Are you *with* me?!"

That place would have been sold out the next time, because you can get the people to commit to attending and supporting you right then and there. It wouldn't even have mattered that Tito Santana was the Intercontinental champion at the time, and both of us were babyfaces. In situations like that, you can almost force the hand of the bookers and make your own matches and angles. Unfortunately, my bowels had other plans that night.

I was paired with Tony Garea in a tag team for a while, and we had several matches against Afa and Sika, the Wild Samoans. Working in tag matches against those two was like taking a master class in tag team wrestling. They were *never* selfish, and they sat down with us to explain what they wanted to do before our matches and established a rapport with us prior to every single match. They would always ask us what moves we wanted to perform so that they could work them into the outline of the match.

The Samoans were so skilled at tag team wrestling that their confidence was contagious. If things ever got out of control during a match, they would simply reel me in and quickly say, "Okay, kid… just listen to me." Every time I wrestled against them, I *knew* the match was going to be great.

We also worked with Mr. Fuji and Tiger Chung Lee around the same period of time. Mr. Fuji excelled in the role of the sneaky Japanese heel, and he would do and say things during matches on a regular basis that made it hard not to laugh out loud at his self-deprecating sense of humor. There was one time in particular that Fuji was standing outside of the ring and a ringside fan flipped his middle finger in Fuji's direction.

B. Brian Blair: Truth Bee Told

"Thank you! Me numba one!" Fuji said, as he bowed respectfully toward the fan. It took all of my strength to not crack a smile at Fuji's intentional misinterpretation of that fan's rude gesture.

If there was one certainty about working for the World Wrestling Federation, it was that Mr. Fuji would eventually get around to ribbing you. We were wrestling at a spot show in New York, and I was in the final match. I was also responsible for driving my group of wrestlers out of there, and someone mentioned that I needed to hurry up with my shower and get moving. I handed the keys to my car over to them so that they could keep the car warm in the chilly weather. When my match was over, I rushed to get out of the shower, towel dried my hair as quickly as I could, and then went scouring the place searching for my cowboy boots, which were nowhere to be found.

Finally, Iron Mike Sharpe asked, "Are those your cowboy boots up *there*?"

"Where?" I asked, looking over at him.

"Right *there*," said Mike, as he pointed upward.

I looked up and saw that my beautiful, $300 elephant-skin cowboy boots were padlocked to the top of a pipe. I had to throw on some old tennis shoes, toss my boots into my bag while they were *still* padlocked to the disconnected segment of pipe, and waited to remove the pipe until much later on when I could find a bolt-cutter.

When Fuji finally confessed to the rib, he said, "We had to initiate you, brudda! We *like* you!"

Fuji was good friends with Don Muraco, so that meant he naturally favored me. This worked out to my advantage, because it prevented me from being subjected to any of the *truly* nasty ribs that Fuji was known for. He was one of the most legendary ribbers in the history of the wrestling business.

Buzz Sawyer and I wrestled in a 20-minute Broadway match in New Haven, Connecticut during May of that year. Buzz had just come into the territory and was a powerful and athletic worker, befitting his background as a state champion wrestler from St. Petersburg, Florida. Our styles blended together perfectly, and the match was extraordinary. Chief Jay Strongbow was the booker that night, and on two different occasions during that run I had in the WWF, Chief told me that a match I was in was one of the best matches he'd ever seen. *This* was one of those two times.

"Brian, that match between you and Buzz was one of the best matches I've ever seen in my life!" Chief said. "Forget 20 minutes; you guys should have gone an *hour*!"

B. Brian Blair: Truth Bee Told

I was very proud of that match, and I was proud of Buzz, too. He stayed right with me the entire time, and he provided more than enough movement in the match to help me keep it exciting. A couple weeks later, Buzz made me reconsider the amount of pride I took in our performance. Buzz and I were at the bar with Orndorff and Adonis, and Buzz was as drunk as a skunk. While we were there, Buzz jostled me out of the blue and said to me, "You stiff bastard!"

I started laughing, thinking he was joking.

"What's wrong, Buzz?" I asked him with a smile.

"No, I'm serious!" Buzz replied. "You're a stiff fuckin' bastard!"

Buzz stepped closer to me, then leaned in and shoved me. That's when it became crystal clear to me that he was actually *serious* about wanting to fight me.

"Don't fuck around like that, Buzz," I said calmly. "Don't push me."

In my mind, there was no reason for any hostilities. Buzz had never complained that I'd worked too snugly with him before, and I had no idea what he was taking exception to at that moment.

Paul and Adrian tried to hold Buzz back, but he shoved past them and took a drunken swing at me. He missed wildly, and I leaned in and grabbed him. We fell to the ground and rolled around for a bit. Since I wasn't nearly as drunk as Buzz was, I was able to get my bearings and rise to my feet much faster than him. I quickly spun back toward him, kicked him in his stomach, then gave him a short uppercut to the chin. That was all it took to put Buzz to sleep that night. Buzz *never* said anything unkind to me after that. He knew he was definitely in the wrong.

It was in the middle of 1984 that Vince Jr. made it obvious that his ambition was to turn the WWF into a true national wrestling promotion. In May, Vince McMahon Sr. passed away from pancreatic cancer. Any of the alliances that Vince Sr. had negotiated with his fellow wrestling promoters died with him, and now there was really no one around to prevent Vince Jr. from expanding the borders of his wrestling empire.

I recorded an interview segment with Gene Okerlund in early July, and I had no idea that it would be included right in the middle of the WWF's infamous "Black Saturday" debut in Georgia Championship Wrestling's established time slot on the TBS cable network. Frankly, I had no way of knowing where or when *any* of my interview segments would be airing. It was only on the rarest of occasions that I actually got to watch one of my matches when it aired on television. We were always eating, training, traveling or sleeping, and the odds were unfavorable that we would be stationary and in front of a television when WWF programming was on the air.

Behind the scenes with Mr. #1derful and singer Bryan Adams

Behind the scenes, Vince had purchased the controlling interest in Georgia Championship Wrestling from Jim Barnett and the Briscos, along with the TBS time slot. The Black Saturday broadcast proved to be quite controversial; fans of Georgia Championship Wrestling didn't appreciate the disappearance of many of their favorite wrestlers from the airwaves.

Later in that same Black Saturday broadcast, Paul came out for an interview wearing a robe with a red-and-black color scheme that was reminiscent of his old University of Tampa football uniform. Gene referred to Paul as "Mr. Wonderful," and from then on he would forever be known nationally by that name.

Right after Black Saturday, the WWF co-promoted a show called *The Brawl to End It All* with MTV. Only the match between Wendi Richter and the Fabulous Moolah aired on television – and it attracted an incredible number of viewers – but there was a full Madison Square Garden show that buoyed the Richter-versus-Moolah bout, and both Paul and Terry were featured performers on that card.

Vince Jr. took a rapid liking to Paul and wanted him groomed and pushed rapidly as a respectable foil for Hogan. Paul was big, strong, fast and athletic enough to make Hogan look vulnerable without being a towering, 400-pound monster like the One Man Gang.

B. Brian Blair: Truth Bee Told

I was tasked with making Paul look dangerous while also delivering entertaining matches.

Paul and I were so familiar with one another by 1984 that we could have wrestled each other blindfolded, but that didn't always mean things went smoothly. We had a match in Boston with Dick Worley as the referee. The fans in Boston had a reputation for being quite vicious, and it could be a challenging place to wrestle. I don't know if we ever had a full-blown riot there, but that hardly mattered. Even as I walked out to the ring as a *babyface*, the fans would say awful things to me like, "I'm gonna slice your throat!" or "I'm gonna fuck your old lady!" They were *horrific* threats, for sure.

The match between Paul I was just getting started when someone threw an elbow pipe that just narrowly missed Worley. It hit the wooden barricade instead, and the banging noise the pipe made against the barricade sounded like a gun was going off. When we heard that noise, all three of us dropped to the mat because we all *actually* thought a shotgun had been fired at ringside. There was a big hole in the wood where the elbow pipe had struck it, and the pipe was lying on the floor next to it.

It didn't make any sense for the fans to be throwing things at *me*; they must have been trying to hit Orndorff. After that happened, Paul was so pissed off that he kept turning in the direction that the pipe had been thrown from. He looked as if he was scanning the crowd to locate the guy who had thrown the pipe so that he could charge into the crowd and punch him out.

I took Paul down in an armbar early in that match. As I held him to the mat, I saw something whiz right past my eye.

"Oh *shit*!" I heard Paul scream.

Blood suddenly trickled onto the mat, and I saw a broken miniature vodka bottle lying on the canvas. Then I looked up and saw that Paul had sustained a nasty cut to his lips. Blood was streaming from his face.

Paul touched his lip, looked down at his hand and yelled, "*Fuck*!"

"Can you keep going?" I asked him.

"Yeah!" Paul replied, very angrily.

Paul was so livid as a result of his cut that he started laying in all of his shots on me most savagely, as if *I* had been the one that had lacerated him with the broken glass bottle.

"Paul, *I* didn't throw the bottle!" I whispered to him. "Stop hitting me so damn hard!"

B. Brian Blair: Truth Bee Told

That match was in the Boston Gardens arena, which was significant to me because the Boston Celtics had a great basketball team back then, and it was a big deal to us to be in their legendary stadium. I always made it a point to get dressed at Larry Bird's locker even though it was locked. I was such a mark for Larry Bird that I went out of my way to do it. He probably has no idea who I am, let alone that I always got dressed at his locker.

There were other nights where things went perfectly in the ring with Paul. We had a bout at the Kiel Auditorium in St. Louis that had the fans leaping out of their seats and screaming with excitement. Both of us looked magnificent in the ring that night, and Paul got tremendous heat when he dropped my neck across the top rope and covered me for the three count.

Paul and I embraced in celebration after we had walked back through the curtain. We were told ahead of time that the bout would be televised, and the combination of our execution and the reaction of the crowd would go a long way toward helping us get attention across the country.

While the two of us changed, Chief Jay Strongbow marched into the dressing room.

"Hey, Paul... BBB... Caesar wants to see you!" announced the Chief.

Backstage, everyone knew that "Caesar" was Vince McMahon Jr., and we couldn't imagine that he would be asking for us for any reason other than to commend us for our performance. We were right.

"I've got to tell you something, gentlemen," began Vince after we arrived at his makeshift office. "As you know I was sitting right there at ringside doing commentary during your match; that was the best match I've seen in my life! I'm *serious!*"

"Thank you, sir!" I told him. "That's probably the best compliment I've ever gotten in my whole life!"

"I'm not joking," continued Vince. "That was the *greatest* match."

"We had an even better one last week in Massachusetts!" said Orndorff. "It blew this one away!"

I was worried that Paul was overdoing it just a little bit, but Vince just nodded.

"That's what Chief told me," concurred Vince. "But I don't see how that match could have been any better than *this* one."

If my job had been to help get Paul Orndorff over, I'd say I accomplished my mission... *wonderfully.*

B. Brian Blair: Truth Bee Told

Fortunately, there were some people who were paying attention to my efforts in the ring even if I wasn't always the person getting his arm raised at the end of my matches. It was a huge honor for me to get voted as 1984's "Most Underrated Wrestler" in the *Wrestling Observer Newsletter*.

I viewed Dave Meltzer and the voters of the *Observer* like sports analysts who picked apart the techniques being utilized during football games. These voters were smart to the business, they could tell the difference between a good match and a bad match, and they could tell who was getting over and who wasn't getting over with their respective audiences.

They could also tell who was a good worker in the ring as opposed to people who got over with audiences simply because of their gimmicks. To me, getting an award for "Most Underrated Wrestler" was like getting an award for being one of the best workers in the business. That meant *everything* to someone like me who didn't rely on a gimmick at all.

I was already a subscriber to Dave Meltzer's newsletter at the time, but I kept it a secret from the boys in the locker room. Meltzer had a lot of heat with most of the wrestlers because they thought he was giving away too many industry secrets, and they also collectively wondered who was stooging off all of the behind-the-scenes information to him.

On a monthly basis, Dave was printing all kinds of insider information that none of us were privy to, so we would read his sheets to find out what was going to happen. I'm not talking merely about the things going on in other territories; we would read the *Observer* to find out the events that were going to happen in *our own* territories! *All* of the promoters hated Dave. They didn't like how he leaked all the rumors and gossip that they were hoping to keep private from the wrestlers, but I *loved* it!

The purchase of Georgia Championship Wrestling brought Jim Barnett to New York City. Barnett was one of the owners of GCW who sold his share of the ownership to Vince, and he acquired a vice presidential role with the WWF in the aftermath of the sale.

It wasn't long after the acquisition of GCW by the WWF that a special message was passed along to me by Chief Jay Strongbow while we were working at a taping in New York.

"Hey, Barnett left his bag here, and he wants *you* to bring it to him on your way home," said Chief.

I could hear King Curtis Iaukea's warning ringing in my ears: "Never be alone with Jim Barnett."

B. Brian Blair: Truth Bee Told

"No way, Chief!" I told him. "I'm *not* going to Barnett's house by myself!"

"He's not gonna hurt you, Brian!" laughed Chief. "Just take him his bag."

"I'm not worried about him hurting me," I corrected him. "I'm afraid that if he tries something, I'll have to kick his ass! I don't play like that."

In the end, I did as I was told and brought the bag with me to Jim's condo. When I arrived, Jim answered the door in the middle of the afternoon wearing a nice, well-tailored suit. In fact, he was dressed so nicely that it made me wonder exactly whom he had been expecting to arrive.

"Hi, Mr. Barnett," I said. "I've got your bag for you."

"Oh, Brian... my *boy*!" Jim said. "Could you please bring it inside for me?"

Jim stepped aside and I walked past him into his house. He led me to the living room where he had cocktails arranged on the table, along with a fancy plate of hors d'oeuvres.

"Have a seat, Brian," Jim insisted. "I want to *chat* with you for a bit."

I sat down, and Jim began to tell me about his long career in the wrestling business, including his time as a promoter in Indianapolis and Australia. It was fine that he shared this with me, but all of it was information that had already been articulated to me on the road during different conversations with the boys. All the while, I had my radar up out of the concern that Barnett was going to make a sexual advance or tell me about something I could *do* for him that would *really* benefit my wrestling career.

If Jim had been entertaining any unseemly ideas or planning to attempt an advance, my guarded posture and body language probably made it clear to him that I wasn't going to fall prey to him. Out of the blue, he abruptly terminated the conversation and shooed me away.

As he was walking me out, Jim said, "I really appreciate all my young stars. That goes *double* for you, Brian."

I turned around to shake his hand, and instead Jim leaned in and hugged me closely. When I made it back to my car, I was struck by how uncomfortable the whole ordeal had made me. For the first time in my life, I had a fair understanding of how young ladies must feel when they're out at a bar, because I was genuinely afraid that Barnett might have tried to slip something into my drink!

There was just something about that encounter with Barnett that left me feeling uneasy. I never felt even remotely uncomfortable around any of the other openly gay personnel in the wrestling business before, like Pat Patterson or his partner Louie Dondero. Barnett just had a smarmy demeanor to himself at times, and in my opinion, the veterans who had advised me to be vigilant around Barnett had done me a favor.

Another favor those veterans could have done for me would have been to advise me about when to put my own needs ahead of those of others, because that's a series of decisions I would soon have to make when I once again said "Hello" to the Sunshine State.

SEVENTEEN – *Changing directions*

During a brief break in my World Wrestling Federation schedule, I returned home to visit my friends and family in Tampa during early October of 1984. I'd been casually dating a lady back in my hometown, but the relationship had taken a sharp turn into uncomfortable territory. She had a bit of a drinking problem, which made all of our interactions very contentious. Moreover, she was extremely possessive, and felt that she could control me because she had purchased several expensive items for me that I'd never requested in the first place.

Part of the issue was that the relationship between us had never been exclusive; we had seen one another *very* casually when I was in Tampa in late 1982, and a few times during the rare occasions that I would visit Tampa during the intervening years. At the time, the idea that I would have an exclusive girlfriend in Tampa while I was wrestling primarily in Japan and the Northeast United States for two straight years was *completely* ludicrous.

I drove over to her place to permanently break things off with her, but she had already downed an entire bottle of very expensive Moet & Chandon champagne all by herself. This made the circumstances of the evening all the more awkward when she clung drunkenly to me after I told her our relationship was over.

The woman didn't take the news well at all, and she did everything she could to detain me. She tugged, pulled and clawed at me, tearing my shirt in the process. In fact, she very nearly shoved me down the stairs. To get her off of me as I was halfway out the door, I shoved her back into her apartment and she fell over. That was the extent of my physical interaction with her, and she wound up with a bump on her head and a few scrapes.

At that point, I simply took off and never heard another word about it. I never dreamed that this minor incident would come back to haunt me many years later.

During the same visit to Tampa, I went to pay my respects to Eddie Graham at his office at 106 N. Albany. Eddie's eyes lit right up when he saw me, and he greeted me with a *huge* hug.

"I'm so proud of you, Brian," said Eddie. "I've been watching you on Vince's show. You're doing such a *great* job!"

Having Eddie say he was proud of me meant *everything* to me. The words couldn't have been any more meaningful to me if they had been uttered by my own father.

"How are things going with *you*, Eddie?" I asked him.

B. Brian Blair: Truth Bee Told

The smile disappeared from Eddie's face.

"Honestly, they're not that great, Brian," he admitted. "Vince is really hurting our business. I loaned Mike and Barry to Crockett, but I just heard from both of them that they're going to New York soon instead of coming back here. Billy Graham didn't draw like we expected him to, and now we have Scott McGhee and Pez Whatley as our champions. They're not drawing well either."

"Mr. B" is ready for action

Seeing Eddie – the man who'd provided me with my start in the wrestling business – in such a vulnerable state was more than I could bear.

"I'll come back and help you out," I told him. "I can give Vince my notice as soon as I go back to New York, and then I'll start with you as soon as I get back from Japan next month."

Eddie perked up immediately.

"That would be *incredible*, Brian!" exclaimed Eddie. "We could plug you right into the main events!"

B. Brian Blair: Truth Bee Told

Vince was far less enthused with my plans. He had already mentioned his plans for a major show early in 1985, and he'd wanted me to be a part of it.

"I'd planned to have you work against Greg Valentine for the Intercontinental title next year," said Vince. "You've earned it after all of your hard work."

It can't be overstated how significant of a reward that would have been. With Hogan headlining the WWF's "A" shows, the Intercontinental champion usually headlined the "B" shows with support from the tag team champions. There was quite a bit of money to be made with a main-event run like that.

"I appreciate that, sir," I said. "I really feel like I should help Eddie out, though. He needs me."

Vince just nodded and smiled.

"Loyalty is a rare thing in this business, Brian," he said. "It's admirable. Just know that you'll always have a home here in the World Wrestling Federation. If you decide you want to come back, we'll have you work for the Intercontinental title."

I shook Vince's hand and walked out of his office, hoping I hadn't just made a *colossal* blunder.

Eddie was well beyond thrilled to have me back in Florida wrestling for him once again after I returned from my month in Japan. He wasted no time at all in rocketing me right back into a main-event position. Straight out of the gate, he had me working against Jesse Barr for the Florida Heavyweight Championship. However, the most memorable portion of my feud with Jesse didn't take place during a sanctioned match.

Being the genius that he was, Eddie came up with an angle where Jesse would call me a "chicken" during his interview segments, and then he would skedaddle as soon as I tried to confront him in front of the crowd. The hypocrisy of the situation stemmed from the fact that, as far as our storyline was concerned, Jesse was the *true* chicken for refusing to grant me a shot at his Florida championship.

For a solid month, someone dressed in a chicken costume showed up during Jesse's television matches at 106 N. Albany, and Jesse either chased the chicken around, beat him up, or ran him into the ring post. After these assaults, officials would have to come out, collect the chicken's lifeless body, and carry him off to receive medical attention.

People *loved* the chicken because of how he would antagonize Jesse and cause him to have fits. Then the audience started chanting at

Jesse that he was the *true* chicken, which only pissed him off even more.

Arm drag on the Assassin

Finally, Eddie brought a chicken suit to the building that would fit me. I went out into the arena wearing the chicken suit while Jesse was in the middle of a match against Rocky King, and everyone in the audience just assumed it was the regular chicken coming out to get thrashed once more. Jesse went through his usual schtick of chasing the chicken around the ring, except this time the chicken jumped into the ring and ran toward the ropes. Jesse slid into the ring and stood up, and when he reached his feet, he was met by the *best* flying forearm I'd ever thrown. I nailed him straight in his face.

The stiffness of the forearm hadn't been intentional. As I hit the ropes to deliver that forearm, the chicken mask turned to the side, so I couldn't clearly see what I was doing. This resulted in the chicken delivering a *massive* potato shot to Jesse's face with the flying forearm. It looked *beautiful* on television.

When I pulled the mask off, the people in the arena went bananas. From there, I dropped an elbow on Jesse and covered him while Rocky King counted to three. Then I went straight to the locker room with Rocky behind me, and Jesse remained in the ring and threw a tantrum. This provided *all* the fuel we needed for our matches to deliver sellout business all over Florida.

B. Brian Blair: Truth Bee Told

Despite the solid business I was doing with Jesse, and despite the tremendous push I was receiving, there was serious trouble looming. Vince Jr. was now making no bones about his intention to turn the World Wrestling Federation into a true national wrestling promotion, and he wasn't taking any prisoners. That September, he had formally withdrawn his membership in the National Wrestling Alliance, and it was open season on all other wrestling territories as far as Vince was concerned. No matter what friendship Vince Sr. might have had with Eddie Graham, Vince Jr. wasn't about to show Eddie any mercy whatsoever.

The day after Christmas that year, the WWF ran a show at the Knight Center in Miami five miles away from where CWF was hosting a show at the Convention Hall in Miami Beach... on the *exact* same night. To add insult to injury, the WWF card featured key performers that Eddie had played a integral role in developing, like Hulk Hogan, Barry Windham and Mike Rotunda.

To make matters *even* worse for Eddie, Hogan was already actively trying to lure me *back* to New York. Since *The Brawl to End It All* had been such a huge ratings success for MTV, another cable special called *The War to Settle the Score* was in the works for early in 1985, with a massive closed-circuit show called *Wrestlemania* being prepared in its aftermath.

Hogan got in touch with me before our respective promotions went head-to-head in Miami, and he requested that I fly to New York with him to meet with Vince. As luck would have it, CWF had a three-day gap in its schedule, and our next scheduled event would also be in Miami. I would be able to slip off to New York, meet with Vince, and be back inside of Eddie's locker room before anyone even realized I was gone.

Vince and I had another conversation that night about having me come back to the WWF, but he was more than a little bit distracted. Not only did Vince have to manage a sellout crowd at Madison Square Garden, but he also had to deal with an investigative reporter from ABC's *20/20* program – John Stossel, who was poking around in the locker room area. When Stossel interviewed David Schultz that night and told him to his face that he thought wrestling was fake, he wound up getting floored twice by consecutive slaps from "Dr. D" as several of us gathered in the hallway to observe the incident.

Schultz had made it clear to us that he intended to rattle Stossel during the interview, but I don't think any of us suspected things would get physical. We praised Schultz's forthrightness in

B. Brian Blair: Truth Bee Told

standing up for the business, but it proved to be very costly to him when the assault on Stossel aired and Schultz was fired.

I returned to Florida in time for New Year's Day having inked no new deal with the World Wrestling Federation, and within a week I kicked off 1985 by winning the Florida Heavyweight Championship once again. Whatever joy I felt from reclaiming a top spot in my hometown wrestling company was *very* short lived.

Two weeks after I won the Florida title, Eddie Graham committed suicide by shooting himself in the head… *twice*.

It wouldn't be hyperbole to say that January 21st of 1985 was one of the saddest days of my life. I can't say that I saw it coming, but I wouldn't be exaggerating if I said it seemed like *something* was coming. Aside from running a company that had been plagued by a marked downturn at the box office due to direct competition from Vince, and the erosion of his talent base, Eddie's life was also fraught with personal problems.

Eddie was often characterized as a functioning alcoholic, but at that stage of his life he could hardly be described as "functioning." His alcoholism only exacerbated his other problems, including the coinciding stress of being torn between his wife and his longtime mistress.

The death of a close friend or family member wasn't something I had truly had to deal with directly, at least not since the death of my friend Steve Bush way back in high school. Losing Eddie absolutely rattled me to the core. It felt like I'd lost a part of myself that I could *never* get back. I knew I'd thanked Eddie repeatedly while he was living, but this was one of those cases where if you'd known the last time you were speaking with someone was definitely going to be the *very* last time you would ever talk to them, you would have profoundly thanked them 100 times over because of the indescribable benefit they had been to your life.

Professional wrestling lost one of its greatest minds when Eddie passed away. If you'd asked anyone who knew anything about booking a quality wrestling territory, including people like Bill Watts, Gary Hart and Kevin Sullivan, they would have told you that Eddie Graham was one of pro wrestling's *true* geniuses. He could detect things and predict events that were far into the future. That's one of the reasons why he was so successful. It also probably contributed to his death, because he could foresee a future *so* bleak that he didn't want to live to see it.

For what it's worth, the fact that I was the final person to reign as Florida Heavyweight Champion when Eddie Graham still controlled the Florida territory means *so much* to me. If I had left Eddie high and dry and bolted for New York less than one month before he took his own life, I'm quite certain that I *never* would have forgiven myself knowing that my defection might have factored into his depression.

Securing the abdominal stretch on "Ravishing" Rick Rude

Even with Eddie gone, we continued to keep the business functioning in Florida to the best of our ability. Sometime between 1983 and 1985, the Southern Heavyweight Championship had supplanted the Florida title as the definitive top belt in the territory. The decision was made that I should drop the Florida title back to Jesse, and then I would work a program with Rick Rude that would conclude with me capturing the Southern title from him.

The event was meant to be a coronation that was visible to everyone. During one of our April television tapings, I locked Rude in my sleeper hold, and then dodged a swing from Percy Pringle's cane so that he would clobber Rude with it instead of me. After dropping one final elbow on Rude's dazed body, I covered him for the three count while the crowd went crazy. Gordon Solie then presented me with the Southern title belt over at the broadcast table while Mike Graham personally congratulated me.

B. Brian Blair: Truth Bee Told

It all looked great on camera, as if Eddie Graham's golden boy – his homegrown version of Jack Brisco – had finally struck gold and was back in Tampa to stay. Behind the scenes, I was already *gone*.

The Southern Heavyweight Wrestling Champion

The WWF's first *Wrestlemania* had been certified as a major success. Vince had made a financial killing, and he was planning to reinvest that money into the WWF to further fuel its rapid expansion.

When the call finally came from New York, I was expecting it to be Vince calling to offer me a run against Valentine for the WWF's Intercontinental Heavyweight Championship. Instead, it was Terry who made the call.

"Vince wants you back, Brian," said the Hulkster. "He's planning to build the best tag team division ever, and he wants to put you with Jim Brunzell. If it works out, you two are going to get the belts."

I was at a loss for words. This wasn't at all what I had been expecting. What's more, I didn't want to make such an important career decision if it was all dependent upon whether or not I got along with someone I'd *never* met before, and who I had only ever heard about in wrestling magazines.

"What is Brunzell like?" I asked.

"He's a cool guy," Hogan answered. "He's a *great* worker. I hung out with him a lot when I worked for Verne in the AWA. Great tag team wrestler."

"How much will I be making?" I asked.

"A lot more than you're making right now," answered Hogan.

"Yeah... that'll work!" I said. "Being a tag champion sounds awesome!"

At the time, I don't think I viewed the pairing of Jim Brunzell and I for what it really was: part of the second phase of Vince McMahon's talent raid on the nation's wrestling territories. As a matter of fact, it was a simultaneous precision strike against *two* territories at once.

By extracting me from Florida, Vince was stealing Eddie Graham's 28-year-old golden boy just as he was entering his prime as a wrestler, and right when Florida needed him the most. Acquiring Jim Brunzell from the American Wrestling Association had automatically broken up The High Flyers – a main event tag team partnership between Brunzell and Greg Gagne that had lasted for the better part of *11 years*.

In one fell swoop, Vince had eliminated the AWA's foremost main-event tag team *and* stripped the Florida territory of its projected long-term top babyface. Even if Brunzell and I never developed any chemistry as tag team partners, it was *still* a brilliant move on the part of Vince if he wanted to decimate his competition.

In the aftermath of my decision to go to New York, everyone in Florida was understandably upset, not the least of whom was Mike Graham, who felt pretty betrayed at the time. Honestly, I don't see how he could have blamed me. The truly marketable stars of wrestling no longer considered Florida a career-making destination.

Dusty was wrestling for CWF on only the rarest of occasions at that point, and his appearances were growing fewer and farther between with each passing month. Dory Funk Jr. had been spending more time wrestling in Japan than anywhere else. The Brisco Brothers were long gone. Barry Windham and Mike Rotunda – two of the other young stars that were also expected to carry Florida into its next decade of prominence – were already in the WWF competing as the U.S. Express. The territory was a sinking ship that was rapidly taking on water, and if I was going to continue my rise to greater prominence, I would have to say "so long" to the Sunshine State.

B. Brian Blair: Truth Bee Told

I quickly dropped the Southern title to Ray "Hercules" Hernandez, and then the only thing remaining for me to do was to finish out my commitments before I flew to New York. That was more challenging than it sounded, because the atmosphere following the announcement of my departure was not pleasant. I had been in the middle of a hot feud with Rick Rude that management was hoping would keep the territory afloat. When I told everyone that I was heading off to New York to join the team that had just violated decades of convention and run a competing show in Miami, they felt completely betrayed.

All of this amounted to me not feeling excited about wrestling for CWF anymore, and it all came to a head when I was on my way to Fort Lauderdale during the home stretch of my Florida farewell tour. Just 20 miles outside of Tampa, my Monte Carlo suffered a flat tire. Without any means to contact anybody, all I could do was wait at the side of the road until someone was kind enough to offer me some assistance. Eventually that assistance arrived, but the frustration of the flat tire only added to my clarity of mind.

"I'm going to make so much money working in New York that I won't even miss what I'm being paid for this show," I told myself. "Why do I want to drive all the way to Fort Lauderdale to work for a bunch of people who are pissed off at me when I can just enjoy my evening at home and then fly off to New York to see Terry and Paul?"

Instead of pressing onward to Fort Lauderdale after I'd changed my tire, I drove to the nearest service station and called the CWF office from the adjacent payphone to get the number for the building in Fort Lauderdale. From there, I called Mike Graham, left a message for him to call me back on the payphone, and sat there in silence waiting for him to call me back.

A few moments later, the payphone rang and I answered it.

"Beeper, where the hell are you?" asked Mike. "We're sold out!"

"My car broke down," I told him. "I'm not going to make it to the show tonight."

"That's *not* an option, Brian," said Mike. "The building is packed and you were advertised for the main event. Just tell me where you are and I'll come get you."

From where I was sitting, it would have taken Mike three hours to come get me and another three just to make it back to Fort Lauderdale. It was a pretty ridiculous suggestion, but it did underscore how desperate they were to have me there.

B. Brian Blair: Truth Bee Told

"You know what… that's okay," I told him. "I think I can get the car working, and then I'll be there."

"Great!" said a relieved Mike. "I'll see you when you get here."

Honestly, I had no intention of continuing my trip to Fort Lauderdale under any circumstances. The writing was already on the wall as far as Championship Wrestling from Florida was concerned. Without Eddie Graham, Dusty Rhodes, Dory Funk Jr., the Briscos, or *any* of the young talent that was expected to row the boat alongside me, the Florida wrestling dynasty was *dead*.

I turned my car around and drove straight home. It was the one and only time I ever voluntarily missed a booking in my career; I would never wrestle for Championship Wrestling from Florida again.

Paul Orndorff picked me up from the airport in New York in his gray Toyota Celica. He was wearing a big smile on his face.

"Are you ready to make some money, Beep?!" he asked excitedly.

I was *well* beyond being ready to make some money, and Vince put me straight to work. I still had a couple weeks to kill until Jim Brunzell arrived from Minneapolis, but that didn't prevent Vince from booking me in singles contests immediately after my arrival.

I received a quick and brutal introduction to what life was going to be like working for a truly national wrestling territory. After wrestling on three different shows in the New York area within two days, I worked a nine-day stretch that included matches in Pittsburgh, Landover, Columbus, San Francisco, Los Angeles, San Diego, Los Angeles, Phoenix and Miami… in *that* order. In other words, I wrestled in Pennsylvania, Maryland, Ohio, Northern California, Southern California, Arizona and Florida, with only one day off. The cross-continental flights were absolutely *insane*.

Aside from the demanding nature of the travel, this first round of matches was noteworthy for two reasons. The first reason is that I was reunited with Matt Borne for the first time since our brawl in West Virginia. Matt was so over the top with his kindness toward me that I was practically embarrassed for him. What's more, they had Matt put me over cleanly during our match in Columbus, which was probably the company's way of testing to see whether or not we could let bygones be bygones and act professionally.

The second landmark event occurred when I publicly stepped across the battle lines in Florida by wrestling on a WWF card in Miami just one day after a CWF show occurred in the same city. The fact that myself, Barry Windham and Mike Rotunda all wrestled at that same event wasn't lost on me either. The young stars who had been expected to reinforce the dominance of Florida's wrestling territory were now all simultaneously working directly against it.

Over a very brief period of time, the terrain of American pro wrestling had been transformed into a kill-or-be-killed warzone. Fortunately, I was about to be a assigned a partner who would help me to navigate that warzone. Together, we would rise to a level of global popularity that we could only have dreamed about. It was going to be *bee*-utiful.

EIGHTEEN – *The Bees are born*

When I finally connected with Jim Brunzell, it was at the Mid Hudson Civic Center in Poughkeepsie, New York. Jim had achieved the bulk of his career success as a tag team competitor, and I had competed in more than enough tag team matches in my own right. We were both traditional, athletic babyfaces that had instant chemistry as a team. The only thing we didn't have yet was a name, and Vince's vision of wrestling required that every *serious* tag team on his talent roster should have a unifying look, theme and name.

George Scott approached Jimmy and I in the locker room in Brantford, Ontario and said, "Vince wants you guys to come up with a catchy name for your team. I'll be back pretty soon... and by the way, you're *on* in less than an hour."

George provided us with a few suggestions for our name, but none of them stood out as anything that would be catchy enough. All at once, an idea struck me that was owed to the fact that I'd spend the bulk of my life living in Florida.

"Hey, Jimmy, do you remember the Miami Dolphins team that played in the Super Bowl this year?" I asked.

"Yeah... they lost to the 49ers," stated Jimmy, matter of factly.

"Right. You know how their defense is called 'The Killer Bees' because they have all those guys whose last names start with 'B'?" I said.

"Okay..." said Jimmy.

"So, we're Brunzell and Blair... so *we* could be the Killer Bees!" I said with an even bigger smile.

"Sounds good to me!" exclaimed Jimmy.

We presented the idea to George, who disappeared for a few moments and then walked back into the room.

"Vince *loves* it; you guys are now the Killer Bees!" he said.

Lanny Poffo had been listening to the ongoing discussions surrounding our team identity the entire time, and he just happened to have a massive hockey bag with him filled with myriad styles of wrestling tights. In what was a coincidence that could only have meant that divine powers were at work that evening, Lanny reached into his hockey bag and produced two pairs of wrestling trunks with black-and-yellow stripes.

Not only was our name approved, but we would be able to establish the image of our team almost instantly. It was only a matter of time before our look was completed by black-and-yellow boots, and

B. Brian Blair: Truth Bee Told

customized Killer Bees ring jackets designed by the incomparable Olivia Walker, the better half of Mr. Wrestling #2.

Now that we had an identity, Jimmy and I tried to come up with some tandem maneuvers that would mark us as a true team, as opposed to two individual wrestlers that had been slapped together as an afterthought. Jimmy had a *gorgeous* dropkick that he could reach magnificent heights with thanks to his world-class high-jumping ability. I would make it a point to come up with ways to work his dropkick into every match, often by forcing our opponents to leap over me in a way that left them even more exposed to a dropkick from "Jumping" Jim Brunzell.

Connecting with The Bee Sting on Rusty Brooks

As far as our finishing maneuver was concerned, it was decided that I should be the one to administer that to our opponents. At the time, Roddy Piper used the sleeper hold, and Tito Santana used the flying forearm. Stealing the finisher of an established wrestler was completely out of the question, so we came up with something more befitting a high-flying bee. After Jim properly positioned our opponents by bodyslamming them, I would apply The Bee Sting by leaping from the top rope and dropping my butt across our opponents' chests.

This seemed like a good idea at first, but I quickly realized it was a poorly conceived strategy for the long term. Obviously, I couldn't drop all of my weight onto someone's chest from eight feet in the air without killing them, so I absorbed the impact with my knees by locking them out, landing on the mat, and *then* dropping my hips toward my opponents.

The stress placed on my knees from that move was *far* too great. A few months' worth of nightly damage to my knees was all it would take before we decided that The Bee Sting wouldn't be good for the long-term health of my lower extremities. Human knees simply aren't built to absorb that type of stress with any regularity. Instead, we established ourselves as a team with several different ways to put their opponents down for the count.

Aside from our in-ring maneuvers, Jim and I also came up with a gesture to signify to fans that the Bees were preparing to give our opponents the stinger. To the uninitiated, our hand signal looked like an ordinary thumbs up, and it's a gesture I would retain for the remainder of my career.

Another task we were assigned was to decide upon some entrance music. Just about any song was fair game; the Junkyard Dog used "Another One Bites The Dust" by Queen, and The U.S. Express ran out to the ring to Bruce Springsteen's "Born in the U.S.A." Jimmy was the epitome of a rock 'n' roll enthusiast, and Bruce Springsteen is one of his true idols. His first few suggestions were all Springsteen songs, like "Glory Days" and "Dancing in the Dark," but I vetoed those suggestions because none of them really seemed to fit us.

After taking a little more time to mull it over, Jimmy had me listen to a song I'd never heard before by a group I'd never heard of. The group was Phantom Rocker and Slick, and the song was called "Men Without Shame." There was a guitar part in there that Jim and I both really liked, so we went with it and the fans seemed to really enjoy our ring entrance. It wouldn't be too long before Jimmy decided he wanted to change our theme to "The Kid is Hot Tonite" by Loverboy. We ultimately switched back to "Men Without Shame" once again, but it wasn't long after that before the company decided to phase out its unlicensed wrestling themes altogether.

From my vantage point, the WWF locker room at the time was more or less broken into four distinct factions. There were folks who'd enjoyed their most significant runs in the WWF – like Mr. Fuji and Captain Lou Albano – who were still hanging on. Aside from that, you had the crew from Florida, the crew from Minnesota, and the crew from Calgary. If you'd broken into the business through Eddie Graham, Verne Gagne or Stu Hart, you entered the industry with a guaranteed level of respect, and you also had several of your peers and fellow trainees to associate with.

B. Brian Blair: Truth Bee Told

During our opening stretch of matches, the Killer Bees were booked by George Scott to be a dominant, crowd-pleasing tag team. We won almost every match we participated in, including victories over the former championship team of the Iron Sheik and Nikolai Volkoff. We also traded victories with the Hart Foundation – an excellent team consisting of Bret Hart and Jim Neidhart – and just barely came up short in matches against the WWF World Tag Team Champions, the Dream Team. I was even given a victory in singles competition against the Iron Sheik, who had once been the WWF World Heavyweight Champion.

The Killer Bees preparing for action in a 10-man tag match

It was during this stretch of time that I stoked the ire of the Iron Sheik for decades to come. It all started when we were in Hershey, Pennsylvania. Sheik has a world-class amateur wrestling background that he acquired in his home country of Iran, and I had a decent amateur background combined with the shoot-style holds I'd learned while training in Florida. Because of this, we went through an opening-match phase where we would exchange *real* takedowns and holds, and then we would progress into a standard professional wrestling match with suplexes and other worked maneuvers.

At this point of his career, Sheik's conditioning had begun to falter, and he would begin to fatigue *very* early in his matches. Even in his enervated state, Sheik was still *unbelievably* tough. In one of our tag team matches, Sheik got me in a tight front facelock, and he clamped down *way* too tight. In response, I got to his wrist, forced the reversal, and then cinched in an even *tighter* double wristlock. Sheik immediately began to complain, and he was too tired at that point to do anything to improve his situation on the mat.

"You fuckin' jabroni!" he said over and over. "Fuckin' jabroni! You almost break my arm!"

In the opposite corner, Nikolai Volkoff was standing there laughing at Sheik's predicament.

"Sheik get stretched!" taunted Nikolai through his thick Croatian accent. "Brian stretched you, Sheik!"

That was really all there was to it; from there we had a perfectly acceptable match. However, the fallout from that little bit of ribbing was that the Sheik wouldn't talk to me for nearly *two weeks*. Meanwhile, Nikolai definitely wasn't doing anything to help matters. He informed me that at least once a day, he was needling the Sheik by saying "Brian Blair *stretched* you, Sheik!"

Under normal circumstances, in a standard amateur-style wrestling match, the Sheik would probably have beaten me nine times out of ten. Yet that one moment of embarrassment when I had given him a quick receipt for what he had just done to me, combined with the daily teasing from Nikolai, would stick with the Sheik and bother him for many years to come.

Things were moving so quickly that Jim and I never got to watch our matches on the television broadcasts that aired all over the country, so in that sense, we couldn't *see* ourselves becoming more famous. However, when the frequency with which we would get recognized in public increased, or the reactions for us in the arenas seemed to grow louder and louder each week, we could *feel* ourselves growing in popularity. The feeling was most obvious in major cities like Chicago or Toronto, where we could gauge the reactions of the crowds and sense how we were growing increasingly more popular with wrestling fans all across the nation, one month at a time.

At one point during the Bees' initial surge in popularity, George Scott approached me in the locker room.

"Did you ever think about shaving your moustache, Brian?" asked George.

"When I started wrestling, I was clean shaven," I informed him. "I looked *way* too young."

"You'd be so much *better* as a babyface if you shaved," urged George. "Plus, you and Jim would look even more alike. That would be *perfect* for you as a team!"

"I'd *really* have to think about it, George," I told him.

B. Brian Blair: Truth Bee Told

And I *did* think about it. A few days later, I was in the middle of shaving when I lathered up some shaving cream and spread it over my moustache. I stood there staring at the mirror for about 10 minutes, thinking about what a huge step it would be for me to completely shave my precious moustache. Eventually, I thought better of it and washed away the shaving cream. My moustache had become a crucial piece of my public identity, and no amount of coercion was going to get me to shave it off.

At the tail end of the year, Jim and I were selected to go to Australia for the WWF's first-ever overseas tour of the land down under. It felt like a huge vote of confidence in us since Vince was entrusting us with the responsibility to help open up a new market for live WWF events.

Killer Bees and Koala Bears

From the airport in Sydney, Jim and I were shuttled off to the zoo, where we enjoyed ourselves at a photo op by posing for photos with koala bears, wallabies and other indigenous Australian animal species. Afterwards, we checked into our hotel, and then Brunzie and I called a cab so that we could go off and tour the area.

Once the cab arrived, the longhaired driver got out and opened our car doors. Even before our rear ends came to rest in the backseat of the cab, the unmistakable, pungent odor of marijuana had nestled into our nostrils.

Getting the better of Jake "The Snake" Roberts

Brunzie looked over at me and gave me a knowing smile, as if the scent of weed indicated that we were about to embark on a wild experience.

"I'm Willie," the driver introduced himself. "Where will you gents be headed off to?"

"Anywhere we can get something to eat and drink," Jim said. "What do you recommend?"

"I know *just* the place," Willie said.

We continued to converse with Willie as he drove us through the streets of Sydney. Before long, he asked us, "Hey, mates… you mind if I smoke?"

"I'd prefer that you didn't," I told him. "I *really* don't like cigarette smoke, brother."

Willie looked hurt, and also a little confused.

"I was just going to smoke a joint!" he said, as if the specifics of what he smoked would make a huge difference to me. "I'll crack the window for you."

I looked over at Jim, who simply shrugged to indicate that he didn't care one way or another.

"Fine," I replied, not wanting to overrule the guy in his own car. The whole interior of the vehicle had the stench of weed baked into it, so it's not like we could escape from it even if all four car windows were all the way open.

The first Killer Bees t-shirt design ever; Australia Exclusive

Willie tore through joints one after the other during our drive, like a joint chain-smoker. To my great surprise, this had no effect whatsoever on the quality of his driving. I *still* spent the entire time *praying* he wouldn't wreck the car.

B. Brian Blair: Truth Bee Told

Now that he was *supremely* loosened up, Willie began to describe all of the potential culinary options available to us in Sydney. He continued listing off the places we could eat as he stopped the car in the Kings Cross neighborhood of Sydney, and we then climbed out so that the vehicle could be aired out somewhat.

The lighter side (and backside) of the Australia tour

While we stood there with the doors of the cab open wide, two girls approached us.

"Excuse us, but aren't you two of those wrestlers that are in town?" one of them asked us.

"That's us," I replied. We immediately included the girls in our ongoing conversation about what we should be attempting to do and see while in Australia. Eventually, our talks turned to the wrestling event that was taking place the next evening.

"Can you get us tickets to the show?" they asked. "We'd love to go!"

"Sure!" I said. "Do you have a pen? Take down this number."

The girl took a pen and a piece of paper out of her purse. I quickly scribbled down WWF agent Tony Garea's phone number.

"Call this number, and just tell them who you are," I lied. "They'll be *sure* to make sure you get some tickets to the show."

The girls walked away thrilled. It may seem like it would have been uncharacteristic of me to pull a rib like this on girls that were being so friendly, but I couldn't help myself. Besides, they weren't exactly girls that I would have been interested in hanging out with at that stage of my life; they came across like a pair of floozies.

B. Brian Blair: Truth Bee Told

"Hey, mates…" Willie piped up as soon as the girls were out of earshot. "Those two Sheilas have had more pricks in 'em than a second-hand dartboard. *Those* two Sheilas are workin' girls."

"Are you sure about that, Willie?" I laughed.

"I'm not sure, mate… but I sure think so!" he replied.

We never spoke to the girls again, and I don't know if Tony Garea ever received a call from them. However, I'll never forget that incident because Willie's line about the second-hand dartboard is one of my all-time favorites.

Working Jake over on the mat

Every place the WWF toured in Australia was sold out. We went from Brisbane to Adelaide to Tasmania to Sydney and every place in between.

B. Brian Blair: Truth Bee Told

While we were at the hotel getting ready to leave for one of the arenas, Jimmy bolted into the room and said, "Hey, I just talked to George Thorogood!"

"What?!" I responded.

"Yeah! He was just in the elevator," explained Jim. "He wants to know if we can get him a ringside ticket. He *has* tickets, but they're pretty far back."

This was happening at a time when George Thorogood and the Destroyers were a pretty big deal on the international music scene. Their gold album *Maverick* had been released earlier that year.

We asked Tony Garea if he could accommodate George, and Tony secured a seat for George inside of the barricade, which is honestly the best seat possible. After the show, George had a million questions for us and was truly marking out for us. I couldn't believe a rock star like George Thorogood could be such a huge fan of ours. On a personal level, this was one of those moments that underscored how far I'd come professionally, and how popular the WWF was becoming as an international brand.

After the show, we met up with George at a local bar. There was a band playing there called Los Lobos. I wasn't familiar with them, but Jimmy knew exactly who they were. It turned out, they were huge wrestling fans, too. Later in the Los Lobos set, George got up to briefly perform with them, and then pointed toward our table and directed the crowd's attention to us.

"We've got the Killer Bees in the house!" George said.

The members of the band came down off the stage to take photos with us and asked *us* to sign autographs for *them*. Never before had I felt like such a huge star.

Just as I was appreciating the professional heights that I'd ascended to, the phone rang in our hotel room that evening. When I answered, the operator on the other end said that she had my mother on the line, and then she put the call through to me. I was immediately concerned because my mother wouldn't go through the trouble of coordinating a call through a 16-hour time difference to reach me unless something serious had transpired.

"Hey, Mom... is everything okay?" I asked.

"Son, I hate to give you this bad news while you're overseas, but Grandpa passed away," she stated.

A wave of sadness immediately washed over me, and I cried for what seemed like an eternity. I was grateful to have Jimmy there to attempt to comfort me, but I was *completely* inconsolable. The cumulative effect of dipping two cans of Copenhagen every day for six decades had finally taken their toll on my grandfather and caused him to succumb to a sudden, fatal heart attack.

I'd already lost Eddie Graham earlier that year. He had obviously been a stable mentoring presence during my wrestling career. In my grandfather's case, he had been a hero, role model and friend to me throughout my *entire* life. This was the most significant and devastating death I had ever been forced to cope with.

With my grandfather

My dad provided me with the details of the funeral arrangements. I promptly changed my homebound flight to America to bring me to Chicago instead of Tampa, and then I rented a car and drove to Portage, Indiana. I stepped through the door just in time for the beginning of the funeral service.

The same man who went out of his way to ensure that the negative consequences of nicotine use would remain forever etched into the brain of his 10-and-a-half-year-old grandson had died as a result of his own incessant nicotine use. It was a costly lesson learned, and I would never forget it.

I didn't have much time to privately mourn and grieve. I had to hop right back aboard the WWF machine. During our first TV taping after the Australia tour, Jesse Ventura interviewed Jim and I about the tour in front of a live audience.

"The reports out of Australia say that you were spreading a lot of *pollen* while you were out there in Australia, B. Brian Blair!" spewed Jesse.

Jesse then shoved the microphone directly under my nose while I began to stammer. I had *no clue* how to respond to something like that!

On a personal note, I was thoroughly sick of dating women who *only* seemed to be interested in me because I was a recognizable pro wrestler. During one of my trips back home, I complained about this to my former high school wrestling coach, Ken Lloyd.

"If you ever run into a nice girl that isn't a wrestling fan, let me know," I requested. "I'm tired of messing around with girls that are wrestling fans. I can't tell if they like me for me, or just because I'm a wrestler."

"Well, why don't we go to Lorello's?" laughed Ken. "I know a pretty girl who's been true to her boyfriend since high school. They broke up about a month ago and she's been devastated."

Yeah, that's fine," I responded, not really expecting anything to come out of it. "Let's see what happens."

When I finally walked into Lorello's, I saw this *gorgeous*, sun-kissed angel with amazing white teeth. When she stood up to shake my hand, I could clearly see that the rest of her was just as beautiful and appealing as her face.

"Hi, I'm Toni!" she said with a smile.

I'm *sure* the smile on my face at that moment was even larger.

"I'm Brian!" I replied enthusiastically.

Toni worked right next to Ken's wife as an underwriter for Integon Mortgage Home Lending, and the Lloyds began talking me up to her as soon as they found out she was newly single. We had an amazing time on that date, and on each of our *next* four dates. By the time our fifth date reached its conclusion, I decided that I couldn't stand the thought of being with anyone other than *her*.

Being in a stable relationship was a necessary lifestyle change for me. After my first marriage, I'd dated without giving even a passing thought to ever getting married again. I knew I simply wasn't ready for it. When I gradually began thinking about marriage again and all of the women around me were wrestling fans, I had a lingering suspicion that these women would have happily made themselves available to *any* babyface wrestler. Toni didn't know the first thing about wrestling, so there was tremendous comfort in that. It wasn't long afterward that we became engaged.

Getting into another serious relationship also proved to me that I was maturing in other ways. My parents were divorced at a young age, and that made things difficult for my siblings and I. Relationship issues aside, my parents were still very loving, and I knew there would come a point in my life when I would want to find someone to have a family with. Fortunately, Toni was the ideal person for me to marry.

"Macho Man" Randy Savage arrived in the World Wrestling Federation from Memphis right around the same time I did. On a few of the nights when I got a break from teaming with Jim, I was able to wrestle Randy. These matches were *just* before he captured the Intercontinental Heavyweight Championship from Tito Santana.

Randy was one of the greatest in-ring performers of all time, and was legitimately a very tough man who never backed down from a fight. However, he was never very comfortable when true, amateur-style wrestling tactics were used in his matches. To be blunt, Randy flat-out hated any implementation of true wrestling. Since I was tipped off to this ahead of time, I absolutely made a point out of taking him down a few times during the opening moments of our first-ever match just to get under his skin a little bit.

After that match concluded, Randy waited for me to walk back through the curtain and met me with a handshake.

"Hey, uhhhh, B?" said Savage. "That was cool, but do you think that we could maybe cool it with the *amateur* stuff a little bit? Let's just work around. Dig it?"

Knowing that Randy hated shoot-style wrestling so much just made me want to do it more. From then on, I always tried to shoot on Randy a little more than he liked, or I would continue to take him down just to add to his discomfort. He was always good-natured enough to laugh about it afterwards. Besides, he always got the win over me anyway, so it was a fair trade for me to annoy him and make him sweat a little bit before he got his eventual victory.

As *Wrestlemania 2* approached, all of us were excited that the event was going to be held in three different locations – New York, Chicago and Los Angeles – to showcase just how colossal the WWF had become during its year of national expansion following the first *Wrestlemania*. The shot at the tag team championships at that year's *Wrestlemania* was granted to the British Bulldogs.

Jimmy and I had no problem with this; we liked Dynamite and Davey Boy, and the two of them had been together in the WWF long before the Killer Bees were paired together as a team. We figured our time would eventually come, and we were content to participate in the battle royal in Chicago pitting WWF wrestlers against stars from the National Football League.

Prior to the show, Jimmy and I were asked to tease our eventual ascent to championship contention during our interview segments. Wearing a *Wrestlemania 2* shirt, I got on the microphone and explained how Jimmy and I wanted to win this battle royal as a way of boosting our candidacy for a future title shot.

That was a ridiculous claim, of course. The British Bulldogs were slated to win the belts from the Dream Team, and the WWF had a rather strict policy of never permitting babyface wrestlers to compete against one another during that era. As long as the Bulldogs had the belts, the Bees wouldn't even get a chance to *sniff* them. All we could do was keep working hard, wait for a heel team to eventually win the championship, and strengthen our position as the next babyface tag team in line by continuing to have great matches.

In the weeks prior to *Wrestlemania 2*, Hogan's buddy Mr. T began to make some appearances at shows in order to hype up his scheduled boxing match against Roddy Piper. After hanging out with me alongside Hogan a few times, Mr. T seemed to really enjoy being around me. This was during the height of Mr. T's popularity as a star of the weekly TV series *The A-Team*, so I was thrilled to be recruited into the entourage of a mainstream star for that brief period of time.

When you traveled with Mr. T, you did *everything* in a first-class fashion. We all flew into Montreal, and T had me ride with him to the famous Chez Paree Gentlemen's Club, where he proceeded to order a dozen bottles of Dom Perignon and flirt with *all* of the dancers. From there, we took a limousine all the way to Buffalo, and we went to *another* topless club. When we finally left the club, we were accompanied by two of the club's Russian dancers that T had personally selected for himself.

I got to stay in the suite with T and the girls, but he had his own room with them. As I sat around the suite, T went to the bathroom to get himself warmed up, and then walked out of the bathroom over to me and said, "Hey, Brother B! Check *this* out!"

Suspended in front of him, T had what appeared to be a pile of laundry, except he *wasn't* using his hands to hold the pile up.

"I can put *two* bath towels on *mine*!" Mr. T proclaimed proudly. "How about *you*?!"

For the record, I'm sure I *could* have hung two bath towels on mine, but I declined T's invitation to try right then and there.

B. Brian Blair: Truth Bee Told

Hanging with Mr. T on a road was like living the life of a rock star. To my great surprise, things were going to get even grander for me in the very near future.

B. Brian Blair: Truth Bee Told
NINETEEN – *To be fined, or NOT to be fined*

When *Wrestlemania 2* finally occurred, it consisted of a lot of sitting around and watching the monitors. The broadcast shifted its coverage from New York to Chicago to Los Angeles, which meant all we could do was sit back and act as spectators to what was going on in the other cities until it was showtime in *our* arena. It probably wasn't the most crowd-friendly format for the show, but I don't think anyone watching the event was too disappointed.

Competitors of the *Wrestlemania 2* WWF vs NFL Battle Royal

One of the most enjoyable elements of the early Wrestlemanias was the opportunity to rub shoulders with the stars who were invited to participate. In our case, the majority of the stars consisted of the players from the National Football League who were involved in the battle royal. This included William "Refrigerator" Perry and Jimbo Covert, who were members of the legendary Chicago Bears team that had just finished dominating the New England Patriots in Super Bowl XX. They were both over in front of their hometown fans, but Perry was *nationally* famous at the time, and he was probably the most over performer in the bout.

B. Brian Blair: Truth Bee Told

Other celebrities present for the Chicago segment of the show included famous rock star Ozzy Osbourne, who was there to accompany the British Bulldogs to the ring for their championship match, and Clara Peller, a diminutive old woman who had become a national sensation due to her delivery of the line "Where's the beef?" during commercials for Wendy's Hamburgers.

My former Louisville Cardinals teammate Otis Wilson was also in attendance at *Wrestlemania 2*. He was fresh from being a participant on the Bears' Super Bowl team, and he was in the building to cheer on his teammates. The two of us embraced in the locker room when he tracked me down before the show.

"I told my buddies to keep an eye on *you* in the ring tonight!" Otis informed me. "I *still* remember when you hit me so hard that it almost caved in the practice field!"

Andre the Giant ultimately won the battle royal, which came as no surprise to anybody. His victory was followed by the Bulldogs dethroning the Dream Team to win the tag titles. This would mean that Jim and I would finally be permitted to score some clean pinfall victories over Beefcake and Valentine at house shows, ensuring that fans also saw *us* as viable contenders for the titles. During one of those matches, we had the crowd on their feet and losing their minds at Madison Square Garden. When Jimmy finally reached out and gave me the hot tag, the roof just about blew off of the building.

Right as I was in the middle of my explosive comeback, the bell just started ringing out of the blue. The crowd had been with us, we were booked to win the match, and just like that, all of the electricity just dissipated from the atmosphere. All five of us, including manager Jimmy Valiant, just stood around in the middle of the ring, visibly irritated and upset.

Two nights prior in New Jersey, a 20-minute time limit draw had been the approved finish to the match. Professor Elliot, the timekeeper, had *also* been the timekeeper during that match, and he forgot that we would be using a completely different finish this time. Everyone in our match had been on time and on cue. We had built to a superb crescendo, and just like that, it was all *gone*. When Elliot rang that bell, it killed everything we had worked so hard to build.

I was *so* livid that I chased Elliot around the outside of the ring to try to get an explanation from him. I must have looked as upset as I felt, because he actually ran away from me! It was a very strange sight to see a babyface wrestler stalking the timekeeper around the ring. When I finally caught up with Elliot, I asked him point blank, "*Why* did you ring the bell right then?!"

B. Brian Blair: Truth Bee Told

"I thought we were doing the finish from East Rutherford!" he said. "I'm so sorry! I just thought it was a good time to ring the bell!"

Aiding Pedro Morales as he fights with Greg Valentine

I couldn't hide how devastated and upset I was that a mistake of that magnitude had happened at a venue as significant as Madison Square Garden. To his credit, Professor Elliot called me numerous times to apologize. Once I accepted Elliot's apology, he *still* called me every year for *20 years* to apologize anew, and it became a running joke between us.

Mistakes aside, it was clear to both Jim and I that we were being groomed to be the next babyface tag team to receive a run with the championships. Yet, Jimmy seemed to be inadvertently doing everything he could to rub Vince the wrong way. In fact, the animosity

B. Brian Blair: Truth Bee Told

between the two had begun soon after Jim and I got rolling as a tag team.

According to Jim, when the American Wrestling Association put together their action-figure deal with Remco, his old tag team partner Greg Gagne had authorized Remco to make action figures of the High Flyers. This meant the AWA was actively producing figures with Jim's likeness even though he was under a WWF contract.

This was the first source of tension between Jim and Vince, and the two fought over whether or not Jim should be entitled to any money from the sale of those Remco figures; Jim told me that Vince wanted to keep the money for himself. This was definitely a consequential lawsuit, and Jimmy actually won it.

As perturbing as that must have been for Vince, I'm sure that was a *minor* dispute compared to what happened next. Right around the time of *Wrestlemania 2*, Jesse Ventura attempted to start a wrestlers' union, and Jim was Jesse's most ardent supporter in those efforts. Vince got word of the attempt to unionize and quickly put the kibosh on everything, but not before Jim had been singled out as one of the masterminds behind the unionization fiasco.

From then on, I would have thought Jim would have gone out of his way to get back into Vince's good graces, but something deep within him just prevented him from ingratiating himself with Vince. One of the most obvious examples of this occurred when Vince pulled the two of us into his office to unveil the design of the first official Killer Bees shirt to be sold in the U.S.

"Here it is, guys!" Vince announced, proudly. "What do you think?"

Vince then held out a white ringer t-shirt trimmed with black ribbing. The design in the middle of the shirt said "Killer Bees" in black font with a yellow 3D shadow. Protruding from those words were two blue, jelly-bean shaped ovals that were supposed to be wings, and some grey eyes that more closely resembled the eyes of a fly. It was underwhelming, but Vince was obviously very excited about the design.

"Those are *awesome*!" I said.

The bee *was* confusing, I couldn't figure out the logic of the design, and it didn't look all that appealing to me, but I wasn't about to tell my boss that I thought it looked like shit.

Jimmy didn't have the same filter that I did, so he looked disapprovingly at the shirt design and finally said, "I dunno…"

"You don't *know?*" Vince said, it stunned disbelief.

B. Brian Blair: Truth Bee Told

"Come on, Jimmy!" I said, trying to get him back on track. "It's awesome, man. You just need to open your mind up! Look at that! It's a bee with the eyes and the wings!"

"I guess...," shrugged Jimmy.

No matter what the shirt looked like, it would be nice to finally get some money from merchandise sales, and if we remained popular, there would always be a chance to get a different design made. Moments like that made me worry that Jimmy would cause Vince to be even less excited about pushing the Killer Bees all the way to the top of the company.

Our shirt may not have had the coolest design, but it still sold very well with the fans as our popularity grew. However, not everyone was appreciative of our newfound popularity. Big John Studd and King Kong Bundy – two gargantuan wrestlers who were frequent adversaries of Hulk Hogan, and who could believably put the 300-pound champion in peril – were asked to put over Brunzie and I in Nassau Coliseum.

"Vince wants the Bees to go over," Chief Jay Strongbow explained to them. "That's how it's gonna be."

That didn't sit well with Bundy *at all*.

"We've got a title match in Madison Square Garden in two weeks!" objected Bundy. "A lot of these people go back and forth! How are they gonna expect us to win the title match if the Bees beat us and we're two times bigger than both of them!"

"It's a *work*," piped in Strongbow. "*Anybody* can beat *anybody* in this business."

"But it has to *look* like a shoot though!" Bundy replied.

"Well, if you do your jobs right, you can *make* it look like a shoot!" Strongbow said. "Put the Bees *over*!"

Bundy moaned and groaned for an entire week starting from the moment Chief gave us the finish to the match, and then he continued complaining for *another* full week after the match ended.

It was around this time that Billy Red Lyons suggested what would become the most memorable calling card of the Killer Bees. We were in the locker room in Toronto, and Billy was describing for us how he and Dewey Robertson used to rely on masks to pull off the illegal switch against the babyface teams when they wrestled as the heel Crusaders.

"You guys are such good babyfaces," Billy said. "Why don't you try to *outheel* the heels? You can beat the heels at their own game."

B. Brian Blair: Truth Bee Told

Gaining the advantage with Masked Confusion

Not only did Jimmy and I both absolutely *adore* this idea, but Vince loved it as well. We quickly arranged for Olivia Walker to design some masks for us, and the response from the fans was pure elation whenever we used the masks to pull off a switch.

We always made sure the heels got sufficient heat on us before we donned the masks. That way the people in the arenas were so incensed by the cheating the heels were engaged in that they didn't care how we went about pulling out the victory. As long as the *heels* didn't win, they were happy. In fact, they were overjoyed that the bad guys had received a taste of their own medicine. Before long, Lord Alfred Hayes coined the term "masked confusion" to describe our actions whenever we donned the masks to outsmart the heels.

If we had just come straight out with the masks on and started doing illegal switches throughout our matches without provocation from the heels, the fans undoubtedly would have turned against us. At best, it would have been a 50-50 reaction.

There was also a hidden upside to the gimmick: If the Killer Bees ever needed to become a heel team, the masks that the fans enjoyed so much would cause them to become *irate* if it was ever implemented against the other babyface teams.

B. Brian Blair: Truth Bee Told

The masks only added to our already soaring level of popularity. There were a few times we even came to the ring already wearing the masks, but then we would take them off before the matches got underway. The idea was to show the masks to the fans to let them know the masks were available, and to add a bit of intrigue to the match. Fans would then be watching the entire time wondering whether or not the masks would become a factor in the outcome.

The Killer Bees fly high at *The Big Event*

Orndorff and Hogan had been on-screen friends for about a year by the middle of 1986, but then Paul suddenly turned against Terry during a nationally televised tag team match, and most wrestling fans were out for his blood. Their subsequent feud resulted in some record-breaking box office numbers, including a show called *The Big Event* on August 26th, 1986, at Exhibition Stadium in Toronto, which attracted a mind-blowing 74,000 fans to the venue.

The Killer Bees squared off against Jimmy Jack Funk and Hoss Funk in the opening match, and we beat them in just under seven minutes. Hoss Funk was the legendary Dory Funk Jr., but Jimmy Jack Funk was a *fake* Funk. It was actually Jesse Barr, one of my favorite-ever opponents from back in the Florida territory.

Aside from gaining the Bees a victory on such a prominent stage, this match resulted in one of my favorite photos ever taken of the Killer Bees during our run as a tag team. The photographer caught

Jimmy at the apex of his leap – a full six feet in the air – dropkicking Hoss Funk directly in the face. To this day, it is perhaps the most awesome dropkick I've ever witnessed. All of this was framed perfectly amidst the sea of humanity in the background while flashbulbs flared throughout the crowd. It's an *awesome* scene.

Right in the middle of a period when it seemed like nothing could go wrong, an incident occurred that would reshape the complexion of Paul's career, and also reshape his body. Terry did his typical move where he would hurl Paul into the corner turnbuckles, and then he followed that up with a big clothesline to the chest. This time, Terry clipped Paul on the chin, and it caused a severely pinched nerve in Paul's neck. Once the soreness from the match wore off and the pain still lingered, Paul began to complain to me about it. About a month later, Paul noticed that his arm was measurably weaker than it had been before the initial damage had occurred.

"You'd better go get that checked out!" I warned him.

Paul did *not* get it checked out, and it's difficult for me to fault him. During that main-event run with Hogan, Paul was showing me his weekly payoff checks, which were all between $25,000 and $35,000. When you were raised in a chicken coop, and now you're making unfathomable money every week, you simply don't do anything to jeopardize that. I can understand why Paul wouldn't want to put a halt to the highest-earning period of his career. We had *never* seen money like that being made in wrestling before.

Granted, I was in the process of making about $200,000 that year – *without* merchandise – which was an absolute *killing* for someone that was used to making as much as $2,000 a week during *very* good weeks. By main-eventing against Hulk Hogan, Paul was able to top my best yearly payoff total ever in just *two* months.

Blinded by the money, Paul refused to take *any* time off to either heal his arm or have it examined, and the arm began to atrophy more and more. It wasn't long before Paul was working with a right arm that was noticeably smaller than his left arm.

As usual, Paul and I were in the dressing room throwing around different ideas prior to one of his matches against Hogan at the Cap Center. I'd always make suggestions to Paul before his matches, and he welcomed the input. Sometimes he'd take the suggestions and sometimes he wouldn't. On this occasion, Paul was preoccupied with the posing routines that Terry typically performed before, during and after his matches.

"You know how Terry goes out and does the bow-and-arrow and all those other poses?" Paul began. "*My* body blows *his* away!"

B. Brian Blair: Truth Bee Told

There wasn't the slightest bit of a joke evident in Paul's tone. He was dead serious.

"Yeah, Paul... you *do* have a better body than Terry in *some* ways," I responded, attempting to provide him with a fair assessment. "You d*efinitely* have better abs than him. And your legs look a *lot* better than his."

"Yeah!" agreed Paul. "He *never* shows off his legs. I've got awesome quads. I need to show those more!"

"You should go out and mimic him," I instructed Paul. "Do the bow-and-arrow thing and do everything else he does. Then you should show your abs, but make sure you're sweaty so that all the definition can be seen."

"Yeah!" Paul replied, as he admired himself in the mirror. "This is *good*!"

"Then you can point to his quads, and then flex and point to *your* quads," I continued.

"This is great!" Paul said. "I like it; I like it!"

"Then, to really pop the crowd... You know how Terry does the big crab flex with his lats out, and he pops his deltoids and his chest?" I asked Paul.

"Yeah, I know what you mean," Paul said.

"Okay... well that's when you break out the *fiddler* crab!" I suggested.

"Yeah, okay!" Paul said.

Then Paul's face sank as the meaning behind my suggestion suddenly dawned on him.

"Fiddler?" Paul erupted. "*Fiddler*?! You no-good cocksucker!"

The boys in the locker room who had been listening in really popped when they heard my comment to Paul. A fiddler crab has one little arm and one big arm. It was *just* like Paul. As obsessed with his appearance as Paul was, that comment *crushed* him. He *really* got upset over it. From that point on, Paul would regularly ask me, "Do I *really* look like fiddler crab? How bad is it getting?"

Paul probably would have made a lot more money in the long run if he had gotten his neck fixed in the early stages of his injury. In his prime, Paul was undoubtedly one of the greatest heels in the history of the wrestling business, and getting surgery would have extended his career and his marketability. I have nowhere near the knowledge of a doctor, but I'd had enough operations by that point to know that the longer you wait, the less likely it is that your body is going to heal properly. Injuries are a part of the wrestling game, and you *need* to take the time to recover and get your body fixed so that you can extend your career.

I'm not sure to what extent the years of constant steroid use exacerbated Paul's injury, if at all. Back then, guys were lining up in the locker room to see Dr. George Zahorian and purchase steroids from him. I was in line with everyone else, and even had steroids sent to my house, but I *never* used steroids to the extent that many of the other guys would. Every once in a while, Jimmy and I would get six bottles of deca-durabolin, primarily because it helped our joints to heal so effectively. We would take one shot every two weeks or so strictly for that purpose, and the prodigious steroid users in the locker room would *laugh* at us.

"Come on, man!" Hercules would say. "You guys need to get on the juice *for real!*"

Demonstrating some holds with Coach Ken Lloyd

B. Brian Blair: Truth Bee Told

For what it's worth, I never had any intention of becoming a big muscle guy. I wanted to look more like my hero Jack Brisco, and just work out hard, eat right and take less intrusive supplements. I always wanted to be strong, but the heaviest bench press I've ever performed in my life is 385 pounds, with a squat of 400 pounds.

The squat figure of 400 pounds was just an ego number for me. I performed *one* rep at 400 pounds exactly *one* time in my life to Paul Orndorff's strict, exacting standards simply to get him off my back and to fulfill my own ego. Other than that, I preferred to play it safe and do reps with 225 pounds. Meanwhile, Orndorff could do squat reps with 550 pounds, with *strict* form, like it was nothing. He was an absolute *animal* in the gym.

As 1986 drew to its conclusion, Vince showed his clear support for the Killer Bees in some less obvious ways. In November, the WWF allowed me to use their television program to promote a Tampa-area wrestling tournament I was hosting with the Police Athletic League for kids under the age of 15. Coach Lloyd helped me to get it organized, along with Corporal Larry Siegel of the PAL.

Vince went all the way with his support, permitting us to use the WWF logo, and even purchasing t-shirts and trophies for all of the kids. The week after the tournament, I did a quick follow-up interview about the event alongside Jesse Ventura. They aired footage of the event while Jesse – in classic heel form – insisted to me that instead of hosting the event for charity, I should have been "... doing it *for the money!*"

Later that same month, on what was essentially the Thanksgiving edition of *Saturday Night's Main Event* on NBC, a national television audience watched the Killer Bees as we picked up our most meaningful victory to date. In the highest-rated segment of the night, and in what was billed as a match to determine the top contenders for the WWF World Tag Team Championship, Jimmy and I utilized a bit of masked confusion to defeat the Hart Foundation.

During a critical juncture of the match, the Hart Foundation hurled Jimmy to the outside of the ring and out onto the floor. From there, the two of us donned our masks. I took Jimmy's place in the ring, unbeknownst to the Harts, and began to pound away at them. At the very end of the bout, Jimmy and I pulled the switch again, and Jimmy was able to secure a small package on the unsuspecting Bret Hart to garner the pinfall victory. The fans *erupted* over the finish. They were elated, and so were we.

Yet, despite the promise that the winner of that match would receive a shot at the tag titles, that opportunity never came. Perhaps

B. Brian Blair: Truth Bee Told

Vince had the thought in his head of having the Bees turn heel and use the masks to score a title win over the Bulldogs, but it was never brought up or came to pass. Dynamite Kid suffered a horrific back injury in the middle of December, and he missed all of his remaining dates in December and January.

Reportedly, Vince wanted the Bulldogs to hand the belts over to him, and Dynamite declined. Then Vince asked the Bulldogs to drop the belts to the Iron Sheik and Nikolai Volkoff, probably so that they could transfer the belts over to us a few months later at *Wrestlemania III*. Once again, Dynamite refused, and then he insisted that he would only come back to publicly drop the belts if the Bulldogs were going to be losing them to the Hart Foundation.

Killer Bees featured in the national Toyota Hilux commercial

I was okay with this, because we had just beaten the Hart Foundation on national television, and we were logically next in line for the titles after they held them. In the meantime, everything that transpired behind the scenes was simply a further indication to Jim and I that we were destined for great things. We were featured in a national television commercial for the 1987 Toyota Hilux pickup truck, while Gene Okerlund provided the voiceover. We were also the most prominent wrestlers in that year's commercial for the WWF's LJN action figure line. Next to Hulk Hogan, we were receiving more mainstream moneymaking opportunities than any of the other talents on the WWF roster.

B. Brian Blair: Truth Bee Told

In March of 1987, we were all back in Toronto for the Frank Tunney Sr. Memorial Tag Team Tournament, and Mr. T stood in the corner of the Killer Bees during the tournament. We were such good friends at that point, and he always insisted on riding with me.

The field for the tournament featured the reigning tag team champions, the British Bulldogs, along with newcomers Demolition and the Can-Am Connection – a team comprising former AWA World Heavyweight Champion Rick Martel and Tom Zenk. In the first round, Jim and I defeated Sika of the Wild Samoans and Kamala the Ugandan Giant, who was actually my old buddy Sugar Bear Harris painted up and recast as a Ugandan headhunter.

**Champions of the 1987
Frank Tunney Sr. Memorial Tag Team Tournament**

In the second round, Jim and I earned a victory over King Kong Bundy and Paul Orndorff, while Paul was still at the height of his success as a heel. In the final match, we defeated Demolition to claim the tournament championship. This major victory in a tag team tournament just two weeks before *Wrestlemania III* further cemented the idea in our minds that Vince McMahon intended for us to be the next babyface team to capture the gold. In fact, Vince had even gone so far as to *promise* the belts to Jimmy and I, and this promise was subsequently confirmed by George Scott.

B. Brian Blair: Truth Bee Told

Even without the belts around our waists, Jim and I proved we could perform at a high level under duress. Moreover, we proved we could deliver great matches even on nights when the WWF management team made us miserable before we ever stepped into the ring.

Athletic commissioner Richard Herring offered Toni and I the opportunity to spend some time together at an awesome ski resort in the Catskill Mountains, and we readily accepted his kind offer. However, the result of this was that I was late arriving to Madison Square Garden because we had been forced to slowly navigate ourselves through the Catskill Mountains amidst a snowstorm.

Our car was slipping and sliding all over the roads, so we had to slow things down dramatically just to get through it all safely. As a result, I was *very* late for that night's scheduled match featuring the Killer Bees against the Hart Foundation. Toni and I arrived at the Garden with barely any time left for me to get dressed before I was due to step in the ring.

When we finally ran into the building, Vince was *really* pissed off at me.

"Goddammit!" Vince yelled. "I can't afford to hold up a show in the Garden because *you* want to take your time getting here. There's *no* excuse for it!"

As I rushed to change into my ring gear and Jim stood nearby, Blackjack Lanza approached us.

"You're getting fined $500 for being late, Brian," he said.

I was already stressed out from having to drive in through the blizzard. Finding out I was being fined on top of it definitely dampened my mood even further. I would simply have to suck it up and jog out to the ring as a babyface while pretending to be exuberant and happy. That was asinine timing on the part of Lanza.

The agents always seemed to enjoy slamming you with bad news as expediently and directly as possible, even if it meant compromising the quality of your in-ring performance. And, if you *did* have a bad performance, they would have blamed *that* on you as well. It would have been a much fairer move for Lanza to wait until I had already gone out and worked my match before delivering the unwelcome news to me.

Jack's timing really could not have been much worse. The Hart Foundation was standing in the middle of the ring waiting in front of a sold-out Madison Square Garden, and Howard Finkel had already announced the entrance of the Killer Bees. Meanwhile, my boots weren't even laced up yet, and I was in a state of *sheer* panic.

B. Brian Blair: Truth Bee Told

"Come on, Beep!" Jim yelled. "We gotta go!"

We hadn't discussed any of the spots for the match beforehand, and we only knew the finish. Fortunately, we had worked with the Hart Foundation so many times that it really didn't matter at all. We had a *tremendous* match that went to a time-limit draw. All four of us busted our asses in the ring that night. The fans were into everything we did, and the electricity in the building was palpable.

The Hart Foundation Vs. The Killer Bees

Our match went so well that I had *completely* forgotten about the fine that had been levied against me. Brunzie and I hugged when we came back through the curtain, and we were joined by Bret Hart and Jim Neidhart a few seconds later. Vince didn't say anything to Jim and I directly, but we could tell from his expression that he was *very* impressed with what he'd just witnessed.

"Great match, guys!" Bret said. "*Hell* of a match!"

From there, I hit the showers, and as I was getting dressed, I saw Lanza marching back over to me. That's when it dawned on me that I had pretty much just delivered one of the best matches of my career at a drastic discount, since $500 would be deducted from my $1,250 payoff.

"Hey, Brian," Blackjack said. "Vince loved that match so much that he's *not* gonna fine you!"

"Really?" I asked.

"Yeah," Lanza confirmed. "He said you guys worked too hard in that match, and that he couldn't fine you with a clear conscience."

B. Brian Blair: Truth Bee Told

"Please tell him I said I really appreciate that, because I've been worried the whole time," I said.

"How did you have a match *that* good if you were worried about being fined?" laughed Jack.

"I have *no* idea, Jack!" I said, as bitterly and sarcastically as I could. "It just happened!"

Jim and I had proven everything we ever needed to prove in order to be rewarded with a title reign. With the biggest event in the WWF's history – *Wrestlemania III* – coming right around the corner, we knew the Killer Bees were destined for great things over the course of the next year.

In the end, both of us would be extremely surprised by the huge difference just *one year* could make.

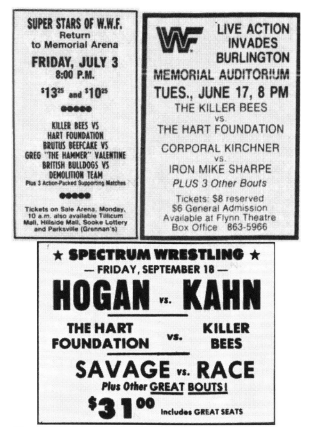

Everywhere we went: The Bees Vs. The Harts

TWENTY – *Peaks and valleys*

Since I was such good friends with Terry, and Terry was so close to Vince, I was frequently riding around with both of them during the buildup to *Wrestlemania III* and the looming main-event showdown between Hulk Hogan and Andre the Giant, with the WWF World Heavyweight Championship on the line. That meant I got to hang out with them in Learjets and limousines while listening in on all the inside gossip as the big event drew nearer.

When we got to the hotel the night before the show, Vince had reserved a big suite for himself on the top floor. Throughout the evening, Vince was sharing some of the show's projected performance numbers with us, and we were having difficulty grasping what he was telling us. He told us he was expecting close to 100,000 people to show up, which sounded like an impossible number. We were all drinking champagne, getting tipsy, and celebrating the success of the event *before* it had even happened. It was also a nice time to connect more closely with Vince and to get to know him on a personal level. He was fully relaxed and reveling in the extraordinary achievements of his company.

Receiving the Toyota commercial had been too good to be true for the Bees, but Jim felt compelled to up the ante a little bit more. He purchased black-and-yellow high-top shoes for both of us to wear during our bout at *Wrestlemania III*. He rightly assumed that more sets of eyes would see *Wrestlemania III* than had viewed any other wrestling event in history, and wearing those shoes might help us to secure sponsorship from Nike for the two of us.

Without a doubt, when *Wrestlemania III* ultimately occurred on March 29th, 1987, it was the most significant event in the history of professional wrestling at the time that it happened, and maybe even to this day. It broke all sorts of attendance records and box-office records. There were more than 93,000 fans in attendance, and Vince pulled out all of the stops with that show. The spectacle included celebrity appearances from singers like Aretha Franklin and Alice Cooper, and extended to the inclusion of special ring entrances for almost all of us. We were shuttled to the ring while standing on motorized carts that had been customized to look like miniature wrestling rings, complete with turnbuckles and ring ropes.

Sadly, none of the same care and creativity that went into the planning of the show was devoted to the matchup between the Killer Bees and Volkoff and the Iron Sheik. The buildup to our match bore all of the signs of the calamity and indecision that marred the tag team championship scene at the time.

B. Brian Blair: Truth Bee Told

In order to make good on his promise to Dynamite Kid, Vince had to hold off on transitioning the belts to the Hart Foundation until the end of January. There was no time to get the belts off of one heel team and then onto the Killer Bees in a meaningful way, and Vince didn't seem to want to diminish the significance of the moment when Jim and I were ultimately crowned as the tag team champions.

The Killer Bees at the Wrestlemania III press conference with Ricky "The Dragon" Steamboat

Because of this, Jim and I faced the Sheik and Volkoff in the penultimate contest of the evening with *no* tag titles on the line. This distinction critically lowered the intrigue of the bout, because the match was now a grudge match instead of a title match, and the booking of the show hadn't established any reason why the Killer Bees were supposed to *hate* Volkoff and the Sheik.

Vince's idea to counteract this was to insert Hacksaw Jim Duggan into the equation. Hacksaw had just arrived, fresh out of the Universal Wrestling Federation, which was how Bill Watts had rebranded his Mid South promotion in his own attempt to promote nationally. Duggan would be playing the role of a flag-waving, patriotic babyface, and that cast him as a natural foil for the Sheik and Volkoff, who symbolically represented two of the United States' chief adversaries: Iran and the Soviet Union.

B. Brian Blair: Truth Bee Told

As Brunzie and I waited to be introduced to the crowd, Nikolai Volkoff began singing the national anthem of the Soviet Union, and boos from the crowd rained down upon him. Duggan then stormed into the ring brandishing a wooden 2x4 board with a miniature American flag taped to it, along with a stars-and-stripes headband wrapped around his head. From there, Duggan grabbed the microphone and made a patriotic speech that turned the boos of the crowd into cheers. Frankly, the presentation of the scene probably did more to shift the crowd's focus to the interaction between Duggan and our adversaries, and deemphasized the involvement of the Killer Bees.

With all of that being said, when Jimmy and I were ushered through the curtain and were within view of that awe-inspiring crowd, it was an *indescribable* feeling. It was impossible to feel like we hadn't made it to the pinnacle of our profession. Howard Finkel introduced us to the crowd, and the roar from those 93,000 fans was earth-shattering.

"At a total combined weight of 474 pounds… here are B. Brian Blair… "Jumping" Jim Brunzell… The Killer Bees!" announced Finkel, as the crowd exploded into cheers and applause.

The match itself lasted less than seven minutes. Nikolai was somewhat limited in terms of what he could do in the ring, and the layout of the bout did more to elevate Jim Duggan than it did the Killer Bees. The Sheik put his camel clutch submission hold on Brunzie, and Duggan chased Nikolai in and out of the ring before turning around and whacking the Sheik on the back with the 2x4 for a disqualification ending. Duggan got to look strong, Volkoff and the Sheik were awarded the disqualification win, and the Killer Bees received *no benefit* from the outcome of the match.

For the record, *Wrestlemania III* would be the *only* Wrestlemania event of the first *twenty* Wrestlemanias that did *not* include a match for the tag team championship. The luck of the Killer Bees was historically bad.

However, there were honestly no *true* losers at *Wrestlemania III*. Simply by being a participant on that show, it seemed like everyone became an even bigger star than they had previously been. Jimmy and I received a deluge of fan mail from people who had watched wrestling for the very first time as a result of the hoopla surrounding that show, so we were even bigger stars than we had ever been before.

It seemed like we were on a high that we could never come down from. Little did we know, we would come crashing down from that high in just two short months.

B. Brian Blair: Truth Bee Told

Things took a sharp turn for the Killer Bees shortly after *Wrestlemania III*. The WWF's schedule was very demanding. Vince placed us on a tour where we wrestled for 67 straight days, and the travel schedule included stops in Australia and Italy. I was feeling *so* burnt out, but that was nothing compared to how Jimmy was feeling. I would hear him talking on the phone with his wife Mary every night about how he was routinely missing important family events like middle school graduations and elementary school graduations.

Mary would describe these milestone events to Jimmy while he sat tethered to the phone in our hotel room, and I would see the tears welling up in his eyes. I could clearly see the toll that our schedule was taking on him. Tours for the American Wrestling Association had allowed Jimmy to take sufficient time off, and they always concluded their tours in Minneapolis. This allowed Jimmy to spend relatively large amounts of time at home with his family. Staying out on the road for months at a time, often overseas, with no breaks in between required a superior level of mental *and* physical endurance than many of us simply weren't used to mustering up.

The psychological pain had far less to do with the time spent in transit, and far more to do with the absence of loved ones and familiar surroundings. When you wrestled in a territory like Florida, wrestling for 67 days in a row was nothing because we still got to sleep in our own beds every night if we wished to. The WWF's schedule didn't allow for that convenience under any circumstances.

There were certainly some enjoyable nights during that period of time. There were a few nights when we put a Killer Bee mask on Koko B. Ware (Vince had brilliantly added a "B" initial to his name) when he tagged with us, and the fans absolutely ate it up. Those were definitely some fun nights to go to work in the ring, but once the shows were over with, the misery would set in once again.

As that long stretch of matches was winding down, Jimmy asked Vince if we could take some time off, and I think that spelled the end for our chances of ever winning the tag team championships. In mid '80s, the WWF had three different crews running shows simultaneously, and the tag team champions were commonly relied upon to wrestle in the main events of the "B" or "C" shows. Saying you wanted to take time off was equivalent to letting Vince know you lacked the mental toughness to endure life on the road and do what was required of a title holder.

To top it off, Jimmy already wasn't the sort of guy that Vince was going to go out of his way to push at that point. He had already drawn the ire of Vince due to his direct participation in Jesse Ventura's attempt to unionize the wrestlers just prior to *Wrestlemania 2*, and he also hadn't exuberantly embraced all of Vince's marketing plans for us.

Entering with my groomsmen:
Kevin Blair, Paul Orndorff and Hulk Hogan

Toni and I pose with my groomsmen in our Swatch sunglasses

B. Brian Blair: Truth Bee Told

Last but not least, Jim had personally contacted Nike after *Wrestlemania III* requesting sponsorship from them after we had worn those black-and-yellow Nike tennis shoes in the ring. Nike wrote him back to inform him that professional wrestling was beneath their standards, and they would not be allocating any money toward sponsoring a pair of wrestlers. I'm not sure if Vince ever found out about this, but if he did, I'm *sure* he wasn't thrilled.

Either way, when Jimmy asked for time off it was probably the final straw for Vince. In the blink of an eye, we went from winning all of our matches against everyone prior to *Wrestlemania III*, including our matches against Demolition, to losing to Demolition almost every night for *four* consecutive months. During that same period of time, all of the momentum that we'd once had as the top babyface tag team seemed to slide over to Rick Martel and Tom Zenk of the Can-Am Connection.

In the midst of my professional demotion, a pleasant, life-changing event occurred in my personal life. Toni and I got married that July in a beautiful ceremony in Tampa. The event was better attended than some of the shows I'd wrestled in during my career. It was standing room only in the church, with at least 500 people present. Paul Orndorff and Hulk Hogan stood next to me as my groomsmen, alongside my middle brother Kevin. All of us arrived fashionably late to the wedding. Hogan's wife at the time, Linda, insisted on getting some giant Swatch sunglasses for all of us.

At the appointed time, the four of us marched straight up to the pastor, John Debevoise. We all wore the Swatch sunglasses during our walk to the front of the chapel and struck a pose once we reached the front of the room. Then we all took the sunglasses off in unison and stuck them in our pockets. It was a highly choreographed moment, and the audience popped *big* for it.

It definitely broke kayfabe for Terry and Paul to be my groomsmen at that point in time. Paul was still working as a heel then, and the feud between him and Terry had been seasoned by betrayal and bitter hatred. Wrestling fans would have lost their minds if they'd seen the two of them together in a friendly setting that summer.

I can't say that being a lifelong friend of the biggest star in wrestling history didn't have its perks. I was hanging out in the locker room during an event at the LA Memorial Sports Arena when Terry came up to me and said, "I want you to meet a friend of mine: Willie G. Davidson."

Being the fan of motorcycles that I am, I became absolutely *giddy* when the Hulkster said that.

B. Brian Blair: Truth Bee Told

"You mean the Harley-Davidson guy?" I asked.

"Yeah, brother!" said Terry. "Come with me."

Terry walked me over and introduced me to Willie, and I was grinning from ear to ear as I was shaking his hand. I'd owned motorcycles ever since I was 14 years old, starting with my Yamaha 200. By that point, I'd also owned a Husqvarna 360, a water-cooled Suzuki 750, and both a Suzuki 125 and Suzuki 175. For me, this was like meeting a member of the royal family, and in a sense it was. Willie Davidson was *undoubtedly* motorcycle royalty.

The conversation between Willie and Terry was very humorous because each man kept trying to steer the topic back to the *other* man's claim to fame. Willie was interested in wrestling and had all kinds of questions about what went on in the ring and behind the scenes, but Terry was equally as interested in learning about motorcycles.

In the midst of the conversation, Willie stared at Terry and me for a moment, and then he casually asked, "Hey, do you guys want *bikes*?"

Terry and I both looked at each other with perplexed expressions, because neither of us truly grasped what Willie was offering us.

"If you guys want bikes, I can get you the bikes at cost," Willie clarified. "We've got the new Softail customs coming out."

"Hell yeah! *I'll* take one!" Terry said.

Terry could afford whatever he wanted, but in my head, I was making some rapid calculations. I knew a Harley like the one Willie was describing was probably going to cost between $12,000 to $15,000. Without knowing what the cost of the bike was, I wasn't sure I could just casually agree to that offer, no matter how generous it was. I also wasn't sure if I would even be around to ride the bike given how much time we were all spending on the road. All of this raced through my head, but in the end, there was only one acceptable answer I could give.

"Yeah, sure!" I finally replied to Willie. "Thank you *so* much!"

It wasn't every day that one of the Davidson family members *personally* offered me a custom motorcycle, even if it wouldn't be totally free. I didn't see how I could possibly refuse him.

Shortly thereafter, we met a friend of Willie's by the name of Tony Carlini, who was a renowned designer of motorcycle handlebars. We then drove over to Tony's house and met another man there named Arlen Ness, who was himself a famous motorcycle designer. To put this into its proper perspective, this was like meeting an entire wing of the Motorcycle Hall of Fame!

Collaboratively, the three men sat around inside Tony's massive garage and brainstormed with Terry and I to try to develop the custom motorcycles of our respective dreams. Obviously, Hogan was the star in that equation, and the three motorcycle specialists were all doing their best to appease the Hulkster. I was more or less along for the ride, but they were all still very kind to me.

While we conversed, the phone rang inside of the garage, and Tony pressed a button on his speakerphone. This moment stands out so clearly for me because it was my first time seeing a speakerphone in action, even though they would soon become commonplace. On the other end of the line was Tony's stockbroker calling him with some investment advice regarding a particular stock.

"If you sell right now, you'll make about $300,000," the stockbroker advised Tony.

"Hey, I don't have time for *this*!" Tony replied, sounding truly annoyed by the interruption. "I'm with my friends: Hulk *Hogan* and B. Brian Blair. I'll call you back later!"

The receipt for my custom Harley-Davidson motorcycle

Terry and I exchanged amused glances. This guy was willing to jeopardize a potential payday of $300,000 just to spend time designing motorcycles for the two of us, for which he would make *no* money! It was *incredible*. Either this guy had money to a degree that we couldn't fathom, or he was simply *that* delighted by the idea of spending time

B. Brian Blair: Truth Bee Told

with two WWF wrestling stars, one of whom was the biggest wrestling star in the entire world.

A few months later, the two bikes that Arlen customized for Terry and I arrived in Tampa under the name "Terry Bollea." I had to swing by Barnes Harley-Davidson on Hillsborough Avenue to pick up my Harley-Davidson with a custom paint job featuring a customized killer bee on the side of its tanks. The bee was shown to be emerging from a hive with an Uzi submachine gun in its hand. The total price came to $4,589 including the shipping and customization. I still have that bike to this day, and it runs like a charm. It only has 14,000 miles on it, and the receipt sits in a frame above my desk.

It was very nice of Terry to include me in the deal, because this was clearly all arranged out of the desire of Willie, Tony and Arlen to make the Hulkster happy. In 1987, *everyone* wanted to make Hogan happy. His popularity was literally at the same level as a rock star's. It isn't at all far-fetched to say Hogan was the Michael Jordan of wrestling, except in 1987 Terry was probably an even *bigger* deal globally than Michael Jordan was.

Terry *certainly* made out very well in this deal, too. Tony Carlini customized a long, stretch motorcycle for Hogan, befitting a world heavyweight champion. It had a giant, red-and-yellow logo on it that said "Hulkster," and featured huge, ape-hanger handlebars. The front and back end of this monster were both extended. Tony and Arlen had built this behemoth for Terry piece by piece.

I think the fact that the bike was so heavily customized made Terry a little bit nervous, because by the time we got the bike back to Terry's house, he was actually *afraid* to ride it.

"Hey, Beeber… how 'bout *you* go ahead and ride this thing for me, brother," Terry offered. "See how it runs."

"You want to make *me* the guinea pig?!" I laughed. "Okay!"

I climbed on the Hulkster's motorcycle, started it up, and sped off toward the Sunshine Skyway – a beautiful bridge that wasn't too far from Terry's house. It's the highest of the three bridges that connect Hillsborough County and Pinellas County. I reached the top of the Skyway, and the bike started shaking a little bit. It was the evening, and there wasn't a whole lot of light up there. I was concerned about the departing daylight, but I became far more alarmed when I became aware of the gradually increasing heat that crept into my crotch. Pretty soon, it felt like my *balls* were burning.

When Arlen and Tony built the bike, they built it with a gap between the seat and the gas tank. That meant the head of the motor – the hottest part of the vehicle – was placed right where my crotch sat.

B. Brian Blair: Truth Bee Told

All the heat from the motor was building up and then being funneled *directly* into my groin.

I slowed the bike down to 60 miles per hour in the hopes that it would cool off a bit, and people began to pass me all along the Skyway as they zoomed by at 80 miles per hour. At a height of 300 feet above the waters of Tampa Bay, it felt like the entire bridge was swaying. By the time I reached the bottom of the Skyway, I couldn't even sit down on the seat of the bike because I would have been seriously burned.

Admiring the custom Killer Bee Harley with Koko B. Ware

After pulling into Terry's driveway, I leapt off the bike as quickly and unceremoniously as I could while still bringing the Frankenstein motorcycle to a safe stop. I then bounded along the driveway in incredible pain as I lowered my head to assess the damage to my crotch.

"Are you okay, Beeber?" Terry asked. "What happened?"

As I stepped into the light of Terry's driveway and took a closer look at my nether regions, I could see that Terry's custom bike had burned my jeans and left black-and-brown marks in all of the areas where the jeans had made contact with the Harley.

"Are *you* okay?!" repeated Terry.

"Yeah... I *think* so!" I lied.

Terry decided this gave him the permission he'd needed to finally let loose with the belt of laughter he had been suppressing.

B. Brian Blair: Truth Bee Told

"Damn!" Terry said. "It's a good thing I let *you* ride it first, brother!"

As cool as custom-made motorcycles are, there are risks involved with them. They're more likely to have problems that need correcting in comparison to bikes that are all the same and roll out of the factory by the thousands. When everything is pieced together in a unique configuration, it's less likely that the designers have tested out that specific arrangement of parts. In short, *that's* how I wound up with scorched balls.

After my painful experience with Terry's custom motorcycle, I was in so much pain that I had to sleep with my legs apart for an entire week in the aftermath.

During those rare occasions when I did get to spend time in Tampa, I tried to make appearances at different schools around the area. Vince put together a highlight tape with some footage from my matches in Madison Square Garden for me to show the kids whenever I gave presentations at the local schools.

The kids *always* seemed spellbound by the sight of a sold-out Madison Square Garden, with fans packing the aisles and screaming their heads off. I accentuated the presentation of my highlight reel with the story of how I'd attended big-people's church and prayed for God to turn me into Superman.

"Be careful what you pray for," I'd warn them. "You just saw me on the television, which is where Superman lived. No, I didn't have a blue-red-and-yellow outfit on with a big "S" on my chest, but I did have a black-and-yellow outfit on with a *bee* on my back. I could run the ropes like a speeding bullet and leapfrog over a man in a single bound. I could withstand a 300-pound man leaping off of the very top rope and landing on my chest, and I could still walk away from it. I lived through *all* of that so that I could be here with you guys today. That's about as close to Superman as I think *anyone* can truly get."

From there, I would tell the children to be confident in themselves, to not be cocky, and to *never* act like bullies.

"When you believe, you achieve, and when you achieve, you *receive!*" I encouraged them.

The eyes of the kids in those classrooms would light right up, and they would nod along with me in agreement. Professional wrestling created such a controlled, colorful, athletic environment that children truly believed in our ability to execute superhuman feats of strength, endurance and agility. There was no other display of entertainment on Earth that was anything like it, and it was a privilege to be able to convince kids that superheroes were real, and that they could all become heroes as well.

Enjoying my special bike

TWENTY-ONE – *The master ribbers*

My ex-wife Mike McGuirk arrived in the WWF early in 1987 and shared ring-announcing duties with Howard Finkel. I was honestly happy to see her. It's not like there hadn't been good times between us, and Mike's mother Dorothy had always been especially kind to me. There was no longer any ill will remaining from our failed marriage, and both of us had moved on. For the entire duration we spent together as WWF employees and coworkers, we got along perfectly well.

Another person who arrived in the WWF in early 1987 was Outback Jack, and as the year progressed, he gradually grew to be *extremely* cocky and arrogant. He was the *ultimate* story topper. No matter what you said you'd accomplished in life, Jack had *always* done it better. This helped him to mark himself as a clear target for the British Bulldogs and Mr. Fuji, who would routinely collaborate and then go out of their way to rib Jack. Typically, Fuji was the mastermind behind the ribs, and then the Bulldogs would venture out to execute the ribs at Fuji's behest.

We were in San Francisco during the West Coast leg of a long tour, and Jack was relentlessly antagonizing Fuji and trying to rope him into a drinking competition later that evening.

"Why don't you have drinking contest with one of Bulldogs instead?" offered Fuji, in his semi-broken English.

"No way, Fuji!" said Outback. "You're the one who keeps saying you can drink *so* much beer. I want to drink against *you*!"

"Okay! We meet at bar after the matches," Fuji agreed.

We were all staying at one of the Holiday Inns near the San Francisco International Airport. Once we got back from wrestling that evening, we all went to the bar to observe this drinking showdown between two of the WWF's most colorful personalities.

Mr. Fuji and Outback Jack took up positions at the far corner of the bar that would enable the pair to stare directly into one another's eyes as they faced off. The Bulldogs were appointed as the official referees of the contest, while Brunzell and I were watching closely from behind Mr. Fuji.

"Get the beer flowin', mate!" Outback instructed the bartender.

A pitcher of beer was presented to the men, which they used to fill their glasses to the brim. They then clinked their glasses together to salute one another, and then downed the golden liquid as rapidly as they could.

B. Brian Blair: Truth Bee Told

While Davey Boy kept Jack distracted, Fuji handed a tiny bottle of about 10 crushed halcyon tablets to Dynamite Kid. When it was apparent that Outback's attention was hopelessly diverted, Dynamite poured a tiny bit of the powder into Outback's glass.

Unaware of what was happening all around him, Outback consumed his second glass of beer. Meanwhile, the bottle full of crushed sleeping pills kept changing hands between Dynamite and Davey Boy behind Jack's back, and the two kept swapping the duties of keeping Outback occupied and slipping intoxicants into his beer.

"Okay!" Outback gurgled. "Let's have *another* one!"

The look on Jimmy's face became increasingly more concerned as he leaned in close to me.

"They're gonna *kill* him!" Jim whispered into my ear. "We should tell them to stop!"

Jimmy was right. I liked ribs as much as the next guy – and usually a lot *more* than the next guy – but most of my ribs had a truly funny element to them. *This* was clearly dangerous.

Without any warning, Jack suddenly fell backwards off of the barstool and onto the hard, wooden floor. It looked like he was taking a textbook back bump.

"Alright… you blokes have been messin' with me," slurred Outback as he attempted to pull himself up along the side of the bar. "I *know* I can outdrink you, Mr. Fuji! I'm not done yet!"

Fuji responded by presenting Jack with his usual mischievous smirk as he patiently waited for Jack to climb off of the floor and back onto his barstool. It took quite a great deal of effort on Jack's part to successfully reassume his place on the stool. The Bulldogs doggedly taunted Outback during the entire process.

"C'mon, Jack!" Dynamite goaded. "What's wrong with you? Fuji is an *old man!*"

"Yeah, Jack!" Davey Boy joined in. "I thought you said you could outdrink him! He's *20 years* older than you!"

Meanwhile, Brunzie was growing increasingly more upset.

"This isn't right, Brian!" Brunzell said. "This is going to be *really* bad…"

After that remark, I was fully on Jim's side of not wanting to be an accessory to a murder.

"Guys, we have to get him back to his room," I said, stepping forward. "He can't be here like this."

Brunzie, Dynamite, Davey Boy and I each grabbed a hold of an appendage, and we lugged Jack all the way back to his room. Fuji, the obvious victor of the drinking exchange, never left his barstool the entire time. He also *never* stopped smirking.

Once we'd arrived at Jack's room and sat him down on his bed, Dynamite suddenly unzipped his fly, whipped out his *dick*, and began to urinate all over Outback. He took great care to get as much of it on Jack's face as he possibly could.

Backstage with Davey Boy Smith of the British Bulldogs

"Hey, man!" Jim objected. "Cut that out! That's *really* wrong!"

Davey Boy and Dynamite cackled in response as Dynamite continued to empty his bladder right in Jack's face.

"I've been pissed on by better blokes than *you*, mate!" Jack sputtered defiantly.

"We'd better stay with him for a while to make sure he doesn't die," Jim warned me.

The Bulldogs left, but Jim and I remained behind as we chatted with Outback to make sure he wouldn't die.

"Are you okay, Jack?" Jim asked him. "You're not gonna die, are you?"

"No, mate," said Jack, weakly. "I'm not gonna die. I'm just *really* sleepy."

After staying for a tiny bit longer to assure ourselves that Jack truly wasn't going to die, Jim and I went off to find something to eat. There was a memorable restaurant at the Holiday Inn that had palm trees and a nice counter-top dining area. It was also open late, so Jim and I chose to grab some food from there and then head back to our rooms.

As we were getting ready to leave the restaurant, Outback Jack stormed through the door totally *naked* except for his boots and his hat with alligator teeth protruding from it. He staggered past a few of the 15 guests who were still eating at the restaurant and lurched about as if he was in search of something very specific.

"Pretend you don't know him," I whispered to Jim.

Jack walked straight over to the first palm tree he came to inside of the restaurant and nonchalantly began pissing on the tree as if there was nothing unusual about it, and as if he wasn't doing so to the horror of *all* of the other patrons of the restaurant. From there, Jack walked right over to the restaurant's countertop, unaware that Jim and I were already seated there, and sat down as casually as he would if he was sitting on his home sofa.

"Let's go," I said to Jim.

Jim and I got up and exited the restaurant just as some police officers were walking in to handle the disturbances that Outback had wrought during his nude midnight stroll through the hotel. Brunzie turned around and followed the police back inside. Somehow, Jim talked the officers into simply helping Jack back to his room and leaving him there without further incident. I hope the restaurant's staff *thoroughly* scrubbed the stool that Jack sat on before the next round of guests arrived.

Even after the incident at the hotel, where Jack was humiliated and urinated on, Fuji and the Bulldogs wouldn't leave Jack alone. They simply couldn't help themselves. During one of our TV tapings during that same swing through California, the Bulldogs cut Jack's crocodile right off of the jacket he used as entrance attire prior to his matches.

When Jack went to slip his shirt on, the crocodile slid right down his back and smacked onto the floor. Outback flew into a rage and began to do laps around the building looking for the Bulldogs with a huge knife in his hands that resembled a miniature machete. I truly believed Jack when he said he would have killed Dynamite and Davey Boy if he had found them. *That's* how livid he was.

At a later house show in California, Don Muraco and Mr. Fuji were conversing in a corner of the locker room, while the Bulldogs and a few other people were sitting around chatting with Jim and I. Outback left the room to go to work his match, and the Bulldogs quickly stood up and huddled together with Mr. Fuji. That was *never* a good sign.

B. Brian Blair: Truth Bee Told

Outback had a routine that he went through every single night: He took a quick shower, dressed rapidly, and turned his hat upside down to rest it on something while he packed his gear away prior to his departure. This time he put his hat on top of the lockers before he walked to the showers.

When Outback concluded his shower and began to get dressed, Fuji said to him, "Jack…. Come here."

Jack walked over, and Fuji began to play the role of mediator.

"Bulldogs go *too* far with you," Fuji said to him. "I tell them to quit messing with you."

"Well, I appreciate that, mate," Jack said. "I was about to kill those buggers."

Meanwhile, on the opposite end of the locker room, the Bulldogs were busy lining Jack's hat with super glue.

Jack turned around and walked over to collect his things. He grabbed his hat and placed it on his head, then took a few moments to further situate himself before turning around to address everyone in the room.

"See ya, blokes!" Outback said.

Under normal circumstances, Jack would have removed his hat, bowed to the room, and then departed. This time, Jack reached for his hat and tugged at it, but it wouldn't budge. Jack yanked away at the hat a few more times before it occurred to him that it was glued to his head. Jack's face instantly turned as red as a tomato. Then he kicked the locker room door open and stormed off without uttering another word.

As Jack left the building, I'm sure he heard everyone in the locker room howling in laughter.

Somehow, Fuji could rib people with impunity, but if anyone ribbed Fuji, they could expect the response from Fuji and the rest of the boys to be severe. That's just my theory, anyway. *No one* wanted to be in Fuji's crosshairs if he opted to double down on the ribbing! Not even the Bulldogs were immune; Fuji once fed Ex-Lax to their pet bulldog, Matilda. He would rib anyone, or any *thing*.

When Tom Zenk left the WWF right in the middle of a tour, Vince had Tito Santana replace him as Rick Martel's tag team partner and dubbed the pair "Strike Force." That was probably the true beginning of the end for the Killer Bees' hopes of ever winning the WWF World Tag Team Championship.

Again, Rick was a former AWA World Heavyweight Champion, and Tito was a former WWF Intercontinental Heavyweight Champion. What's more, Rick was one of Vince's favorites from years ago when he teamed with Tony Garea, who was now a WWF agent. With Martel and Santana on a team together, Vince had two established, reliable babyfaces as champions who wouldn't do anything to rock the boat if he promoted them heavily.

A short time after they were put together, Strike Force captured the tag titles from the Hart Foundation, which also meant the Killer Bees wouldn't be getting any more shots at the championship... at least not as long as we remained a babyface team.

Granted, there were some whispers and signs that turning the Killer Bees into a heel team might have been in the works. That year, the WWF held its first-ever *Survivor Series* pay-per-view event in Cleveland. It was built around an elimination-style match concept, and we were placed in the tag team feature match along with Strike Force, the Young Stallions, the British Bulldogs and the Fabulous Rougeau Brothers.

Despite being the champions and former champions respectively, Strike Force and the British Bulldogs were eliminated during the match, along with the Rougeaus. At the conclusion of the match, I benefited from a bit of masked confusion to slingshot myself into the ring and pin Tama of the Islanders with a sunset flip. We celebrated with the Young Stallions as the only teams to survive our *Survivor Series* contest.

If Vince ever had any plans to turn the Killer Bees into a heel team, *that* would have been the opportune time to do it. We could have relied on a masked-confusion switch against Strike Force to screw them out of the championship; the heat for it would have been *off the charts*. Ultimately, we weren't permitted to turn heel, which was a shame. Instead, we started losing lots of matches to the Islanders, before trading victories with the Bolsheviks – Nikolai Volkoff and Boris Zhukov.

In the middle of our run of matches against the Bolsheviks, Jimmy and I got to participate in a memorable eight-man tag team match on *Prime Time Wrestling* as members of the Killer Bee Family with Animal Bee and JYD Bee, who were clearly George Steele and the Junkyard Dog wearing Killer Bee masks. It was one of those special moments that was clearly designed to bring smiles to the faces of everyone in the building, and the four of us captured a victory against the Bolsheviks and Los Conquistadores.

George was a lot of fun outside of the ring as well. During one of the times when Toni was visiting me in New York, George approached me and asked if I could give him a ride.

"Sure, but can you do *me* a favor?" I asked him.

B. Brian Blair: Truth Bee Told

"Yeah, what do you need?" replied George.

"When you get in the car, can you do the gimmick to my wife where you lick somebody's head?" I asked him.

George looked shocked at that request.

"Ummm... yeah," he said. "I mean, if you *really* want me to, I can!"

Toni really wasn't all that familiar with George's gimmick, or with who most of the wrestlers were for that matter. When George climbed into the back seat of the car, he licked the back of Toni's head and she *shrieked*. From there, he started acting like his crazy self until we got to his stop. Toni would later tell me that was the *longest* car ride of her life!

Another sign that there had been at least a little bit of thought given to turning the Killer Bees heel occurred in early 1988. We defeated the Bolsheviks in a tag match in the Philadelphia Spectrum, and then we turned heel on Hulk Hogan during his lumberjack match later that night against Ted Dibiase. We beat Hogan up outside of the ring, and the fans were absolutely *furious*.

The two of us were pleased to have elicited that level of heat from the Philly fans. Backstage, Terry wasn't nearly as thrilled.

"Hey, guys!" Terry said. "That was a little *stiff!*"

Jim and I had wanted to lay our shots in pretty well to make our attack on Terry look convincing, but at that stage of his career, the Hulkster was very protective of himself. Most of the people he worked with *barely* touched him during his matches, which was how he preferred it. If there had been a plan to turn Jim and I heel and then have us challenge Strike Force for the tag team championship, pissing off Terry might have further soured Vince on that idea.

Wrestlemania IV took place on March 27th, 1988, at the Convention Hall in Atlantic City. There were only two tag team matches scheduled: a championship match between Strike Force and Demolition, and a six-man match with the British Bulldogs and Koko B. Ware against Bobby Heenan and the Islanders.

Almost everyone who wasn't involved in that night's WWF World Heavyweight Championship Tournament was placed in the 20-man battle royal at the beginning of the show, including Brunzell and I. At *Wrestlemania III* we were in the match just prior to the main event between Hogan and Andre, and now we would be an afterthought in a throwaway match at the beginning of the show.

Toni was given clearance to be backstage, and we both walked around before the show and took photos with some of the celebrities who were helping out that night, like Vanna White and Bob Uecker.

B. Brian Blair: Truth Bee Told

My responsibilities that night would be over with early, and then there were plenty of post-*Wrestlemania* events and parties that we were planning to attend.

Toni and I behind the scenes at Wrestlemania IV with "Mr. Baseball" Bob Uecker and Vanna White

B. Brian Blair: Truth Bee Told

Billionaire Donald Trump, the sponsor of that night's show, was seated dead in the center of the front row for nearly the entire show, along with his wife at the time Ivanka, and his son Donald Jr. All of the wrestlers involved in our battle royal stood in the ring and were introduced either one by one – or as a team in the case of the Killer Bees – and then the bell rang and the action ensued.

Both Jim and I were set to be eliminated at the midway point of the battle royal. I dramatically prolonged my elimination by hanging onto the ropes while taking punches in the face from Jacques Rougeau and Bad News Brown, before finally dropping off the apron. The problem was that Jim Neidhart was standing behind me arguing with one of the ringside referees, and when I fell off the apron, I landed partially on the referee and my chin got carried into the steel barricade that separated the ringside area from the fans. I felt my legs go wobbly, and then I collapsed onto the arena floor.

I regained my bearings just in time for Brunzie's elimination, but when I rose to my feet, I was still very unsteady. Jimmy legitimately had to help support me as I staggered all the way back to the dressing room area.

When we got to the back, we realized my chin had been split open a bit, and we found a doctor to evaluate me. As the doctor was assessing my injuries and Toni was standing by, Donald Trump wandered over. He glanced at me for a moment, then he extracted his clean, pressed handkerchief from his suit pocket and held it under my bleeding chin.

"How are you doing?" he asked. "Are you okay?"

"I'm fine, sir," I responded.

That's good," he said. "Are they taking care of you?"

"They are; thank you," I answered.

"Very good," Trump said, and then he patted me on the back. "We have an ambulance here that's ready to take you to the hospital if you need to go, okay?"

"I appreciate it, Mr. Trump," I told him. "Thank you very much."

Sadly, I *did* end up needing to go to the hospital that night. The medical personnel monitored me for potentially having a concussion. Once I was cleared, they stitched up my chin and sent me back to the hotel. By this time all of the show-related festivities were over with, so Toni and I had missed the coronation of Randy Savage as the new world champion, along with all of the afterparty events.

"Well, we can *still* go to the casino," urged Toni. "Let's do a little bit of gambling!"

B. Brian Blair: Truth Bee Told

Honestly, I wasn't in much of a gambling mood. I had stitches in my chin, and it was all bandaged up, but at the same time, I wanted to make Toni happy. I also had a laundry list of things I *never* wanted to be labeled as, and "gambler" was on that list right beneath "drug addict" and "alcoholic." I was conditioned by my upbringing to think of money as a resource that is terribly difficult to attain, and even harder to keep. Asking me to gamble was like asking me to get my *teeth* pulled. I really didn't like to spend money if it could be helped.

However, I knew I would soon be the recipient of a solid *Wrestlemania IV* payoff, so I took $200 or $300 down to the casino to play blackjack alongside my wife. I figured that I wouldn't be too upset about losing that amount of money because my wife would be in a good mood from the experience, and if she would be happy, then I would be happy.

To be honest, the blackjack table was one of the few places in the casino where I felt somewhat comfortable, and that's because blackjack was the only game where it seemed like I had some sort of control over the outcome. After all, I could choose to hit or not to hit. I also knew the bare minimum required to be able to play blackjack: I wanted to get my score to 21 if possible, and if I exceeded that number, I would automatically lose.

Toni sat next to me at the blackjack table with a rag in her hand because I was bleeding through the stitches in my chin, and she had to dab at my chin with that rag every so often.

"Sir, are you okay?" one of the casino employees asked. "Are you one of those wrestlers?"

"Yes, sir," I answered. "I'm one of the Killer Bees."

"Why don't you come on over to *this* table?" he pointed. "There's more room for you over here."

The casino worker escorted Toni and I over to a blackjack table where nobody was sitting and ushered us into the vacant seats. As the dealer doled out the cards, he began to ask me questions about the wrestling business. During that exchange, I divulged to the dealer that I had never played blackjack in a casino before.

"It's easy," the dealer said. "I'll help you out the best I can."

Probably acting against the policies laid out the casino, the dealer began to advise me when I should hit, and when not to hit. Almost unfailingly, I was winning hand after hand. Yet I stupidly limited my bets to only $5.00 at a time.

"Now that you're winning, you should bet a little more," the dealer advised me. "Like 50 percent more."

B. Brian Blair: Truth Bee Told

In my mind, the dealer was just setting me up so that he could take all of my money in one fell swoop, but I did raise my bets from $5.00 to $10.00. The dealer *never* screwed me, and I left the table with over $1,300 that night even though I never bet more than 10 bucks at a time. The way I had it figured, I could have left the casino that night with maybe $5,000 if I'd continued to raise my bets as the dealer had advised. Then again, it's also safe to remember that the games are all rigged in the casino's favor, and that this dealer was just being nice to a wrestler, but he was only willing to stretch his kindness so far. All the same, to take $200 and stretch it to nearly $1,500 caused a lot of elation for us that night.

Strike Force lost the tag titles to Demolition at *Wrestlemania IV*, which offered the Bees a brief ray of hope that we might be able to work our way into a fresh round of championship matches as the new babyface contenders. However, we were kept far away from Demolition, and began to lose matches far more regularly than we had in the prior three years.

During that period of time when the Killer Bees seemed to be in career limbo, two new babyface tag teams entered the WWF: the Powers of Pain and the Rockers. The Powers of Pain were a visual replica of the world-famous Road Warriors – Hawk and Animal. The Warlord and the Barbarian were massively muscled, wrestled in face paint, and even had hairstyles that were identical to Hawk and Animal. After Demolition finished a round of title defenses against Strike Force, they began squaring off against the Powers of Pain in a series of matches that probably resembled Vince's dream scenario of colossal men throwing one another around, even if the quality of the matches wasn't very good.

In contrast, the Rockers were the polar opposite of the Powers of Pain. Shawn Michaels and Marty Jannetty were lightning-quick, likeable babyfaces who battered their opponents and captivated the fans with an impressive arsenal of aerial maneuvers. Vince had tried to bring them into the WWF during the prior year, but things quickly went awry. Shawn and Marty walked into a restaurant in Buffalo, New York without saying a word to any of us.

All of us were already seated at the bar; the two Rockers looked like they'd had a little too much to drink prior to their arrival. They both found empty chairs to sit in and asked for a few more drinks. Seemingly out of nowhere, Marty took a glass and *threw* it against the fake fireplace by the bar and it shattered into a thousand pieces.

B. Brian Blair: Truth Bee Told

"What the hell did you do *that* for?!" the woman behind the bar asked.

In response to her, Shawn picked up his own glass and lobbed it against the fake fireplace. The two of them then walked out without uttering another word.

Lowering the boom on Raymond Rougeau

Word of that incident got to Vince, and the Rockers were fired. Now that they were back, they were another fresh babyface tag team that we would have to compete with for attention. It was definitely an uphill battle. Being positioned as a mediocre tag team caused the fans to believe the Killer Bees were never going to be featured as title contenders ever again. The crowds' reactions to us grew less passionate with each passing week.

The final two televised matches for the Killer Bees in the WWF were against the Rougeau Brothers and the Hart Foundation. We lost to the Rougeau Brothers and were given a disqualification win against the Hart Foundation. However, our unconvincing win against the Hart Foundation was only intended to provide the backdrop for the Hitman and the Anvil to split from their manager, Jimmy Hart, and become a babyface team. After June of 1988, Jimmy and I *never* appeared together on WWF television as a team again.

In retrospect, Jimmy and I may have inadvertently cursed our pairing by adopting the name "The Killer Bees." The incredible defensive unit from which we had inherited our team name lost in its two Super Bowl outings against the Washington Redskins and the San Francisco 49ers. Much like those Bees, Jimmy and I seemed to be snakebitten, and cast as the memorable team that could never quite seem to win the big one.

Fortunately, there is much more to life than professional wrestling. Even though I would never say goodbye to wrestling permanently, I would quickly learn a brand-new set of skills, and discover other ways to make money that didn't involve dressing in tights and spending two thirds of my time away from home.

TWENTY-TWO – *When one door closes, another opens*

Behind the scenes, the writing on the wall was clearly visible to me when the WWF was planning its first-ever *Summerslam* show, and Jim and I were left completely off of the card. There were three matches at the event featuring established tag teams, and the babyface side was represented by the British Bulldogs, the Powers of Pain and the Hart Foundation. When I realized we were no longer factored in as one of the company's top *three* babyface teams, it was clear to me that we were finished as a meaningful attraction in Vince's eyes.

In the weeks just prior to *Summerslam*, Jim and I worked at house shows in a series of babyface-versus-babyface matches against the Young Stallions. Before the matches began, we were told to react to the crowd and let the *audience* decide which team should work as heels during the match. Despite the fact that the Stallions were the younger team with the more muscular physiques, the crowds were consistently behind us to the point where we were always forced to assume the babyface role.

We were the better-established team, so I wasn't at all surprised by this. My guess is that Vince wanted to see if the crowd would naturally turn the Killer Bees into heels, but I didn't see much of a point to it by then. I didn't see much of a future for us in starting from scratch as a heel tag team, especially when a heel team like Demolition was already holding the tag team titles. *That's* when I went to Jimmy and told him I was leaving.

"Jimmy, I've got to go," I told him over dinner. "I hate to leave you, but the writing is on the wall. Vince is *never* giving us the belts."

Collectively, George Scott and Vince McMahon had promised us the belts to Jimmy and I *three different times* during our three-year run. Jim totally understood my frustration, but he also told me he couldn't afford to leave. He had a full-blown family, including two beautiful children. Honestly, if Jim had saved his money a bit better, he probably would have felt comfortable enough to leave the WWF right alongside me and never look back. However, when we were on the road, Jimmy ate what he wanted, when he wanted, and he didn't care if there was a room-service fee attached to the bill or not, never mind the fact that he had a family to feed.

B. Brian Blair: Truth Bee Told

"Jimmy, you've *got* to save your money," I'd tell him, echoing the same sentiments that veterans like Bruiser Brody had inculcated in me when I was a very young wrestler.

"Awwww don't worry about it!" Jim would respond. "You should just *enjoy* yourself. Tomorrow isn't guaranteed to any of us!"

That was true, but if tomorrow *did* arrive, I wanted to ensure that I would face tomorrow in comfort by saving money *today*. I felt like I was financially secure enough to leave the certainty of a WWF paycheck behind.

My dad's brother – Uncle Jim – always advised me to live as if I was going to die tomorrow, but to save as if I was going to live forever. I listened to my uncle's advice and tried to split the middle *very* precisely.

In Salisbury, Maryland, I pulled Vince aside, and I said, "Vince, we've been promised the belts three times and it hasn't happened. I don't know what the problem has been, but I've busted my *ass* and things just don't seem to be working out. I've enjoyed working for you, but I'm giving you my notice."

Vince *immediately* frowned.

"I'm sorry to hear that, Brian," he told me. "Let's talk about this, because we have options. We can turn you heel. If this is because you don't want to tag with Jim anymore, we can also put you in singles competition."

"I'm burned out," I explained, shaking my head. "I'm *tired* and I need to figure out what I want to do with my life."

Vince nodded and then said, "I respect that, Brian. Did you have anything in particular in mind to do?"

"Well, I've thought about getting a business going," I told him, and then I smiled. "Maybe I could even become a businessman like you."

Vince chuckled at that one.

"You've been a tremendous asset to us, Brian," Vince said. "You're a terrific talent. Your work has always been top-notch. Let me know how I can help you out. You'll *always* have a home here in the World Wrestling Federation. We'll work out the right time for you to leave."

I *can't* say that Vince intentionally lied to Jim and I when he said he would put the belts on us on those three separate occasions. There were a lot of factors involved with operating the WWF, and circumstances were constantly evolving. I'm certain there were several times he had every intention of letting us have our run as champions –

including when Dynamite Kid got injured – but circumstances prevailed that prevented it from happening.

At the same time, I'm certain that Vince did his fair share of overpromising to *a lot* of guys. He recognized that he needed to drain every territory that he intended to compete against, and that meant he had to lure a lot of talented wrestlers into the WWF by offering them opportunities that they couldn't match if they remained where they were. If he had to overpromise things to a few key wrestlers just to get them to sign contracts, and *then* underdeliver once they'd agreed to those deals, so be it.

The WWF was making enough money at the time that it could afford to carry its bloated talent roster, but there were only so many belts to go around. There was absolutely no way Vince could have conducted his business without disappointing several wrestlers. Unfortunately, the Killer Bees became casualties of some of those business decisions.

Once the Bees split up, Vince seemed to relish the idea of mercilessly jobbing Brunzell out to everyone in sight during the next few months. It all started innocently enough, with Jim competing respectably on television against Ted Dibiase, although Ted pounded on him for *an eternity* before Jim finally got in some offense of his own. Andre interfered toward the end to cost Jim the match. For most of his matches after that, Jim returned to wearing his tie-dyed High Flyers tights and then lost the majority of his matches on his way out of the WWF that year.

We did have some memorable moments as we winded down our WWF tenure, some of which were enjoyable, and others that were downright tragic. One of Jim's frequent opponents during this period was "Mr. Perfect" Curt Hennig, an outstanding second-generation wrestler who had just arrived from the American Wrestling Association. Curt was *magnificent* in the ring, and he also had a penchant for ribbing everyone in sight, just like Mr. Fuji. One of his early targets was Koko B. Ware.

Koko had a room on the first floor of one of the hotels we were staying in. As usual, he propped open the window of his room so that his parrot, Frankie, could stand by the window and get some fresh air. Unbeknownst to Koko, Curt had been monitoring him from his own second-floor room across the courtyard, which provided him with a clear view of Koko's room. When Koko went to the bathroom to take a shower, Curt donned a dark-colored mask, snuck across the courtyard and hid behind the giant tree by Koko's window.

B. Brian Blair: Truth Bee Told

While Koko was in the bathroom, Curt picked the screen off the window and then hid beneath the windowsill. Then, when Koko returned from his shower and went to the window to tend to Frankie, Curt leapt through the window and grabbed at Koko. Fearing he was about to be murdered, Koko *screamed* at the top of his lungs. In the process, Koko knocked Frankie's cage down onto the floor. Bird excrement spilled out and littered the room.

Curt turned around to flee from the scene, but his mask had been jarred loose around the eyeholes. Curt couldn't see anything in his path, and before he could fully readjust his mask, he wound up sprinting headfirst into a low-hanging branch on the tree he had initially hidden behind. This resulted in Curt nearly knocking himself cold, and he opened up a nasty gash on his forehead in the process.

Koko noticed Curt sporting the huge gash on his face the next day in the locker room. He remembered how his assailant had smashed his head on the tree branch, and also recalled that Curt's room had been directly across from his. Koko put two and two together and confronted Curt forthwith.

"Curt, *why'd* you do that, man?!" Koko said. "That *wasn't* funny!"

"I have no idea what you're talking about!" Curt deadpanned.

Curt denied it until his dying day, but everyone knew he was behind it.

One of the most tragic episodes occurred in Fort Wayne, Indiana. I had already wrestled that evening against Barry Horowitz, and a group of us were sitting around the locker room and chatting. As usual, there were plenty of people in the locker room for the *Superstars* taping even if they weren't booked to appear. That included both the British Bulldogs and the Rougeau Brothers.

Dynamite Kid loved to drink coffee, and whenever he had it, he always put tons of cream and sugar in it. The coffee pot was situated right around the corner from where we had all been congregating.

"I'm gonna go get some more coffee," Dynamite said, and then he disappeared around the corner.

There really wasn't much else to it, but after a few moments, one of the referees burst into our room screaming.

"Dynamite just got beaten up!" he hollered.

We were all looking around wondering what was going on, and then Dynamite came staggering around the corner with blood *pouring* from his face. His teeth were all knocked in, except for one that

B. Brian Blair: Truth Bee Told

had been completely knocked out. Somehow, he was still able to squeeze out a few choice words.

"That *fookin* Rougeau!" said Dynamite, unintentionally spitting blood out of his mouth with every utterance. "He *fookin* sucker punched me with a roll of quarters!"

A group of us ran over to see which Rougeau it was that had done this to Dynamite. *None* of us supported bullshit like that. Cheapshotting a fellow wrestler, especially as violently as that, was completely against the informal code of ethics that wrestlers were taught to abide by. When we arrived at the scene of the crime, we discovered that both of the Rougeaus had already exited the building.

We also confirmed that Dynamite *had* been punched with a roll of quarters, even though he would still write in his autobiography *Pure Dynamite* that Jacques Rougeau had tagged him with brass knuckles. Quarters littered the floor where Dynamite had been ambushed, as did drops of the Englishman's blood.

Truth be told, Dynamite kind of had it coming. The Rougeaus were strait-laced guys that weren't really ribbers, and it certainly wasn't in their DNA to be involved in the sort of nasty ribs that Dynamite enjoyed. I don't know exactly what Dynamite did to upset Jacques so badly. Raymond was the clear leader of the Rougeau Brothers, and *he* wouldn't have sucker punched anyone; he would have fought anybody man to man.

Unlike his brother, Jacques was not a fighter, and it's unsurprising that he wouldn't have wanted to fight Dynamite in an unregulated, no-holds-barred situation. Of course, you can beat up *anybody* if you catch them unaware with a roll of quarters in your hand.

Sadly, it seemed like getting punched by Jacques led to the ultimate decline of Dynamite. Everyone respected him for what he had done in the industry, both in the U.S. and overseas. He was an absolute legend everywhere he went, and to see him shaken so badly during the latter stages of his career was downright depressing.

It was agreed that I would make my final departure from the WWF following back-to-back tours of Italy and Canada, and then I would wrap things up with one final appearance at the 1988 *Survivor Series*.

If I hadn't been ready to leave the WWF already, my final day of working for the company would have sealed the deal. On November 6th, we had to work a double shot, with one show at the Maple Leaf Gardens in Toronto, and another show at the Ottawa Civic Center. I was wrestling Iron Mike Sharpe in both of my singles matches, and the Young Stallions were booked against the Brain Busters – Arn Anderson and Tully Blanchard.

There was a *massive* snowstorm in the area, very reminiscent of the snowstorm that left me incommunicado in my dorm room at Louisville. Only about 70 percent of the fans who'd purchased tickets for the show actually made it to the Civic Center that night. The situation became even more dire, because a lot of the boys were late getting to the second show, and several wrestlers who had piled into one of the cars never made it to Ottawa at all, including the British Bulldogs and Jimmy Powers. As a result, I had to fill in for Powers and team with Paul Roma against the Brain Busters immediately after I'd finished working with Mike Sharpe *twice* that same day.

I'd worked with Arn Anderson plenty of times in Georgia, but this was the first time I'd wrestled against him when he teamed with Tully Blanchard, who was a tremendous second-generation wrestler from Texas. They'd been a legendary pairing in the Mid Atlantic region, and Roma and I had a *great* match with them that night.

In the latter stages of the bout, Roma gave me the hot tag, and I exploded into the ring. I immediately hit Arn and he fell through the ropes and out onto the floor. That resulted in me being left in the ring with Tully. I'm certain that I wasn't in the most pleasant mood at that moment. I'd been fed up with working in the WWF in general, I was irritated by the snowstorm, and I was pissed off at the fact that I'd had to wrestle *three times* that day. Apparently, all of that frustration was manifesting itself on my face in the ring that night.

I went to punch Tully with one of my normal working punches, which meant that I kept my fist a bit loose and let the punch strike my opponent in the neck. This time, as I went to make contact with Tully's neck, he stuck his arm up to cover his face at the last moment. When he did that, I caught his arm with my thumb, and my thumb got yanked all the way back to my own wrist. All of the nerves and tendons in my hand were torn along the way.

If I hadn't already been leaving the WWF, I *would* have required time off to have surgery on my hand no matter what.

"I don't know what happened, Brian!" said a very apologetic Tully after the match. "I'm *so* sorry! You had this look on your face and it just scared me at the last second!"

By that point, the WWF had already aired a segment where I came out on the set of the *Brother Love Show* along with my *Survivor Series* teammates: Jake Roberts, Tito Santana, Jim Duggan and Ken Patera. Obviously, my wrist injury precluded my participation in that match, so Scott Casey was brought in as my replacement.

B. Brian Blair: Truth Bee Told

I was only 31 years old, and for the first time in 11 years I would be waking up in the morning without a full-time wrestling career taking precedence over everything else.

Before my wrestling career really peaked, I read an old book by George S. Clason – *The Richest Man in Babylon* – that advised its readers to save 10 percent of their incomes no matter what, and also to abstain from making any outlandish luxury purchases.

I wisely did both of those things, and by the time I left the World Wrestling Federation in November of 1988, I had accrued a substantial amount of money in my savings account. I'd purchased my modest house on a Tampa lake back in 1982, and everything was *completely* paid off. I had perfect credit, had never missed the payment of a bill, and had never swindled anyone out of a dime. I felt like I'd done everything necessary to put myself in a solid financial position just in case I declined to ever wrestle again.

I had to ask myself, "What do I really want to do?" Thanks to my own life experiences and some great mentors along the way, I had a solid understanding of the dollars and cents of business, and I knew I had enough money saved to invest in a franchise of some sort. In my mind it was a simple matter of deciding what sort of franchise to invest in.

My first thought was to open a Chick-Fil-A or a McDonald's franchise, which seemed like relatively safe investments to make with established brands. However, there was *nothing* about opening a fast-food restaurant that truly excited me.

Once I gave the situation a little more thought, it occurred to me how I was constantly concerned with what time I was going to be able to get to the gym throughout my life, no matter whether I was a high school student, a college athlete, or a professional wrestler. I also remembered how my friend Pete Gronkowski – who owned more than 50 percent of Gold's Gym's corporate offices at one point – had once offered me my first year of licensing for *free* if I ever agreed to open a Gold's Gym location.

At the time, the Gold's Gym licensing fee was $7,500, and it *surged* to $10,000 the following year. The combination of my passion for working out and the offer from Pete made me lean heavily toward entering the gym business.

One of my very good friends, Dr. Stephen Propper, owned a business that used to be called "The Racquet Club," but he and his partner Michael Spielvogel were in the midst of converting the building into a gun range called "Magnums." Even with their gun range fully installed and situated within the building, the place was so huge that they *still* had enough space left over in the building for someone to fit a well-stocked gym inside of it. When I realized this, *everything* clicked together in my mind.

I called up Pete Gronkowski and asked, "Pete, is that offer still good?"

"What offer?" he asked.

"That no-licensing-fee offer if I open a Gold's Gym," I answered. "I think I've found the *perfect* place for a gym!"

"Are you *serious*, Brian?" Pete said, with excitement evident in his voice. "That's great! We'd *love* to have you as part of the Gold's Gym family!"

Pete was true to his word, and he waived the first-year licensing fee. For $115,000 cash, I opened my first Gold's Gym in 1989 at the old Racquet Club location at 7815 N. Dale Mabry. At the risk of sounding egotistical, I took to gym ownership like a duck to water. I'd been in and out of gyms for the better part of my life, and I *loved* being inside of them. At a minimum, this opportunity provided me with a business that I could be passionate about, an environment that I would be comfortable in, and a nearby place where I could go to train *whenever* I felt like it.

Even though I felt very comfortable with the idea of operating a gym, I still had *a lot* to learn. When you buy a Gold's Gym, you're really only buying the name, and the licensing agreement comes with a requirement that your club needs to contain a specified amount of equipment. Everything that says "Gold's Gym" on it needs to be purchased directly from them. Beyond that, they didn't offer any guidance on how to run your business outside of some suggested pricing structures. I was given the freedom to put together a gym that fit my vision, so I gained the experience of developing my own flow charts, policies and procedures.

The sense of pride I got from watching the business grow was immeasurable. We started with zero members and had to build the operation from the ground up, one member at a time. I operated on three principles that I explained to *everyone* who worked for me: We're going to have the *cleanest* gym in town, we are going to be the *friendliest* gym in town, and we are going to be the most *knowledgeable* gym in town.

Being a professional wrestler certainly paid off when it came time to promote the gyms. I had enough name recognition that my decision to open a gym was deemed noteworthy enough to receive coverage in the local newspapers.

B. Brian Blair: Truth Bee Told

Terry supported me by making a publicized appearance at my grand opening, and we had *thousands* of people show up to see him. The line extended out onto the street and stretched for more than a quarter mile. Vince provided 2,000 photos for the Hulkster to sign for the people who walked through the doors of my brand-new gym, and there were only about 200 unsigned photos remaining when the event reached its conclusion.

Once my gym was established, all of the wrestlers who lived in Tampa or visited the area would stop by to get their workouts in. If there was a wrestling event within hailing distance of Tampa, there was a very good chance you would see several of the top wrestling stars in the world training at Gold's Gym Tampa.

Over the course of the 12 years I had already spent in professional wrestling, the landscape of the industry had changed monumentally. The vast territorial system that had predated Vince's national expansion attempt was now a veritable wasteland. In the same month that I left the WWF, the Crockett family sold their company to billionaire media mogul Ted Turner. This gave rise to World Championship Wrestling, which was headquartered in Atlanta. It was the only legitimate competitor left in Vince's path. All of the other major wrestling territories were either out of business or working on it, and *none* of them were attracting interest at the levels they once had.

That didn't mean there weren't still plenty of great opportunities to wrestle if you knew where to look for them. One outlet available to wrestlers with name recognition was the overseas scene. During one of the overseas tours I was booked on in 1989, I experienced the *scariest* in-ring moment of my entire wrestling career. I was actually teaming with Jim Brunzell as the Killer Bees during that tour, and the two of us were in the middle of a match against the Nasty Boys in Kota Kinabalu in Sabah, Malaysia. Thousands of rabid wrestling fans were in attendance.

Mahar Singh, the local promoter for that tour, was refereeing the bout, and Frenchy Martin was at ringside as the heel manager of the Nasty Boys – Brian Knobbs and Jerry Sags. The Nasty Boys did something to enrage the massive crowd, and the people in attendance all got fed up with the dastardly antics of the heels. The fans charged the ring in protest, and we quickly found ourselves being overrun.

Here I was, in the middle of a wrestling ring in a third-world country, in mortal fear for my own life, and in a city that *no one* I knew had ever even heard of. Of all the places where I could have died, I *never* could have imagined my life would come to an end in Kota Kinabalu.

B. Brian Blair: Truth Bee Told

In the middle of the melee, Mahar Singh grabbed me from behind and yanked me down on top of him.

"Get me *out* of here!" he screamed.

I pulled Mahar off the ground and jerked him through the ropes and onto the ground outside of the ring. From there, I dragged Mahar with my left hand and threw punches with my right hand as I worked my way back up the aisle to the locker room, slugging rioters in their faces the entire way. It was a *truly* terrifying moment, and one that I'll *never* forget.

Kota Kinabalu event ticket

During that same tour, Frenchy and I visited a top-quality Malaysian tailor. We requested that the local tailor create several exquisitely crafted, hand-woven, custom-tailored suits for us for $120 each. *Everything* in this operation was first class. Each suit came with a shirt, which was also custom made, and if you chipped in an additional $10, they would customize a tie for you as well. These were the same quality of custom-made suits that Ric Flair would spend thousands of dollars on, and we were getting them for bargain-basement prices.

B. Brian Blair: Truth Bee Told

I purchased two suits, and Frenchy ordered six. When the time came for us to pay up, I paid cash, and there were no issues. When it was Frenchy's turn to make his final purchase, his credit card was declined at the register, and he *bolted* out of there with the six suits as the tailor threatened to have him arrested. Somehow, Frenchy managed to abscond out of the country with the suits in his possession, and he wound up getting all of them for free.

During one night of the tour, Frenchy got really drunk with the Nasty Boys, and while he was in his drunken stupor, Frenchy began to berate Knobbs and Sags while using some very colorful language. Then Frenchy stood up on his bed, whipped out his penis, and began to urinate directly on top of *both* of the Nasty Boys. I thought Knobbs and Sags were going to kill Frenchy, but they seemed to be so amused by Frenchy that they decided to have mercy on him.

The Nasty Boys did *not* look back on those tours very fondly. They complained about their inability to sleep being owed to the fact that their hotel room faced the prison that stood directly across the street from the hotel. Every morning, a prisoner would be dragged outside in shackles and publicly caned with a kendo stick. Knobbs and Sags found it impossible to sleep through the piercing screams of those prisoners.

The framework of what would eventually become a vibrant North American independent wrestling scene was beginning to take shape, and there was no shortage of wrestling promoters hosting events who were willing to offer me decent money to appear at a show, even if they weren't able to do much to follow up on some of those initial shows. Almost all of these small promotions were lacking something critical, like the support of a regular television show, or a home venue where they could regularly host events.

Al Burke worked as an underneath talent on WWF broadcasts from time to time, but he also worked for other wrestling companies when he wasn't being booked to put over members of Vince's roster on national television. Al gave me a call in 1989 and asked me if I was interested in working for a wrestling promoter based in Denver, Colorado named Tom Shade.

Things truly got rolling for Tom when he connected with both Ed Wiskowski and I and asked us to headline a show for him at Ellsworth Air Force Base in Rapid City, South Dakota. Tom sold the show to the base at cost – meaning he didn't profit from it at all. He was trying to get his foot in the door, and it worked *precisely* as he'd envisioned. Tom was provided with a letter of recommendation from the folks at the Air Force base, which he then photocopied and mailed out to the MWR (Morale, Welfare and Recreation) departments at countless other military bases.

The interest from those military bases was almost instantaneous, so Tom reasoned that he might as well see if there was any interest from Indian reservations as well; several of the military bases we wrestled at were positioned right next to Indian reservations. Before long, Tom had formed a stable, profitable, under-the-radar wrestling territory composed primarily of military bases and Indian reservations.

This is how the International Wrestling Alliance was born. Tom's shows were "sold shows," which meant they were completely financed up front. Under normal circumstances the people who purchased sold shows would attempt to recoup their money from the paying attendees. In the case of the military bases, this wasn't a factor at all; the shows were purchased by the U.S. government solely for the purpose of entertaining American troops.

Behind the scenes, an IWA show resembled a traveling circus. Tom had a 15-passenger van that wrestlers would pile into, and on the side it said "La Petite Academy." We all laughed about that label, as if it was somehow a rib imposed on all of us for working on the *petite* wrestling show. The van hauled a trailer behind it that contained the ring. Some wrestlers would ride in the trailer, and still more were stuffed into Al Burke's Suburban.

I was far from the only recognizable wrestler working on the IWA's shows. Paul Orndorff, Rick Rude, the Honky Tonk Man and Jimmy Snuka were all featured IWA performers at one time or another in the late '80s and early '90s. However, Ed Wiskowski (wrestling as Colonel DeBeers) and I were regularly featured as Tom's stable main event on shows that typically entertained between 500 and 1,500 fans. Ed and I were both content with our lives outside of wrestling and weren't looking to use the IWA as an intermediary territory before we jumped to one of the two national companies. This made us reliable talent to book in the main events; Tom wasn't afraid that we would no-show our matches if he advertised us.

I was concerned that the main-event matches lacked intrigue because there were no championships on the line, so I asked Tom to spring for some championship belts.

"I don't think so, Brian," said Tom. "Belts cost *a lot* of money. Our shows and attendance are guaranteed whether we have belts or not, so I don't really see the point."

Tom was a smooth talker, and his point was a difficult one to argue against. Fortunately, Al Burke also agreed that belts would be a nice touch. He contacted Reggie Parks – a former wrestler and the maker of just about every championship belt from that era – and paid Reggie to create new championship belts with money out of Al's own pocket.

The result was that the IWA received two new championship belts representing the IWA World Heavyweight Championship and the IWA Intercontinental Heavyweight Championship. The belts were physically almost identical to the belts that represented those respective titles in the WWF at the time.

The bouts between Ed and I were then upgraded to "world title" matches, and I became a long-term holder of the IWA World Heavyweight Championship. No, this accomplishment wasn't nearly on the level of being the WWF champion or the NWA champion, but a real argument could be made that the IWA was the third most stable national wrestling company in the U.S. at the time.

Not only was the IWA profitable – a rarity in early '90s wrestling – but it also held regular shows in about 40 states without having to rely on the support of a television program. Being at the top of the IWA was like being the world champion of the minor circuit, so to speak. Besides, when the crowds inside of those military gymnasiums got engrossed in our matches to the extent that they seemed to believe the fate of the world was riding on the outcome, it was *almost* enough to make me believe that I was really the champion of the world when I held that belt aloft at the end of the night.

We found that the military personnel were among the easiest audiences to elicit tremendous crowd reactions from. Many of them had been cooped up for long stretches of time without any form of entertainment, so they appreciated the release and relaxation that came from kicking back and watching our wrestling matches.

In contrast, the crowds at the Indian reservations were usually *far* less receptive and responsive than the military audiences. We would usually meet with the tribal police forces at checkpoints and then get escorted to a high-school-style gym on the tribal properties to set up the shows. Some of the events were almost treated as a daycare; parents would drop their children off when the show started and pick them up when it was all over with.

Aside from the mainstream wrestling talent, the IWA's events also showcased women and midget wrestlers on the shows. The women included wrestlers like Sabrina Fury and Nyah Kennedy, who were relative newcomers to the business. They were very green, but they worked diligently to improve, and they gradually became better as the touring increased.

B. Brian Blair: Truth Bee Told

I probably wrestled on just 50 IWA shows each year, but the lengths of some of the tours would rival WWF tours in the rigor of the travel involved. On at least one occasion, an IWA tour lasted for 21 days in a row. We piled into Tom's van and drove from military base to military base, or from Indian reservation to Indian reservation. The team developed into a very tightly knit clique, where everyone looked out for one another, and the veterans consistently coached the rookies.

I wrestled for plenty of other promoters over this same time period, but Tom Shade's IWA provided a very stable and reliable outlet for my pro wrestling energy for a few years, without grinding me into the dust the same way the WWF's schedule had done. His company would continue to operate for about 20 years, and it was convenient for me, because I was able to accept regular bookings with Tom and still spend a more than adequate amount of time back in Tampa tending to my gyms.

Little did I dream that I was about to be lured off to wrestle for one of the most colorful, reckless and *infamous* wrestling promoters who ever lived.

TWENTY-THREE – *Meeting Mr. Electricity*

My first Gold's Gym quickly reached the point where it could be considered successful, so I opened a second club at 3689 W. Waters Avenue. I consolidated the W. Waters location with my original gym after about three months, and then I opened *another* gym in South Tampa on S. Dale Mabry. All of my clubs had phone numbers that ended in 2-6-3-9, which spelled "body." This allowed us to promote ourselves using some very catchy advertising slogans, because I could conclude all of our advertisements by telling people to call a number that ended in "body."

A Gold's Gym visit from Rick Steiner, Lex Luger and Sting

When I was in the process of changing club locations and consolidating gyms, wrestlers Glenn Jacobs and Rico Federico literally picked up *thousands* of pounds worth of weight, placed it on dollies, and loaded it into trucks for me. It was some of the most taxing and demanding physical labor I've ever personally witnessed. Rico was actually the manager at one of my clubs before he took a stab at the professional wrestling business.

It was during one of those periods while I was at home in Tampa during July of 1990 that I went out for some recreational enjoyment on Coopers Lake with fellow wrestler Ed "Brutus Beefcake" Leslie, who also lived in Tampa. We were enjoying a day of parasailing over at the lakefront home of Mike Hannis, along with my friend Ed Barbara, and Ed's girlfriend Tracy.

Brutus was manning the rope, and standing in water that was about waist deep. Tracy was preparing to take flight in the parasail. I was holding the parasail steady, along with a redheaded kid named Paul who owned a hardware store not far from the house. Mike was at the helm of his very powerful speed boat. Brutus had the responsibility of signaling to Mike when he should throttle up the boat and take off. Everyone was in the position they were meant to be in, and Brutus signaled for Mike to fire up his boat and take off.

Posing for some young fans with Brutus Beefcake

When you're the line man, you're always supposed to turn to the right, which means that your body is supposed to turn to the outside, and away from the person with the parasail. On this occasion, Brutus accidentally turned to the *inside* and placed himself directly in Tracy's path of acceleration. Instinctively, Tracy lifted her legs to protect herself from colliding with Beefcake, and her knee struck Brutus square in the *face* at about 30 miles per hour. The limp body of Brutus plopped into the water as if he'd been smashed with a sledgehammer.

I dashed into the water, splashed my way out to Brutus as quickly as I could, and pulled him up to the shore. It was all dead weight. In our wake, a crimson trail of blood mixed with the blue waters of the lake.

"Brutus!" I screamed frantically. "Are you okay?! Are you *okay?!*"

I don't know that I'd ever been that scared for someone else's well-being like that before in my entire life. I thought Brutus was either dead, or about to be. His face was mashed and swollen, and blood was *pouring* out of it. My fear subsided somewhat when I began to hear low, guttural, gurgling noises emanating from Brutus' face.

"Can you talk?!" I asked him. "Open your mouth!"

"Ai 'out *ih* o'en," said Brutus, dazedly.

The words didn't come out clearly, but I could tell that Brutus was trying to say, "My mouth *is* open." The problem was, his mouth *hadn't* opened. When I used my fingers to open Brutus' mouth, I could plainly see the damage that Tracy's knee had caused. Brutus' skull had been shattered, and although his tongue could move freely, his upper row of teeth was *resting* on his bottom row of teeth, because the framework of his skull had been disconnected from all of the soft tissue in his face. It was a *terrifying* sight.

I sat there with Brutus and tried to keep him comforted for what seemed like an hour, even though I'm sure the paramedics made it to the lake house in about 10 minutes. In the end, Brutus' skull had to be completely rebuilt, and he was forced to convalesce for years just as his popularity in the WWF was peaking. Having a firsthand view of this tragedy etched into my mind that I should do everything I could to maximize my ability to earn money outside of the wrestling ring, because a wrestler's ability to make money inside of the ring could be snatched away at *any* moment.

The first time Herb Abrams called me, it was to ask me if I wanted to work on a show for him in Reseda, California. I had no reason to suspect this trip would amount to anything out of the ordinary. At best, I figured this would result in one or two show dates for me at a maximum.

"How would you like to come out and work with Bob Orton Jr.?" Herb asked me.

"I would *always* love working with Bob Orton Jr.," I told him.

It was true. Bob Orton Jr. was as smooth of a wrestler as they came, and one of the most criminally underrated wrestlers of all time. When Herb dangled the carrot of wrestling Bob, in addition to the payoff for the match, there was no doubt whatsoever that I would be willing to wrestle for him in Reseda.

The match itself was great. Bob and I tore the house down in Reseda despite the size of the crowd not being all that impressive. I'd grown accustomed to sparse crowds since leaving the WWF. To me it didn't matter if there were 50,000 people or 50 people in attendance; I was always going to do my best. I grew up poor and knew what it was like not to be able to afford a ticket to see the wrestlers I wanted to see. Because of that, I always wanted to give people their money's worth. I was one of those kids who had literally cried because he wasn't able to afford entry into the arena on some nights. I didn't want to deprive *any* of those families of a good show.

Executing a sunset flip on Bob Orton Jr.

Around the building, there was plenty of signage for the "Universal Wrestling Federation" hanging around. All I could think about was how that had been the name of Bill Watts' former Mid South territory right before he sold it to the Crocketts in 1987.

Herb was a short, wide-eyed Jewish guy with a pot belly, a big nose and curly, picked-out hair. When I first laid eyes on him, his hairstyle reminded me a little of Christopher Lloyd's from *Back to the Future*. After my match with Bob, Herb started asking me questions about how my gym business was going. Then he transitioned to asking me if I knew people who might be interested in making an investment in his wrestling company if he could get all of his ducks in a row.

"I've got a friend named Ed Barbara," I told Herb. "He might be interested in hearing about this."

"Great!" said Herb. "I'll fly out to Tampa the *first* chance I get!"

Ed had been with me when Brutus Beefcake's tragic parasailing accident occurred. He was one of my best friends and also one of the most trustworthy businesspeople I'd ever known. His connections were *extraordinary*. If Ed believed in you, he was also *very* trusting. There was a time when I had my savings tied up in my business or in some investment properties and needed some quick cash; Ed loaned me $25,000 on a handshake. I went out of my way to pay him back with *$35,000* just to let him know how much I appreciated his generosity. Paying Ed the additional $10,000 was a symbolic gesture, because he certainly didn't need my money. He had plenty of cash, and he wasn't afraid of losing it.

When Herb arrived in Tampa, we arranged to meet at Donatello's, an expensive Italian restaurant on N. Dale Mabry. I brought Ed along with me, and the two of them hit it off almost immediately. Herb had enough charisma to put a smile on anyone's face, in part because his face would burst into a huge grin whenever he saw somebody he liked. It was difficult not to reflect that level of affection right back in Herb's direction.

From there, Ed brought Tom Kenny into the equation and introduced him to Herb. Tom owned a company called CMI, and much like Ed, Tom also had plenty of money at his disposal. With the four of us sitting around a dinner table, Herb explained his master plan for the development and expansion of his Universal Wrestling Federation. The more Herb talked, the more excited *he* got, and the more I could see that Tom was *really* going for everything Herb was saying... hook, line and sinker.

"There are more stars *outside* of wrestling right now than there are *in* wrestling," Herb explained. "If we can get all of those stars together, *and* get a national television show, we could be bigger than the WWF in less than two years!"

Even during that initial meeting, Herb's chemical dependencies were obvious. He would repeatedly excuse himself from the table to use the restroom, then return to the table looking wired to an uncanny extent. Then Herb would pick on a few of the items on his plate, down a few glasses of scotch, and then excuse himself to use the restroom once again. It was clear that whatever Herb was eating was of secondary priority to the cocaine he'd been snorting. At the end of the night, he asked to have his meal boxed up; he had *barely* touched his food.

Soon after the dinner meeting at Donatello's, Tom flew Herb, Ed and I to Atlanta to meet Tom's brother, Larry, who served as Tom's personal accountant. Larry's reaction to me was the most markish reaction I had *ever* seen from an adult male.

"B. Brian Blair!" he screamed. "I'm such a big fan of the Killer Bees! It's an honor to meet you! I *can't* believe it!"

B. Brian Blair: Truth Bee Told

Tom laughed. He'd already warned me that his brother was going to get a huge kick out of meeting me in person.

A discussion about funding the UWF ensued, and Herb and Larry rapidly became very good friends. The meeting concluded with Herb being granted unfettered access to a mountain of Tom Kenny's cash. Tom purchased 49 percent of the UWF, and I believe it cost him somewhere in the neighborhood of $3 million.

Getting interviewed by Herb Abrams on an early UWF show

To his credit, Herb initially made some solid business decisions. He negotiated to secure a regular time slot for the UWF's *Fury Hour* television show on SportsChannel America. He also managed to secure some true, top-notch wrestling talent for our shows. Bob Orton Jr. and I were quickly joined by Paul Orndorff, "Dr. Death" Steve Williams, Bam Bam Bigelow, Don Muraco, Terry Gordy, Cactus Jack and Danny Spivey. Herb also managed to acquire the services of legendary former world champion Bruno Sammartino for the commentary booth, and manager Captain Lou Albano for the hosting of interview segments.

Herb opted to hold a press conference in New York to announce his aspirations and vision for the UWF, and he wanted it to be a noteworthy event.

"We need something to *spark* things," Herb said. "We need to do something at this press conference that will get us some type of attention."

B. Brian Blair: Truth Bee Told

I suggested that we should stage a brawl between Danny Spivey and I during our press conference, and Herb was all for it. As the interview portion of the press conference unfolded, I implied to Danny that he wouldn't be very successful in the UWF without the support of Sid Vicious, his one-time tag team partner in WCW. Danny didn't take too kindly to that; he threw a pitcher of water into my face, smashed my head into the table, and then threw me headfirst into the wall. It all looked *very* realistic.

Our press conference showed the promise of our new wrestling promotion, but it soon became evident that Herb was the wrong person to be steering the ship for a few obvious reasons. First, despite all of his financial backing, Herb never seemed to be capable of signing anyone to a contract. Danny and I wrestled in only one match together, and then Danny bolted for Japan to work for All Japan Pro Wrestling for the next *four* months. From there, Danny immediately signed with WCW when he returned to the U.S. because Herb didn't have anything in writing that could force Danny to stay with the UWF.

Another problem Herb had was that he simply didn't know anything at all about booking. That's not a crime, but he truly believed that he knew *everything* about proper booking. He didn't have the guts to ask any of the established stars to lose matches to one another.

In my opinion, this reluctance on Herb's part was because he wanted all of the wrestling stars to remain fond of him, and he thought that would change if he ever asked anyone to convincingly lose a bout. As a result, there were seldom any UWF matches that ended with famous wrestlers definitively losing. There were *far* too many count-out finishes and disqualifications, and those are match endings that almost never send the fans home feeling satisfied.

By comparison, Vince McMahon's roster was composed almost entirely of wrestlers who had been stars in other territories, yet Vince wielded *total* control over his booking decisions, and ruled the WWF with an iron fist. Agents and wrestlers could make suggestions to Vince, but in the end the wrestlers were going to get in the ring and deliver the exact matches and finishes that Vince required of them. Herb tried to appease everyone, and it resulted in the UWF presenting fans with a mediocre product.

I can't say that there wasn't an upside to working with Herb. One of the benefits to having a wrestling promoter who was so receptive to suggestions was that I was able to get Toni involved in the wrestling product. It struck me how there were very few women on the UWF roster, so I started thinking up a gimmick for my wife.

B. Brian Blair: Truth Bee Told

"Hey, Toni… would you like to be my valet?" I asked her. "We can call you 'Honey' and I can get a bee outfit made for you, and we can give you a cattle prod and call it your 'stinger.'"

Toni agreed, and I got to work assembling her outfit. I got the cattle prod idea from the days of working on my grandfather's farm. When we wanted the bulls or cows to get moving after they had been given their shots, we had to zap them with the cattle prod to get them out of their pens or into their head holders. I was always smart enough to never get shocked by the prod, because if it was strong enough to convince a 2,000-pound animal to get moving, it was likely to do considerable damage to a 150-pound kid.

I got black-and-yellow tape to decorate the cattle prod and made it look striped like a bee. The cattle prod wasn't just for show; it was the *real deal*. It fired off electricity in an arc formation with the strength of six DD batteries, and it could deliver an *agonizing* shock.

Herb *loved* the idea of Toni being my valet and okayed it immediately. He always placed additional emphasis on the name "Honey" every time he said it during his broadcast commentary. There were times when I would throw my opponents into the corner, or they would back into the ropes, or they would be getting ready to leap from the top turnbuckle to finish me off, and then Honey would jab them with the stinger and turn the tide of the contest. My opponents would then *convulse* on the ground. The fans ate it up whenever the cattle prod came into play.

More often than not, wrestlers from my era who had women in their corners as managers – like Jimmy Garvin with Precious, Randy Savage with Elizabeth, or Tully Blanchard with Baby Doll – were heels. On top of that, the fact that Toni carried a cattle prod as a weapon absolutely *screamed* "heel gimmick" to most wrestling fans. It all sounds like something Tully Blanchard might have done with Baby Doll during their heyday.

I didn't have any plans to ever turn heel in the UWF. I viewed the whole gimmick through the same lens as the masked-confusion gimmick that the Killer Bees used. Once the heel gets enough heat on you, fans don't really care what the babyface does to get revenge. Fans didn't mind if Honey jabbed at the heels with a cattle prod after they had been cheating me throughout a match.

We worked in an angle where Orton headbutted Honey in the ring and laid her out, which drew a lot of heat, because violence against women in the ring was taken *very* seriously back then. Toni was a terrific sport about getting headbutted by Orton, although Bob had to reassure her that the headbutt wouldn't do any actual damage to her head. It worked perfectly, because fans quickly understood the justification behind her carrying a weapon to defend herself against the brutal wrestlers that her husband was competing against.

Honey usually accompanied me to the ring without any batteries in the cattle prod, so there was never any chance that my opponents could actually get hurt from it. However, I simply *couldn't* help myself, and I reasoned that it would be a brilliant idea to rib Honey *and* Orton by actually sneaking *live* batteries into the cattle prod during a few of my matches. There was an inquisitive part of my mind that was enamored with the idea of seeing what would happen if someone actually got stung with the cattle prod.

Toni "Honey" Blair zapping Bob Orton Jr. with the cattle prod

I got my answer to that question during a match against Bob Orton Jr. in California. Honey zapped Orton with the stinger, discharged *live* voltage into his body, and he sold it like a *son of a gun*. Bob whirled around, looked at Toni and pointed at her like he was going to kill her. Bob wasn't working at the time, either. He was well and truly pissed off, and Toni had a terrified expression on her face as if to ask, "What did I do wrong?!"

"I'll tell you what..." Orton told me afterward. "You don't *ever* want to get shocked with that thing!"

Toni didn't see much humor in the incident. She was so scared after the match that she actually started crying in the locker room.

B. Brian Blair: Truth Bee Told

"*Why* would you do that to me?!" she cried. "Why would you think *that* was a good idea?!"

"It's *funny*!" I told her. "Orton didn't expect it!"

I tried to explain to her that ribs were just a traditional part of the business, and a requirement to help wrestlers occupy their time, but she failed to see things from that perspective. I probably should have considered it from the standpoint of the 115-pound woman getting an accusatory finger directed toward her by a 250-pound wrestler.

It was nice to have Toni on the road with me during that period, because it allowed us to spend even more time together. We didn't have any children yet, and being at my side helped her to experience the business as a performer. She also experienced what it felt like to have fans chanting approvingly for her. Ultimately, it just wasn't something that captivated her the same way it appealed to me.

"I don't want to disappoint you, but I'm *not* really comfortable doing this," Toni admitted after a few months.

I immediately told her it was okay, and that I understood her decision. The wrestling business simply isn't for everyone.

Since I was helping Herb with recruiting talent to the roster, I approached him and asked, "Why don't we bring Jimmy Brunzell in, and you can let us tag up again? We can be your flagship tag team here."

"Sure, Brian!" Herb said. "That's a great idea!"

Herb might have felt pressured to agree that *all* of my ideas were great ideas. I had the most direct connection to the people that were funding his operation, and if I'd demanded to become the UWF World Heavyweight Champion, Herb probably would have acceded to my wishes. I would *never* have done that, though.

We had respected, established main eventers like Steve Williams and Paul Orndorff on our talent roster, so I was more than happy to play a secondary role. With that being said, I believed my suggestion to build a tag team division around the Killer Bees had merit. We were a team that still enjoyed instant name recognition with knowledgeable wrestling fans all over the world.

Not only did I want to help Jim out by bringing him into the UWF, but this decision was also important to me for purposes of preserving and enhancing our team's legacy. Jim and I had never held tag team gold together, and this was an opportunity for me to somewhat right what I considered to have been a grave injustice of WWF booking. After being promised the world tag titles on three occasions in the WWF, the least I could do would be to get Jim and I a run with the UWF World Tag Team Championship. That way, no one would ever be able to say that the Killer Bees *never* held a world tag team title.

The Killer Bees reunite in the UWF

In addition, I'd hoped to somewhat rehabilitate Jim in the eyes of wrestling fans. One full year after the two of us left the World Wrestling Federation, and three years after our signature victory over the Hart Foundation on *Saturday Night's Main Event*, Jim returned to work for Vince as an underneath talent. He was now simply one of the guys who stood in the ring and awaited the arrival of the stars so that they could squash him and get themselves over with the viewing audience.

I totally understand that Jim needed the money, but it was *sad*. Jim was a star and a tag team pioneer, so this mistreatment of him didn't sit well with me. What's more, the perception being created of Jim during that time probably erased any opportunity that the Killer Bees might reunite *and* be taken seriously in a WWF ring.

Jim and I reconnected in the UWF for a few matches, and our team chemistry was still intact. However, we were nervous about continuing to wrestle as the Killer Bees. Vince had been fine about permitting me to wrestle as "The Killer Bee" Brian Blair, but his disdain for Jim might have tempted him to take legal steps to block our use of the Killer Bees tag team name in the UWF. Our thinking wasn't without justification. Herb *hadn't* escaped Vince's notice by any means; the WWF took legal action against the UWF to prevent Rick

B. Brian Blair: Truth Bee Told

Rude from appearing on one of our shows. Therefore, Vince might have retaliated against us as well just to be spiteful.

Instead of going as the Killer Bees, we wrestled as "The Bees" and then "Masked Confusion." We still used our same masks and Killer Bees ring jackets, but we occasionally wrestled in jaguar-patterned tights instead of our customary black-and-yellow stripes. We figured it was better to be safe than sorry when you were dealing with someone like Vince McMahon.

It was around that time that Tom Kenny, the man who was funding the UWF, held a golf tournament called the CMI Challenge at the Horseshoe Bend Country Club on July 15, 1991. The tournament was in Roswell, just north of Atlanta.

Each team was required to have a competent golfer and a celebrity, and Ed Barbara selected me as his celebrity partner. I was a serviceable golfer, but I was never great. On the other hand, Ed was a scratch golfer, and he was *incredible*. On that day, Ed was golfing at the top of his game, and I was putting the ball as well as I ever had in my entire life. We captured the first-place trophy that day, and it is still displayed proudly in my office.

After the tournament, Tom asked Ed and I if we wanted to grab some food and drinks. We agreed, of course, and wound up on the outdoor patio of a local restaurant surrounded by plenty of other people who were drinking and having a good time. It was a lively place with a boisterous atmosphere. Somehow in the middle of all that merrymaking, Tom got into a heated argument with one of the other patrons at the restaurant. Instinctively, I rose from my chair and came to Tom's aid.

"Hey!" I interjected, while inserting my arm between the two men. "You better leave him alone right now!"

The man drunkenly stared at me for a moment as if he was sizing me up, but then he appeared to think better of fighting me and walked away. Tom and I sat back down at the table, and everyone's attention returned to food, drinks and laughter.

The patio was elevated slightly and fenced in by exterior railing. Beneath the railing there were some bushes adjacent to the parking lot. It was very dark out there, but there was just enough lighting coming in from the parking lot that I was able to notice when a shadow disturbed that lighting. The flicker of light was just enough to catch my attention before I turned and noticed that the man Tom had been arguing with was slinking through the bushes and on the verge of ambushing him from the cover of darkness.

B. Brian Blair: Truth Bee Told

In one motion, I pivoted and rose from my chair, and I knocked the man to the ground with a quick forearm to his forehead. I hadn't hit him *that* hard, but it was sufficient to stagger him and knock him off balance. The man then stood up and lunged toward me. I hopped over the railing and into the bushes, fully intent on battering Tom's would-be assailant. All of a sudden, I was blinded by a bright light.

"Stop and show me your hands!" boomed a voice from the parking lot.

Two Fulton County Sheriff's deputies – one White and one Black – had been sitting in the parking lot, and they had caught the tail end of the incident.

"Turn around and put your hands behind your back!" the Black deputy instructed me.

"Are you *serious?!*" I protested. "That guy was *attacking* my friend!"

"I saw *him* walk through the bushes, and I saw *you* deck him in the face," the deputy responded. "Turn around and put your hands behind your back."

"I don't believe this!" I said, but I did as I was told.

The Black deputy escorted me over to his squad car. The White deputy handcuffed Tom's attacker and departed with him in the opposite direction. I never saw the assailant again after that.

The deputy opened the door to the squad car, plopped me down in the back seat, and then walked around and sat down in the driver's seat. I glanced down to my left and saw a plastic bag with something green and leafy in it. As I leaned over and peered closer, it looked to me like a bag of marijuana.

"Holy cow!" I thought to myself. "This is a *setup!*"

I started freaking out worse than I'd ever freaked out before. Going against everything I'd ever been advised to do about making sure I had a lawyer present or asserting my rights and so forth, I instead began to spill my guts to the deputy about what had transpired at the restaurant. I also told him that I was a professional wrestler, which seemed to improve my situation slightly because the deputy responded by saying he was a wrestling fan.

It was a *long* drive to the Fulton County Sheriff's Office, so I had plenty of time to build a rapport with the deputy and to tell him some road stories. All the while, I still figured something was up, and I remained on a heightened level of alertness all the way to the jail. I didn't know if someone who was in the car before me had left the bag of marijuana so that he wouldn't get caught with it, but *I* sure didn't intend to take the blame for it.

In my state of panic, I did something extremely stupid: I wriggled and contorted myself over to the bag of weed and attempted earnestly to jam it into the crevice between the seat cushions. In the best-case scenario playing out in my mind, the deputies hadn't known the weed was back there, so they wouldn't know that it was missing. In the worst-case scenario, they knew it was there, and now they had proof that I'd tampered with it. Again, it was an asinine decision.

When we finally arrived at the jail and I was escorted inside, I was still just as paranoid as I could be. Then a major from the Sheriff's Office materialized in the room mere seconds before I was about to be booked.

"B. Brian Blair!" the major shouted through a grin. "You're one of my *favorite* wrestlers! Golly! Never thought I'd ever meet you! What brings *you* out here?"

This guy was *so* happy to meet me that he seemed totally oblivious to the fact that I was standing in front of him with my hands cuffed behind my back.

The major casually motioned for the deputies to uncuff me, and then as soon as my arms were free, he gave me a big hug.

"Hey, somebody bring a camera over here!" the major ordered. "I want to get my picture taken with B. Brian Blair!"

I posed for as many photos as the major requested, and then he sent me on my way. I felt like God had rescued me from obvious peril. In my mind, I was certain that I was about to be convicted of aggravated assault in a country town in Georgia, *and* I was going to get booked for possession of marijuana. My name would have been dragged through the mud in all of the papers, and then I would have served *10 years* in prison. Instead, I didn't even get a slap on the wrist because that major was on duty, and he was such a diehard wrestling fan.

I was the only White guy in the building, so I half expected everyone there to use me as the scapegoat in order to exact vengeance against historic injustices perpetrated by White people. To my great relief, they were *very* kind. It just goes to show you that you shouldn't always assume the worst in people because everyone has a heart.

Once I disappeared from Roswell, I never heard from anyone regarding the incident again. To play it safe, I also *never* went back there. However, it wouldn't be too long before my continued involvement in wrestling would land me in all sorts of outlandish predicaments.

TWENTY-FOUR – *High-heeled hookers and cocaine*

After only a few months in operation, the Universal Wrestling Federation went through an obvious rough patch and discontinued its television shows on SportsChannel America. Simply stated, Herb did *not* run a tight ship. Between failing to lock talent down with exclusive contracts, to shoddy production, to spending all of Tom Kenny's money to maintain his destructive habits, Herb capsized the UWF through a wide range of miscalculations and misbehaviors.

On top of this, Herb developed an unshakeable reputation for bouncing checks to both wrestlers and contractors. Had he not had the backing and support of Lenny Duke, the incredible producer that Herb had smuggled away from Vince McMahon, Herb probably would have been drawn and quartered by all of the creditors he owed money to. Lenny repeatedly served as an intercessor to keep people from strangling Herb over missed payments.

I tried to assist Herb with booking decisions during the UWF's early stages, but it only grew increasingly more difficult to talk sense into Herb as time progressed. One day I just got fed up, screamed at Herb, and told him I wasn't going to give him any more booking advice since he simply dismissed it all.

"You've *got* to have winners and losers!" I advised Herb. "*I* do jobs here. *Everybody* does jobs here. As long as we know it's leading to something good in the end for all of us, nobody will have a problem if you just do it *right!*"

"I *know* what I'm doing, Brian!" Herb insisted. "Don't worry about it. I've got it *all* under control."

"You know what, Herb… I don't want anything to do with booking anymore," I told him. "You don't listen to me anyway. You *clearly* know better than I do. Just put me in matches and I'll take care of my own matches."

"Come on, Brian!" he protested. "It's not like that at all!"

"Nah… I think we'll all be better off if you just do it yourself," I said.

As bad as Herb's hairbrained booking practices were, they represented only a miniscule fraction of the UWF's problems. At no point was this more evident to me than when I went to collect some of the money that Herb owed me for my matches.

Herb was staying at the Causeway Hotel in Tampa, which is about 20 minutes from my house. I arrived at the hotel, took the elevator up to Herb's floor and knocked on the door to his room. Lo and behold, two *naked* women opened the door for me, in a scenario eerily reminiscent of when David Von Erich sent a girl to open the door for me at his house in Dallas.

"Is Herb in here?" I asked the women.

They stood aside and I stepped into the room. Herb was lying on the bed wearing black, silk socks that were pulled right up to his knees. He had some strange quirk about never wanting to be seen without socks on. Aside from the socks on his feet, Herb was stark naked, and it *wasn't* a pretty sight.

Backstage at the UWF tapings, Herb would go to great lengths to describe the sex acts he would have prostitutes perform on him. I guess he thought we were impressed by the fact that he was having sex with beautiful women, though the accomplishment was made far less impressive by the fact that he was obviously *paying* for all of the fun he was having.

Sex consumed Herb's thoughts to such an extent that even when we were supposed to be discussing how we were booking our shows and the finishes to matches, Herb would be preoccupied with shifting the discussions back to sex. It was the epitome of a one-track mind, even more so than Paul Orndorff in his younger years.

"Hey, Brian," Herb said with a smile. "Ya wanna join us?"

"*No*, Herb," I replied, sternly and impatiently. "My *wife* is at home. I've got to get going."

"Okay, okay..." Herb said. "Ladies, go get cleaned up and I'll get you your money."

Admittedly, I stared at the girls a *little bit* as they walked by in their high heels. One had fishnet stockings on, and the other was totally nude. As far as hookers went, they were definitely in the upper echelon, and Herb had probably agreed to pay a handsome sum of money for their services.

Once the door to the bathroom closed, I lit into Herb.

"Dammit, Herb!" I yelled. "Why the fuck are you spending all your money like this?! It's not even *your* money! It's *Tom Kenny's* money! You'd better write me a check right now, and this check better not fuckin' bounce!"

"No, no, no..." Herb said, with his palms facing me. "I've *got* your money."

"I know you've been bouncing checks to different people!" I told him. "You'd better *not* do that to me!"

It was true; Herb *had* been bouncing checks to at least half of the UWF's talent roster. He had developed a reputation as one of the most unreliable promoters in wrestling... which covers a *vast* stretch of territory.

With Herb Abrams and Ric Flair

"*Your* check isn't gonna bounce," Herb said, remaining calm.

The girls opened up the door to the bathroom and came out to collect their money from Herb. I used that as an opportunity to walk past them and grab a big, white hotel towel from above the toilet. Then I walked back into the room and tossed the towel onto Herb's midsection.

"Here, Herb," I said. "Put that on your lap."

"Oh, Brian," laughed Herb. "Why are you such a fuckin' *prude?*"

I stepped over to one side of Herb, and my eyes widened as I watched him write two $2,000 checks, tear them from the checkbook, and hand them to the hookers.

"Don't spend it all in one place, ladies!" he said.

After a little more chatting, the girls left the room. I was *pissed* to see Herb blowing all of my friend's money on floozies.

"Herb!" I yelled.

"Just a minute," Herb said, cutting me off. He reached for the phone and began to dial while studying a page of his checkbook.

"Herb..." I said again.

"Just a minute, Brian!" Herb screamed. "*Shit!*"

After a couple more seconds, someone on the other end of the line answered Herb's call.

B. Brian Blair: Truth Bee Told

"Hi! This is Herb Abrams," he said. "I need to cancel a couple checks. I've looked everywhere for these lost checks, and I just can't find them. Please void the checks or cancel them. Do whatever you have to do, but I need to stop payment on them."

I stood there dumbstruck as Herb recited the check numbers to the bank employee. When the phone call reached its conclusion, Herb hung up the phone, flopped back down on the bed, kicked his feet into the air, and cackled like a maniacal supervillain.

"Brian, I just had the greatest night of my life for *free!*" he declared.

Instead of helping Herb celebrate the scam he had just run on two young prostitutes, I capitalized on the opportunity to draw his attention to something else I'd noticed since I had entered the room.

"Herb, there's two *giant* piles of cocaine right there," I said, pointing them out. "One on *that* table, and one on *that* table! How much did *that* cost you? *That* wasn't free, was it?"

"Awww, don't worry about that," Herb said. "I have a friend that sells coke. I got a good deal on it."

Herb handed me my check, and I drove straight to the bank with it. To my great shock and relief, the check cleared. I *couldn't* believe what I'd just witnessed. A naked Herb Abrams in silk socks, flanked by high-heeled hookers and cocaine. I couldn't get the image out of my mind. I was mostly frustrated, because the UWF once had a golden opportunity to be successful if Herb could have simply maintained a level head and gotten his act together.

In fairness, Herb *never* bounced a check to me. He might have held off on paying me a few times, but he *never* bounced a check to me. I was the one who'd introduced him to the golden goose that was funding his entire organization, so he knew better than to totally screw me over on a payoff.

The person who *was* screwed over mightily was Tom Kenny. Herb used his relationship with Tom's brother, Larry, to gain an additional $2 million of Tom's cash later on. This drove a permanent wedge between the two brothers that was never removed.

Herb used this latest influx of cash to assist with the staging of *Beach Brawl*, a pay-per-view event that aired on June 9, 1991. A pay-per-view show can generate a ton of money if it's promoted properly, *and* if the talent level is sufficient. In the case of *Beach Brawl*, the talent was definitely accounted for. Wrestlers like Steve Williams, Paul Orndorff, Bob Backlund, Terry Gordy, Cactus Jack and Bam Bam Bigelow were all present and accounted for, along with Jim and I, who competed against the Power Twins.

B. Brian Blair: Truth Bee Told

The event itself wasn't bad, but it didn't matter a whole lot; *no one* watched it. Only about 500 people showed up in Palmetto, Florida in the Manatee Civic Center, a venue that was designed to seat 4,000 people. A small, passionate crowd packed into a tiny building can improve the overall atmosphere of a wrestling event, but when a large building is only a little more than 10 percent full, it can be very deflating to both the wrestlers and the audience.

What was even more devastating was the incredibly low number of orders the broadcast received. An average WWF pay-per-view event during that era was attracting about 400,000 buys; *Beach Brawl* had fewer than 18,000. There were plenty of reasons for the failure, but most of the blame would deservedly fall at the feet of Herb. Instead of managing Tom's money responsibly and making rational business decisions, he was hopelessly preoccupied with hookers and cocaine.

I was preparing some lunch for myself in the kitchen that summer when the doorbell rang. I hadn't been expecting any guests, so I was very curious about who might have been stopping by unannounced. So many wrestlers lived in Tampa that it could have been absolutely anybody. Instead, when I opened the door, I was surprised to discover a gentleman wearing a dark suit, a black tie, and sunglasses. He held a briefcase in one hand, and in the other hand he was holding something that looked like a black wallet.

"Hi," I said politely.

"Hi...Brian Blair?" the man asked.

"Yes?" I replied.

The man raised his wallet to my face so that I could clearly see the shiny badge on one side of it that bore the words "Federal Bureau of Investigation."

"I'm from the FBI, and I'd like to ask you a few questions about some packages you received in the mail," he explained. "Do you mind if I come in?"

I led the agent into my house and we both took a seat at the kitchen table.

"Are you familiar with Dr. George Zahorian?" he asked me.

"Yes, I am," I told him.

The agent nodded, set his briefcase down on the table, opened it, and extracted some documents from within it.

"We've tracked some packages sent by Dr. Zahorian to your residence, along with the homes of several other wrestlers," he informed me. "I want to be perfectly clear: *You* haven't done anything illegal by buying steroids and valium when you did. *Zahorian* did something illegal by selling those drugs to you in the way that he went about it."

"Okay, so what do you want from me?" I asked him.

"We want you to *testify* against Zahorian," he said. "All we need you to do is admit under oath that you ordered steroids from him. It's as simple as that."

"Is anyone else testifying?" I asked.

"Yes… we have several other people lined up to testify," said the agent. "Like I said, you weren't the only one that received a package in the mail that we tracked."

The other wrestlers that were lined up to testify included Hulk Hogan, Roddy Piper, Rick Martel and Danny Spivey. Of the five of us, Danny and I were the only two that weren't actively wrestling for the WWF at the time.

"I'll help you in any way I can," I told him. "I've got nothing to hide."

I did exactly as I was instructed, and I testified that I had ordered steroids and valium from Dr. George Zahorian through the mail. Then they got around to asking me about Vince McMahon.

"Did Vince McMahon have any knowledge that Dr. Zahorian was selling steroids to wrestlers in the locker room?" the prosecutor asked me.

"I can't speak to that," I told him. "I have no idea what Vince did or didn't know about."

Zahorian was sentenced to serve three years in federal prison. Subsequent to that, the Federal Government pivoted and pursued Vince McMahon for his alleged role in a conspiracy to distribute steroids, but I had no role in that trial whatsoever. Frankly, I had the sense that the feds always viewed McMahon as the bigger fish, and they seemed disappointed that my testimony wouldn't be useful in their efforts to put him behind bars.

Aside from wrestling for the IWA and UWF, there were several other opportunities presented to me and other former WWF wrestlers to earn paychecks in the world of professional wrestling in the early 1990s. Many of those opportunities involved wrestling overseas in environments that would be difficult for North American wrestling fans to comprehend.

While it's true that I had been absent from network television wrestling events for a few years, many countries were only just starting to receive mid-'80s wrestling broadcasts and video tapes in the early '90s. These distribution delays benefitted WWF veterans a great deal, and created touring opportunities for us in many countries.

B. Brian Blair: Truth Bee Told

For example, I was invited to go on a few tours of Guam and the Northern Mariana Islands during some of my downtime from the IWA and UWF. The wrestling promotion that operated there was called the National Wrestling League. In Saipan we wrestled in an outdoor arena in Cowtown. In Guam, the largest show was at the University of Guam Fieldhouse. Depending on the location or the venue, anywhere from 1,000 to 10,000 rabid fans were in attendance for these events.

Posing with Bam Bam Bigelow and other wrestlers in Guam

The Mariana Islands were a little less developed than Guam, which had American-style shopping centers and other amenities. In both places, we had very comfortable accommodations. Promoter Dick Caricofe placed us in huts along the water, consistent with the sort of huts you envision when you think of a place like Tahiti. The roofs were made of frontons, and we had all of the provisions we would ever need in order to feel comfortable.

The highlight of my time in the National Wrestling League was winning the promotion's tag team championship with Paul Orndorff. Cactus Jack and Bam Bam Bigelow were two of the other recognizable names on those tours alongside us.

After one of the shows in Saipan, Brady Boone and I wandered into a local bar. In addition to being a wrestler, Brady also worked for me in one of my Gold's Gyms. We were the only White, non-native patrons in the entire place. A live band played loud rock 'n' roll music in that smoky bar. A uniformed security guard was also present in the area, which struck me as odd and left me with an uneasy feeling. I'm used to seeing bouncers at bars, but this was the first time I could recall seeing a uniformed security guard *openly* brandishing a firearm inside of a bar.

Out of the blue, a Saipanese girl came by, introduced herself to Brady and I, and sat down to converse with us. As we all talked, a couple of drinks arrived at our table. We were told that the girl had purchased the drinks for us. Then two more girls wandered over and invited themselves to take a seat at our table. That's when a cigarette butt struck me in the back of the head, which I glanced at and chose to ignore. A few moments later, a couple more cigarette butts landed on our table, which we *also* ignored.

The next event that happened was *impossible* to ignore: A Saipanese man stormed over to our table, smashed a bottle against the edge of it, and began berating us in his native language as he waved the broken end of the bottle in our faces. We couldn't understand a word he was saying, but it was quite clear that he didn't appreciate our presence in the bar one bit. It was later translated for us that his grievance had something to do with us being White men that were chatting with a table *full* of Saipanese women.

As Brady and I were being berated, someone lobbed a large chunk of ice in our direction; it crashed into the back of Brady's head. All at once, more of the male onlookers stood up and worked their way over towards us. Sensing the obvious danger, one of the tiny Saipanese girls at our table also stood up and smashed a bottle at the edge of our table and waved it threateningly in the faces of our potential attackers. As she did so, *blood* began to drip from her hand. Evidently, she'd cut herself during the act of smashing the bottle.

I sized up the situation and realized that Brady and I were vastly outnumbered, and probably faced with a life-or-death struggle if we didn't make a move to escape immediately.

"Brady, get your back against the wall *right now!*" I yelled.

We both quickly moved against the wall. The girl holding the broken bottle continued to scream at the men who hovered in front of us in a semicircular formation. I looked over at the uniformed security guard in the hope that he was headed over to de-escalate the altercation. To my horror, he was clearly content to stand as a spectator over by the bar's entrance and watch as we died.

"To the door!" I said to Brady. "*Quick*! Get to the door!"

A couple more girls joined our cause and inserted themselves into the fracas. One of the girls, who went by the name "Saipan Rose," balled up her fist and popped one of the men right in the nose. Only then did the security guard begin to move closer, and Brady and I slowly inched toward the side door of the establishment.

Glass bottles and other debris began to fly toward us. When we found an opening, we sprinted out through the door and straight to our rental car. Fortunately, our rental car was modern enough that a key fob would unlock the doors, which saved us a few critical seconds. The Saipanese men were still able to do plenty of damage to the car as we made our escape. They pelted the vehicle with bottles and other debris as we absconded from the scene. Brady and I could easily have wound up disfigured or dead simply because we were approached by the wrong girls at the wrong bar on the wrong island.

Early the following year, in 1992, I got a call from my old mentor Afa of the Wild Samoans.

"Hey, do you want to come to Russia?" Afa asked me.

"I *could*, but how much are we getting for the tour?" I responded.

"Ten thousand dollars for six days," he said.

"Okay... I'm *in*!" I told him.

The tour actually wound up being closer to eight days long given the two days of flying. With all of the accommodations and expenses taken care of out of the promoter's pockets, $10,000 was a more-than-adequate payoff.

When we landed at the airport in Moscow, the Russians didn't take us through customs. Instead, they brought us all in through a room that had no windows. It resembled a giant prison cell.

Afa was holding onto all of our passports before we entered the room, and from there we were locked inside of the room for a solid half an hour. That was a *long* time to spend in the windowless room of a Russian airport when you have *no idea* what's going on, and we all started getting pretty antsy.

"Hey, Afa!" said Bam Bam Bigelow. "Do you know what's goin' on? Are they *ever* gonna let us out of here?"

"It's okay," answered Afa. "They probably just need to double check everything with the promoter."

I'm not sure whether or not Afa really knew what was happening. Eventually the door was soon opened for us, and we exited the room to discover that a crowd had gathered outside of our detention area. Standing out from the crowd were two Russians who spoke to us through an interpreter.

"All of you stand next to your assigned roommate," the interpreter ordered us. "Each pair of you will be given a bodyguard for the duration of your stay."

B. Brian Blair: Truth Bee Told

Ken Patera was assigned to me as a roommate, and we were introduced to our bodyguard, Arnold. Like the rest of the bodyguards, Arnold was fluent in English. Every grouping of wrestlers and bodyguards was ushered into its own limousine as the Russian press snapped photos of us. Hilariously, the limos were merely for the sake of a photo op. As soon as we'd traveled a comfortable distance away from the hotel, we were all shuttled over to a large bus, which we piled into before continuing on our way.

As we arrived in Red Square, we passed the first McDonald's to ever open in Russia, which happened back in January of 1990. The restaurant was still very popular; it had a long line of customers waiting well beyond its entrance, and the line extended all the way around the corner. At that point, we were confident that there would at least be food nearby that we would be comfortable consuming. Little did we know the sorts of meals the promoters had in store for us.

We pulled into the hotel parking lot of what was supposed to have been the nicest hotel in Moscow. The exterior looked ancient, but I didn't want to judge a book by its cover. A group of bedraggled-looking people gathered outside of our bus as soon as it came to a halt. Once the doors to the bus opened, the crowd of beggars drew closer and nearly blocked the doorway.

"Gypsies," Arnold said. "They are *always* looking for money. Don't give them any."

We stepped off of the bus, and several of the children in the group stepped forward.

"American... *one* penny!" the children pleaded. "Please! *One* penny!"

I felt awful at the sight of children who were so desperate to collect as little as one penny from us. As soon as I was certain that no one was looking at me, I dropped a couple dollars to the children. I'm sure their parents had taught them to do the asking because they assumed it would be far more difficult for American tourists to decline the requests of children. They were *correct*.

When I dropped the money, two of the children began shoving one another, and they nearly came to blows over the two dollars I'd let fall to the ground. Some of the other wrestlers turned around to see what was causing the commotion, so I put my head down and walked faster so that they wouldn't suspect that I'd given money to those poor children.

At this stage of the day, between being detained, shifted from one mode of transportation to another, seeing the dilapidated-looking building we would all be staying in, and *then* watching a brawl ensue over just *two* U.S. dollars, I was feeling very nervous about the entire trip, and desperately hoped that the U.S. consulate knew where we were in case any trouble ensued.

When we arrived at the hotel's lobby, Afa said, "Get the keys to your rooms and get checked in. We'll meet in the conference room in an hour."

Right away, we learned that the hotel had no elevators, which was brutal because Ken and I were given a room on the third floor. Fortunately, the interior of the hotel was in better shape than the exterior. The accommodations were nothing special, but they were adequate. Our room had two, comfortable double beds. The hotel also had a huge bar in its lobby, which is where Ken Patera would spend the majority of his free time during our trip. Even as we were entering the hotel, we could see *obvious* hookers stationed at the bar, anxious to separate the inbound wrestlers from their cash.

Once the wrestler meeting was underway, two Russian diplomats entered the room and requested to pose for photos with us. One of them pulled out the most absurdly massive wad of cash I'd ever seen. It must have been $10,000, all in $100 bills. That display of wealth undeniably got the attention of *every* wrestler in the room very quickly.

As this man leaned in for photos with each wrestler, he would hand off a $100 bill to the wrestler. When it was my turn, he extended the bill, but I waved my hand dismissively and shook my head.

"That's okay," I smiled. "No money."

In response to that, the man smiled and shook my hand.

"Thank you!" he said, and then we took the photo together.

From there, we were taken to the Moscow Auditorium to see the venue where the matches would be held. That's when I found out that I'd been booked to work with a former Olympic champion, because I was the only person on the tour with legitimate amateur-style wrestling experience.

Bam Bam also worked with the same Russian guy, who was far from an experienced worker. Professional wrestling opportunities had been few and far between in Russia. In fact, I'm guessing the style was nonexistent there prior to the fall of the Soviet Union. I worked out with the wrestler in the ring a little bit, and he was eager to learn.

The stadium was configured in a very interesting arrangement. There was a ringside section, and then there was a raised section. The raised section was filled with Russian diplomats and dignitaries. We wrestled in that same building for four nights in a row, and it was sold out all four times.

B. Brian Blair: Truth Bee Told

Wrestling in front of a Russian crowd was the easiest thing in the world. Since I was facing the Russians' star heavyweight, Vladimir, all I had to do was step through the curtain and the people were already amped up to *murder* me. It was the *best* crowd heat you could possibly get. Tapes of 1980s WWF shows had circulated prior to our arrival, so the audiences were familiar with who we all were.

Bam Bam and I both had very good matches with Vladimir. He was very stiff and clumsy for a worker, but it was easy to make up for. He understood that if I gave him "the office" – which meant I squeezed his wrist – it let him know that he was to reverse a hold. If I put him in a front facelock, I would wait until the time was right, and then I would squeeze his wrist to signal the reversal to him, and he would immediately comply.

"We have to eat breakfast, lunch and dinner with these guys, *every* day," Afa informed me.

"Okay, fine," I said.

Different public officials were rotating in and out of the meals each day, but every single meal was prepared by professional chefs, and they consisted of the most eye-popping quantities of delicious food I'd ever seen in a single location. *Anything* that you wanted – whether it was steak, lobster, or some other delicacy – they had it. They didn't care how much you ate and drank. In fact, they encouraged us to drink as much vodka as we possibly could. Fresh bottles of vodka and red wine were set in front of us during breakfast, lunch and dinner.

The food was only one part of the spectacle at these meals. Las-Vegas-quality stage shows accompanied every dining experience. Elite ballerinas, gymnasts and other high-wire performers entertained us on a nightly basis. Four of the nights were punctuated by incredible aerial displays from different acrobats.

Every night after the matches, the $100 bills flowed as freely as the vodka. Dozens of men with wads of cash darted back and forth throughout the room, openly flashing their money and looking for opportunities to impress us with it. We were also taken to a Russian dance club that was probably 300 yards in length. I've *never* seen another place like it. It was absolutely humongous and packed full of people dancing to rave music. Everyone was dancing and having a great time as we listened to music supplied by a band that performed behind a glass partition well off in the distance.

All of us were treated like absolute royalty during that trip, and I was in *no* hurry for that tour to ever end. That tour of Russia was *easily* my favorite tour *of all time*. To top it off, we were all paid *in cash* on the final night. I received an envelope with the full $10,000 of cash inside of it – *all* in $100 bills – as it had been agreed in advance.

The Russians *also* offered us girls, but I'm not aware of any wrestlers on the tour who partook in any of that. Not that I would have done anything with prostitutes anyway, but the girls that were being offered to us all looked like they had something *clearly* wrong with them. Several of them even had thick hair under their armpits, which just wasn't very appealing to me.

I went up to my room to start packing up, and Patera wasn't there, which was no surprise. I changed my clothes, and then went back downstairs to eat and enjoy the entertainment. Ken didn't show up at the dinner table either, which *was* surprising because he had been present for every other meal during the tour. Finally, it got late, and I decided to call it a night.

I reached the landing area between the first and second floors. As I turned to head up the second set of stairs, I saw a pile of $100 bills lying on the ground. From that spot, a trail of money led up the stairs, almost like Hansel and Gretl's breadcrumbs. I picked up all the money at the bottom of the stairs, and then gathered the rest of the bills together as I climbed the steps. There were *so many* $100 bills scattered everywhere, and they were in such disarray that it took me a full five minutes to gather them all together. The trail came to a halt right at the door of our hotel room.

I opened the door to the room to discover Ken Patera passed out on his bed, drunker than Cooter Brown. As fate would have it, I happened to be the first person to walk up the stairs after the money had trickled out of Ken's envelope. If anyone else had come by and seen that money, Ken almost certainly would have left the Russian tour with nothing.

I handed Ken his money as soon as he woke up the following morning.

"I got *so* drunk last night," Ken moaned.

"*Obviously*, Ken," I laughed. "You were snoring so loudly I could barely sleep."

"I met this Russian girl, and she took me to her room," he said. "I didn't want her to get my money. I hid it, but I didn't remember where I put it."

Ken was eternally grateful to me that I'd scooped up his money from the stairwell. Considering how happy the beggars outside of our hotel had been with mere pennies, I can only imagine how they would have reacted to seeing $10,000 in loose bills scattered along the interior stairway. It would have changed their entire lives.

B. Brian Blair: Truth Bee Told

At the airport, Arnold said, "I have present for you."

With tears running down his face, Arnold unfastened the watch from his wrist and handed it over to me.

"I wish I could go to America with you," he said.

"That would be *great* if you could come visit," I told him.

I scribbled down my address and phone number on a piece of paper and passed it over to him.

"If you ever make it to the U.S., you should give me a call," I told him. "If you need a recommendation for a job or anything like that, I'd love to help you out."

From there, Arnold handed me a 25-pound bag filled with the most *expensive* beluga caviar that money could buy. Even a small can of caviar of that quality would have cost around $50 in the U.S. at the time. What I was holding in my hands was worth at least $1,000... and probably a *lot* more.

At our airport gate, there was a sign that said, "These items will be confiscated, and you will be arrested." One of the items on that *very* specific list was caviar. I had the caviar packed very tightly in my bag, and I assumed I was in the clear, but I had a niggling feeling in my gut that kept urging me to ditch the caviar somewhere in the airport. I sat there with the caviar for a full half an hour struggling with myself about what to do with it. I thought about placing it somewhere that a Russian citizen might be able to pick it up and get some value from it. Even if its value was only $1,000, that *still* represented half of an average Russian's wages for an *entire year* back in 1992.

As discreetly as I could, I walked over to a nearby trashcan and regretfully dumped the caviar into it. In my mind, I was being watched on a camera somewhere, and Russian police were just waiting for me to attempt to board the plane with the caviar so that they could swoop in and nab me. I don't think Arnold was trying to set me up, but by no means would it have been worth it to serve time in a Russian prison over 25 pounds of caviar.

The one souvenir I did leave Russia with was a set of the stackable Matryoshka dolls. *All* of the guys on the tour bought them. When you opened the large wooden doll, the rest of the dolls each contained successively smaller representations of Russian and Soviet presidents and dictators.

As much as I enjoyed that tour, a few elements of the trip did bother me. The class disparity I saw lingered with me for a long time. It seemed like there was no true middle class in Russia, and that people were *either* living in abject poverty, or they were *filthy* rich. There was *no* middle ground. It was hard not to feel at least somewhat guilty when you'd received a $10,000 *cash* payoff in Moscow, after a week of being on the receiving end of massive feasts, all on the same day that you saw average Russian citizens standing in breadlines.

    Privately, Arnold complained to me about the oppressive government in Russia, and what he described was worse than a modern American could possibly fathom. I never saw Arnold again, but I certainly hope he's living a safe, prosperous life somewhere. To this day, I still have the watch he handed me as I was departing from Russia.

    This experience in Russia laid bare for me how privileged I was to live in a country that afforded me tremendous freedoms. It also left me hoping that one day I would be able to take advantage of my American freedoms to make things better for average people in my own community.

TWENTY-FIVE– The *hardest thing to open is a closed mind*

The early 1990s ushered in my return to New Japan Pro Wrestling for the first time in a long time. When I finally rejoined New Japan in 1992, I was pleased to learn that the company had done a great job of keeping the Japanese fans abreast of the changes in my career. Wrestling magazines in Japan printed photos of my involvement in the UWF, and also apprised them of the change to my ring name.

This was the first year that I wrestled in Japan following my high-profile run in the WWF as one half of the Killer Bees, and I was introduced in Japan as "The Killer Bee" Brian Blair. Of course, the fans in Japan called me either "Hachi" – which is the Japanese word for "bee" – or "Bee-san." Along with the updated name came a boost in pay; I now commanded a $2,500-per-week salary for my work in Japan.

I spent a lot of my time on that tour teaming with super heavyweights like Leon "Big Van Vader" White, Bam Bam Bigelow and Scott Norton in tag team matches and six-man matches. All three of them were extraordinarily talented big men, but all three wrestled with very different styles. Scott Norton was a muscular giant with world-class powerlifting strength. Leon was a former professional football player who threw his weight around a lot in the ring. He was also already one of the most popular and iconic gaijin wrestlers in the history of Japan by 1992. Bigelow was almost as big as Leon, but was *far* more graceful and athletic. He was also so friendly behind the scenes and a total breeze to work with.

On top of that, Bigelow seemed to have been on every independent wrestling tour I was on during the 1990s, no matter where it was, and we developed a tremendous rapport with one another. Without a doubt, I visited and wrestled in more countries with Bam Bam Bigelow as my friend and travel companion than with any other wrestler.

We all hung out in Roppongi quite a bit while we were in Japan. Roppongi was known as the party district of Tokyo. Smoking marijuana was strongly discouraged by the New Japan office, but there were always *plenty* of guys smoking pot on the rooftops of Roppongi. It was nearly as common that someone would go the additional step of trying to urinate from the rooftops of the Roppongi buildings down onto the passersby walking the streets.

B. Brian Blair: Truth Bee Told

On more than one occasion, the person doing the urinating was Terry Gordy, who was a featured performer for All Japan Pro Wrestling whenever he wrestled in Japan. It wasn't at all uncommon for the gaijin wrestlers from New Japan and All Japan to meet up during tours since we all worked together back in the U.S. We'd watch from above as Japanese citizens walking the streets of Roppongi would feel droplets of liquid descending from the sky, and they'd open up an umbrella thinking it was incoming rain, never realizing they'd just been urinated on by famous American wrestlers.

The more time I spent in Japan that year, the more I could sense that there was a bit of professional jealousy brewing between Bigelow and Vader, but *all* of the jealousy seemed to rest on Leon's side of the equation. Despite enjoying unmatched popularity, Leon was very self-conscious about how he was perceived by both the fans and wrestlers in Japan. He seemed to be on a mission to ensure that everyone regarded him as a superior super heavyweight to Bigelow.

In my opinion, Leon was *nowhere near* the worker that Bigelow was. Bigelow was as quick and agile as a cat despite weighing close to 400 pounds. He was acrobatic enough to perform cartwheels inside of the wrestling ring, and he could leap high enough into the air to dropkick most wrestlers in the face. He was also *very* gentle, and never actually hurt anyone despite how devastating his maneuvers appeared to be.

It seemed to bother Leon that he lacked the agility and athleticism of Bigelow, and he appeared to compensate for his shortcomings by becoming the polar opposite of Bigelow in one *crucial* way: Leon made sure his moves looked as stiff and believable as possible because he would *actually* hit people *full blast*. That's a problem, because you're *never* supposed to injure the men you're working with who are entrusting you with their physical well-being. Leon didn't seem to care about this at all if it meant ensuring that he remained at the top of the list of the industry's big men.

To conclude our tag team matches, Leon liked to do this finish where I would hold one of our adversaries in a double chicken wing. With our opponent trapped in the hold, Leon would hit the ropes and come off with a clothesline. Our opponent would duck out of the way, and I would get clobbered with the clothesline instead. It's a very simple finish to execute, and the reason Leon loved that finish so much is because it made *him* look incredibly strong. In essence, Leon's teams were only losing because he was *so* powerful that his own teammates couldn't withstand the impacts from his blows.

B. Brian Blair: Truth Bee Told

Friction arose when Leon clocked me so hard with his clothesline that I rotated about 270 degrees before I crashed to the mat. Seriously, I flipped all the way around and landed on my *knees* without even attempting to help Leon with the bump.

Everything about the ending looked real because the Japanese wrestlers were always great with their timing, but Leon added an *unnecessary* level of realism to it by endangering me. This didn't just occur once, either; Leon did it *two more times*. When the two of us returned to the locker room after he'd done it for the third time, I had no recourse other than to confront him about it.

Teaming with Leon "Big Van Vader" White in Japan

"Leon, that was *ridiculous!*" I told him. "You know this is a *work*, right? You don't have to knock my dick in the dirt with the clothesline every time! Don't *ever* hit me that hard again!"

"Oh, I'm sorry, man!" said Leon. "I *won't* do it again."

Vader loosened up a little bit for the next three or four shows, but then he smashed me with a *stiff* clothesline yet again toward the end of the tour. I was pissed off, and Leon could tell.

"The next time you hit me like that, Leon, it's going to be the *last* time you ever hit me," I warned him.

"What do you mean by *that?*" Leon asked.

B. Brian Blair: Truth Bee Told

"Just do it *one* more time…" I threatened him, and then walked away.

Dropping an elbow on Keiji Mutoh as Scott Norton looks on

At the airport with Yokozuna, the Steiners and Scott Norton

That was one of those nights where we didn't even go out to eat sushi together afterwards, which was Vader's favorite thing to do. After that warning, Leon lightened up, and we never had another problem. Then again, I *also* didn't have many matches with him after that either.

B. Brian Blair: Truth Bee Told

I always liked Leon outside of the ring, and when we went out to eat and drink after the shows, all of the ill will was quickly forgotten. However, you always had to be mindful of your safety, because Leon would stop at nothing in his efforts to stay over with the Japanese crowd as a monster. If you *didn't* confront him, he would just keep clocking you as hard as he pleased. Despite his immense size, Leon was actually a very sensitive guy. There was one night on the tour when I noticed Leon crying in the locker room and I checked on him.

Posing for Japanese fans with Scott Norton and Chris Benoit

"What's wrong, Leon?" I asked. "Are you okay?"

"Yeah... I'm fine," Leon replied. "I just talked to my wife at home. I just miss being home."

"It'll be okay, man," I told him. "I get it."

I understood what Leon was dealing with. The two-week tours of Japan were like working vacations where you were in and out quickly with money in your pockets. Most tours of Japan were four weeks long, which was also fine. However, the six-week tours of Japan could be *brutal*, and they seemed like they were even longer when you had children at home, which Leon and I both did by the end of that year.

Toni gave birth to our first son in 1992; I named him Brett after Bret Hart, although Toni *insisted* that we should spell his name with two *T*s. I wanted my own set of Killer Bees, so we were off to a great start. To be quite honest, I had literally prayed to God that He would bless me with sons. I wanted boys to hang out with so that I

B. Brian Blair: Truth Bee Told

could have fun with them and help them develop into men, and I *also* knew that I would become a very strict parent if I had daughters. Any time a daughter of mine went out on a date, I would have been riding in the back seat of the car, watching everything like a *hawk*.

Leon wasn't just sensitive when it came to his family, though. He was a rather insecure guy at times. He would complain about where his match was positioned on the card, or who would be the person in the ring to take the loss if his team was booked to lose a match; he did everything in his power to make sure it was never him.

When Hulk Hogan took some time away from the spotlight of pro wrestling, he had several opportunities open up for him in the form of motion pictures and television appearances. Hogan managed to secure a starring role on the show *Thunder in Paradise*, which seemed to be built around his desire to stay closer to home. Everything was either shot in and around Tampa, or at Disney's studio in Orlando. As one of Terry's friends, I was fortunate enough to be recruited to the set for a cameo appearance, and in one of the *Thunder in Paradise* episodes, I played a thug and got my head smashed into a car door.

While Terry was focused on his acting career, Eric Bischoff was given control over World Championship Wrestling and managed to lure Terry away from acting and back into the persona of Hulk Hogan. This time Terry would be competing directly against Vince McMahon and the World Wrestling Federation. As part of the deal, Bischoff ceded a *ton* of power over to Terry when it came to booking decisions and talent acquisitions.

It seemed like Terry immediately brought several giant, safe heels into WCW so that he could look awesome when he defeated them and not worry about getting injured. This included Kamala, John Tenta, and the One Man Gang. It's much easier to get sympathy as a babyface when you're working with bigger guys as opposed to smaller guys, so there were only so many people that Hulk Hogan could wrestle against that could make him look tiny by comparison.

In terms of babyface wrestlers, Terry also had a hand in bringing in Randy Savage, Hacksaw Jim Duggan and Ed "Brutus Beefcake" Leslie, who had long ago recovered from his horrific parasailing accident. He also brought in the Nasty Boys as a tag team, partly because of his very close friendship with Brian Knobbs. Before long, it looked like Terry had more or less handpicked *half* of the WCW roster.

Terry and I were together all the time back then, even though he lived on the other side of the Bay in Clearwater. At a minimum, we saw each other every weekend, so it was only a matter of time until

Bischoff and I had a face-to-face meeting. It wasn't until I was riding in the car with Terry *and* Bischoff that I learned the two of them had also had a discussion about bringing *me* into WCW.

Eric pitched it as a deal where I would receive $150,000 as a downside guarantee for wrestling only about eight matches each month.

"When can you start?" he asked.

"I don't know," I answered. "Maybe in two weeks. When do you *want* me to start?"

"Two weeks is fine," Eric replied. "In fact, that's *probably* perfect."

I assumed it would take me about two weeks to get everything situated at my gyms so that I wouldn't need to be there very often. Honestly, I was excited about the idea of finally wrestling on a major U.S. network again. At least that's what I *thought* was going to happen until two weeks passed and I hadn't received any phone calls from Eric.

Instead of calling Eric, I decided to ring Terry first and ask him what was causing the holdup with my employment. Terry was Bischoff's most vital acquisition, so I assumed he would be aware of all the decisions that were being made back in Atlanta.

"I'm not sure what's going on, Brian," Terry told me. "Let me go talk to Eric and then I'll check back with you."

"Well, have you talked to him about me *at all*?" I asked him.

"I *did*," said Terry. "I asked him, and he was vague about what he wanted to do with you."

"What do you mean 'vague'?" I asked.

"I think he's got some heat with Ted Turner over spending too much money on talent," he said.

After going another few days without hearing from anyone, I wound up calling Bischoff three times, and I finally got him on the phone with my third attempt.

"Hey, Eric... it's Brian Blair," I said when he answered.

"Brian!" Bischoff exclaimed. "I'm *so* sorry! I've been meaning to call you. Just give me a day. I have a bunch of issues I'm working through over here."

"Okay, Eric," I said. "It's no problem. Just get back to me tomorrow."

I *never* heard from Eric again.

I was pretty dejected about the whole thing. I'd given a lot of thought to what I was going to do, the type of character I was going to be, and how I should be introduced to the viewing audience. My

B. Brian Blair: Truth Bee Told

contingency plan for the operation of my gyms was also fully established by then, so all of my bases had been covered. When Bischoff never got back to me, I was probably depressed for an entire month.

To this day, I don't understand how you could look someone in the eye, make them an unsolicited offer to work for you, agree to a dollar amount, shake their hand, have witnesses present, and then *never* even return that person's phone call. To me, that was a very low-class move on Bischoff's part. Eventually, I got over it, but it stung for quite a while.

It was during this time that I thought about making an overture to Vince about returning to wrestle for the WWF, but WCW's flirtations with me had caused me to grow enamored with the idea of earning a six-figure wrestling income while working fewer than 100 dates a year. Also, when it came to Vince, you *never* knew how many days you were going to end up working. The WWF's business was in the midst of a slump at that point, and Vince might have had me working *300* days a year and making as little as $50,000 depending on the priority I was given on the cards. In my eyes, it just wasn't worth it.

I also had one young son at home and another on the way, and I didn't want to be gone 25 days out of every month. I had vivid memories of sitting in hotel rooms and listening to Brunzie crying on the phone with his family, and then *continuing* to cry long after he'd hung up the phone. I just wasn't prepared to make that sort of personal sacrifice at that stage in my life, especially when things were going so well for me and I could control my own destiny, as opposed to placing my professional destiny back into the hands of a wrestling booker. The gyms were making *very* good money, and we were even expanding into additional locations.

One of the things I think about the most from that era is the approach taken by Vince McMahon and the WWF during the mid 1990s. Several members of the tag teams I worked with in the '80s – including Bret Hart, Jacques Rougeau, Shawn Michaels, Marty Jannetty and Davey Boy Smith – all had reigns as either the WWF Intercontinental Heavyweight Champion, or as the WWF World Heavyweight Champion.

As the younger of the two Killer Bees, I think I would have meshed very well with the top singles wrestlers during this period, and I'll admit that it's interesting to consider what might have occurred if I'd returned to the WWF during this period. I was only a few months older than Bret Hart, and a series of singles matches against him definitely would have been a career highlight for me. He did an *unbelievable* job of carrying the WWF through tough times, and he is rightly credited with elevating the overall quality of the company's main event matches.

In the end, I think I made the right decision to stay home, build my business, and take whatever low-commitment wrestling opportunities were presented to me along the way.

Killer Bees/Masked Confusion fan art

One financial opportunity for wrestlers that *was* winding down in the mid-'90s was the Universal Wrestling Federation. The last gasp of the UWF transpired at the *Blackjack Brawl* on September 24th, 1994, in Las Vegas. I was frankly surprised to hear that Herb was planning to hold another event, because I had been under the impression the UWF was completely out of commission. Herb had somehow conned the management team of the MGM Grand into permitting him to host a wrestling show at their Garden Arena – the location for so many memorable championship boxing fights.

I'll admit, the thought of wrestling at a large venue once again was enticing to me, but so was the *next* thing Herb told me.

"Vince didn't reinstate the Killer Bees trademark," said Herb. "*We* own the trademark now. You and Jim can officially start calling yourselves the Killer Bees again."

"Are you *sure* about that Herb?" I asked suspiciously. I was in no hurry to attract the attention and subsequent wrath of Vince McMahon.

B. Brian Blair: Truth Bee Told

"Of *course* I'm sure," Herb answered. "And I've also got some world tag team championship belts for you and Jim."

For me, this all sounded much too good to be true – which meant it probably was – but I was especially enamored with the idea of the Killer Bees finally being crowned world champions in front of a large, cheering crowd at a major arena.

As far as the name was concerned, if Herb was lying about acquiring ownership of the "Killer Bees" name he would have to take responsibility for it. Herb was the owner of the wrestling company *and* an announcer, which meant he had the ability to call us whatever he liked even if he didn't have the legal right to. If a problem emerged as a result of something Herb uttered over commentary or told the ring announcer to say in the arena, it would be *his* responsibility, and not the Bees themselves.

I knew the *Blackjack Brawl* was destined to be an ill-fated event as soon as I met up with Herb in Las Vegas. The first thing he did was to display for me the yellow, ostrich-skin cowboy boots he intended to wear out to the ring at the Garden Arena. They had the letters "U-W-F" embroidered into their sides.

"Check *these* out, Brian!" Herb cackled. "These are fuckin' incredible! People are going to go *nuts* when they see these!"

Here we were with an entire Las Vegas arena that we needed to fill with wrestling fans, along with a wrestling company that was hanging on by a thread, and Herb was primarily concerned about attracting envious pairs of eyes to his cowboy boots.

"Those *are* nice boots, Herb," I nodded. "Except you've got one problem: Your pants are going to hang over the logo and *nobody* is going to see it."

"I've got that figured out," laughed Herb. "Don't worry. They're *definitely* gonna see the boots."

At *that* point, I knew the UWF was absolutely finished. The hardest thing to open is a closed mind, and you couldn't have opened Herb's closed mind with a crowbar and dynamite. He seemed to want all the trappings of success without placing any of the essential hard work behind it, or without taking any of the painstaking steps to achieve that success. He was far more concerned with *appearing* to be successful than actually *becoming* successful.

Despite all evidence to the contrary, Herb insisted that all the information he was privy to indicated that the *Blackjack Brawl* would be a success. He floated around the locker room that night in that cocaine stupor of his, sipping on scotch from a paper cup. I'd be shocked if anyone had believed Herb's projections, but things swiftly progressed to a point where he could no longer have misled us even if he'd attempted to. Fans slowly trickled into the Garden Arena, and then the trickle came to an abrupt halt.

When showtime arrived and we realized no more people were going to be entering the building, it was a heartbreaking feeling. The mood in the locker room was very somber, because the turnout for *Blackjack Brawl* was even more embarrassing than the attendance at *Beach Brawl*. There were only 600 people in attendance within a building that could hold more than 15,000. It was *impossible* to conceal an embarrassing failure of that magnitude.

The Killer Bees: UWF World Tag Team Champions

Despite the miniscule crowd, Jimmy and I prepared to walk out to the ring for our championship match. Not only had Herb brought in the Warlord from the Powers of Pain tag team, but he paired him with Larry Power and rebranded them as "The *New* Powers of Pain." If Herb was willing to flout the trademarks that Vince McMahon may still have owned, he was certainly going all out in his efforts to violate them. Jim and I came out next, introduced as "The Killer Bees," and bedecked in our classic Killer Bees ring attire and ring jackets.

At the end of the match, our opponents attempted an illegal switch, with David Power attempting to substitute himself into the match for his brother Larry. Jim and I outmaneuvered our opponents so that David Power wound up on his back, and I covered David for the pinfall victory. With that, the Killer Bees *officially* captured the UWF World Tag Team Championship. No matter what people might say about the time Jim and I spent in the WWF or how we might have underachieved relative to the fans' expectations for us, they could never say the two of us didn't hold at least *one* championship together.

No matter what the Killer Bees had ostensibly accomplished that night, any joy I might have felt was offset by the circumstances surrounding our achievement. I'd wanted to feel a sense of elation, but all I could think at the time was, "Damn, Herb! *Why* did you mess all of this up?! *Why* couldn't you take care of business?"

Jimmy and I left the championship belts with Herb in Las Vegas that night, and we haven't seen them since. The *Blackjack Brawl* would be the UWF's final show, or at least it was the final UWF show that *I* had anything to do with. Possibly owing to the stress brought about by the mishandling of his money by Herb, Tom Kenny died of a heart attack after years of suffering from crippling stress brought about by the loss of much of his fortune.

As most wrestling fans are aware, Herb died from a cocaine-induced heart attack in 1996. His death is commonly viewed as an innocuous event, and his mismanagement of the UWF is often characterized as consisting of a series of miscalculations by a drug-addled lunatic that really only harmed *that* one lunatic. Well, Herb's financial backers were *real* people, and those people were *friends* of mine. Every day I'm forced to wrestle with the fact that I might have contributed to Tom Kenny's early demise by introducing him to Herb Abrams.

The elimination of professional wrestling's classic territorial structure did plenty of financial harm to a lot of people. One of the people hurt by that downturn was my close friend, Steve Keirn. Steve had attempted to reboot Championship Wrestling from Florida in a collaborative effort with Gordon Solie and Mike Graham.

Their version of CWF – originally called "Florida Championship Wrestling" and later called "The Professional Wrestling Federation" – attempted to become the next major WWF competitor in the late '80s and early '90s by using old and new Florida-based talent before they ran into financial trouble and had to close the company down. From there, Steve briefly wrestled as Skinner in the WWF, but he hadn't lasted too long in that role.

Things only got worse for Steve as the decade progressed. As a matter of fact, things became so dire that at one point Steve and his wife were both mowing people's lawns for extra money... *including mine*. I knew with his disposition and work ethic, Steve would be an incredible asset to my business, so I hired him as the general manager at one of my gyms. Just as I expected, Steve was a huge asset to me in his managerial role. He was *so* beneficial to the gym, in fact, that I offered him an ownership percentage of the next gym I opened in 1995, which was in Tampa Palms.

"I'm opening up a new gym in Tampa Palms, and I'd *love* for you to have ownership," I told Steve. "I'll sell you 20 percent of the club for $20,000, and I'll show you on paper right now that this 20 percent is actually worth $60,000."

Steve agreed to the deal, and we instantly became business partners. I may have done Steve a tiny bit of a favor, but he'd earned *every bit* of the ownership that I offered him, and he busted his ass at that gym to make it successful.

With Keirn and Hogan at Gold's Gym South Tampa

Our Tampa Palms location was a huge success. As usual, the Hulkster was willing to help Steve and I out with a promotional appearance to boost local interest and membership sales for the new gym. This time, he was joined by Randy Savage, Dory Funk Jr., the Nasty Boys and several other wrestlers. The fan turnout was extraordinary. I was always fortunate to have such good friends that I could rely on to assist me with the promotion of my business endeavors.

Having Steve as a partner at the Tampa Palms club was tremendous on several levels. To have the privilege to walk into work every day and be greeted by one of my very best friends was a real treat. At the same time, I *always* had to be mindful of the fact that Steve is one of the boys just like I am, and that meant I always had to be on the lookout for ribs for which I would be the target.

B. Brian Blair: Truth Bee Told

One day I walked into the Tampa Palms gym, and Steve greeted me excitedly.

"I just signed this world-class fly fisherman up for a membership today," announced Steve. "His name is Jim Seagraves."

Steve and I were both avid fishermen, so having a renowned fly fisherman frequenting our club was a cause for legitimate excitement to us. After meeting him, I learned that Jim Seagraves was everything Steve had led me to believe he was and much more. He's among the best fishermen in the entire world and *still* holds dozens of world fly fishing records. When I met him in person, Jim and I instantly became one of my very best friends, and I expressed to him my *strong* fondness for dining on fish.

With Steve Keirn and Jim Seagraves

"I'm heading home to Alaska for a few months," Jim told me one day while he was working out at the gym. "I'll be sure to bring you back some fresh Alaskan salmon. It's the *best* salmon in the entire world!"

"That would be unbelievable, Jim!" I told him. "I'll be looking forward to it!"

"You won't believe this salmon, Brian," Jim continued. "I'm telling you, there's *nothing else* like it."

I counted the days until Jim returned to Tampa from Alaska. I couldn't wait to sink my teeth into the muscle-building, heart-healthy, mouthwatering salmon that he had bragged about so frequently.

B. Brian Blair: Truth Bee Told

Despite my efforts to catch up with Jim on the first few nights he was scheduled to be back in town, I still missed him each time. It wasn't all that surprising; with three different clubs to monitor, I was spread thin visiting a different club every night, and sometimes I visited all three locations on the same night.

Finally, after a few different attempts to track him down, I eventually ran into Jim at the Tampa Palms club. I approached him with great anticipation and excitement for the Alaskan salmon that he would be handing over to me for my culinary enjoyment.

Jim grinned as he saw me approaching him.

"Hey, Brian!" he said. "It's great to see you! How did you like the salmon?"

The smile from my face was instantly replaced by a look of bewilderment.

"I never saw *any* salmon," I told him. "Did you leave salmon here?"

"Yeah!" replied Jim. "I left some *really* nice salmon for you. I left it with *Steve*!"

I turned my head to look for Keirn, and he was already staring over at me with a *massive* grin plastered all over his face. That son of a gun *stole* my salmon!

I was upset that I'd missed out on that Alaskan salmon, but I couldn't really be angry with Steve. He was a ribber at heart, and he just couldn't help himself.

Of even greater importance than my gyms was the fact that I completed the formation of my personal pair of Killer Bees in 1995 with the birth of my younger son, Bradley. Once again, God had answered my prayers with a resounding "yes." No matter how many challenges have accompanied the responsibility of being a father to two sons, those boys have brought me *so* much joy, and I love them both more than life itself.

I continued to make appearances for a host of wrestling promoters in the mid '90s as long as it was convenient for me to do so, and it didn't interfere with the running of my gyms. I wrestled at a show promoted in the Bahamas by Hal Jeffrey in 1995 that was memorable for *two* different reasons.

The first reason it was memorable was because Rocky Johnson was there with his young son, Dwayne. Rocky had been training Dwayne to wrestle, and the pair had made the brief flight from Miami down to Nassau so that Dwayne could gain some quick in-ring experience by working on a show that was fairly close to home. This was the first time the two would be performing together as a father-and-son team.

"I want you to be honest with Dwayne," Rocky told me before the show. "Tell him what you think about the match. He has a little bit of an attitude and I'm trying to get that attitude out of him."

"What kind of an attitude?" I asked.

"He acts like a bit of a know-it-all," explained Rocky. "He doesn't realize just how much he *still* has to learn."

Taking a seat along Bay Street in Nassau, Bahamas

Honestly, for it to be one of Dwayne's very first matches, it wasn't all that bad. I gave Dwayne my honest opinion of the match as Rocky requested, and I'm sure it all went in one ear and out the other.

The second noteworthy thing that happened at Hal's Bahamas show was that two of WCW's underneath performers – Brian Logan and Mike Legacy – provided me with a blow-by-blow description of a fight they'd witnessed a couple weeks prior between Paul Orndorff and Leon White.

The story they told was that Leon was late getting to the building, and took his sweet time getting ready. In his role as a WCW agent, Paul approached Leon and told him that he needed to hurry up and get ready for his match. The two kids told me that they were scared about the whole situation because the atmosphere was extremely tense, and they *still* needed to ask Leon – a guy who was notoriously stiff in the ring with underneath wrestlers – what he wanted to do with them during his match.

B. Brian Blair: Truth Bee Told

The two told me that Leon was being generally gruff with everyone, including them, and that nothing he told them provided them with any reassurance that they would be safe during their match. They were also provided with no guidance about what to expect once they stepped into the ring during the taping. Their whole story concluded with Leon mouthing off to Paul, Paul responding to Leon, Leon punching Paul, and then Paul dropping Leon with a few punches of his own before *kicking* him half to death… *barefoot*.

I was so enthralled by the story that I *nearly* missed the introduction for my own match. For Leon to get beaten up by a much older, much smaller agent who only had one good arm must have been very embarrassing for him. To add insult to injury, Leon was fired for instigating the whole incident. Knowing both men, I can't say that I was surprised. Leon was used to people backing down from him because he was so large, and Paul would never back down from anybody under any circumstances.

Hearing about the incident just further underscored for me why no one should ever mess with Paul Orndorff. Even with only *one* good arm at his disposal, Paul was still more dangerous than most giants with *two* good arms.

TWENTY-SIX – *Quitters never win*

About a year after I wrestled for him in the Bahamas, Hal Jeffrey contacted me and asked me if I would help him arrange a star-studded tour of India. What resulted was a 12-day swing through India in March of 1997. For that specific tour, the roster of talent included me, Tito Santana, Bad News Brown, Bam Bam Bigelow, Cuban Assassin, Tatanka, the Bushwhackers and the Warlord.

The rights to promote and sell tickets for those shows were sold to a different local promoter in every Indian province we wrestled in. In the middle of the tour, one of our events was cancelled outright due to a political assassination. There had been a disputed election result on the local level in that province, and one of the candidates thought the suitable way to solve the conflict would be to simply *murder* his rival. Due to the unrest that followed, it was deemed advisable to simply cancel the show. I've heard of several different reasons for wrestling events to be canceled, but politically motivated murder was a *new* one to me.

During the tour we received a mountain of media coverage throughout all of the Indian provinces we toured in. We advertised the Asia Pacific Heavyweight Championship as our top prize, and I defeated the Warlord at the tail end of the tour to acquire it. Since I had essentially partnered with Hal on the tour, the thinking was that I was guaranteed to stick with the enterprise, so the championship should reside with me.

Everyone booked on that tour of India got paid what they were expected to receive with the exception of Hal and I. Just as the tour was nearing its conclusion, one of the local partners absconded with a significant portion of the ticket revenue and we *never* found him again. That was always one of the hazards of touring in foreign countries; it could be quite simple for local partners to disappear with your money, leaving you with *zero* clue how to track them down.

Hal soured on the idea of continuing to tour the Asia Pacific region after the fiasco with the theft of our money, but I managed to connect with a few other promoters in the area and continued touring in places like Singapore and Malaysia. I was also able to maintain a roster full of well-known wrestlers for those tours, and we continued to provide professional wrestling to the region for several years.

It just so happens that I was standing in one of my Gold's Gyms when I received a phone call from Hal Jeffrey, and he had been contacted by an Indian man named Dylan who wanted to speak with

B. Brian Blair: Truth Bee Told

me about bringing the Asia Pacific crew on a second tour of India. For some unknown reason, Dylan was absolutely *adamant* about securing Rhonda "Bertha Faye" Singh – a rather large women's wrestler who had appeared on WWF's worldwide television programming – for the tour of India.

An advertisement for our Asia Pacific wrestling promotion

Despite not knowing why Dylan was so hopelessly infatuated with Bertha Faye, I called her up and ensured her participation on the tour.

When we all arrived in Bangalore, India, Dylan greeted me and requested that the two of us chat about the tour we would be embarking upon. He was a stout, chubby, hairy, middle-aged Indian man. The two of us quickly became comfortable with one another to such an extent that Dylan was willing to divulge his ulterior motive for requesting Rhonda Singh's presence on the tour.

"Brian, I asked you to bring Rhonda because I am very much *in love* with her!" exclaimed Dylan.

"*Really?*" I said, with legitimate surprise. There *had* been some women's wrestlers over the years for whom it wouldn't have shocked me to learn that promoters had been willing to move heaven and earth just to meet them, based solely on the physical beauty of those ladies. Rhonda Singh was *not* on that list.

"Okay, Dylan," I said, after recovering from the initial shock caused by his declaration. "Let me see what I can do."

It should come as no surprise that the devious parts of my mind instantly went to work cooking up a rib. For a few days, I allowed Dylan's hopes to marinate. Every time he asked me whether or not I had put in a good word for him with Rhonda, I assured him that I was working on it.

After those first few days, I'd managed to form the foundation of a phenomenal rib in my mind, and I was prepared for Dylan's predictable question.

"Have you said anything to Rhonda about me yet?" queried Dylan.

"Dylan, I'm working on it," I told him, before continuing in a hushed tone. "You've got to remember that Rhonda and Bam Bam are a *thing*. You know what I mean? They're *together*."

"No!" cried the crestfallen Dylan, clutching at his chest. "Oh no! My god! I *can't* believe it! No way!"

"Don't worry," I reassured him. "I'm trying to work with her to set up a time where the two of you can get together, because she likes you, too."

Dylan perked up after receiving this reassurance from me, so I knew I had him right where I wanted him. I made the decision to gather all of the wrestlers together to concoct a suitable rib to pull on the lovestruck local wrestling promoter.

In Bangalore, everyone's room was on the same floor. Rhonda's room happened to be on one side of Dylan's, and Bam Bam's room was a further two rooms down. I called a wrestlers-only meeting in my room, and that's when I unveiled my scheme to trick Dylan.

"Rhonda, I've got a *hell* of an idea," I began. "Dylan is in love with you. *Totally* obsessed. We can pull an incredible rib on him if you'll be in on it."

"I'm in!" Rhonda said quickly. "What do you need me to do?"

"Okay, great!" I said. "Call him and tell him you want him to order a bottle of that *really* expensive scotch we saw at the hotel restaurant. I think it's the Johnnie Walker Blue. Get some shaving cream, a razor and athletic tape. You've got to tape his wrists up so he can't move, and also tape a sock over his eyes to *blind* him!"

All of our rooms had double beds and end tables. They were *perfectly* configured for tying someone up.

B. Brian Blair: Truth Bee Told

"Tell Dylan you're going to tie him up and massage him," I suggested. "Tell him *whatever* you need to tell him to get him to come over so you can tie him up and blindfold him!"

With the rest of us listening in, Rhonda called Dylan and presented her indecent proposal to him. The only step of the plan that gave Dylan any pause at all was the price tag of the Johnnie Walker Blue, which was over $150.

"Oh, that scotch is *so* expensive!" remarked Dylan.

However, for the love of Bertha Faye, Dylan agreed to everything, and he forked over the cash in exchange for the scotch. The two of them made plans to meet the following night. Tim Thompson, Bam Bam Bigelow, and several other wrestlers agreed to be in on the rib.

As the time for the rendezvous neared, Rhonda called Dylan, with seduction dripping from her voice, and asked, "Dylan… did you get the stuff I asked you to get?"

"Oh, *yes*!" Dylan said. "I have *everything*!"

From there, Rhonda described several sex acts she intended to perform on Dylan while he was bound and blindfolded, including shaving his body, and licking the expensive scotch off of his freshly shaved skin.

"Please, Rhonda!" replied Dylan. "Oh, yes! *Please* come over!"

Once Rhonda hung up, I gave her a final set of instructions.

"Get him all tied up," I advised her. "Before you put on a show for him, leave the door open, and then tell him you need to get something out of your room, like the scotch."

The rest of us were all waiting in seclusion, including David Sierra and Tim Thompson. Tim had his camera and tripod at the ready, prepared to record the entire episode. At the appointed time, Rhonda opened her door and ushered us all into the room. Sure enough, Dylan was bound and blindfolded, lying on the bed as *naked* as a jaybird. Every appendage of Dylan's that was capable of being secured was fastened by athletic tape to either the bed or the end table. Rhonda was even creative enough to devise a makeshift pulley system, which allowed her to tug at the tape and hoist Dylan's legs into the air. I don't know where she got that idea from, but it was a nice touch.

Tim began recording, and Rhonda went through the motions of making Dylan think he was actually going to get lucky with her.

"Oh, Rhonda!" Dylan proclaimed. "I'm *so* excited! I've been in love with you for *so* long!"

B. Brian Blair: Truth Bee Told

After Rhonda made it seem like she was preparing to initiate some rather deviant sex acts with Dylan, he admitted to some trepidation.

"Rhonda, I have *never* done anything like this!" said Dylan. "Everything feels good, but this is kind of scary for me!"

"Don't worry, Dylan!" Rhonda reassured him. "It will feel *so* good!"

From there, Rhonda doused Dylan with a sizable amber splash of expensive scotch from the bottle of Johnnie Walker Blue.

"Rhonda!" cried the alarmed Dylan. "That's *very* expensive! What are you going to do with that?!"

"I'm gonna *lick* it off you," stated Rhonda, matter of factly.

"Oh, okay!" responded Dylan, satisfied that the scotch was ultimately being sacrificed for a worthwhile purpose.

From there, Rhonda liberally applied the shaving cream to every place on Dylan's body that can be imagined; his vocalizations in response made it clear that he was enjoying himself immensely.

Meanwhile, Tim, David and I all had *snot* running down our noses from our attempts to stifle laughter as Tim recorded everything.

Right when I felt like Dylan might be getting suspicious that nothing overtly sexual had transpired yet, I signaled to Bam Bam – who had been waiting in the hallway the entire time – that it was his cue to make an emphatic entrance.

CRASH!

Bam Bam exploded into the room, nearly separating the door from its hinges as it swung open violently and dented the wall.

"*Rhonda!*" roared the angry Beast from the East. "What are you doing with this man?! What are you doing?! That's *Dylan!*"

The taped-up Dylan couldn't have been any more vulnerable, and his fear of Bam Bam was so great that he actually managed to tear his right hand free from its restraints and curl himself up for protection as best he could despite the tape that was tightly secured to his other three appendages.

"No, it's *not* me, Bang Bang!" cried Dylan. "Please, Bang Bang! It's a dream! It's a *dream!*"

"I'm gonna kill you!" promised Bam Bam. "I'm gonna *kill* you!"

As Dylan cowered in total fear, Rhonda disappeared with the scotch, the rest of us bolted from the room, and Dylan was left behind blindfolded with the murderous threats of Bam Bam Bigelow ringing in his ears.

B. Brian Blair: Truth Bee Told

At breakfast the next morning, a sulking Dylan made a somewhat veiled confession to me.

"Brian, I did a *very* bad thing," he lamented.

"What happened, Dylan?" I asked.

"I have to go to the mosque and repent," he said. "I shouldn't tell you."

"Please tell me what happened," I coaxed him.

"I was with Rhonda last night," he said. "It was a bad dream. Bang Bang came in and burst the door down. I know it was a dream, but I still need to go to the mosque. Rhonda... she tied me up... but I know it was a dream. *You* enjoy breakfast. I need to go to the mosque. My wife... she will be *very* upset."

With that, Dylan departed for the mosque, and I didn't see him again until he arrived at the next show. As far as I know, Dylan never learned that his bad dream had actually been a well-executed rib masterminded by yours truly.

At a press conference in India with Bigelow, Jeffrey and others

On one of our subsequent tours, the Nasty Boys – Brian Knobbs and Jerry Sags – kept teasing the nearly 60-year-old veteran Bulldog Bob Brown while he was in the presence of his nephew, Kerry Brown. Knobbs and Sags were so over the top and obnoxious with their taunts that I had to ask them to cut it out. Both Brian and Jerry are good friends of mine, but back then they went to great lengths to needle people until they'd elicited the negative reactions from them that they were looking for. Jerry was the more laid-back personality of the two Nasty Boys, but Brian had a *special* gift for getting Jerry worked up. When the two were together, it often spelled trouble for whomever landed in their crosshairs.

In this case, Brian and Jerry both kept calling Bob Brown senile while cracking jokes about his age, lack of mobility, and fading memory right in front of his nephew.

"Guys, knock that off!" I told them. "You really shouldn't be saying things like that about a guy in front of his nephew. You wouldn't want someone saying insulting things like that about you in front of *your* relatives."

They backed off a little bit, but then they changed the insult to "serility," as a substitute word for "senility." In all fairness, Bob started out on the wrong foot by acting cocky toward the rest of the group because he was the elder statesman of the tour. To Brian and Jerry, that sort of attitude made Bob a prime candidate for mocking and widened the target on his back. When it came to the Nasty Boys, words like "respect" and "reverence" could be thrown right out of the window.

Things were far less contentious on some of my other tours, including tours of the Caribbean orchestrated by Dick Worley. I'd met Dick many years prior when he worked as a referee for the WWF in most of the company's New Jersey towns. He was a *great* referee, a straight shooter and an honest guy.

Somewhere along the way, Dick made connections with several local event promoters in the Caribbean. For all intents and purposes, our tour was a glorified pleasure cruise. We enjoyed our time at sea, and then we would disembark on a different island every few nights to wrestle in front of a local audience.

I'm not sure exactly how Dick coordinated everything, but what I *do* know is there was a ring awaiting us on every island, so we weren't forced to travel with it or go through the rigamarole of setting one up. Every location was jam-packed, so Dick made money, and so did everyone that worked for him.

During our stop in Bonaire, I rented a fishing boat with Bob Orton Jr. and Paul Orndorff. We were trolling in the water for dolphin fish when the line suddenly started *flying* out of the rod. The first stage of our fight with that monster fish lasted for a full 15 minutes… until the captain of the boat started flipping out because he realized our "fish" was more likely a shark or a whale. He couldn't confirm that though, so instead he started backing the boat up and continued to let us battle whatever was on the other end of the line.

From there, we kept up the battle *for an hour and a half.* All of our arms were thoroughly blown up and fatigued from trying to reel this monster in. While all three of us were locked in mortal combat with the mysterious beast hidden deep below the water's surface, the captain called in to port, bragging that we might have a world-record fish on our hands. Out of the blue, a gigantic, speckled fin popped up out of the water about 30 feet behind the boat. We had been battling with a *whale shark* the entire time. It had been swimming through plankton when Orton had accidentally hooked it.

When the whale shark coasted by us, we realized that we never had a rational chance of winning our struggle. Our boat was 32 feet long, and this whale shark was *much* longer than the boat we were riding on! After we snapped some photos of the whale shark, we unhooked it and let it go. It lingered behind for a little while before deciding it felt like departing from the scene. It probably could have snapped the line and left whenever it felt like it, but it must have continued swimming toward our boat out of pure curiosity over what it was connected to.

Orton had continued to pull on his line to keep it taut while the whale shark was battling our boat, and when we collected Orton's hook afterwards, we discovered that the whale shark had *completely* straightened it out.

It should come as no surprise that's the biggest thing *any* of us ever came close to catching. I managed to catch some wahoo during the same excursion, and there was a place back on the island that cooked the fish for all of us for three days. I had never eaten wahoo before; it was *delicious*. Really, I was just happy to get something worthwhile out of that fishing trip, instead of simply getting toyed with by a whale shark.

By that point, things were looking up for professional wrestling companies back in the United States as well. The popularity of wrestling boomed once again in the late 1990s thanks to the TV-ratings war between the World Wrestling Federation and World Championship Wrestling. It seemed as if many of the young pro wrestling fans from the national wrestling boom of the 1980s were now all grown up and ready for a new round of wrestling programming. The flagship programs of both the WWF and WCW – *RAW* and *Nitro*, respectively – raked in mind-blowing ratings on Monday nights, and were regarded by many viewers as must-see television.

One of the fortunate side effects to wrestling becoming hot on television once again is that a lot of national fan interest trickled down to the regional level, and also overseas. My pay in Japan swelled to $5,000 per week, and several stateside wrestling promoters were able to run consistent shows that attracted regular fans to their local venues.

Among those promoters was Howard Brody, who was able to run a series of successful shows at the Fort Homer Hesterly Armory in Tampa. Between 1998 and 2001, Howard's NWA Florida promotion got so hot that he had standing-room-only crowds at several of his events. He had a deal at the Armory that only required him to compensate them for every chair that was filled, and there were nights when they literally ran out of available chairs.

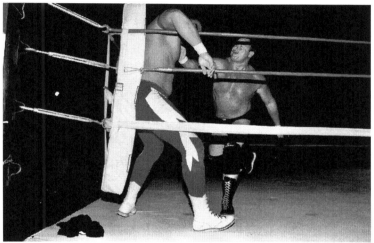

Firing off on the opposition in Tampa

In essence, Howard's Florida territory became the flagship NWA promotion of that era, and he was able to bring in several wrestlers who had made national names for themselves, like Dan Severn and Steve Corino. On the local level, Steve Keirn and I were the stabilizing presence that bolstered the company by competing in tag team title matches at many of Howard's shows.

I ceased working for Tom Shade's IWA around this time, and Keirn and I put everything we had into our matches for Howard even though they were only intended for the local audiences in Tampa. We *definitely* weren't afraid to bleed for the sake of providing compelling entertainment for the fans.

During one of the matches in which we defended our NWA United States Tag Team Championship, I was left in the ring as a bloody mess. Later, we pulled off a surprise angle in the midst of one of our title defenses against the Bushwhackers, where Steve *turned heel* on me in the middle of the ring and the crowd came unglued. The people in the arena knew that Steve and I were real-life friends and business partners, and they couldn't fathom what they were seeing.

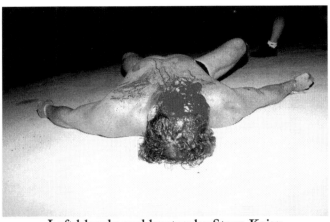

Left bloody and beaten by Steve Keirn

Steve beat me to a bloody pulp, and *that* wasn't even the half of it. When the paramedics arrived to tend to my wounds, Steve beat *them* up, too. From there, my 14-year-old brother Mike – my father's youngest child – hurdled the barricade and shoved Steve in the back. Steve spun around and was *stunned* to see that it was my brother.

"Leave him alone!" screamed Mike, thinking that my lifelong friend had truly just thrown our friendship away and assaulted me in the ring.

In response, Steve *shoved* Mike so hard that my brother's feet involuntarily left the ground. It's a miracle that he wasn't hurt. Furthermore, my young sons were both in the crowd sitting with Toni, and the sight of Uncle Steve beating on their dad *and* their Uncle Mike had them *sobbing*. The level of heat in the building that night was off the charts. It was like we were back in the 1980s with everyone believing wrestling was real again. It's just a shame that my sons thought their father was *actually* being murdered.

Without fail, a hot wrestling promotion is going to attract attention. Howard ran everything on a shoestring budget, and that opened the door for Marti Funk – Dory Funk Jr.'s wife – to gain leverage over him. In exchange for the use of the Funks' lighting system and sound system, Howard provided Marti and Dory with *far* too much control over his wrestling product.

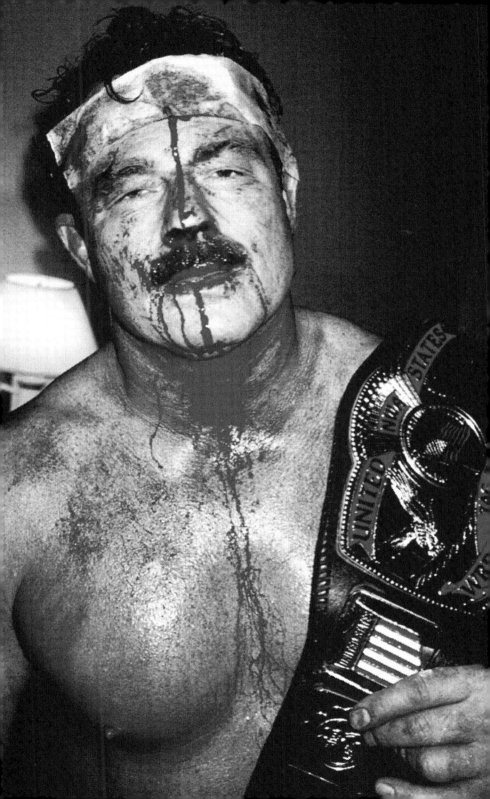

B. Brian Blair: Truth Bee Told

On the night of my revenge match after Steve turned heel on me, and with the building already packed solid with rabid fans, Dory and Marti decided the best thing to do would be to send Dory to the ring to wrestle for 90 minutes with some of the students from his wrestling school, the Funking Conservatory.

What resulted was an interminable match between Dory and some of his very *green* wrestlers. About 40 minutes into this abomination of a contest, and long after the arena had first begun ringing with chants of "boring," fans simply started leaving. As a matter of fact, the fans kept on trickling out as the bout stretched to 50, 60, 70 and 80 minutes. By the time Dory's match reached its 90-minute conclusion, the size of the audience had been cut by a full two thirds, and there were *still* two matches left on the card.

The entire episode played out like the inverse of a Herb Abrams' scenario. Herb was famous for his profligate spending. In *this* case, Howard had permitted a husband-and-wife team to gain an undue influence over his show and cripple his company simply because he'd wanted to *save* a few dollars.

In the time that has elapsed since this incident, Dory and Marti have become *close* friends of mine, and I wouldn't have it any other way because my countless matches against Dory in Florida helped me to progress into the seasoned wrestler that I eventually became. It's simply unfortunate that their actions on that particular night played a role in hindering the growth of a developing local wrestling company right within my own hometown.

Despite how contentious Steve and I may have made our relationship look in the ring, things were going swimmingly behind the scenes. My Gold's Gym locations had performed tremendously well for me, and when rumors began swirling that Gold's Gym was going to become a publicly traded company, I was approached by a set of interested buyers. I had been thinking about getting out of the gym business for a couple of years by that point.

All of the debt associated with the gyms had been paid off a long time ago, and I was able to simultaneously sell *all* of my locations for a $2.1 million profit in December of 1999. It was an *incredible* return on the initial investment I'd made back in 1989. Even after the sale, I negotiated a six-figure management contract with the new owners of the gyms to help iron out the unavoidable bugs that would pop up after the transition occurred.

Steve benefitted from the sale as well; I was able to write him a check for about $175,000 – a *fantastic* return on his initial $20,000 investment. What made the whole thing even more satisfying is that

B. Brian Blair: Truth Bee Told

Steve and I *never* had a contract on paper; all of that business was done on a handshake. It's tough to find friends you can trust well enough to do business with in such an informal fashion. It worked out unbelievably well, but I seriously doubt I would ever do a deal like that again. There are simply too many risks involved.

Becoming a business owner created a natural bridge for me to develop an interest in politics. Owning a set of local businesses had forced me to assess how the actions of governments directly influence business owners, and how those actions either contribute to the running of a successful business, or how they make it more difficult for business owners to manage their operations smoothly.

Particularly in Tampa, I analyzed a lot of government spending practices that appeared to be wasteful. That was when I decided that I could make the greatest difference in my community if I ran for public office.

In 2002, I set my sights on running for the county commissioner seat occupied by Pat Frank; several people advised me that Pat would be *impossible* to unseat. I wasn't interested in what the naysayers had to say, however, because I *truly* believed I could defeat her and acquire her commissioner's seat.

The role of a county commissioner is to determine land use taxes, rates and fees, while also establishing a variety of different public policies. In addition, county commissioners are required to sit on between five to eight County Boards, like the Port Authority Board, the Airport Authority Board, the Environmental Commission, and numerous others.

Running for a seat on the Board of County Commissioners in Hillsborough County was a major undertaking. For one thing, Hillsborough County isn't a county with a mayor or an executive position occupied by a sole individual, so the county commissioners effectively wield all of the authority at the county level. In addition, Hillsborough County has a landmass larger than Rhode Island, and a population greater than those of 10 U.S. states. That meant my campaign had to be robust enough to cover a *wide* area and reach a large number of voters.

Before I ran for political office, most of the people living in Hillsborough County seemed to have a very favorable opinion of me. I'd spoken at several schools, was a fixture in the community, and had logged *thousands* of hours of community service time over the years. The instant I declared myself to be a candidate for county commissioner, half of the people in Hillsborough County automatically began to hate me when I placed the "R" for

B. Brian Blair: Truth Bee Told

"Republican" after my name. That *definitely* took some time for me to grow accustomed to.

My own father was even forced to compromise in order to cast his vote for me. He was a lifelong Democrat, and after he finished voting for me, he told me that I was the only Republican he had *ever* voted for in his life.

Despite having to share the services of my campaign advisor with several other candidates running for assorted offices, the early polls showed that I was outperforming Pat Frank, and was the favorite to win the race. It was at that point when *The Tampa Tribune* opted to publish a hit piece about me with the headline "Sheriff's Report Haunts Blair." It was about me supposedly beating my girlfriend brutally in 1984. Underneath the headline in much smaller print, it said, "Domestic abuse alleged; never charged, arrested."

The article reprinted the lies of my ex, claiming that I'd punched her "10 or 12 times in the head." Realistically, if any 230-pound professional wrestler punched a 110-pound woman in the head a dozen times, she would have been *dead*. At a *minimum*, she would have had black eyes, a broken nose, missing teeth and potential brain damage. Her *only* injuries were a few scratches on her from when I pushed her off of me after she'd climbed on me, clawed my back until it was bloody, and torn my shirt.

Someone had obviously searched to see if any charges had ever been filed against me, because they were looking for material to weaponize against me. The allegations by my ex had been totally preposterous at the time the incident occurred, and now her baseless claims were being dredged up 18 years after the fact, and totally devoid of any context.

The officers didn't investigate the incident any further at the time because they knew bullshit when they heard it. Again, when I'd hit the 6'3", 245-pound Doug Somers in the head, he wound up on a couch, wearing a full facial cast, and getting fed with a spoon. I'd also knocked Buzz Sawyer *unconscious* with just *two* punches to the face. I'd clearly done *nothing* to this woman.

The irony of the headline is that nothing about the incident "haunted" me in the slightest bit until the biased journalists at *The Tampa Tribune* went looking for any excuse they could muster to write a hit piece against me. Sadly, it did its intended damage. I lost to Pat Frank by roughly half of a percentage point. It was a *painfully* bitter pill to swallow.

The world of politics is unimaginably dirty, and I was caught completely off guard. Even though the two mainstream Tampa Bay newspapers would occasionally admit to the anti-Republican bias in their coverage, I still wondered why I *never once* saw a negative article aimed at any Democrats.

What made the whole ordeal even worse were the phone calls that poured in from people expressing their disappointment with me over what I was alleged to have done nearly two decades prior. Yet, when I challenged those callers as to whether or not they'd read the entire story, including the portion that explained how I was never questioned, charged or arrested, they all said, "No." It was just further evidence that a simple headline can do untold damage to a person's reputation.

Instead of sitting idly by until the next election cycle, I accepted the nomination of Commissioner Ken Hagan to a Board position on the Hillsborough County Citizens Advisory Committee, and was approved by the entire Board of County Commissioners.

This role was extremely beneficial to me, because Hillsborough County had more than 30 governmental departments at the time, and I was able to learn how each of them functioned. The members of the Advisory Committee listened directly to the complaints of Hillsborough County's citizens, and acted as a sounding board before complainants spoke directly to the county commissioners. In this sense, I was able to familiarize myself with the inner workings of government while deciding if I wanted to seek office again in 2004.

When 2004 did roll around, I targeted the at-large county commissioner's seat, and my opponent was Bob Buckhorn, a Tampa City Council member who had just finished in third place in Tampa's mayoral race.

Buckhorn's political attacks on me backfired *wildly*, especially when he sent out a political mailing that referred to me as "a dumb wrestler" and prominently displayed one of my LJN action figures that was released while I was in the WWF. First of all, Bob had tremendously underestimated the popularity of professional wrestling.

Second, Bob didn't understand how big of a *favor* he had done for me by including that action figure in his mailing. Very few living people have had action figures made of themselves that were sold all over the world. By familiarizing the voters of Hillsborough County with the fact that I'd been awarded with my own action figure at one point in time, Bob had actually *enhanced* my status in the eyes of many voters. He made me look like a *true* celebrity.

Once again, I ran as a pro-business candidate. In the general election, I defeated Buckhorn by about 2,400 votes after more than

430,000 total votes were cast. I was *thrilled* by this outcome, and on a personal level, it was one of the proudest moments of my life.

Campaigning for County Commissioner alongside my son Brett

I was raised in a broken home, had been financially destitute and lived off of food stamps during stretches of my youth. Thanks to a combination of hard work and the guidance of a few people who had been interested in helping me to achieve my goals, I enjoyed amazing success in professional wrestling, transitioned from that into a profitable business career, and then leveraged *that* into a prominent local political position. The moment was steeped in the validation that I had truly come from the gutter and made something of myself. Also, I knew that all of my absent mentors and role models – like my grandfather and Eddie Graham – would have been *very* proud of me.

Another crucial moment in my life also occurred in 2004, and that was the death of Ray "Hercules Hernandez" Fernandez. Herc had broken into the business by training with Hiro Matsuda shortly after Hogan, Orndorff and I had. He had been battling addictions and other assorted demons for quite a while before he finally passed away.

Ray also became somewhat emblematic of a performer from the 1980s heyday of pro wrestling. He had seven children with his wife Debbie, yet he had a penchant for blowing his money on the road despite having so many mouths to feed. He was the polar opposite of a bargain hunter like Bruiser Brody, who was often the *highest paid* wrestler in whatever territory he was working in.

B. Brian Blair: Truth Bee Told

Instead of searching for discounted hotel rooms and strategizing about the cheapest methods of protein consumption, Herc lived life on the road like a *king*. He frequently stayed in the nicest hotels he could afford, ate at all of the finest restaurants, and spent a *ton* of money on drugs and alcohol. In the end, Ray was one of those wrestlers who worked in the WWF for almost seven straight years and had almost nothing to show for it when his time working for Vince reached its conclusion. Wrestlers often believe the money from the best run of their careers will last forever, only to quickly find themselves struggling financially when they suddenly stop getting booked.

Earning a victory in New Japan with the Barbarian and Hercules

    Despite the hardships he went through, Herc was a *very* proud man. During the height of my business success with my gyms – which also coincided with some of Ray's most taxing financial hardships – he would frequently visit my house just to hang out with me. Never once did he ever ask me for a dime.

    Shortly after Ray passed away, his widow Debbie drove over to see me before the funeral.

    "I'm sorry to come to you like this, Brian, but I don't know who else to talk to," she said, with tears in her eyes. "We don't have *any* money. I can't even afford to pay for a pastor to preach at Ray's funeral."

    "I'm so sorry, Debbie," I told her. "How can I help?"

    "You were Ray's friend, and you're a Christian," she explained. "Do you think you could give the eulogy at the funeral?"

B. Brian Blair: Truth Bee Told

"Absolutely!" I replied. "I'd be *happy* to do it. It would be an honor. Don't worry about anything."

At Ray's funeral, I stood up in front of the roomful of mourners and asked everyone to recite the Lord's Prayer in unison. From there, I uttered some additional words on Herc's behalf, talking about what he'd meant to me individually, what he'd meant to his family, and how much he was going to be missed. When it was over with, I thought it was a fitting and respectful sendoff for Ray.

It was on the day of Ray's funeral that I recalled the attempt by Jesse Ventura and Jim Brunzell to start a union while we were all in the WWF. It struck me that more could be done to help the families of the wrestlers who sacrificed and decimated their bodies in the wrestling business, so that they weren't left destitute or incapable of paying for even the most basic funeral arrangements. It was something that I hoped I would have an opportunity to rectify one day.

B. Brian Blair: Truth Bee Told
TWENTY-SEVEN – *Bumps, bruises and addictions*

In my role as a county commissioner, I developed a reputation for taking very pro-business stances, and I did my best to eliminate what I viewed as government waste. For that aspect of my service, I received several awards, including an award for helping to save Hillsborough County over $5 billion in four years, which is virtually unheard of on that level of government. I fought for – and achieved – the *largest* property tax reduction in the *history* of Hillsborough County.

Being sworn in as a member of the Tampa Port Authority

However, my *greatest* contribution came from a moment of divine inspiration in 2006. John Knox Village is an assisted living facility a few miles from my house, and a few senior citizens had been struck by vehicles and died while leaving the facility after venturing out into heavy traffic.

I sent the traffic engineers out there to look into getting a traffic light placed in front of John Knox Village. When they returned, the engineers informed me that they couldn't legally place a traffic light there because it would be too close to the University of South Florida's crossing traffic light, and too close to the traffic light at the nearest intersection. I was advised that an additional traffic light would cause *far* too much traffic congestion in the area.

This outcome of that investigation greatly bothered me, because it meant the lives of more seniors would be knowingly sacrificed in order to maintain a steady flow of traffic. A while later I was traveling down the street and ventured into a school zone. When I saw the flashing lights my natural response was to slow down.

A plaque listing several of my accomplishments as a Hillsborough County Commissioner

That's when it popped into my head: *"Senior Zones."*

Right then and there, I came up with the senior-zone concept. I convened a meeting with the engineering department and presented them with a description of the type of zone I had envisioned. I wanted the zones to be marked with a bright color that could easily be seen on dark asphalt at all hours of the day and night.

The goal was to find a solution that would instantly slow the speed of traffic from 45 miles per hour to 35 miles per hour. Also, there could be no U-turns permitted in front of John Knox Village. The engineering department took all of my ideas, packaged them all

B. Brian Blair: Truth Bee Told

together, and presented the concept to the Board; it passed unanimously, 7 to 0. Hillsborough County was able to install five senior zones at a cost of $35,000 as opposed to the $350,000 it would have cost to install one *single* traffic light. This is just one example of what out-of-the-box thinking can do.

That one idea won Hillsborough County a national award for generating the most innovative new program in the entire United States that year. There are senior zones all over the U.S. now, and there hasn't been a traffic-related death by John Knox Village since then, nor have there been any such deaths in any of the other senior zones that have been implemented in Hillsborough County.

As well as things were going for me professionally, not everything was blissful in my household. The elder of my two sons, Brett, was a phenomenal athlete from the time he was very young. Tragically, he developed a crippling addiction to painkillers at only 16 years of age. Brett had six separate operations for kidney stones, and he required those painkillers to maintain the high caliber of his pitching performances out on the baseball diamond, and the quality of his golf game, as well as to alleviate the pain caused by all of those operations.

I hadn't realized how serious the problem had become until Brett reached what would unfortunately be the pinnacle of his athletic success. Brett's baseball team was the first PONY Baseball team in the history of Florida to emerge from the Tampa region and capture the state championship, and it *hadn't* been an easy accomplishment to attain.

During the state championship game in Miami, the umpires blatantly called the game in a biased fashion in favor of the hometown team. Then they feigned as if they could only understand Spanish and refused to listen to our objections over questionable calls. Despite everything that was working against them, Brett's team prevailed. From there, the team competed successfully at the zone championships in Georgia, and advanced to compete in the nationals, which were in Irving, Texas.

Brett's team was a park ball team, and at nationals they found themselves competing against a field of competitors composed almost entirely of organized Amateur Athletic Union teams. This included their opposition from Houston. In essence, Brett's group was composed of neighborhood kids, and they were competing head-to-head against an all-star travel team. The other team had an incredible pitcher going up against Brett, and our team was winning five to three when the coach of the other team pointed out that Brett was out of innings and wasn't allowed to pitch anymore. After substituting our number-three pitcher into the game, we wound up narrowly losing the game seven to five.

With my son Brett's championship baseball team

Understandably, Brett was despondent after the game, so I did my best to console him during the car ride back to the hotel.

"Brett, you seem very upset," I told him. "I'm *very* proud of you. You played a *great* game. I appreciate you taking your teammates and all the rest of us on that incredible trip through your performance."

"Dad, I just can't get that *pump* off my mind," Brett responded.

I honestly had no idea what Brett was talking about.

"What do you mean?" I asked him.

"I have this pump that I press when I'm in pain, and I know I'm getting another operation next month," Brett said. "I just *can't* wait for that feeling."

My heart *sank*. Brett was talking about the pump that increased the quantity of pain medication that entered his body. I was horrified that my son was on the verge of becoming addicted to painkillers.

I mentioned my concerns to Toni. Her response was, "Well, what is he supposed to do? If he's in pain, he's in *pain*."

B. Brian Blair: Truth Bee Told

My wife made a fair point: The pain from all of Brett's operations must have been *excruciating*. With this in mind, I did my best to mellow out about it, but elements of Brett's life steadily grew worse as his dependency on pain medications increased. Before long, he was ignoring his schoolwork, sneaking out at night, breaking his curfew, and buying Oxycontin pills and *harder* drugs off the streets. Toni and I would go through Brett's room and find needles and empty bags that had once contained drugs.

Brett had even agreed in principle to play golf at Rollins College just outside of Orlando on a scholarship, but the addiction to pain pills caused both his academic and athletic interests to take a backseat to his drug cravings.

As the 2008 election loomed, I was faced with having to make a difficult vote that required me to choose between the interests of the mom-and-pop hauling companies, or the interests of the three largest corporate haulers in the area. The chambers were packed with interested parties on the night of the voting, and even the closed-circuit seating area upstairs was filled to capacity. Very powerful, influential businesspeople in the Tampa area were placing tremendous pressure on me to vote in favor of the large haulers, but I voted in a way that would allow me to live with myself and sleep well at night. The fallout from this vote turned several of my allies against me in my bid for reelection, as I provided the swing vote in favor of the small business operators.

Despite the animosity caused by my vote, I went into my 2008 campaign on solid financial footing. I had around $250,000 reserved to defend my commissioner's seat, and I needed *every* penny. My opponent, Kevin Beckner, distributed nasty campaign fliers accusing me of three supposed offenses against the people of Hillsborough County that were all patently false.

Beckner's first accusation was that I had tried to vote to give myself a pay raise. In actuality, all I had done was to publicly state that I opposed the freezing of commissioner's salaries. Our salaries were set by the State. We couldn't have voted to increase our salaries if we'd wanted to, and Beckner knew it.

Second, Beckner's flier accused me of spending $1 million of Hillsborough County money to clean the private lake behind my house. My house isn't the only house on that lake, but that's the least of what was wrong with Beckner's assertion. The commission spent *far less* than $1 million to clean up an *entire chain* of lakes throughout Hillsborough County; the lake I live on happened to be just one of the *many* lakes that was cleaned as a result of that vote.

B. Brian Blair: Truth Bee Told

Finally, Beckner accused me of being a racist who supports the Confederate flag. What I had actually done was to join with other commissioners in signing a proclamation recognizing the existence of a Confederate heritage group in the area. There was no support given to the organization by me, no direct or indirect support given to the Confederate flag, and *certainly* no suggestion of racism. However, none of this mattered to Beckner, who pulled out all the stops in his malicious efforts to slander me.

I thought about retaliating, but the people closest to me advised me not to counter Beckner's efforts by resorting to similar tactics. They also informed me that I had had a 20-point lead in the polls, so there was no sense in dabbling in any negative campaigning strategies. I shouldn't have listened to this advice, but I did, and it cost me huge. I was at Iavarone Steakhouse in Tampa for what I'd expected to be a victory party. Instead, I *lost* the election by a 10-point margin.

I don't know if I had ever felt more dejected in my life. From the loss of support, to the assurances of a big lead that I supposedly had, to all of the slanderous campaigning done against me, I felt like I'd been set up to take a huge fall. My instinctive response was to file a lawsuit against Kevin Beckner for slander.

Behind the scenes of everything, Brett's drug use had ballooned into a major issue, and it was beginning to compromise every aspect of his life. His dependence on drugs caused him to sneak out of the house to spend time with the wrong crowd. Toni was forced to file six different reports with the Hillsborough County Sheriff's Office between late 2008 and the middle of 2009 because Brett would simply disappear without warning to go do drugs with his friends and then not return home for days at a time.

That was bad enough, but on one occasion Brett brought his 13-year-old brother Bradley along with him. In my mind, all of my worries were fully justified. For my 16-year-old son and his 13-year-old brother to arbitrarily leave our house and then not return until 4:00 a.m. was totally unacceptable to me under *any* circumstances, but the fact that Brett was doing *drugs* with the circle of friends he'd fallen in with only worsened the circumstances in my eyes.

This all reached a cataclysmic end on – of all days – Father's Day of 2009. The doorbell rang between 3:00 a.m. and 4:00 a.m. My sons were at the door, and this was at least the second time Brett had taken Bradley out with him at an obscene hour of the night to do whatever it was they were up to.

"Are they *really* doing this again at four in the morning?!" I asked my wife, Toni. It was far more of a complaint than a question.

B. Brian Blair: Truth Bee Told

When I opened the door, my two sons were standing there in front of me, as bold as brass. I *couldn't* suppress my rage and I verbally unloaded on them.

"Goddammit!" I yelled. "*What* are you doing out at this time of night?! I told you *not* to go out this late! *Why* would you think it's a good idea to take your brother out with you this late at night?!"

In response to my fatherly tirade, Brett chose to *spit* at me. When the saliva struck my chest, I stood there stunned, and then stared at Brett with blinding rage in my eyes. Before I could even take one step forward, Brett ran out into the front yard. I went right after him and gave chase. My goal was to grab him and stretch him to teach him a lesson, the same way Hiro Matsuda and so many other wrestlers had done to me years ago in Tampa's Dungeon.

I chased Brett completely around the car that had dropped my two sons off, which was still in my driveway. Brett managed to stay a few paces ahead of me and ran into the house. I followed him inside, but he didn't stop running once he entered the house. Instead, he continued to race straight through the house and into his bedroom. Just as I was closing in on Brett with my arms outstretched and was about to grab a hold of him, I felt something strike me from behind. I turned around and saw my son's 17-year-old, skin-headed friend Shawn standing before me. Before I could react to grab that kid, Brett hit me in the back.

Once my attention was once again trained on Brett, Shawn kicked me in the balls from behind with his cowboy boots on, which caused me to drop to the ground. From there, *all three* of the boys, *including* my 13-year-old son, Bradley, converged on me and began to rain punches and kicks down upon me. One particularly *brutal* kick delivered by Shawn with the cowboy boots caught me squarely in my ribs and cracked them.

Finally, Toni arrived on the scene and began to pull the boys off of me one by one, but she got roughed up a bit in the process. Fortunately, none of the boys struck her directly, and they all scattered. While I was initially lying on the floor, Toni had called the police. My mother, who was living in my guest house, also came by to see what was causing all of that commotion. The scene was one huge dysfunctional *mess*.

That's when the Hillsborough Sheriff's deputies arrived and assessed the scene, as well as my injuries. My left eye was swollen, I had red marks all over my neck, and I could barely stand up straight due to the pain in my ribs.

B. Brian Blair: Truth Bee Told

One of the deputies eventually approached me and asked, "Mr. Blair, do you want us to arrest your son?"

By *no means* did I want my son to have any sort of criminal record with the authorities.

"No, sir!" I told the officer. "I've got to try to work this out in my own household. My wife and I can manage this."

The deputies were extremely courteous to Toni and I. It may have been partially attributable to the fact that the county commissioners handle their budget, and there was still the potential that I might retake my seat one day.

One hour later, my doorbell rang while I was sitting down holding a bag of frozen corn over my eye. I walked over to the door and opened it to find three new uniformed Sheriff's deputies standing there. I was terrified that they had reconsidered their position and had returned to arrest my son.

"Yes?" I asked them.

"Mr. Blair, we have to arrest you," the lead deputy said.

"Arrest *me*?" I stammered. "For *what*?!"

"In a domestic dispute, one of the parties has to be taken to jail," he replied. "In our report, it says that you requested that your son shouldn't be arrested. That means we have to arrest *you*."

"This doesn't make *any* sense!" I protested. "It's been an hour. Nothing has happened. It's fine. I'll deal with this tomorrow."

"If something happens tonight because we failed to act, we'd be responsible," the deputy said. "We need to take you downtown. Turn around and put your hands behind your back."

My protests were to no avail. The deputies placed me in their car and drove me to the Orient Road Jail. Once I arrived there, they slapped me with two counts of child abuse. I was asked to change into an orange jumpsuit, and then I limped my way before Judge Walter Heinrich of the Hillsborough County Circuit Court.

With news cameras recording, Judge Heinrich – who had always been very friendly to me when we'd interacted on a personal level – told me that it would be up to the Division of Child Services to decide whether or not I would *ever* get to see my children again. I simply could *not* believe what was happening.

When I was released from jail, the news cameras were present once again. With Toni beside me and reporters hounding us, I staggered my way out to the car, and then the two of us drove home. To call the whole situation "embarrassing" wouldn't do it justice. It was a family *tragedy* that was put on public display.

B. Brian Blair: Truth Bee Told

I still considered myself to be a viable political figure, and I wanted to get my public reputation back under control. However, I didn't want to simply disclose to everyone that my elder son was struggling with a serious drug problem. That only would have made things far more difficult for him at a key stage of his life.

Receiving an award from the Hillsborough County Sheriff's Office

As I handled questions from reporters about the fallout from a Father's Day confrontation that had spun irretrievably out of control, I did everything I could to explain things away without outing Brett for his drug addiction. It was a virtually impossible task. People are apt to embrace the very worst things that are publicly disclosed about others, because the worse the details are imagined to be, the more entertaining the story becomes.

This is the point where Mike Graham did one of the kindest things for me that anyone has ever done. Without my knowledge, Mike contacted the local Fox News affiliate in Tampa and sat down for an interview. From there, he did his best to explain the full situation, including how Brett had repeatedly gone missing from the house, and how I was attempting to do what I could to correct my son's behavior. Still, Mike *never* divulged any details of Brett's drug use to the public, which I *also* appreciated.

What I *didn't* appreciate was the conduct of the Iron Sheik around this time. I'm very sympathetic with Sheik's station in life. He already wasn't in a sound financial position at the beginning of the

B. Brian Blair: Truth Bee Told

2000s, but then he seemed to spiral totally out of control after his daughter was tragically murdered in 2003. Sheik admittedly turned to cocaine and other drugs, and gained a new level of popularity over the internet by going on profanity-laden tirades against wrestlers he hadn't shared a wrestling ring with in *decades*. Posting videos online and making himself available for crazy interviews was the only avenue the Sheik had to make any money at all.

My name was dragged through the mud during several of these tirades, which were somewhat humorous in the beginning. In my opinion, the Sheik had singled me out for ridicule because I'd briefly embarrassed him in the ring way back in 1985, and he clung to that grudge for more than 20 years. However, when he posted a video shortly after my family fracas and publicly ridiculed me for being an alleged child abuser, he undeniably crossed the line. It was downright *wrong* of him to do it.

The Sheik's outbursts captured so much online media attention that the production team of the infamous shock jock Howard Stern called me on two separate occasions to invite me to appear as a guest on *The Howard Stern Show* to verbally spar with the Sheik. I declined on both occasions; I had no desire to fall into that trap, or to draw even more attention to my problems.

The news coverage of the event eventually subsided when the child abuse charges against me were dropped. It was very simple for the State Attorney's Office to reach that conclusion when they reviewed the medical report and found that I'd been the one who sustained *all* of the injuries from the incident, all of my wounds were *defensive*, and my sons had essentially *no* injuries.

I was reunited with my sons in Key West just a short time later. However, I felt like irreparable damage to my reputation and my political aspirations had been done, at least for time being. Certainly, there wasn't much point in continuing the lawsuit against Kevin Beckner or trying to regain my seat on the Hillsborough County Commission now that the tide of public opinion had swung so wildly against me.

I opted to run for a seat in the Florida State House of Representatives in 2010, but one month after I qualified for the race – and one month before the primary election took place – Brett was arrested and charged with possession of oxycodone, marijuana and other drug paraphernalia. Because of Brett's connection to me, and because of the incident that happened just one year prior, his arrest and the details surrounding it circulated in the news. Despite my best efforts to shield Brett from the public eye and take the consequences for his drug abuse upon myself, it was exposed to the public, nonetheless.

I can't confirm that this is the reason I lost my bid to claim a seat in Florida's House of Representatives, but it *certainly* didn't help. I lost by a little over 1,000 votes in a four-person race of notable candidates. Unfortunately, second place doesn't matter in scenarios like that. No one likes it when political leaders speak about the specific paths they would like others living in a society to follow, but then they don't appear to have their own houses in order.

One of the reasons I can understand the lure of painkillers and the hold they have on so many people's lives is because I once had my own opioid addiction. Over a relatively short span of time between 2009 and 2010, I had *three* separate operations: a knee replacement, a shoulder surgery that resulted in the collapse of a lung, and an emergency appendectomy that *almost* killed me.

Even after surviving the appendectomy, it felt like my entire body had betrayed me. The pain and inflammation from all of these maladies and surgeries was driving me completely insane. Even when I tried to rest, that simply worsened my condition. The more sedentary I became, the more the pain set in.

My doctor, Michael Cromer, provided me with a prescription painkiller that was incapable of keeping pace with the pain I was experiencing. When it reached a point where Dr. Cromer couldn't extend my painkiller prescription any further, I knew I was in *big* trouble.

Without any drugs in my system to control my discomfort, I began to sweat profusely and get chills. My instinctive impulse was to run out of my house and acquire some form of chemical pain relief by any means necessary; either from a friend, or from someone on the street.

I went out and bought some Percocet and used that to control the pain. Once the pain subsided somewhat, the presence of pain was replaced by overwhelming feelings of guilt and hypocrisy. I had been blaming my son's painkiller addiction for my public embarrassment and the setbacks to my political career, and here I was caving in and purchasing drugs illegally off the streets *just* like my son had done.

When I made an appointment and returned to Dr. Cromer's office, it was like going to the confessional at a Catholic church.

"I think I'm addicted to that pain medicine I'm taking," I admitted to him.

"Oh *really?*" he asked with a note of concern in his voice. "What makes you think so?"

B. Brian Blair: Truth Bee Told

"I started sweating when I ran out of pills," I said. "I sweat *all* the time when I'm not taking them. When you wouldn't give me any more of them, I ran out on the street and bought some. My whole body is hurting. I *hate* this feeling!"

Dr. Cromer simply nodded along as I rattled off my list of concerns.

"*What* can I do?" I pleaded. "Is there *anything* I can do?"

"Of *course* there is," said Dr. Cromer. "Tomorrow, don't take any pain pills in the morning. Come straight to my office."

Dr. Cromer scribbled on his prescription pad, tore off the top sheet of paper, and handed it to me.

"Get this prescription filled before you come see me," he ordered. "Bring it with you."

Dr. Cromer gave me a prescription for Suboxone, which is also known as Buprenorphine. I did exactly as he advised: I got the prescription filled first thing in the morning and brought the Suboxone with me to the clinic. Dr. Cromer led me to a small room with white walls and an examination table. Then he opened the door and ushered me inside of the room as I stood there, already shivering and exhibiting symptoms of withdrawal from the pain medication.

"If you knock on this door, someone will answer," said Dr. Cromer. "But I don't want you to knock on this door until you absolutely *can't take it* anymore. Hold out as long as you can. Only knock if the sweat, cold and pain gets so bad that you can't handle it anymore."

Then Dr. Cromer held a hand out in front of my face with his open palm turned upward.

"Give me the pills," he commanded.

Dutifully, I handed over the small, orange bottle full of Suboxone. Dr. Cromer accepted the pill bottle from me, exited the room, and shut the door behind him.

I curled up on the examination table and attempted to get comfortable. As the moments passed, I began to feel simultaneously chilly and sweaty, and the pain in my midsection, shoulder and knees became excruciating. When I reached my breaking point, I pulled myself up from the examination table and pounded on the door.

As promised, Dr. Cromer opened the door a few moments later. Upon entering, Dr. Cromer unscrewed the lid to the Suboxone bottle, emptied four round, orange tablets out into his hand, and then placed them into my palm.

"Put four of these under your tongue *right now*," he said.

B. Brian Blair: Truth Bee Told

I did as I was told. As soon as I put the pills under my tongue, the pain magically began to drift away. It was as if the sun had figuratively risen within that tiny room. My sweating ceased; my body heat rose; my mind was clear; I felt at ease.

"Now, we're going to ween you off the meds until you only need to take the lowest dose possible in order to control your pain," said Dr. Cromer. "In *your* case, it will probably be two pills. There's no tolerance to these. They're not going to hurt you, but there's also no high to it. Whatever amount takes your pain away is fine. What we're trying to do is get you to a point where the pain is manageable, and you don't need to take those pain pills."

Suboxone turned out to be like a miracle drug for me. Since receiving my treatment, I've advised several other wrestlers to speak to their doctors about Suboxone treatments when they've come to me lamenting their own painkiller addictions. Following my recommendations, *four* wrestlers have successfully stopped abusing opiates as a result of completing Suboxone therapy, and a few of them call me regularly just to thank me for informing them about it. The therapy helped them to reclaim control of their lives, the same way it helped me.

Danny Spivey once told me that he bought an ounce of cocaine, drove his car out to California, continued all the way to Venice Beach, finished off the cocaine, and then passed out in his car right there facing the Pacific Ocean.

"When I woke up from that, I told myself I was *done* with cocaine," Danny told me.

Suboxone was the drug that also eliminated Danny's dependency on painkillers and other drugs. It took that extreme of an incident for Danny to make a sober choice, which is why he opened the Sober Choice drug rehabilitation center. He has helped numerous people to rid themselves of their debilitating drug addictions.

As miserable as it was, my one-month experience as a painkiller addict was totally worthwhile. Because I went through it, at least I know what painkiller addiction feels like on both a physical and a psychological level, so I can relate to my son, and also to my fellow wrestlers who are struggling through their own battles with dependencies.

Speaking of wrestlers battling dependencies, the Iron Sheik managed to beat his own drug addiction a few years later, and was feeling very apologetic when he ran into me at a wrestling convention.

"Brian… maybe you forgive Sheik?" said the Sheik as he approached me, supporting most of his weight with his cane.

B. Brian Blair: Truth Bee Told

I shook his hand and leaned in for a hug.

"I never had a problem with *you* to begin with," I replied. "I forgive you."

To top it all off, my battle with painkiller addiction gave me an even more profound appreciation for my mother and everything that she endured during her life. She suffered through a divorce, poverty and alcohol addiction, and persevered through all of it. In the process, she raised several children into upstanding adults, and never shirked her responsibilities as a parent.

Mom emerged on the other side of it all completely free of everything that plagued her, including her addictions. It couldn't have been easy for her, and she provided me with a prime example of what the enduring love of a parent is supposed to look like.

Pretty soon, I would have an opportunity to reflect that enduring love right back at my wrestling peers.

With my mother in 2021

My father celebrating his 89th birthday

TWENTY-EIGHT – *Aging gracefully*

When I was approached by Morgan Dollar at the Gulf Coast Reunion in 2014, I had no idea that one of the reasons he had been sent there was to recruit me to fill a critical role with the Cauliflower Alley Club – pro wrestling's only 501(c)(3) non-profit corporation, which raises money to help former full-time wrestlers, referees and other contributors who are in need of financial assistance.

"Hey, Brian," Morgan said. "Can I talk to you outside for a minute?"

"Yeah, sure," I said.

Once we got outside, Morgan cut right to chase.

"As you know, I'm the vice president of the Cauliflower Alley Club," he said. "You also probably know that Nick Bockwinkel will be stepping down as president due to health issues as soon as we find the right person to take his place. We've been talking about who we feel would be a good president for us, and you came highly recommended. One of the reasons I'm here is to see how you'd feel about becoming the CAC president."

"Oh, wow!" I replied. "That's a *huge* honor. I have a lot on my plate. I'd need to know everything that's involved with the job before I could make a decision."

"It's mostly a figurehead position," Morgan said, *severely* downplaying what the CAC president was actually responsible for. "The thing is, you can be as hands-on as you want to be. It's really up to you. We just think you have the background and the personality that are suited for the job."

"Again, that's a huge honor, Morgan," I told him. "I'm just going to need a little more time to think about it. I'd like to talk to Karl Lauer and get a better idea from him about what the job entails."

Only five men had ever served as the president of the CAC in the organization's 40-year history: Mike Mazurki, Art Abrams, Lou Thesz, Red Bastien and Nick Bockwinkel. I was honored to learn that it had been Harley Race of all people who had planted the thought in the heads of the CAC Board members that I would be a suitable choice to fill the role as president of the organization.

The combination of my business background, my political background, and my respect for the business gave Harley the impression that I would put forth a respectable effort in managing the CAC.

B. Brian Blair: Truth Bee Told

What ultimately made me agree to assume the responsibility as the CAC's president was my recollection of Hercules' funeral, and how his family had been without the financial resources to even pay for a pastor. I realized this would be a perfect opportunity to put my money where my mouth was, to do something to improve the lives of my fellow wrestlers, and to assist the family members left behind whenever my friends passed on from this life.

Posing next to a poster of former CAC president Nick Bockwinkel

Morgan also told me that as president of the CAC, I would *also* have the option to assume the mantle of CEO. That's why I ultimately agreed to accept the position: I didn't want to be merely a figurehead as the CAC president like Nick Bockwinkel and others had been. It's not like they had done nothing of value in their presidential roles, but Karl Lauer and Dean Silverstone had honestly done the overwhelming share of the leadership work for the CAC in their respective roles as the CEO and Secretary/Treasurer of the organization. Simply put, I didn't want to have my name attached to an entity that I had no true control over. That would have been contrary to *everything* I'd learned in business.

B. Brian Blair: Truth Bee Told

No matter what position I held with the CAC, all of the work involved would be entirely voluntary. None of the members of the CAC Board receive any financial compensation for their duties whatsoever. In fact, they are even required to cover all of their own expenses at official CAC events, like the annual reunions.

The CAC Board ultimately approved me to assume both roles, as president and CEO, but I don't think I grasped the full scope of what I was getting myself into at that time. About 50 percent of my responsibilities could be classified as CAC business, but *another* 50 percent could be regarded as duties that are above and beyond the duties of the CAC presidency.

When you assume the role of CAC president, past and present pro wrestlers will call you for assistance and guidance to help them through just about any situation you can imagine. Many of their questions are solicitations for advice on how to find work or get help, but other conversations have delved into more serious concerns, like how to handle a divorce without your spouse taking you to the cleaners.

Other wrestlers may be searching for advice about which surgeries they should opt for, or even advice about the best ways to wean themselves off of drugs. In short, the position calls for you to be an amateur counselor much of the time, and if I didn't have an enduring love for my peers, it would be a very punishing role.

Without exception, the most daunting moments of managing the CAC all involve the fallout following the death of a fellow wrestler. Brian Lawler, Nikolai Volkoff and Brickhouse Brown all passed away on the same weekend, and aside from the personal toll of having three associates pass away, I had to field many calls in connection to those deaths.

Right at the point when I'm most inclined to mourn, I'm forced to delve even *further* into the sadness in order to collect all of the crucial details about the deaths and funeral arrangements, and distribute that information to my fellow wrestlers so that they can make plans to attend the funeral or send flowers and condolences. From there, I *also* have to submit information to the Executive Board so that we can determine what type of financial support can be offered to the families of our departed colleagues.

Managing the CAC isn't only about assisting wrestlers and families who are struggling with financial challenges. I am now *far* more cognizant of just how little it takes for a wrestler struggling with depression to be figuratively nudged over the edge into contemplations of suicide.

B. Brian Blair: Truth Bee Told

Aside from my dear friends the Von Erichs, who succumbed to three suicides – by Mike, Chris and Kerry – in the midst of their additional family tragedies, self-imposed deaths amongst pro wrestlers used to be exceedingly rare. I'm of the opinion that cyberbullying from fans has contributed immensely to the spike in suicides amongst former wrestlers.

Toni and I in Hawaii with Kevin and Pam Von Erich

Many wrestlers are already reeling from financial distress caused by a lack of financial planning, the absence of insurance, medical expenses, divorces, and myriad other issues. From there, wrestlers often go online in search of support, only to become targets for ridicule right when they are in their most vulnerable states. If they're already feeling depressed and take the mean-spirited comments to heart, there can be *disastrous* consequences.

If someone is struggling in life, the wrong comment from the wrong person at the wrong time can be all it takes to make a person decide that life is no longer worth living. A lot of wrestlers go online in search of either love or positive reassurance, and instead they are frequently met with crushing remarks. It may sound shocking, but that sort of bullying has been a significant contributor to some of the wrestler suicides that have occurred during my presidency of the CAC.

For the most part, being the president of the CAC is a joy, but one of the most challenging situations of my presidency occurred when "Superstar" Billy Graham sued the CAC.

B. Brian Blair: Truth Bee Told

Ironically, it all started when the CAC raised about $17,000 to help Billy pay for his medical procedures. Later, at the CAC's annual convention, Billy left a lot of clothing and other assorted items in his hotel room. I was told by Karl Lauer that Billy applied for even more money, but Karl was adamant about not providing Billy with any further financial assistance because he'd already received plenty of monetary aid. By that point, Karl had faithfully served the CAC for well over 27 years, and his integrity was unimpeachable.

To make matters worse, Billy had never thanked the CAC or its members for any of the aid he received; he seemed to think he was entitled to it. In fact, Karl said that Billy had been very rude to him at the convention, and when the CAC had to ship all of Billy's clothes back to him at the organization's expense, Billy never thanked anyone at the CAC for doing that for him either.

That was the extent of it: Karl didn't want to give Billy any more money, so we declined his subsequent benevolent request. In response to that, Billy wrote about us online, referring to us as "white trash punks" and "low life assholes." He also referred to me as "the biggest pile of dung," and "the biggest phony of them all." Please keep in mind, this was *after* the CAC had *already* raised about $17,000 for him and provided it to him to help him pay for his medical bills.

Billy continued making threats to the CAC online, and bragged about how much money he was going to take from the organization. He then filed a defamation-of-character lawsuit against me and the CAC for $3.5 million; his lawsuit didn't even make it past the initial stages. The judge overseeing the case ruled that Billy's lawsuit was frivolous and issued a summary judgment in the CAC's favor.

At no point was I worried about his lawsuit, because I'm familiar with the law. I knew that neither myself nor any other member of the CAC's Board of Directors had done anything that could be construed as breaking the law. No other event in my time overseeing the CAC has been nearly this negative.

I had always gotten along with Billy, and I never imagined that he would turn heel on me – let alone the CAC – in real life.

Unfortunately, Billy's prominence and influence as a notable wrestling figure led to a lot of fans jumping aboard his bandwagon and cheering for him to put the CAC out of commission. I'm sure very few of them realized that eliminating the CAC would have erased the organization that most actively cares for the needs of retired wrestlers, as well as active wrestlers who find themselves saddled with financial problems.

B. Brian Blair: Truth Bee Told

In the midst of serving as the CAC's president, I remained an active wrestler. I was scheduled to compete against Bushwhacker Luke on one of George South's shows, and Luke explained this spot to me that he wanted us to perform during the match.

"I'll hip toss you, but I want you to block it and headscissor me over," Luke explained in his New Zealand accent.

"No problem, Luke," I said, almost dismissively. "I've got it!"

Everything was going as planned during the actual match, except I didn't get up high enough in the air to do a proper headscissor takedown. I blew the spot, and Luke and I simply wound up tumbling over in a heap.

"Hey, mate," Luke said afterwards. "I'm gettin' older. *You're* gettin' older, too! If you can't do the spot anymore, just tell me. We'll do somethin' else."

"Hey, I *can* do the spot!" I insisted. "I just messed up!"

Luke was right, though; I was *definitely* getting older.

From that point on, I found that I had to change my in-ring repertoire quite a bit. A lot of the aerial stuff I used to do needed to come out of my arsenal. Leaping was a challenge, because I'd already had *six* operations on my knees *alone*.

The one good thing for me was that I hadn't maintained a grueling travel schedule during what might have been considered the prime years of my career – in my 30s and 40s – to the point where my body was completely broken down and decimated. Still, that didn't mean I wasn't occasionally placing myself in vulnerable positions that I probably shouldn't have.

The further I moved away from the heyday of my WWF career – where almost every wrestler in the company had been involved in at least 2,000 matches before they earned a roster spot – the more likely it became that I would be working with younger wrestlers who had participated in only the merest fraction of the matches that I had.

This was most easily exemplified by some of the matches I had with young independent wrestlers who were determined to engage in risky moves *before* they were competent enough to perform them safely. These wrestlers were the most dangerous of all, because they always wanted to test out the latest daring thing they'd seen on television, or on the internet.

When I broke into the wrestling business, I worked an average of six nights per week for three years – which amounted to far more than 900 days of wrestling in front of paying fans – and I *still* felt like a total rookie after all of that. As my in-ring career progressed into its fourth and fifth decades, I found myself working with guys who had wrestled only twice a month for five years, yet believed themselves to be experienced in-ring workers. I wrestled more in the first four months of my career than these guys had wrestled in *five years*.

I was involved in a six-man tag match in Iowa at the Pro Wrestling Hall of Fame show in 2017. Wes Brisco and Myron Reed were on my team, and our opponents spent some time with us before the match describing all of the crazy maneuvers they wanted to do to me. Their plan was to get some spectacular heat by executing a bunch of flashy maneuvers on the established veteran wrestler in the ring. The one move they *desperately* wanted to deliver to me was a double backbreaker, combined with an elbow drop across my chest from another wrestler who intended to dive from the top turnbuckle.

"Have you guys *ever* done this before?" I asked, warily. "This is a *really* dangerous move you're talking about."

They insisted they'd done the move several times. I considered that claim to be rather dubious.

"Guys, I *can't* afford to get my neck broken," I warned them.

Wanting to keep myself from getting crippled, I started doling out instructions to ensure that I would be able to walk out of the ring under my own power that night.

"If you do this move, you're the short one, so *you* need to be in the back," I said, pointing from one wrestler to another and attempting to diagram the delivery of the move. "*You're* the tall one, so you need to be in the front. My neck needs to have room to come over. Cup my neck with your left hand and make sure that you grab my ass, my legs, or whatever. When he hits me with the elbow, *you* need to flip me while holding my neck and guiding me over gently."

Everyone in the room insisted it was no problem. As it turned out, it was a *huge* problem.

In their haste and excitement to perform their fancy tag team move, the *short* guy got in the front, and the *tall* guy got in the back. To top it off, their backs were turned toward the wrestler on the top turnbuckle, so they couldn't look directly at him and time the spot correctly. By that point, it was already too late. I was at their mercy, and they didn't cup my neck. I was left totally unprotected, so when my opponent came off the top rope with the elbow drop, he drove my head *straight down* into the mat.

The first thing I can recall after my head hit the mat was the numbness of my toes. Initially, I thought I was paralyzed. After a few seconds of attempting to bend my knees, I was very grateful to discover that the signal from my brain finally got through and that my legs were still capable of movement. All the same, some obvious damage had been done to my body.

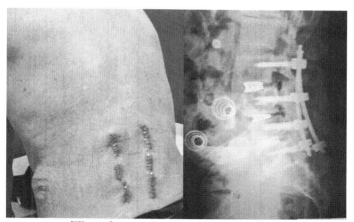

The aftermath of my back surgery

The young wrestlers I had been working with attempted to apologize to me in the ring, and then they continued their apologies to me in the locker room afterwards as I was nursing my neck. Not to sound like a jerk, but after warning them about what might happen if they attempted that dangerous move, and *then* having it go just as disastrously as I imagined it might, I wasn't in the mood to accept any apologies. Apologies don't fix *paralysis*.

"I told you guys if you don't know how to do the freakin' move, *don't* do the freakin' move!" I screamed.

I wound up requiring a neck operation, which was expertly handled by Dr. Rashid Kumar. Instead of going through my throat – which was the standard surgical pathway – Dr. Kumar performed a cervical laminectomy by operating on my spine through the back.

The $500 payoff from that match didn't even come close to offsetting the damage that was done to my body as a result of that one move. Recklessness in the ring is very costly, and I hope the next generation of wrestlers remembers that the first order of business in the wrestling ring is to protect the person you're working with.

I've continued to wrestle sporadically, but the injuries have continued to mount. To my great disappointment, this often prevented me from delivering the caliber of matches that I'd hoped to. The fans remained supportive, but there is a special kind of disappointment that comes from losing the ability you once possessed, and that you worked so tirelessly to acquire.

B. Brian Blair: Truth Bee Told

One notable event that demonstrated this occurred in July of 2019, when I wrestled for promoter Troy Peterson against James Jeffries in what was billed as my retirement bout. The event was the sold-out Impact Pro Wrestling Hall of Fame Show in Iowa. I accepted this booking despite also being scheduled for a major back surgery the following month.

I was relatively immobile during that match, and I was not up to my usual performance standards. I just wish Troy would have mentioned my injuries and pending surgery to the commentators who voiced over the match so that they could have communicated how much pain I was feeling to the viewing audience.

Speaking at a Tampa elementary school

Even if I never wrestle in the ring again, I've had a very long and satisfying wrestling career. I performed and made friends with some of the most wonderful and entertaining people who *ever* lived, including many guys who started out as my childhood heroes and became closer to me than blood relatives. In my opinion, professional wrestling was the greatest industry in the world, in my lifetime.

Not only did I get to live a life that most people can only dream of, but my exploits also permitted me to spend countless hours mentoring children. I coached baseball, football and wrestling for at least 25 seasons, and I've spoken at more than half of the schools in Hillsborough County. Even if all of that effort only managed to keep one child from going down the wrong path, it was worth every second.

When I prayed to be Superman as a young child, I think God really answered my prayers by allowing me to be a participant in the wrestling world. In my eyes, being a professional wrestler was as close as anyone could get to being a real-life superhero.

EPILOGUE

In 2020, I made a surprise visit to Paul Orndorff's house in Atlanta during the COVID-19 pandemic. The purpose of the trip was to pay a visit to Diamond Dallas Page, but I couldn't turn down an opportunity to see my good friend Paul. In fact, I extended my trip by an extra day just to see him since he's been a fixture of my life for such a long time.

When I arrived at Paul's home, he was sitting on the porch, looking like he hadn't shaved in a month. Paul gazed quizzically at my unfamiliar rental car as I pulled into his driveway, but when I hopped out of the car, he said "Beeper!" very loudly.

At this point in his life, Paul doesn't remember too many people, aside from family members, and maybe some of his grandchildren's significant others. The fact that he even recognizes me *at all* these days is a tremendous testament to our enduring friendship.

Paul struggled mightily in his effort to rise to his feet and greet me. As I approached Paul, I noticed his nose had been scraped up.

"Paul, what happened to your nose?" I asked him.

"I don't know," Paul said, hazily. "I *don't* know."

These memory-loss issues were nothing new with Paul. When I went with him to the Pro Wrestling Hall of Fame induction ceremony, he needed help remembering Gerald Brisco's name five separate times – and he and Gerald are *lifelong* friends. When Paul got up to deliver his speech, I stood with him and helped him along as he struggled his way through it.

Paul was one of the primary wrestlers involved in the concussion lawsuit against World Wrestling Entertainment because he had experienced at least two concussions while working for Vince. However, Paul also played football for several years, as a fullback no less, and probably had a few concussions from his football days as well. That's one of several reasons I didn't participate in the concussion lawsuit. Many wrestlers from my era and the era that preceded it suffered concussions across multiple sports, or at least in multiple territories. In my view, it isn't fair to attach 100 percent of the blame to Vince for all of the concussions and concussion-related consequences when *many* of those concussions were suffered outside of wrestling, let alone outside of the WWE's wrestling rings.

I helped Paul to his feet and we hugged one another. Then, as we sat down on Paul's porch and began the process of getting caught up with one another's lives, Paul kept rubbing his shoulder and complaining about soreness.

"Why are you so sore?" I asked him.

"I *can't* remember," Paul said, sadly. "I *think* I fell down, but I'm not sure."

While we were chatting, the boyfriend of one of Paul's granddaughters pulled up in his vehicle and then approached the house with two big bags of Chick-Fil-A in his hands. I hadn't even been in the house yet to greet Paul's wife, Ronda – a rumored meth addict who no longer has any teeth.

The young man carrying the food walked right past Paul, who remarked, "I'm hungry," and entered the house. We continued to sit there and talk for a little while. The young man then exited the house, and we waited for someone to walk out onto the porch to give Paul some food. No one ever came.

Finally, I got up and entered the house. Ronda Orndorff was lying on the couch with some sort of blue handkerchief or rubber cap on her head. She raised her head when I walked into the room.

"Hi, Ronda," I said, attempting to sound cordial.

"Hi, Brian," she replied, curtly.

"Did you get something for *Paul* to eat?" I asked her.

"Well... uhhh... he had four sausages and four eggs about an hour ago, and he said he wasn't hungry," she stuttered.

I knew better than that. Ronda lies like a *rug*. She has gone so far as to tell me that she has never done a drug in her life even though her son has personally shown me video footage of her coming down the stairs so inebriated that she couldn't even walk straight.

The occupants of the house had consumed *all* of the food. Feeling heartbroken for Paul and pissed off at his clear mistreatment, I drove him with me to Chick-Fil-A and told him to order whatever he wanted. It was just like old times. We frequented the very first Chick-Fil-A all the time when we were working for the NWA's Atlanta office back in the early '80s. Paul was so hungry that he ate *three* Chick-Fil-A sandwiches *and* a large fries, and washed it all down with a large milkshake. He'd been *starving*.

When Paul had finished his meal, we returned to his house. The two of us took up a position on Paul's porch and spoke for quite a while. It was somewhat heartbreaking, because it's very difficult to reminisce when Paul's mind is in such a sad state. I determined that it was worth the effort to confront Ronda about the condition of her husband, so I accompanied Paul into his home and looked around. There were *huge* piles of laundry occupying the dining room. The house was a total mess.

B. Brian Blair: Truth Bee Told

I figured the best thing to do would be to ask Ronda some direct questions.

"Hey, Ronda… are you giving Paul his medicine?" I asked her.

"No," she stated. "He won't take it."

"What do you mean I *won't* take it?!" Paul asked, accusingly.

"Oh, Paul!" she said. "You *know* you won't take it!"

"Give it to me!" Paul challenged. "I'll take it *right now!*"

I'm certain that if Ronda had been giving Paul his medicine for the last three years like she should have, his memory would be a lot better.

"You know, Paul hasn't taken a shower in *over* a month," Ronda said.

"Oh really, Ronda?" I replied, growing increasingly angrier. "Don't you think you could *help him* take a shower?"

"He can take a shower on his own," she spat. "It's just getting him in the shower is the problem."

Things were becoming contentious, so I de-escalated the situation just a tad. It wasn't worth having a major argument with her in front of everyone in the house. However, between Paul's frail physique, his poor hygiene, and what I perceived to be an intentional effort to deprive him of his essential medicine, it almost seemed like a deliberate effort to gradually kill Paul on the part of his own wife.

I opted to call the authorities on Ronda, which made me at least the *second* person to do so. According to Paul's son Travis, the authorities had been alerted about his father's mistreatment on at least one other occasion.

Sadly, no amount of intervention was able to prevent the worst from happening. Paul Orndorff passed away on July 12, 2021 at the age of 71. I had certainly known about the dire nature of Paul's condition for a long time, but I had *always* hoped against hope that he would recover.

Just three days prior to Paul's death, Travis Orndorff called me from his father's bedside and held the phone to Paul's ear while I said my final goodbye to him. It was the third time I'd spoken to Paul while he was lying in that hospital bed.

By that point, Paul was no longer able to physically speak when he was listening to my words. The first two times I had talked to Paul, he had made a few sounds and raised his arm, but no one around him understood what he was attempting to say.

A treasured photo signed by my Wonderful friend

Following my final message to Paul, Travis informed me that the sound of my voice had brought a faint smile to the lips of his dying father. Hearing that gave me goosebumps. From that moment on, in the days leading up to Paul's inevitable passing, I spent much of my time reflecting on our friendship and crying my eyes out.

As magnificent and legendary as Paul had been in the prime of his life, it seemed *so* unfair that he would spend his final years of life in such a gaunt, frail and vulnerable state. It's a sobering reminder that we need to enjoy the time we have as much as we possibly can, but we also need to prepare our hearts, minds and souls for when it all eventually comes to an end.

Paul was my childhood hero, and then he became one of the best friends I've ever had in my life. It was the wrestling business that made our friendship possible. It turned heroes of mine that I revered into men that are as close to me as many of my own family members. The bonds of brotherhood run deep through the pro wrestling community, and as long as I'm alive, I'll do whatever I can to make sure my fellow wrestlers are treated with the dignity and respect they deserve, no matter what stage of life they're in.

Even though the cheers from fans in dimly lit arenas are long gone for many of us, if you are one of my fellow wrestlers, I'll always be there to lend you a helping hand, and I'll always continue to be *your* biggest fan. And, if I'm remembered more for the assistance I provided for my fellow wrestlers as the president of the Cauliflower Alley Club than for anything I did inside of a wrestling ring, I'll count it as a blessing that I was able to give so much back to the industry *and* the people who gave so much entertainment, direction and meaning to me... *Truth Bee Told*.

EPILOGUE #2

The motto of my son Brett's baseball team during their run to Nationals was "Believe, Achieve, Receive." When you believe, you achieve, and when you achieve, you receive. More specifically in their case, if you believe in yourself, then you will achieve the ability to win, and when you achieve that ability, then you will receive exactly what you worked for.

Brett's team bought into that mantra, and their season was highlighted by incredible successes and memorable performances that spanned several states.

The Blairs: Brett, Toni, Brian and Bradley

All of that occurred back in the mid-2000s right before my son's serious problems with painkiller addiction began to destabilize his life. Over a 14-year stretch, Brett progressed from using pain pills to heroin, and then to meth. A lot of darkness and negativity encircled Brett's life during that time despite his constant efforts to improve his circumstances, and everyone in our family prayed earnestly for my eldest son to turn his life around.

Early in 2021, I skimmed through Brett's diary like the concerned father I was, and I found a recent entry that said this:

"I'm done. No more drugs. I've messed up. I've hurt people, and I've hurt my family. I'm not doing drugs anymore."

B. Brian Blair: Truth Bee Told

It was a comforting sight to see that Brett was fully cognizant of the fact that his life hadn't been everything it could have been, and that he was desperate to make a change. Brett's resolve would be put to the test. On July 4th, Brett was in Marathon, Florida was his cousins, the McKeons. Brett went out on the water on the large boat of his cousin Kevin, accompanied by a bunch of girls. It was an obvious party setting, but I trusted Brett. I trusted him knowing full well that my nephews would stooge on him if he did anything untoward; his cousin Matt was also with him, and Matt is a counselor at a drug rehabilitation center.

The day after the party, I asked Matt, "How did Brett do?"

"You would not believe it!" exclaimed Kevin, proudly. "There were two people there that wanted Brett to party with them and do meth, but Brett wouldn't have anything to do with them."

Brett always had faith in God, and I knew that one day the lightbulb would be turned on in his head and in his heart. Brett had Biblical scriptures and symbols tattooed all over his body, and I knew that the meaning behind those tattoos was in his mind and his heart as well. I was simply waiting patiently for the day that it would manifest itself through his actions. Well, it was all starting to come out in obvious ways.

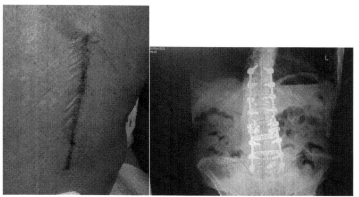

The aftermath of my 2021 back surgery

I had back surgery scheduled for later in July, and Brett brought a girl along with him when he came to visit me two days before my surgery. The far-off look in the eyes of the girl conveyed all of the obvious signs of drug use. She didn't have the appearance of someone I wanted Brett associating himself with.

B. Brian Blair: Truth Bee Told

"Brett, what's the deal with this girl?" I asked him. "She looks all knocked out. I thought you quit that stuff!"

"I did, Dad," Brett replied earnestly. "Don't worry. *She's* the one who needs help."

With that Brett kissed me and hugged me very tightly.

"Daddy, I love you so much," he said. "You're gonna be okay, and I'm gonna visit you in the hospital."

"Thank you, Son," I told him. "I know you're going to be good. I believe you, and I love you so much."

I *did* believe Brett, because I had read what he had written in his diary, and I had also seen the evidence of the improvements in his life.

Two days after my back surgery, and two days after not hearing another word out of Brett, the doorbell rang at our home. Standing at the door were two detectives carrying a heartbreaking message with them. They were the hardest words that any parent could ever hear.

"Mr. Blair, your son has been murdered," the Sheriff's deputy said.

Naturally, I instantaneously broke down in tears. Brett's body had been discovered, wrapped in a sheet, and intentionally buried at a remote construction site in Pasco County.

In the aftermath of Brett's murder, several people approached me and asked me if I was angry at God.

"No," I told them. "I have never been mad at God for a single day of my life."

I will never be angry with God because there is evil that exists in the world, and *that* is the source of the pain and suffering that happens to people. I also know that no matter how sacred your loved ones are to you, they're not truly yours. They belong to God. Our family will never truly let Brett go, but we can rest assured that he is in the arms of our Heavenly Father. I believe that with all of my heart and soul, and I believe that we'll see Brett again one day.

I also believe that if Brett could say anything to you, he would ask you to not cry for him because he's in a better place, and that God has set him free. He would urge you to believe in God. He would tell you that when you have that belief, you will achieve wisdom, knowledge and understanding. And ultimately, Brett would tell you that when you achieve those things, then you will receive Jesus Christ as your savior. When you do that, you will *truly* win the big game.

The final photo ever taken of Brett Blair

> 10/11/2019
> "A DAD is someone who wants to catch you before you fall but instead picks you up, brushes you off, and lets you try again." DAD i love you more than you'll ever know and i look up to you in so many ways... youre my idol - thats the TRUTH.
> Love, Your Son — Brett L. Blair

A cherished message from my eldest son

AFTERWORD

B. Brian Blair: Truth Bee Told

For those of you who don't know Brian Blair, or can't possibly understand what this guy is all about, he's what I would call "The Real Deal." I'm not talking about Brian Blair the wrestler; I'm talking about Brian Blair the human being.

I met Brian many years ago when I was first attempting to get into the wrestling business. He was very kind to me from day one. Now, after knowing him for over 40 years, I can tell you that he's the same person he was all those years ago. He has always been there for me through thick and thin.

We've spent tons of time together on the road, wrestling all over the country and all over the world. Brian Blair has always been

B. Brian Blair: Truth Bee Told

there for me as a friend. I don't have to tell you how good of a wrestler he is because his resume stands for itself – he was one of the *best* wrestlers that ever stepped into the ring. As a person, Brian Blair has always been a friend, and will *always* be a friend.

When I had my ups and downs – when I was on top of the world and then crashed and burned in a big way more than once – Brian was there for me. Then I went through a crazy divorce and was lost for about 10 years, and I went through all kinds of other tough events in my life. I didn't talk to Brian for about nine years while my life was in turmoil, but when I needed Brian and reached out to him, he was there for me once again. He has no idea what his friendship means to me, or how valuable his friendship has been over the years.

When you got in the ring with Brian, you *knew* what he was all about in that arena. What's more important is that he's the real deal as a quality human being. As a man, Brian is absolutely incredible, and that's the *most* important thing that everyone needs to know about him.

Hulk Hogan

Terry Bollea, AKA "Hulk Hogan"

B. Brian Blair: Truth Bee Told
BONUS STORIES AND OUTTAKES

A Special Dedication to My Two Sons

I so vividly remember when my wife Toni and I wanted to start a family. Enjoying my tag team years as a Killer Bee, I prayed to the Good Lord that He would bless me with two boys – maybe twins or maybe through two separate pregnancies – because I wanted to have my own "Killer Bees," as I really liked my tag team partner "Jumping" Jim.

Several of my other colleagues also had names that began with the letter "B," like Bret Hart, who was my favorite tag team opponent, and Brad Rheingans, who was a very good amateur wrestler, a solid pro-wrestler, and one of the nicest guys in the business. Most of the other wrestlers that I really liked and got along with – which included 99 percent of the guys I worked with – had names that began with other letters, and I honestly didn't want to have more than two children anyway.

I have to say that I have never felt as elated as I did when I watched both of my sons come into this world. It's an indescribable and an incredible experience. The deliveries were handled by Dr. Howard Johnson, who was a great OBGYN – a brilliant man with a great personality, a passion for his job and an affable human being!

So after a little haggling with my wife over our first boy's name, Brett (named after Bret Hart... but my wife insisted on two T's in Brett) was born in May of 1992. Then exactly three years later, almost to the day, in May of 1995, Brad was born, and I had no problem with the name "Brad," other than the fact that Toni insisted it was Bradley. What the heck; you have to make room for compromise in many situations.

I was fortunate enough to not be working a steady daily schedule on the road, so I was able to coach both sons for about 20 seasons (two seasons per year) in various sports, and they were both *excellent* athletes. Brad actually got to play in Raymond James Stadium as an offensive tackle on the undefeated West-Chase Colts Bay Area Champions in the 14-to-15-year-old division, and was an all-star baseball player during most of the seasons he played.

Brett excelled in baseball and golf, and was a starting pitcher and utility player on the only Park Ball team in the history of the Tampa Bay area to go all the way to the Nationals in the 13-to-14-year-old Pony division.

B. Brian Blair: Truth Bee Told

Although my Killer Bees have stung me a few times, I would not trade them for anything in the world. I love them with all my heart and soul, now and always.

An Apology to My Parents

I've given my parents a lot of gifts over the years, and one of the reasons I've been so adamant about giving them things is because of the inconvenience I caused when I blew out the transmission of our family car back in high school. It was *so* irresponsible of me, and it set our family back big time. It cost about $1,000 to fix the transmission; I wanted to be sure to pay it back *20 times* over.

At one point I bought my mother a Toyota Avalon. Hopefully that will take some of the sting off of the news of how the transmission really got blown out.

Mr. Titan and Best All Around

I won a ton of athletic awards at Tampa Bay Tech High School. When the 1975 yearbook was being prepared, editor Buzzy Scott approached me and said, "You won in *two* categories. Do you want to be most athletic or best all around? You *can't* be both."

I opted to be named "Best All Around" because it seemed less limiting. I was also voted "Mr. Titan" during the annual homecoming football game.

Strongbow, Garea and Lanza

The job of the WWF agents was to make sure the matches at our shows got off and running as smoothly as possible, to report on our matches and rate them for quality, and then to *stooge* to Vince about anything that wasn't copacetic.

Of all the agents, Chief Jay Strongbow was the one who praised my work the most. He was also considered by many wrestlers to be the *biggest* stooge of all the agents. Still, it was nice to have people on my side and sticking up for me with Vince. Despite Chief being such a supporter of mine, Tony Garea was the agent I was probably closest to.

B. Brian Blair: Truth Bee Told

The one agent I *didn't* get along with was Blackjack Lanza. Any time someone brought something up, Lanza would always interject by chiming in and mentioning some milestone that he had accomplished in his heyday. Yet, Lanza and Brunzell got along very well together, and it probably had to do with all of the time they spent together in the AWA.

I was approached by Tony Garea one time, and he asked me, "What did you do for Chief?"

"What do you mean?" I asked. "I didn't do anything."

"Chief is *always* talking good about you," Garea asserted. "Chief doesn't talk good about *anybody*. He keeps telling Vince that he loves your work."

"Well, I'm happy to hear it!" I said with a grin.

The Hunting Story

I once went hunting in Rhine, Georgia with Ed Barbara, Paul Orndorff, Rick Rude and Steve Keirn. It was at the ranch of a guy named Mike Williams. Ed, Rick, Steve and I all rode up together from Florida and met Paul in Rhine, since Paul lived in Georgia.

Preparing to go hunting

Paul was a remarkable hunter, but he was *very* strict about it. He was one of those guys that wouldn't take a shower for two days before he went hunting so that the animals couldn't detect the unnatural body-care products on his skin. He was also a huge stickler

B. Brian Blair: Truth Bee Told

for what tools and props were permissible to use in order for a hunter to legitimately be credited with making an honorable kill.

Rick Rude showed up for the occasion sporting every hunting accessory imaginable, including a slick mosquito face protector, a full set of camouflage clothing that covered him from head to toe, and even a scent-elimination spray to mask his odor from the animals. From looking at him, you never would have guessed that he was a *total* rookie when it came to hunting.

While we were preparing for the hunt, a 50-pound pig strolled out into the middle of where we were stationed, and that poor pig got attacked *so* savagely. It was like facing a firing squad; the pig probably wound up with 100 rounds in its body. Out of all of us, Rude was the most aggressive. He simply would not stop shooting this pig despite the fact that it was inarguably dead. It's as if he felt he could claim it as his kill if he managed to get more bullets into it than anyone else.

"*Quit* shootin' the pig!" Paul screamed at Rick. "Stop it!"

Rick stopped shooting and beamed at the pig's bloody carcass with pride as he admired his handiwork.

"We gotta *eat* that thing, man!" Paul shouted. "That's half the point! If you put all that lead in it, we *can't* eat it!"

Rick's proud face dissolved into a pout.

"Oh... ummm... I'm sorry," was all Rick could muster. "I just got excited. That was my *first* pig."

Later on, all of us were driving around on three-wheelers when Keirn and I hit a mud bog and tipped over in it. When we pulled ourselves out of the bog, we were covered from head to toe in muck. We also opened fire on a 300-pound boar as it wandered across a very boggy creek. Both of us managed to hit the boar, but the darn thing *still* managed to get away.

Rick and I had driven up with Ed Barbara in his brand new 735i BMW, and then Paul swiped Ed's keys right after we arrived. There were a lot of deer-head trophies in the lodge we were staying in, so Orndorff hung Ed's keys from one of the antler sets as a rib. Ed tore the *entire* place apart looking for his keys, never realizing that they were suspended just above him on the antlers of a deer. We teased Ed about misplacing his keys to the point where Ed was just about ready to cry.

Finally, Rude looked up and said, "What the hell is *that?*"

Ed glanced up, spotted his keys, and shouted with great relief, "*Those* look like my *keys!*"

Ed stepped on a chair to get a closer look.

B. Brian Blair: Truth Bee Told

"Yeah, those are my keys!" he confirmed. "Man, I know we were drinkin', but I *sure* don't remember putting my keys here!"

Ed wasn't used to spending time with people who had nothing better to do than to come up with creative ways to play practical jokes on each other. It never dawned on him that the wrestlers he was hanging out with would hide his keys from him just for the sake of watching him go insane with worry as he wasted an hour searching for them.

Asset Performers vs. Enhancement Talents

I've *always* hated the term "enhancement talent," and especially the way it's retroactively applied to people from my era. I would venture to guess that 75 percent of the talent in the WWF in the mid 1980s had been main eventers in at least one territory before then, if not *more* than one territory.

If you're defining main eventers based on the regularity with which they appeared in the main events of shows after all of the talent in the territory was gathered together under one roof, that would mean Hulk Hogan and Randy Savage were the only *true* babyface main event wrestlers in the WWF between 1985 and 1988. From there, whichever heel wrestlers they defended the WWF Heavyweight Championship against would rotate into the other main event slots on a *very* temporary basis.

If being able to claim main-event status mattered so much, it would have been far better to be a heel than a babyface in the WWF. At least that way, you could have been in the rotating cast of heels that Hogan and Savage defended the world championship against and claimed main-event status for yourself.

If asked to do so, at least 60 percent of the talent in the WWF had the wherewithal to capably perform in the main events of shows during that era. They simply weren't selected to do so. Financially, it made more sense to voluntarily give up main-event opportunities in other territories – as I did in Florida – to perform on the undercards of Vince's shows. That doesn't mean we weren't main-event caliber talent. We were simply being wise businesspeople and going where the money was.

With that being said, every one of the main-event-caliber talents in the WWF played an important role in the success of the company. You couldn't just promote a one-match event of Hulk Hogan versus Randy Savage and expect to draw tens of thousands of

B. Brian Blair: Truth Bee Told

people to a venue. There *had* to be wrestlers in supporting roles. Fans are paying to see the entire presentation and not solely the main event.

The people I know who've worked in the wrestling business almost universally despise the term "enhancement talent," and using that term makes the people who say it appear to be more markish than I can put into words. The acceptable way to refer to wrestlers who did favors every night would be "underneath performers." Overall, it was a *team* effort, and everyone should be referred to as an "asset," because *everyone* was an asset to the overall entertainment quality of the card no matter what position they were featured in.

ABC Pizza

Sometime around 2010, Toni and I were enjoying some of the best pizza we'd ever had at ABC Pizza in Tampa with my friend Steve Keirn and his wife Terry, and mutual friend Albi and his wife Susan. There was so much pizza left over from the meal that I requested a takeout box for it. I knew I would be hungry around midnight, and the pizza would serve as my late-night snack.

When the takeout box arrived, I decided to run to the bathroom before we all hit the road.

"Hey, Toni, can you put the pizza in the box for me?" I asked my wife. "I'll be right back."

"Sure!" answered Toni.

The payment was handled in bitsu-bitsu fashion – everyone paid for their own food. "Bitsu-bitsu" is an expression that gaijin wrestlers needed to learn very quickly in Japan in order to avoid getting stuck paying for everyone else's meals.

When I returned to the table, everyone was holding onto their takeout boxes, and Steve pointed over to the remaining takeout box to indicate that it was mine. I picked it up, and all of us began making our way toward the entrance to ABC Pizza.

Out of nowhere, I heard a voice coming from behind me.

"Excuse me... sir?" the voice said.

I turned around to see the manager of ABC Pizza standing before me.

"Yes, sir?" I answered.

"I don't really know how to say this," he began, "but why did you steal all of our tableware?"

"What do you mean?" I asked him.

B. Brian Blair: Truth Bee Told

"Well, our salt and pepper shakers are missing…" noted the manager. "Our pizza slicer is missing. All of our fine eating utensils are missing…"

"Wait a minute!" I objected. "Are you accusing me of *stealing*? I'll know you something: I haven't stolen *anything* since I was 12 years old, and the last thing I'd ever do is steal anything from you, you *jabroni*!"

With that, I turned to exit the restaurant once more, only to feel the ABC Pizza manager's hand latch onto my shoulder.

"No, sir!" the manager pleaded. "You *can't* steal that!"

People were looking over towards us, and I was outraged and embarrassed at the suggestion that I would stoop to theft, especially at such a low level.

"Look you son of a bitch!" I yelled, as I whirled around and opened up the pizza box.

The lid of the box was lifted, revealing the pizza slicer, the salt and pepper shakers, and all of the other tableware I was being accused of stealing. I felt about two inches tall. Keirn had seized upon the opportunity that presented itself while I went to the bathroom, stashed all of the tableware into my takeout box, and then stooged to the manager about my attempt to ransack the establishment.

That's just the way Speedo was. He was one of the consummate ribbers in our business, and he could never let an opportunity for a rib pass by.

The Sheriff Rib

As I mentioned earlier in the book, Steve Keirn is always ribbing people. He is also the perpetrator and mastermind behind one of my *favorite* ribs of all time. I couldn't resist taking this opportunity to have that story told in my book, so here to tell one of my favorite rib stories is the one and only Steve Keirn!

The following story is told by Steve Keirn, with the assistance of Ian Douglass:

Curt Hennig was flying into Memphis, Tennessee to wrestle there for the first time. Along with a few other guys, I came up with a plan to rib Curt from the moment he arrived at Memphis International Airport.

B. Brian Blair: Truth Bee Told

Back then, airports didn't have the same level of security as they do today. In Memphis, this meant that I was able to go right out onto the tarmac and watch Curt get out of the plane.

I arranged for this humongous cop – a true redneck who stood 6'4" and weighed 400 lbs. – to be waiting at the airport in uniform with an *authentic* arrest warrant to serve to Curt.

I remained hidden behind a huge, round pillar, and I could hear everything that was being said as Curt descended from the steps leading from the plane to the tarmac, and the burly cop approached him.

"Are you Curt Hennig?" the cop asked.

Curt thought the cop was a wrestling fan and extended a hand to shake hands with him.

Staying perfectly in character, the cop followed up by saying, "I don't wanna shake your hand, *boy*! You're under arrest!"

Curt was caught completely off guard and scanned the cops face for signs that he was joking.

"*What?!*" Curt replied.

"Here you go; *read* it!" the cop said, as he shoved the warrant right under Curt's nose.

Curt studied the arrest warrant for "Kurt Hennig," and read all of the details. It explained that Curt was being arrested for statutory rape, and that a father had sworn out the warrant because he had overheard his daughter elaborating about her sexual escapades with Curt Hennig to one of her friends over the telephone. The father then confronted his daughter, and she reluctantly confessed that she'd had sex with Curt.

Curt's face gradually grew more contorted as panic seeped into his features. His face flushed a deep shade of red; I couldn't tell if the color change was due to embarrassment or worry.

"I've never even *been* to Memphis!" protested Curt.

"I can beat *that*!" replied the cop, sarcastically. "I've never arrested anyone who was actually *guilty* either!"

"What do we do?!" asked the nervous Curt.

"Well, you've got *two* ways to leave the airport," began the cop. "I can handcuff ya, and we can walk up there and get your bags, and you can go out and get in the back of my patrol car. We can take the drive. Or, if you *don't* want me to handcuff ya, I'll handcuff ya by force and drag your phony wrestlin' ass all the way through this airport. How 'bout *that*, boy?"

B. Brian Blair: Truth Bee Told

Once again, Curt studied that cop's face for any hint that the whole thing might be some sort of prank, but the cop didn't crack in the slightest bit. He sold it unbelievably well.

"I'll come with you, officer," said the defeated Curt. "But I *promise* you I've never been to Memphis!"

"Like I said, and I've *never* arrested anybody who's guilty," repeated the cop.

The officer handcuffed Curt's wrists in front of his body, and then he marched him right past the pillar where I remained obscured from Curt's view. The officer proceeded to walk the handcuffed wrestler through the airport and over to baggage claim to collect his bag. In the meantime, I ran out and got in my car, and then pulled it up and parked it behind the police car and waited.

Eventually, the officer emerged from the airport with the handcuffed and dejected-looking Curt Hennig still in front of him. He opened up the door to the backseat of the squad car and helped Curt get situated inside of it, and then he walked around to the other side, started up the car, and pulled off.

I followed closely behind them, and I could see Curt gesticulating wildly in the officer's direction. He was clearly in full freak-out mode, pleading his case to the massive officer. Meanwhile, in my own car, I was laughing so hard that my sides were aching.

It was a long drive to downtown Memphis, but we didn't quite make it all the way there. I found out later that Curt stammered when he told the officer, "I have a wife and four kids... *No!* I have a wife and *five* kids!"

The officer responded with, "See? You don't even know how many *kids* you've got!"

"I *do*!" Curt pleaded. "Isn't there *anything* I can do?"

"We can pull over, and you can call the dad's phone number and explain to him that it must be a case of mistaken identity cuz you've never been here," the cop answered. "His number is right on the warrant."

"Oh, man!" said Curt. "Let's do that! That's great!"

They pulled off the road and into the parking lot of a 7-Eleven that had a Shoney's Big Boy restaurant attached to it. I did the same, and pulled my car in alongside the squad car.

As I remained hidden behind the blacked-out windows of my vehicle, the officer opened Curt's door, and when Curt stood up, I heard him say to the officer, "I don't have any change."

"So now you want me to lend ya a quarter, *too*?" asked the annoyed officer.

B. Brian Blair: Truth Bee Told

"Could you?" pleaded Curt. "I have some dollars in my bag…"

The cop reached into his pocket, extracted a quarter and handed it to Curt, whose arms were still handcuffed in front of his body.

At that moment, I rolled down my window.

"Hey… where are *you* goin'?!" I asked Curt.

Curt looked at me with startled eyes, hesitated for a second, and then appeared to be simultaneously relieved and excited when he recognized the face of a friend.

"Oh, man!" exclaimed Curt. "The *shit's* on! The *shit's* on!"

Curt must have thought I was there by pure coincidence. I emerged from my car as if I had no clue how it was that Curt had found himself detained in the back of a Memphis police officer's patrol car. The two of us stood face to face between the two cars, while the officer stood on the walkway adjacent to the 7-Eleven.

"What's the matter?" I asked innocently.

"I've been arrested," answered Curt.

"You got arrested at the airport?" I chuckled.

"Yes!" said Curt.

"Well, what did you get arrested for?" I pressed him.

"*Statutory rape!*" he yelled.

"You know… Curt…" I began. "I've been tellin' you for *years* that you need to leave those young girls alone."

My statement seemed to confirm the cop's initial suspicions that the charges against Curt were true. Curt glowered at me as if he wished death upon me.

"I'm just kiddin' officer," I said, in the hopes that it would lessen Curt's hatred for me somewhat.

"Here… read the warrant!" Curt said, and he shoved the warrant toward me.

I scanned the warrant line by line and said, "Yeah… okay… Curt Hennig… yeah… this is *your* phone number… yeah… Ooooo, *that* doesn't sound good…"

Curt looked altogether exasperated by the time my eyes reached the bottom of the page. Finally, I held the warrant in front of his face and said, "And see? Here's where *I* signed it! The *judge!*"

Curt stared at me as the revelation took a moment to sink in. I had signed the warrant as Judge "Stevens." Then Curt looked at the cop. As if to signal the end of an acting performance that had been worthy of an Academy Award, the officer *finally* burst into laughter. Then I started laughing, too.

"Son of a *bitch!*" screamed Curt.

The warrant for Curt Hennig's arrest

    Still handcuffed, Curt began to chase me, and I took off running completely around the Shoney's Big Boy restaurant. Curt was hot on my tail the entire time. I completed a full lap around the Shoney's and 7-Eleven, and Curt was *still* right at my heels, so I took a *second* lap.

    By the time we'd completed the second lap, Curt was laughing uncontrollably.

    "Stop! Stop!" laughed Curt. "I'm blown up! Just forget about it!"

    This is one of the reasons it paid off that I always made friends with the cops who watched our matches. Because of the great relationships I formed with those cops, I was able to regularly rib guys by having them arrested during my career. It always works tremendously well. After all, who's going to argue with a *cop*?

With my best friend, Steve "Speedo" Keirn

Hercules and the Fire Hose

Spending habits aside, Ray "Hercules" Hernandez (real last name Fernandez) was incredible to be around, and he was constantly trying to make everyone around him laugh. We were in Green Bay, Wisconsin once with Andre the Giant and Ken Patera sometime in 1987. Herc snatched the fire extinguisher hose out of its cabinet after breaking the glass that held it in place.

Somehow, Hercules had gotten it into his head that it would be a good idea to blast the wrestlers with water from the fire hose while their match was still in progress. I *truly* believe he was under the influence of something at the time. There was a set of steps that led down to the ring, and they were made of a greenish-colored cement. Fortunately, somebody came by and prevented Herc from going through with it, as Herc managed to get all the way down the stairs and was heading right for the ring when he was finally halted in his tracks. That probably would have been the end of his WWF career right then and there.

B. Brian Blair: Truth Bee Told
The Flair Flop

When Ric Flair was involved in a match, you *always* got great wrestling. Granted, I never really cared for that one goofy bump he did, when you would hit him hard with a punch or an elbow in the corner, and then he would take three or four steps forward and fall flat on his face like a cartoon character.

With Ric Flair: Possibly the greatest wrestler of all time

To me, it seemed like after all of the hard work he would do to make his matches seem as real as possible, Flair would turn around and do something that was ludicrous in my opinion. There were times I wanted to say something to him about it, but I always decided against it. After all, he was one of the best in the world – the *world champion* – and there was no question that he was going to make more money in the wrestling business than I would ever even come close to making.

B. Brian Blair: Truth Bee Told

Down the line, there were plenty of times where Ric and I would be riding in the same car or sitting at the same bar, and I'd want to say something to him about it, but I would never quite muster the courage to get the words out. It was clearly a spot he loved to do in his matches, and I didn't want to annoy him with my opinions.

Honestly, though, I thought if Ric just took that *one* comedic bump out of his repertoire, he would have been far more credible and believable as the world champion. And I'm *not* the only person who has said that about him. Other people have said the same thing. That one bump was the *only* thing about Flair's wrestling style that clued in people to the fact that our business was truly showbiz.

Because Flair was such a preening, strutting guy with immaculate hair and shiny robes, I'm sure that bump was designed to give the local crowds in the territories a chance to laugh at a world champion who seemed to take himself *far* too seriously. It was fine when it was confined to that local audience, but when wrestling went national and Ric did the same thing on national television every week, I think it outlived its original purpose.

That was the *only* criticism I ever had of Ric. Other than that, I thought he was *perfect*. He had every necessary tool, and was tremendous with all of them. In Flair's prime on a 1-to-10 scale, his interview was a 10, his body was at least an eight, and his work was a 10. In every area that you would grade a wrestler to determine his competency, Ric was an eight or better. I don't know if there has ever been anyone else who was that good in *every* category. At his best, Flair was the epitome of a true superstar.

Quickdraw and the Elevator

Quickdraw McGraw got wasted on gamma-hydroxybutyrate – popularly known as GHB – while he was staying at the Keio Plaza Hotel in Tokyo. While Rick was passed out, someone got to him, stuck him in a wheelbarrow naked, then drew a moustache on his face and painted him up.

Once this mystery person had ushered Rick into the elevator through the use of the wheelbarrow, he pressed *every single button* inside the elevator and then walked out. Everyone waiting to ride the elevator in the hotel that night was treated to quite a sight. As the doors opened on every floor, they unveiled Rick McGraw, naked and passed out with a moustache drawn on his face in dark ink, and with his body decorated by magic marker. The words on his body were *all* obscene, and there were even a few animal faces drawn on him for good measure, including a rabbit's face.

As we waited in the lobby, we could see the horrified reactions of the Japanese hotel guests as they exited the elevator after having been treated to the unexpected sight of Rick's colorful, naked body. We couldn't understand a word they were saying, but the shocked expressions on their faces spoke volumes.

From there, Rick's body was taken over to the other elevator, and he went on a similar ride back up to the top floor of the hotel so that the rib could be repeated for a brand-new set of hotel guests.

Rick was always entertaining and was a very good worker. Had he been five inches taller, he would have made a lot more money in his career. I miss his voice, and the way he would always say to me "Hey, Triple B!" in that Southern drawl of his.

Orndorff and the Elevator

One of my favorite ribs in Japan was one that I wasn't there for, but Keirn and Hogan were both present for it and can vouch for it.

During Paul Orndorff's physical prime, he had the epitome of a one-track mind. The only thing he cared about doing during his spare time was finding women to hook up with. That desire often proved to be his undoing.

Paul got to Japan for a New Japan tour that included several top American wrestlers, including Don Muraco, Steve Keirn, Ron Starr and Hulk Hogan. They were all downstairs registering at the desk of the Keio Plaza Hotel, and some American Airlines flight attendants began their own check-in process at the hotel's front desk. Paul decided to approach the most attractive flight attendant in the pack, and then he returned to the boys, bragging about how the flight attendant was going to be giving him a call after that night's show.

Keirn arranged for either Leilani Kai or one of the other female wrestlers to call Paul, introduce herself as the flight attendant he'd met downstairs, and lure him upstairs to her room. Posing as the flight attendant, the lady wrestler seduced Paul by telling him she wanted to perform unspeakable sex acts on him. Once she'd gotten Paul worked up, she explained how she wanted Paul to set the mood for her. She asked him to do his hair perfectly and to put some cologne on, but she didn't want him to wear anything at all except his

B. Brian Blair: Truth Bee Told

yukata robe so that she could tear it off of his body once he walked through the door.

At this stage of the game, Paul was absolutely raring to go. He got the girl's room number, which was 2103, while *his* room was in the upper section in the 3500s. Paul did exactly as the girl asked and prepared his hair perfectly, applied the cologne, wrapped himself in his yukata, placed his sandals on his feet, descended the elevator to the lower floor, walked all the way down to the opposing elevator shaft, and then took that elevator all the way back up to the 21st floor on the opposite end of the building.

Paul told me he stood out in the hallway and knocked on the door for an eternity with no answer. Giving up, he made the whole trip in reverse and went back to his hotel room on the other side. While Paul was moping back in his hotel room, the phone rang again. This time, the woman's voice asked Paul where he was, and she made it clear that she was practically bursting at the seams with excitement in anticipation of his arrival. She wanted to know what was taking him so long because she was going *crazy*.

"I was *just* there!" Paul said. "I knocked on the door just like you told me, and you didn't answer!"

"What room did you go to?" the woman asked.

"I went to 2103 just like you told me!" Paul said.

"I'm in 2105!" the woman corrected. "I'm *right* next door!"

"Oh my god!" Paul said. "Okay! I'll be right over!"

Paul traveled all the way back to the other side of the hotel, certain that he knew what awaited him this time. He knocked on the door to room 2105. Instead of having his knocking answered by a sexy flight attendant, Paul was surprised to see the door opened by an elderly Japanese man.

"What you doing here?" asked the man, surprised to find a burly American man dressed in sandals and a yukata standing in the hallway outside of his room.

"I'm sorry," Paul said. "My mistake."

Defeated, Paul made the long trek back to his room.

Once again, the phone rang in Paul's hotel room, and he practically ripped the receiver off of it.

"Paul, where *are* you?!" the woman asked, pleadingly.

"I was *just* there!" Paul cried. "I went to 2105!"

"I didn't say 2105! I said *2107!*"

"Dammit!" yelled Paul as he slammed down the receiver.

Undaunted, Orndorff made his way back through two sets of elevators to the far end of the hotel for a *third* consecutive time. With

B. Brian Blair: Truth Bee Told

thoughts of sex clouding his mind, it somehow never occurred to him that he was *clearly* being set up. This time, Paul knocked on the door to room 2107 with total confidence. When he did, the door to the room was quickly jerked open by Ron Starr, and Paul was greeted by the emissions of two trash cans that had been filled with water, courtesy of Hulk Hogan and Steve Keirn.

Paul was now standing in the hallway, drenched in tap water, with his yukata stuck to his body. The thin, silk fabric of the robe, *now* soaked by water, had been rendered almost completely transparent. To cap the rib off, Ron shut the door on Paul, forcing him to walk all the way back to his room sopping wet, embarrassed and functionally naked. According to Paul, that was one of the most humiliating moments of his life.

The Spoiler and Mabel

Don Jardine was tremendous in the ring. He was a large man who was agile enough to perform a tightrope walk along the top rope like a cat. He liked to do it following a strength challenge where he would transition to holding just one of your arms, or while holding you by the hair. Then he would walk across the top rope and drop a big forearm on you. He was the first true big guy that I ever started clicking with in the ring and having quality matches with.

"You need an equalizer in our matches," Don advised me.

"What's an equalizer?" I asked him.

"A weapon," said Don. "Something that you can get your hands on and hit me with that will take me down a peg. The crowd will *love* it."

During our match that night, Don started out by hitting me with some illegal object and almost pinned me, but I got my foot on the bottom rope. Annoyed by my persistence, Don chucked me to the outside of the ring. I crawled under the ring, produced a giant board from beneath it, and proceeded to start whacking Don with it. He sold the beating like I was *killing* him. The people went crazy for it, just like he said they would.

Don was always easygoing with me, and he was true class whenever I had the good fortune to be around him. He was also the first guy that the infamous Mabel rib was ever pulled on.

When Don was a young wrestler in Canada, he was told that there was a woman who really enjoyed the company of young wrestlers, and that the woman had singled him out as the next wrestler she intended to sleep with.

Don met up with the woman, who owned a house out in the woods, and the husband supposedly was off on a hunting trip. Don and the woman excitedly stripped off all of their clothes. Just as they were beginning the lovemaking process, the front door slammed.

"Honey, I'm home!" bellowed the voice. "Wait... is there *someone* here?!"

"Oh, *no!*" the woman reportedly screamed. "My husband is home, and he has a *gun*! If he sees you, he'll *shoot* you!"

Jardine supposedly grabbed a sheet to wrap around himself, and then ran through the snow barefoot to flee from the wrath of the jealous husband. The story goes that Don developed severe frostbite on his feet as a result of this incident. Of course, there was no husband. The whole thing had been a setup to scare Don.

The girl's name was Mabel, so this incident and similar ribs came to be known as "The Mabel Rib" all over the professional wrestling world.

The End of Ron Bass

One of my most memorable late-career matches was an eight-man elimination match involving Ron Bass. Ron brought his son with him that night so that his son could watch him work, but the two of them took some wrong turns and arrived late to the event. Ron was already looking pretty rough back then. He wasn't in any condition to be working in a match, and the added stress of being late and wanting to perform well in front of his son truly affected him.

Mike Rotunda and I were both still in decent shape at the time, so we set the tone for the match by tagging in and out quickly and accelerating the pace of the bout. This didn't sit well with Larry Zbyszko, who was on our team, and who wasn't really in the mood to move around very much that evening.

"Slow it *down!*" complained Zbyszko. "There's no need to work *that* fast!"

Ron was over on the heel team, and the very first time he climbed into the ring, he stumbled and fell over. He also wound up tripping and falling another two times later in the bout. The whole ordeal was quite embarrassing for him.

"This is my *last* match," he sulked afterwards. "I'm done. I'm *never* working again."

B. Brian Blair: Truth Bee Told

One of the last things Ron Bass did in his life was to appear in a film called *Silent Times*. It was a black-and-white film that both of us participated in, with Ron playing an old 1920s football coach. He helped to draw a lot of money during the prime of his wrestling career, and it was pretty much a night off whenever I worked with him.

Straightening Out Rick Rude

Rick Rude was always one of my favorites to work with, and we had many great matches together. However, if Rick's wrestling career had been any longer, and had he lived to see old age, he certainly would have suffered from his practice of intentionally over-rotating his body whenever he took backdrops and landing countless times on his rear end. Those landings were *always* brutal on his spine.

Rick wanted to be superior to everybody when it came to his performance in the bedroom. He would spend as much time with a woman as he possibly could. He referred to it as "sport fucking." His ultimate goal was to be so good in bed that every woman he was with would declare him to be greatest lover she had ever been with. To accomplish this, he would inject his penis with chemicals that allowed him to last for one to two hours at a time. These injectable chemicals were a pretty new innovation at the time, and I honestly didn't see the appeal. At the point where it's going two hours, it's no longer fun, and it simply becomes exercise.

I remember when Rick came into the WWF locker room one time, and he had an erection that was slanted off to the side. Before anyone could say anything, he said, "*Look*! I've been injecting my dick with this shit for weeks. I've been injecting it on the right and now my dick curves to the right. I need to start injecting it on the *left* now just to straighten it out!"

Title Reigns and the WWE Hall of Fame

It bothers me when every modern fly-by-night tag team seems to be awarded a run with the WWE tag team championship, especially when the average fan judges the success of a team by whether or not you held the tag team titles.

Unlike a lot of the modern teams, Jim and I would headline "B" and "C" house shows and were expected to actually draw money. Whether or not you were given a tag team championship run or a title opportunity back then had more to do with your ability to draw money on the road, and had almost nothing to do with wrestling storylines. Belts were seen as rewards for individual wrestlers or tag teams that had proven they could draw money, or had at least provided strong evidence that they would be able to draw money.

These days, teams are given the WWE tag belts simply to enhance storylines, or worse yet, in order to further comedy sketches. *All* of the prestige is gone from those titles.

It also bothers me that to most fans I'm thought of primarily as a tag team wrestler, and *almost* exclusively as a Killer Bee. I had a lot of tag team partners during my career other than Jim Brunzell, including Len Denton, Tony Garea, Bulldog Bob Brown and Al Madrill, and I had *far* more singles matches in my career than I had as a tag team wrestler.

Also, modern wrestling fans generally don't realize the magnitude of what it meant to hold the Florida Heavyweight Championship or the Southern Heavyweight Championship, or even the significance of the territories themselves. It was a *big deal* to hold the top title in one of the old NWA territories.

As an illustration of this point, people have lauded the accomplishments of wrestlers who were champions in the Extreme Championship Wrestling promotion run by Paul Heyman in the 1990s and early 2000s, and that company *was* very innovative. However, in 1982, the Florida territory was attracting an average of 4,000 fans to local arenas for *every* show, *seven* days per week. ECW ran far fewer shows, and even in its prime as a promotion, when they held events in several different states, they were very lucky whenever they had even 2,000 fans at an event.

Wrestlers and Money

During the WWF heyday of the 1980s, I was making between $150,000 and $250,000 every year, depending on the year. This was a very healthy income during the '80s, but there were also a lot of ways that you could eat away at your profitability. One way was to get married and bring your spouse along with you. Wrestlers' wives tended to have higher quality-of-life requirements on the road than the wrestlers did. That means you couldn't scrape by on eggs, toast, tuna and potatoes if you really wanted to cut costs, and you also couldn't stay in dirt-cheap motels or heel a room.

There were certainly wrestlers who had issues with very problematic drugs like cocaine, and those could be huge drains on their finances. Others would blow huge sums of money on booze and women in bars and nightclubs.

If you'd learned to save a significant portion of your money and didn't squander it all, you could have socked away a solid amount of cash. It all depended on your lifestyle and your discipline with saving money. We also didn't have health insurance or a 401(k), which was unfortunate. You might end up giving anywhere from 10 to 40 years of your life to the wrestling industry, but in the end there's no financial safety net for you. You simply had to do your best to be a disciplined saver who lived within a set budget. A lot of guys simply didn't understand that.

I know there are former WWF wrestlers from that era who claim they weren't well paid, and there is *some* truth to that in terms of the pay disparity between main eventers and midcarders. You certainly couldn't have had a one-match event featuring Andre the Giant against Hulk Hogan with no other matches propping up the show. However, there wasn't a single main-roster talent for the WWF during that era who would have led a life of total discomfort after leaving the business if they'd *simply* saved their money.

Could things have been better, and *should* things have been better? Yes, by all means. Still, you have to work with the cards that you're dealt.

Every wrestler on that roster earned enough money to make a down payment on a home somewhere, and since they knew they were going to be on the road, they could have rented their homes out and made some money from them. Once they were *off* the road, they would have a place to stay that they owned, and once they retired, that house would have been an asset. Whether you're a wrestler or not, owning a home should be one of your first investments. To top it off, many of my fellow wrestlers also didn't understand the importance of maintaining good credit.

In general, I can safely say that a pure lack of financial literacy was the root cause for many of the problems that a lot of wrestlers from my era would experience later in life.

The Political Motivations Behind My Arrest

The boyfriend of Commissioner Kevin Beckner was Sheriff's deputy Gilbert Sainz. At the time of the Father's Day incident at my

B. Brian Blair: Truth Bee Told

house, I had a lawsuit pending against Kevin Beckner, and I'm *convinced* that Sainz was responsible for having me arrested.

That's the only explanation that makes sense to me as far as how drastic the change had been when the deputies returned to my house to arrest me. Sainz was the sergeant of the Hillsborough County dispatch unit in my district, and he didn't want me to run against his boyfriend again. He *certainly* didn't want me continuing with my lawsuit against him, either.

I was sitting in the office of my attorney, George Lorenzo. Beckner and Sainz had already done the damage they wanted to do by getting me arrested, even though the whole thing was total bullshit. While I sat in George's office, two of Sheriff David Gee's henchwomen came in with the paperwork for me to sign to have all of the charges against me dropped. By then, I'm sure they had already realized there were no charges they *could* file against me that would stick.

One of the ladies stood up and said, "If you're thinking about suing us, our deputy said that you threw up in the back of his car, and *we* have the vomit to prove it."

I stood up, got right in that woman's face and said, "Ma'am... you are *lying* through your teeth! I *never* threw up, and that's bullshit!"

George tugged on my arm to prompt me to sit back down, and said "Brian... *Shhhhhh!*"

"You'd better sit down right now, Mr. Blair, or we might have a change of heart," the woman goaded me.

Grudgingly, I retook my seat. I was *so* pissed off. I had no idea what that meant, anyway. The entire episode had been sickening. I don't know what having my *vomit* would have proven in the first place.

The whole ordeal was very meanspirited. It upset me to know they would lie right to my face like that. I had done so much to support the Sheriff's Office while I was a commissioner, not to mention the fact that I had donated money to them for decades and also been an honorary deputy for 16 years. The whole episode was highly discouraging. I felt *completely* betrayed.

The Undertaker and the Crime Dog

I have a friend named Darryl Manarty, who owns Yellow Cab. He is a member of Avila Golf and Country Club in Tampa, which is one of the nicest country clubs in the area. Darryl is a big wrestling fan, so we made plans to put together a group for golf that included "The

B. Brian Blair: Truth Bee Told

Undertaker" Mark Calaway, Brian Adams, Danny Spivey and myself. We started off with lunch, and that's when we learned Danny Spivey wouldn't be able to make it.

Darryl phoned to let us know he would be running late, and he provided us with his membership number so that we could get whatever we wanted at the club, including snacks and beer.

"This is a *very* strict course," Darryl warned us in advance. "Please repair your divots, and whatever you do, *don't* leave any litter on the course. No wrappers or anything. You need to be on your *best* behavior, and you need to use complete golf etiquette."

With "The Undertaker" Mark Calaway

That was fine with us. Aside from some colorful language, which was unavoidable considering the people involved in the event, we swore we wouldn't be the cause of any trouble.

Our game of choice was Bingo Bango Bongo, where there were three points available for players to earn: first person on the green, closest to the hole, and then first one in the hole. In terms of money, points were worth 50 cents apiece.

B. Brian Blair: Truth Bee Told

We were on the front nine of the course, and probably on the seventh hole. Brian wasn't playing very well that day, and Taker was razzing Brian like crazy, which only served to frustrate Brian even more.

As Brian was lining up the tee shot on the seventh hole, Taker casually blurted out, "You're gonna go left."

Brian backed up and stared daggers at Taker.

"*Fuck* you!" Brian screamed at Taker with his thick Hawaiian accent. "That's not proper golf etiquette, *Brah*! Darryl said to use golf etiquette!"

"This ain't about etiquette," Taker replied with a smirk. "I'm just telling you you're gonna go left."

On cue, Brian stepped back up to the ball, struck it hard and shanked it left, straight at the cabin where the restrooms were located. It bounced off the top of the cabin, and luckily it dribbled back out to where Brian could play it easily. Still, Brian was *so* pissed at having fired the ball to exactly where Taker said he would, that he was *seething*.

Brian took his club and smashed it into a beautiful bottlebrush tree that was in bloom. Half of the tree fell to the ground.

"You've *got* to control your temper, Brian!" Taker said, half amused. "Why'd you do that?! You heard what Darryl said!"

"Yeah, Brian!" I chimed in. "You're *gonna* get us thrown out of here if you do shit like that! We're gonna get Darryl in trouble!"

We looked around to see if anyone had noticed Adams' outburst and subsequent assault on a bottlebrush tree, and we spotted a golf cart about 100 yards away from us that was beelining toward us. On it were two Black guys wearing blue polo shirts.

"Oh, man!" Taker said. "You did it now, Brian. Here come the course cops."

"Oh, fuck!" Adams said. "I'm *so* sorry, guys!"

Adams knelt down by the tree to try to lift the felled portion, as if it was magically going to reattach itself to the tree's base.

"Anybody got a shoelace or something that I can tie this with?" Adams asked sheepishly.

"Why the hell would anybody have a *shoelace* on them out here?!" Taker responded.

The golf cart rolled closer, and Adams' shoulders sagged in defeat as he realized there was nothing he could do.

"Screw it," Taker said. "Just tell them that we'll pay for the tree. That's all we can do."

As the cart got closer to our group, I said, "Why do those guys look so familiar?"

B. Brian Blair: Truth Bee Told

No one responded. The cart pulled all the way up to our green and came to a halt.

"Undertaker!" came the call from the cart. "I *knew* that was the Undertaker! How are ya?!"

Seated on the cart were Major League Baseball All-Stars Fred McGriff and Daryl Strawberry. McGriff was playing for the Tampa Rays at the time, and the two of them had sped all the way over to our green to try to get the Undertaker's autograph. They were wearing matching shirts because they were both coming from the same charity event. The atmosphere went from tense to relaxed and joyous in an instant. The two of them were stone-cold *marks* for the Undertaker.

Taker couldn't sign enough things for them. When it was all over with, and Strawberry and McGriff had pulled off on their cart, Taker looked over at me.

"Who *were* those guys?" Taker asked, quizzically.

"What?!" I exploded. "You don't know who Daryl Strawberry is?! Fred McGriff… 'The *Crime Dog'*?! Come on, *man*!"

Kmart and the Blue Light Special

One of the many jobs I held during my high school years was in the shoe department of our local Kmart. It was a very entertaining place to work, and one of the reasons for that was because I was able to get jobs there for my high school friends Ralph and James as well.

Ralph was an average-sized Latino guy, who we affectionately nicknamed "Taco," and James was a medium-sized yet muscular Black athlete who we called "Hop Sing." James and I were especially familiar with one another since we were both in the same grade and were fellow members of the football, baseball and wrestling teams at Tampa Bay Tech High School.

There was another guy on the Kmart staff whose name was Randy, except we called him "The Fishman" because he worked in the fish department. He fit the hippy stereotype perfectly; not only did he have the stereotypical hippy look, but he also frequently reported to work smelling like pot.

I was already an ardent ribber by that time, and the rest of my coworkers enjoyed playing pranks as well. On one particular day, I decided it would be the best use of our time to pull a prank on Randy.

"Let's tell Randy we're holding some sandals with marijuana leaves on them in the back of the store for him," I told Ralph. "When he comes to the back to get them, we'll tell him he can have them

B. Brian Blair: Truth Bee Told

because Kmart is sending them back to the manufacturer on a recall because they *can't* sell shoes with marijuana on them."

Ralph delivered the news to Randy, and he excitedly rushed to the back of the store to score the marijuana-leaf sandals.

"Where are they?" he asked with a smile. "Those sandals sound *awesome*!"

Ralph pointed over toward a box on the top shelf of the supply room.

"They're in that box up there," said Ralph. "You'll have to climb up and get them out of there. You can help yourself to them."

Randy went straight over to the ladder and began his ascension to the top shelf. Once we were certain that Randy's focus was squarely on the fictitious sandals we had told him were nestled inside of the box on the top shelf, Ralph and I extracted a pair of fire extinguishers from the place where we'd hidden them and absolutely *blasted* Randy with them once he reached the top of the ladder. We caught Randy completely off guard, and in just a few seconds he resembled a living snowman. Ralph and I nearly fell to the floor with laughter, and then we dropped the fire extinguishers and darted out of the supply room.

Randy scooped up the fire extinguisher that I'd dropped and began to chase Ralph and I straight into the primary retail section allocated to shoes. All the while, he was completely covered in foam.

When Randy came through the door with his body drenched in foam, and with a bright-red fire extinguisher in his hands, he ran *straight* into the line of sight of Mr. Griffin, the store manager. Mr. Griffin's face flushed red with anger when he saw Randy preparing to douse Ralph and I with foam.

"Randy, *what* are you doing?!" screamed Mr. Griffin. "Get out of here! You're *fired*!"

Poor Randy lost his job simply because I'd wanted to play what I expected to be a harmless prank on him. I hope his life wasn't ruined by that incident.

On a separate occasion, Ralph came to work with some PCP and showed it to me.

"What does *that* do?" I asked him.

"It works kind of like an animal tranquilizer," explained Ralph.

There was another guy on our staff who was also kind of a hippy, in the same way Randy was. This guy wanted to try out the PCP, so Ralph invited him to the upstairs office of the Kmart.

B. Brian Blair: Truth Bee Told

"Now remember, you only get to take *one* hit of this," Ralph told him. "This stuff is *really* strong!"

Without hesitation, this guy took *three* hits of the PCP, then departed from the office.

"Man... that was a *big* mistake," said Ralph. "He's gonna be *really* messed up from that!"

A few minutes later, Ralph and I were chatting in the back of the store when an announcement came over the intercom.

"Code one to the Blue Light Special!" blared the urgent voice through the speakers. "Code one to the Blue Light Special!"

We knew that "code one" referred to the store manager, which meant that something serious had occurred. Ralph and I walked very quickly over to the Blue Light Special area to see what had necessitated the impromptu announcement, and we were greeted by the sight of our co-worker – *high* as a kite – standing on top of the Blue Light Special counter.

"Wow, man!" he blurted, while regarding us with eyes that were the size of saucepans. "Wow! *Wow!*"

Understandably, he was *also* fired on sight, which marked the second time that one of our co-workers had been terminated from employment because of something we'd initiated. Ralph and I were a dangerous tandem; our behind-the-scenes work trimmed the Kmart workforce more efficiently than any initiative ever produced by the company's world headquarters in Michigan.

Howard Frankland and my 50th Birthday Party

My friend Howard Frankland has one of the most recognizable names in all of Tampa. Howard shares the name of his grandfather, who was a highly successful banker during Tampa's rise to prominence. The eight-lane Howard Frankland Bridge was named in honor of him. It stretches for three miles across Tampa Bay and connects Hillsborough County to Pinellas County.

Howard has been a friend of mine for at least 40 years, and he is also friends with a lot of the other influential people in Tampa. This includes several of the other wrestlers, and also iconic local athletes like Freddie Solomon, who was a boyhood hero of mine way back when I was a young teenager selling sodas to the football fans of the University of Tampa while he and Paul Orndorff electrified the crowd.

Personal friendships aside, Howard is also well known for his tremendous generosity. Every time Florida stone crab claws were in

B. Brian Blair: Truth Bee Told

season, Howard would invite around 50 people to his house to feed them all stone crab claws. Despite the great expense of hosting such a fancy soiree, there was always *plenty* of food left over.

For my 50th birthday, Howard shocked me by throwing what was probably the best birthday party of my life, and it came as a total surprise. I was lured to Howard's house under false pretenses, only to be surprised by friends from all eras of my life, along with several members of family. The list of attendees included "Macho Man" Randy Savage, Steve Keirn, Freddie Solomon, the Nasty Boys, and even Ralph – AKA "Taco" from my days of working at Kmart. Hulk Hogan also made an appearance later in the evening.

It was incredibly rewarding and humbling to see so many people who meant so much to the development of my life all gathered in the same place to celebrate my birthday.

My 50th Birthday Surprise Party
Seated: Steve Keirn, Jerry Sags, Randy Savage, Brian Blair
Standing: Howard Frankland, Brian Knobbs, Ralph "Taco" Rodriguez, Freddie Solomon, David Boromie, Larry Sabella, Danny Gaudarian

Legends Lunch and the Cauliflower Alley Club

My involvement with the Legends Lunch event predates my involvement with the Cauliflower Alley Club. Legends Lunch was started in 1999 by Jack Brisco and I, when we began taking Hiro Matsuda to lunch as frequently as possible during the last seven months of his life. Shortly thereafter, Gordon Solie became terminally ill, and Gerald Brisco, Buddy Colt, Lou Thesz, Dottie and Don Curtis, Paul Jones and I *officially* cofounded the Legends Lunch events. The purpose of Legends Lunch is to lift spirits and strengthen friendships. We are still going strong with four gatherings per year.

Hanging out with the legendary Rocky Johnson

When the CAC's Board of Directors went through the process of selecting Nick Bockwinkel's replacement at the CAC, the two individuals they zeroed in on as primary candidates were Jim Ross and myself. Jim Ross had been an active, tremendous cheerleader of the CAC for a long time, but for some reason they picked me.

I certainly don't think Jim took any issues with my selection as CAC president. He was always a good guy to me. We were introduced early in my career when we both worked in Mid South, and we got along very well. When the Watts-McGuirk split occurred, Jim wound up going with Watts, of course, because Watts got him started in the business. In my opinion, Jim is second only to Gordon Solie when it comes to ranking the *greatest* wrestling commentators of all time.

When Rocky Johnson passed away, his son Dwayne Johnson personally raised $40,000 for the CAC by telling people to donate to our organization in lieu of sending flowers for his father's funeral. Rocky and I had been friends ever since my last summer

B. Brian Blair: Truth Bee Told

training in the Tampa Dungeon. It was very difficult and emotional for me to speak at his funeral, even though it was a tremendous honor. Both Dwayne and Steve Keirn did a *fabulous* job with their dedications to him.

Vince McMahon is one of the CAC's biggest supporters, and he is a stalwart contributor to the CAC. The WWE buys two tables at our reunion event each year and sends many of their legends to participate at it. On top of that, former WWE wrestlers receive letters every year advising us that the WWE will pay for our rehabilitation services if we're suffering from drug addiction. The WWE often forwards financial-assistance requests from wrestlers directly to the CAC when they don't want to be publicly seen helping certain people. From there, the CAC Board will consider the request, and then investigate to make sure the request is legitimate.

The CAC gives money away on an ongoing basis to members of the pro wrestling fraternity who have spent at least three years of their lives full time in the wrestling industry. Even referees or crew workers who regularly set the ring up are eligible to receive assistance, because everyone who supported the wrestling industry has been important to its success. If someone falls into a tough financial situation, our desire is to help lift them up.

We don't hold or oversee fundraisers at the CAC. Instead, we have a donation button on our webpage, and our contributors often donate money when they get their tax returns.

Anyone who is interested can join the CAC for as little as $25 for one year, $50 for two years, or $300 for a lifetime membership. Fifty percent of the donation total is tax deductible. Members receive four copies of the CAC's award-winning newsletter called *The Ear*. It's four colors and 24 pages, and members also receive certificates suitable for framing.

It's also worth mentioning that you *must* be a member of the CAC in order to attend the reunions, and since I've become president of the CAC, we have sold out *every* reunion. We've also doubled our total membership, doubled the amount of money we've raised, and doubled the amount of money we've given away to wrestlers in need, all within a seven-year period. This is partially due to the fact that I promoted the CAC more, and also due to the fact that I operated the CAC like a business, the same way I ran my Gold's Gyms.

When Dean Silverstone passed away in 2020, it was a huge blow to the CAC. I owe a lot to Dean, and also to Karl Lauer, as two of the driving forces and bright minds that have enabled the CAC to thrive.

B. Brian Blair: Truth Bee Told

We don't just hand people checks at the CAC when it's determined that a wrestler is rightfully in need of monetary assistance. The checks go to pay off delinquent property taxes, to cover medical bills, or to whatever other emergency aid the wrestlers need. The most we will give to someone to spend on their own is maybe $500 to $1,000. We're *very* reluctant to give cash to people because many wrestlers have highly problematic addictions to pain pills. I've watched several of my friends die while struggling with pain pill addictions, including Curt Hennig, Rick Rude, Ray Hernandez and Brickhouse Brown.

Steve Keirn, Bret Hart, Mick Foley, Brian Knobbs, and myself

There have been times in the past when the CAC was functionally insolvent, and people have had to step up behind the scenes and contribute money in order for it to regain its solvency. Fortunately, the CAC is presently in the best financial position it has *ever* been in.

My accountant has told me that we're the most efficient, effective 501(c)(3) in the United States of America. According to him, there's no other 501(c)(3) that gives away 99 percent of what it takes in. We have an incredible, tireless team of volunteers, and I feel for them because they are so dedicated. However, just like myself and the rest of the CAC's officers, our volunteers receive *no* monetary compensation for their tremendous sacrifices of time and energy.

B. Brian Blair: Truth Bee Told
CHAMPIONSHIPS & ACCOMPLISHMENTS

NWA World Junior Heavyweight Champion
NWA Florida Heavyweight Champion
NWA Southern Heavyweight Champion
NWA United States Tag Team Champions
NWA Central States Tag Team Champions
NWA America's Tag Team Champions
Asia Pacific Heavyweight Champion
NWL Tag Team Champions
IWA World Heavyweight Champion
UWF World Tag Team Champions
WWF Frank Tunney Memorial Tag Team Tournament Champions

Participated in:

The Big Event
Wrestlemania 2
Wrestlemania III
Wrestlemania IV
The First Royal Rumble
The First Survivor Series
The First WWF European Tour
The First WWF Australian Tour

Outside of the Ring:

More than 7,000 hours of community service
Gold's Gym Celebrity Owner of the Year
Hillsborough County Commissioner – District Six, Countywide
President of the Cauliflower Alley Club

B. Brian Blair: Truth Bee Told
RING ATTIRE

B. Brian Blair: Truth Bee Told

B. BRIAN BLAIR MERCHANDISE

LJN Figure

JAKKS Pacific Figure

Classic Killer Bees T-Shirt

UWF T-Shirt

B. Brian Blair: Truth Bee Told
AUTHOR'S ACKNOWLEDGEMENTS

I cannot thank Ian Douglass enough for the hard work and dedication that he put into *Truth Bee Told*. Over the past year, Ian has become much more than a co-author; he has become a true and trusted friend whom I both appreciate and admire. Ian is extremely wise and has personality plus! It's no wonder he has such a beautiful wife. I truly believe that Ian has an extremely bright future!

Thanks to the amazing friends that wrote the forewords and the afterword to this book: Steve Keirn, Bret Hart and the Hulkster. We have shared some wonderful times together and I am so thankful to you guys for putting up with me still!

I also have to thank the guy that I have spent the most time with on the road, "Mr. "#1derful" Paul Orndorff, who sadly passed away just as the writing of this book was drawing to a close. In his prime, Paul was the toughest guy that I knew in the business, and I consider Paul to be the *best* wrestling heel of our era.

To the wrestling fans: We would all be nothings in this business without our tremendous fans! Thank you all for your unwavering support!

I want to also thank the man that helped me get started in Championship Wrestling from Florida, Buddy Colt, who truly believed in me and was a tremendous friend until the day he passed on March 20th, 2021, during the writing of this book. Then there was Hiro Matsuda, who could make a man out of anyone that had the tenacity to endure his brutal routine. Believe me when I say that hanging with Hiro was one of the toughest challenges of my life.

The Dungeon at 106 North Albany Street in Tampa, Florida was famous for people that wanted to be wrestlers leaving without even stepping back in the dressing room to retrieve their clothes. Hiro was my primary coach, along with Gordon Nelson, and Jack Brisco – who was like a brother to me and my favorite NWA World Heavyweight Champion. Karl Gotch and Bob Backlund also helped to teach me the art of hooking long before MMA was cool.

As I was beginning to get smartened up several weeks before my first match, besides the aforementioned, there was Don Muraco, Gerald Brisco, Mike Graham and Steve Keirn, who all assisted me with my work, manners and ethics. The times I spent on the road with them are priceless memories.

Eddie Graham was *always* looking out for me in the beginning of my career, and always making sure that I had the best talent to work with. That talent included superstars like Dory Funk Jr., whom I've

B. Brian Blair: Truth Bee Told

had at least a hundred matches with, J.J. Dillon, Pat Patterson, Ed Wiskowski and Ivan Koloff, to name a few important role models who helped me to develop my style. I also enjoyed long talks and great times with Dusty Rhodes and Andre the Giant. To all of them, I extend my deepest gratitude.

I met some of the greatest sets of wrestling parents that anyone could be blessed to have, like Pete and Ruth Bollea, Doris and Fritz Adkisson, and Colonel "Pops" Keirn and his wonderful wife Hazel. Pops is one of only two people to be shot down during *two* different wars and survive both times. He then endured nine months in a Korean prison and seven and a half years at the Hanoi Hilton. Each one of these parents played a special role in my life, for which I will always be grateful.

The awesome promoters, road agents and bookers that helped shape my career include Chief Jay Strongbow, Grizzly Smith, Cowboy Bill Watts, Ernie Ladd, Skandor Akbar, Buck Robley, George Scott, Hal Jeffrey and Gary Hart just to name a few.

It's amazing how much a commentator can do for your career, and with that said, I'd like to thank Gordon Solie, Jim Ross, Lord Alfred Hayes, Vince McMahon Jr. and Gorilla Monsoon, along with Jesse "The Body" Ventura and Bobby "The Brain" Heenan, who always made things interesting and entertaining.

Some of my favorite referees were Bill Alfonso, Tim White, Joey Morella, Dave Hebner, Bronco Lubich, Nick Patrick, Billy Silverman, Pat Tanaka, and Bruce Owens of Florida fame, just to name a few. They were often referred to as "the *third* man in the ring," and rightly so. I've always appreciated the referees, as having a good referee or a bad referee can make a huge difference in the quality of a match.

My career will always be inextricably linked with that of the great "Jumping" Jim Brunzell, my tag team partner in The Killer Bees. Thank you for being by my side when we were the most popular tag team on the planet, and for so many years since.

I'd also like to mention some great families whom I was fortunate to have been friends with, like the Von Erichs, the Guerreros, the Funks, the Garvins, and of course the Briscos.

Without the historians that preserve the memories of all the guys that blazed the trails, wrestling would be like a baseball game without replays, and our history books would have no words. They are all to be commended for preserving the history of this business that I wouldn't have traded for anything, as well as making me feel like I knew all of those who preceded me in this business thanks to the artistry of the historians' writings.

B. Brian Blair: Truth Bee Told

Thank you to my political mentors, Joe Chillura and Ralph Hughes, as well as my fellow board members on the Hillsborough County BOCC. Also, thank you to my aides and all of the fine people that I was able to work with in Hillsborough County.

The great people at Gold's Gym corporate, who assisted me in making our Gold's Gyms of Tampa one of the most successful Gold's Gym licensees in the history of Gold's Gyms. Thank you to Pete Grymkowski and Rich Minzer, as well as Sal Correnti for not only selling me on ABC Financial, but for assisting my staff and I every step of the way.

I'd like to extend a special shout out to Steve Dibbs, Bobby Reymey, Joe Gomez, Pep Prado, Jody Simon, Dan Gaudarian, Joe Eisenberg and Diamond Dallas Page.

A special thanks is owed to Steve Williams, my friend and business partner in our "Celebri-tea" beverage venture. Steve's father Buster had a big motor home that we would all ride in over to Eddie Graham Stadium for several Sunday shows. Buster had a heart of gold.

My cousin Karen and her wonderful husband Steven McKeon, along with their great kids Matt and Kevin, have been the best cousins anyone could ask for. We go to Marathon Key almost every July to visit them and this is where I started writing my notes for Ian to sort out for *Truth Bee Told*. It is also where I was able to write my final few notes to send to Ian. Marathon and the "Kay" Condos where we stay are quiet and beautiful, located right on the Atlantic Ocean. The entire McKeon family have been a great blessing in our lives, and they deserve some credit for this book, as they provided the calm I needed for thought, as well as love and friendship that only certain cousins share.

Every person should have a primary care physician that they trust and can have an honest relationship with. This is so important for many reasons, but I'll spare the lecture.

I would like to thank my primary care physician of many years, Dr. Michael Cromer. As I mentioned in the book, Dr. Cromer has assisted me through my aches, pains, and everything that has ever ailed me. Michael has also helped me recover from most of my 19 surgeries from the wrestling business. He has sent me to the best surgeons in the Bay Area. I would be remiss if I did not thank Dr. Cromer and the many surgeons that have put me back together. As a side note, Dr. Cromer has either been voted "Physician of the Year," or has placed on the list of the top five MDs on several occasions here in Hillsborough County, Florida. I also can't forget my awesome back surgeon, Dr. Steven Tresser.

B. Brian Blair: Truth Bee Told

The Cauliflower Alley Club has been a passion of mine for over seven years, and I would like to thank Karl Lauer, Dean Silverstone, our executive boards, and all of the people that have contributed and continue to give their time and talents to this wonderful organization that has done so much good for so many, and all without receiving any financial compensation for their herculean efforts.

If you are a wrestler or a fan of wrestling, please join the CAC. For as little as $25.00 per year you can become a member. You will receive four full color newsletters, a membership certificate suitable for framing, and the right to attend our reunions, which are a total blast. Just go to www.cauliflowerallleyclub.org and become a member, and you will receive all the information you require to be in the know. You would be surprised to know how many of the folks from the wrestling industry fall on difficult financial times.

To my Pastor Ken Whitten: What a strong, devoted and honest leader. You have made life and death differences in countless lives, including the lives of my family and I. Thank you so much, Pastor Ken!

I have always appreciated and loved my in-laws, Chris and Larry Sabella, who are both tremendous people. My father-in-law, who is Mexican, Cuban and Italian, endured harsh racial treatment; when he'd go to work, all "Spics" had to sit at the back of the bus.

Almost last, but certainly not least, to my Mom and Dad, who were divorced when I was young, but always stood by me through good times and bad: We still have so much fun together! I simply could not have asked for better parents!

Thank you to my two sons, Brett and Bradley. It's a shame that children don't come with instructions, but all in all, things seem to always work out for the best. I will always love you both with my entire heart and soul!

To my wife Toni: We have shared a lot of experiences together, and we have been through many good times as well as many challenges. You have been so strong during the most difficult time of our lives lately, and I can't thank you enough for being a rock of faith, love and encouragement to me. I love you more than you will *ever* know. Thank you for always being in my corner, whether it was as "Honey" at ringside, or simply by being my partner in life. Thanks for being a beautiful soulmate and giving me the freedom to do what I have enjoyed in life, as it has passed so quickly.

Finally, I would like to thank the Father, Son and the Holy Spirit. Without my faith, I could have never accomplished the things

B. Brian Blair: Truth Bee Told

that I have accomplished in my life, nor could I have lived a life in which I can say, if I died tomorrow, I could never complain. My faith has carried me through the most trying of times, and please remember, we all have to be accountable to Someone!

Thank you all for purchasing this book, and I sincerely hope that you enjoyed it. If not, please direct your boos toward Ian! (Just kidding, Ian!) Honestly, every chapter could have been a book in and of itself, and I truly appreciate Ian's writing skills for helping me to structure the true stories you have read! Despite all of the challenges and tragedies that have unfolded over the past year, Ian and I were able to complete this book through God's grace!

I sincerely wish you all nothing but good things!

Sincerely,

B. Brian Blair

Extra Special Thanks!

An extra special thanks is owed to the 85 individuals who helped to offset well over 100% of the expenses incurred during the writing of this book due to their contributions to *Truth Bee Told*'s crowdfunding campaign. Your generous support has made this publication process so much easier.

Special consideration is also owed to Daniel Milne and Ricky Nance, who contributed more financial resources toward our publication efforts than any other individuals. I *can't* thank you enough!

B. Brian Blair: Truth Bee Told
BIOGRAPHER'S ACKNOWLEDGEMENTS

Thank you to everyone who contributed to this book in any fashion, including all of the people listed on the credits page. Apologies to anyone who feels slighted because they didn't get a mention. We interacted with many helpful people during the course of writing this book, and it's a true challenge to remember every person by name.

Also, thank you to everyone who purchased this book. My goal for every project is always to sell just one book to a person who isn't related to me by blood or marriage. My dream comes true anew every time a single book is sold. It means the world to me.

Aside from those directly associated with this project, I'd like to individually thank Dan Severn, Dylan "Hornswoggle" Postl and Michael "Buggsy McGraw" Davis for permitting me to be involved with the telling of their life stories. I'd also like to say "Cheers!" to Ross Owen Williams. He knows what he did for me, and I hope he knows how much I appreciate it.

As always, a special word of appreciation is reserved for Erik Love, my lifelong friend who first challenged and motivated me to become a better writer in the first place. Please show this section of the book to your daughter Aurora Lee, and let her know that Uncle Ian says that this is also *her* book now.

My efforts in creating this book are dedicated to the memory of my grandfather Claire Elmer Douglass. Before I finished my very first book, you told me you knew I could do it. You were right. Both of my grandparents continue to mean the world to me.

James Douglass and Pauline Capron Douglass: You're the best parents who ever lived. Thank you for being mine.

Teisha, thank you for once again suffering through long hours of me staring blankly at a computer screen while you struggled to get my attention. I hope you're as proud to call me your husband as I am to call you my wife.

Romans 12:21: "Do not be overcome by evil, but overcome evil with good."

Regards,

Ian C. Douglass

CREDITS

Author:
Brian Blair

Coauthor/Biographer/Layout:
Ian Douglass

Editor
Jamie Hemmings

Forewords:
Bret Hart
Steve Keirn

Afterword:
Hulk Hogan

Executive Producer:
Kenny Casanova

Cover Art:
Marc Leitzel

Guest Content:
Steve Keirn

Content Contributor:
Scott Stevens

Behind-the-Scenes Help:
Jim Brunzell
Georgia Blair
Barry Rose
John Crowther
Sabrina Ruggiero
Nyah Kennedy
Al Burke
Tom Reeder
Dave Millican
Hal Jeffrey

Photo/Art Contributors:
George Napolitano
Pete Lederberg
Bobby VanKavelaar
Nathan Smith
Bill Otten
Bret Hart

Beta Readers:
Oliver Bateman
Dave Meltzer

Made in the USA
Coppell, TX
20 October 2021